# International Relations

## Introductory Readings
*Revised Printing*

Edward Rhodes
Jonathan M. DiCicco
Dalia F. Fahmy

**Kendall Hunt**
publishing company

Cover image © Shutterstock, Inc.

**Kendall Hunt**
publishing company

www.kendallhunt.com
*Send all inquiries to:*
4050 Westmark Drive
Dubuque, IA 52004-1840

Copyright © 1992 by Kendall Hunt Publishing Company

Revised Printing: 1998, 2003, 2006, 2010, and 2017

ISBN 978-1-5249-1083-9

Published in the United States of America
20   19   18   17   16

# Contents

# Preface

The purpose of this book is to introduce students to the major concepts of international relations. The readings in this volume develop political scientists' basic arguments and theories about how nations and states interact in the modern world. In editing this book we have kept two goals in mind. In the first place, this book is designed to provide students with the tools necessary for understanding the international events that are likely to shape their lives. This book is intended to make the nightly news make more sense—not by providing historical background or an overview of current events but by exposing the basic logic, tensions, and dilemmas of international politics. In the second place, this book aims to provide the solid theoretical foundation essential for advanced coursework in international relations. It lays the groundwork and sets the stage for more detailed studies of American foreign policy, defense policy, international political economy, international law, international organization, and the causes of war.

This book is organized into four sections. The first develops the central concepts of modern international relations: the state, the international system, and international society. Along the way it explores the ideas of anarchy, power, regimes, law, interdependence, and morality and how they may affect international behavior. The second section turns to the central intellectual problem of international politics: war. It examines how the characteristics of the international system and society may provoke or prevent war, how various attributes of particular states or nations may make conflict more or less likely, and how the basic nature of human beings may play an important role in explaining the occurrence of war.

The third section explores challenges to the international system emerging in today's world. Changes in the relationships among sovereign states, between people and states, and among individuals from different states raise questions about how order and security will be provided in the future. Many of these changes seem to simultaneously strengthen and weaken the capacity of the state system. Transnational networks, for example, may increase state capabilities to cooperate while at the same time increasing the power of groups that compete with states and diminish state authority. A brief fourth section raises the fundamental epistemological problems inevitably encountered in the study of international relations: how do we know what we (think we) know, how do we go about thinking conceptually about world affairs, and how are we to understand "history"?

As our students will recognize, this book is a direct product of our experiences in the classroom with them. These are the readings that we have found generally provide the insights that allow our students to answer for themselves the questions that inevitably arise about the nature of international politics. The selections included in this volume have the enormous merit of achieving tremendous clarity without resorting to oversimplicity. In many cases, they are excerpts from classics in the political science literature and, like a deep well, they offer new insights on each reading or re-reading. They do not provide easy, pat answers. But they do suggest valuable ways of thinking about the problems.

# Part I
## The International State System

Since the end of the Cold War, the international political system has entered into a period of rapid change and dramatic transformation. Political institutions such as the sovereign state have been confronted with novel challenges, reflecting extraordinary changes in economic, technological, social, and cultural realities, changes that continue to occur at an ever-increasing rate. The globalization of the world's economy, the emergence of a new international security agenda that includes issues such as health and the environment, the empowerment of individuals thanks to improved education and information technology, and the development of new identities and cross-cutting loyalties have all posed challenges for the existing system. To understand the transformation of international politics that is underway, however, it is important to understand the major continuities that exist as well.

Although a variety of types of actors—individuals, multinational corporations, international nongovernmental organizations, intergovernmental organizations, and so on—are involved in international politics, the principal players in world affairs are *states*. While the terms "state" and "nation" are sometimes used interchangeably, it is useful to distinguish between them, for they represent very different concepts. A state is a corporate body exercising, or claiming to exercise, sovereign political power over a particular geographic area; sovereign political power implies a monopoly on the legitimate use of violence. A *nation*, by contrast, is a group of people who view themselves as sharing a common identity and destiny, perhaps because of some myth of common ancestry or because of

shared history, religion, language, or culture. The confusion between "states" and "nations" arises because of the emergence of *nation-states* as political units. The nation-state is a unique type of state, one in which the state is the political representative of a particular nation: typically in the case of a nation-state, the state's territory encompasses essentially all of the people of one nation and effectively none of those of any other nation.

In chapter 1, Miguel Centeno examines the emergence of the modern state and the interrelated roles of war, taxation, the expansion of state bureaucracies and administrative capability, and elite unity in the development of the European state system. Turning from "states" to "nations," Walker Connor develops the idea of the nation and the problems arising from the conflation of "nation" with "state" in chapter 2; in chapter 3, he considers the historical evolution of nationalism as a mass, rather than elite, movement and the development of the nation-state.

If states interact with each other—if they have interests or concerns that lead them to cooperate or to oppose each other—then they form a *system* of interacting units. Because each state is sovereign, however, the system they create through their interaction lacks any higher authority ruling over it. We call this absence of higher authority *anarchy,* and we describe the international state system as an anarchic one. Obviously, an anarchic system runs on the "self-help" principle: participants must rely on their own strength, and on their ability to make friends, to protect and advance their interests. In this sort of self-help system, *power*—defined as the ability to achieve a desired outcome in a situation of conflicting objectives—clearly matters. States can be expected to threaten and pressure each other to get what they want. This is known as *coercion.*

Chapters 4 through 6 explore these basic features of life in the international state system. In chapter 4, Kenneth Waltz develops the notion and implications of anarchy. In the following chapter, Joseph Nye explains the concept of power, its sources and the different forms it can take. In chapter 6, Thomas Schelling discusses the logic of coercion and the role played by threats.

While the international state system lacks any government over it, certain expectations and obligations may nonetheless develop and strongly influence state behavior. In other words, to some degree there is likely to exist a *society* among states even though there is no super-sovereign government over them to enforce societal rules. This anarchical society affects how states act and facilitates cooperation that would otherwise be difficult or impossible to achieve. In the jargon of political science, what we witness is the development of international *regimes,* or "sets of implicit or explicit principles, norms, rules and decision-making procedures around which actors, expectations converge."[1] Such regimes can be formalized into international law, relying—unlike domestic law—on societal or collective enforcement rather than on sovereign enforcement. The picture of the international system that emerges from this analysis is far more complicated and nuanced than the Realist image of sovereign states interacting like freely moving billiard balls. What it suggests is the notion that states are caught in a web of *complex interdependence,* interacting through multiple channels on multiple issues according to multiple sets of rules and with power that varies by issue.

Chapters 7 through 11 explore these ideas. In chapters 7 and 8, Hedley Bull develops the concept of international society and considers the functioning of an anarchical one. Next, Robert Keohane examines the role of international regimes. Chapter 10, by Hedley Bull, investigates the idea of international law. In chapter 11, Robert Keohane and Joseph Nye probe the meaning and implications of complex interdependence for the interaction of states—and foreshadow some of the transnational and transgovernmental phenomena discussed at greater length by scholars like Anne-Marie Slaughter in Part III of this book.

The study of international politics raises *normative* issues as well as *positive* ones, however: that is, it raises questions about how states and their governments, and other international actors, ought to behave, as well as question about how they do behave. Do international actors possess a range of choice? Or is what they can choose to do so narrowly constrained by what they must do to survive that notions of *morality* are irrelevant? While the idea of international society suggests the relevance of certain moral criteria, such notions are largely dismissed by political *Realists* who maintain that in conditions of anarchy all states must pursue power and that necessity, not morality, does and should shape state policy. Against this position stands the body of Western political thinking collectively known as *Just War Theory*, which establishes moral criteria for decisions to undertake war (*jus ad bellum*) and for conduct in war (*jus in bello*).

Chapters 12 through 16 explore these concerns. Greg Russell discusses in chapter 12 the ideas of Hans Morgenthau, the pioneering political scientist who popularized political realism after World War II. Morgenthau argued that the nature of politics is fundamentally conflictual, and that international relations inevitably involve

---

1   Stephen Krasner, "Structural Causes and Regime Consequences," in Krasner, ed., *International Regimes* (Ithaca: Cornell University Press, 1983), p. 2.

states' egoistic pursuit of the national interest, defined in terms of power.

Chapter 13, an excerpt from the ancient Greek historian Thucydides's account of wars between Athens and Sparta, offers what many political scientists regard as the classic illustration of Morgenthau's vision of the primacy of power concerns, and the triumph of *realpolitik* calculations over worries about morality. In this provocative passage, Thucydides recounts a hypothetical discussion between the very powerful Athenians and their much smaller neighbors, the Melians; this famous "Melian dialogue" is a clear literary exposition of the logic of Realism—that the strong are necessarily driven to do what is required to preserve and advance their power and that the weak must do what is needed to survive. In chapter 14, Michael Walzer examines the moral dilemmas of international politics, offering critical perspective on political realism and the Melian dialogue. Finally, in chapter 15, James Turner Johnson explores the Western "Just War" tradition of thinking about the morality of war and about moral restraints on violence.

# 1: Making the State

## Miguel Angel Centeno

The destructive capacity of war is self-evident. Less so is the manner in which war, or more accurately, the process of going to war, can be constructive. War is rejuvenating. The demands of war create opportunities for innovation and adaptation. Wars help build the institutional basis of modern states by requiring a degree of organization and efficiency that only new political structures could provide; they are the great stimulus for state building.[1] States, in a sense, are by-products of rulers' efforts to acquire the means of war; war is inherently an organizing phenomenon from which the state derives its administrative machinery. According to Hintze, all state organization is principally military in nature. The shape and size of the state may even be seen as deriving from the managerial potential and limits of military technology.[2] So, for example, the advance of bureaucratic forms may be in part a result of increasing demands for administrative efficiency generated by the needs of growing armed forces and the escalating costs of waging war.[3]

The notion that war supports the institutional development of the state is widely accepted in political sociology.[4] This is not a recent discovery, but reflects the importance assigned to war by Weber and Hintze.[5] Wars help build the institutional basis of the modern state by requiring a degree of organization and efficiency that only new political structures could provide. Charles Tilly has best summarized this process with his statement "States make wars and wars make states."

This at least is the scholarly consensus on the European experience. On that continent, wars served as a crucial causal mechanism behind the growth of the state. The rise of the modern European state may be traced to the military revolution of the sixteenth and seventeenth centuries.[6] During this period, three critical organizational developments changed the nature of military struggle: control over the means of violence shifted from private to public control; the size of armies increased dramatically; and their composition became less varied and more based on a specific national identity.[7]

War made the territorial consolidation of a state more feasible and more imperative. Only those states that could wield great armies *and*

1   Huntington, *Political Order in Changing Societies.*
2   Bean, "War and the Birth of the Nation State."
3   M. S. Anderson, *War and Society in Europe.*
4   Andreski, *Military Organization and Society;* Finer, "State and Nation Building in Europe"; Tilly, "Reflections"; Downing, *The Military Revolution and Political Change;* Porter, *War and the Rise of the State;* Ertman, *Birth of the Leviathan.*
5   Weber, *General Economic History;* Hintze, "Military Organization."
6   Outside Europe, the American Civil War both provided the major impetus for state expansion and allowed the industrial North to reshape the antebellum agenda (Bensel, *Yankee Leviathan*). Karsten describes the links between the rationalization of the armed services in the United States and similar organized efforts in other government sectors ("Militarization and Rationalization"). Bendix suggests that the effective rule of early Japanese shogunates may originate in the aristocracy's military experience (*Kings or People*).
7   Finer, "State and Nation Building in Europe"; Porter, *War and the Rise of the State;* Roberts, *Essays in Swedish History;* Parker, *Military Revolution;* Duffy, introduction to Duffy, *Military Revolution and the State;* Ralston, *Importing the European Army;* Kaiser, *Politics and War.*

guarantee control over their own territories could play the great game. Only those states able to impose that central control could survive the military revolution. Countries unable to do so—Poland being one example—disappeared. The decline in the number of European states after the fifteenth century (from fifteen hundred to twenty-five by 1900) is an obvious indicator of the centralization of power wrought by military conflict. Wars pushed power toward the center.[8] War provided both the incentive *and* the means with which the central power was able to dominate. Peter Paret explains that "military force performed the essential task of defeating particularistic rivals to the crown, lending authority to the expanding process of government."[9] Whether in the France of Louis XIII, seventeenth-century Prussia, or Restoration England, violence was used to impose the rule of the center. The means for this violence were provided by war.

The key to the relationship between war and state making in western Europe is what Finer calls the "extraction-coercion" cycle.[10] We begin with the obvious fact that wars require capital: by the sixteenth century, combat became so expensive that the mobilization of an entire country was required. Professional armies clearly outperformed any rivals, but these needed "ample and continuous amounts of money."[11] These changes causally linked military and political development. On the one hand, states penetrated their societies in increasingly complex forms in order to obtain resources. The organizational innovations that occurred during wartime did not disappear with peace, but often left an infrastructural residue that Ardant calls the "physiology" of the state.[12] On the other hand, the new form of the post-Westphalian state was particularly well suited to the organizational task of managing this penetration and channeling the resources thus obtained into "productive" violence directed at some external enemy. Thus, wars both built and were an expression of political power.

Taxation is the best measure of effective political authority and institutional development, both representing and augmenting the strength of the state as measured by the capacity to enforce centralized rule on a territory and its population.[13] Taxes partly determine the very size of states' institutions and shape relationships between these and society; they help mold the eventual form of the state.[14] War is widely perceived as increasing the capacity of a state to tax its population.[15] Combat simultaneously generates greater need for resources and temporary declines in the state's social constraints; it also provides a focus around which the state's organizational capacity may improve. Finally, armies raised for war might also serve as a means with which to collect resources.

The evidence for the positive link between war and the rise of taxes in early modern Europe is exhaustive.[16] The pattern is also evident in the

---

8   Howard, *Causes of War.*

9   *Understanding War,* 41.

10  Finer, "State and Nation Building in Europe."

11  Howard, *War in European History,* 37.

12  Ardant, "Financial Policy and Economic Infrastructure."

13  Peacock and Wiseman, *The Growth of Public Expenditure in the U.K.;* Organski and Kugler, *The War Ledger.*

14  Tilly, "Reflections on the History of European State-Making"; and Ardant, "Financial Policy and Economic Infrastructure"; Schumpeter, "The Crisis of the Tax State"; Gallo, *Taxes and State Power;* von Stein, "On Taxation"; Levi, *Of Rule and Revenue.*

15  Peacock and Wiseman, *Growth of Public Expenditure;* Mann, *Sources of Social Power,* vols. 1 and 2; *States, War, and Capitalism;* Tilly, *Coercion, Capital, and European States;* Rasler and Thompson, *War and Statemaking;* J. Campbell, "The State and Fiscal Sociology."

16  Ames and Rapp, "The Birth and Death of Taxes"; Mathias and O'Brien, "Taxation in Britain and France"; Stone, *An Imperial State at War;* Brewer, *The Sinews of Power;* Aftalion, "Le financement des guerres."

United States.[17] In all these cases, not only does state revenue increase after war; the structure of taxation also changes. For example, wars led both the British state in the eighteenth century and the American in the nineteenth and twentieth to increase both the amount of revenue (which never returned to prebellic levels) and the relative importance of domestic and direct taxes. Military conflicts allow—and force—the state to depend less on the administratively simple, but inelastic, custom taxes and to rely on the more politically challenging, but potentially more lucrative, domestic sources of revenue. The greater bureaucratic complexity required is at the heart of the institutional legacy of war.

Yet how automatic is the relationship between war and increased state strength? Appreciation of historical specificity and structural conditions is vital for the production of truly generalizable models of state development. Only some wars built states, only some states were built by wars. The European experience indicates that warfare in and of itself does not necessarily lead to state making. Until the sixteenth century, several centuries of prior warfare had not produced states in Europe. Rather, as Tilly has emphasized, particular circumstances found in parts of Europe between 1600 and 1800 promoted conflict-led state development.[18]

To an extent, this transformation remains a historical black box. We possess myriad references to the rise of the modern state and countless monographic descriptions of the specific historical sequences. Yet political sociology has generally failed to produce a coherent model of how violence was transformed into order. Sociological and comparative accounts of the relationship between war and state building have also not sufficiently emphasized historical order in their analysis. There is a causal ambiguity in Tilly's famous aphorism: Which came first, states or wars?[19]

I argue in this chapter that wars in and of themselves do not make anything. Rather, they merely provide a *potential* stimulus for state growth. Wars can only make states if they are preceded by at least a modicum of political organization. Without institutional cohesion, wars will make for chaos and defeat. Wars only provide an opportunity for those political organizations that are able to capitalize on them; they cannot create institutions out of thin air. The consolidation of central authority and the creation of a modicum of a bureaucracy appear to have preceded the state-making stage of war in England, France, and Prussia. The venality of the Spanish bureaucracy and the financial leakage of tax farming in a variety of other countries represented critical obstacles to state development.

It is vital to fully appreciate the social resistance that may be offered to state penetration. The combination of coercion and capital symbolized by the military draft and direct taxation, the defining characteristics of a warmade modern state according to Tilly,[20] does not come about simply because a bureaucratic apparatus is in place and wishes it so. The capacity of a state to extract resources will be closely linked to the willingness of the population to accept these burdens. Reluctance on the part of either an economic oligarchy to part with its cash or a populace to move closer to penury may make expansion of taxes simply not worth the effort.[21] Thus, state capacity is not an

---

17 Bensel, *Yankee Leviathan;* Skowronek, *Building a New American State;* David and Legler, "Government in the American Economy"; Hooks and McLauchlan, "The Institutional Foundation of Warmaking."

18 Tilly, *Coercion, Capital, and European States.*

19 Tallett, in *War and Society in Early Modern Europe* (citing I. A. A. Thompson's work on Spain), calls war less a stimulant than a test of state strength.

20 Tilly, *European Revolutions,* 32.

21 On the political costs of pushing too far, a wonderful recent addition is Markoff, *The Abolition of Feudalism.*

absolute phenomenon, but a relational one. It is not merely a question of strength, but also of the potential of the relevant societies to resist (or welcome) intrusion.

Wars only make states when there already exists some form of union between a politically or militarily dominant institution and a social class that sees it as the best means with which to defend and reproduce its privilege. That is, following Perry Anderson, there has to be a prior agreement that the state will be responsible for collecting and disposing of social surplus.[22] European cases demonstrate that the fragmentation of sovereignty, be it through the persistence of local autonomies (Spain), powerful but divided aristocracies (Poland), or direct external control (the Balkans), can and does prevent the solidification of states even when they are surrounded by conflict. In contrast, more successful war-making states established a coalition between central authority and potential aristocratic challengers either through alliance (England) or through coercion (France, Prussia).[23]

Following the methodological logic of the counterfactual, the failure of Latin American wars to generate similar state-building forces as seen in Europe after the seventeenth century can serve to improve our understanding of the relationship between conflict and institutional development. . . .

We must trace successful state developments not to war in itself, but to the presence of a united elite, willing—or forced to—accept the loss of individual prerogatives for a (still elite-defined) collective good, and leading a society not already torn asunder by ethnic or racial divisions. Europe has been exceptional not only in the immense amount of organized violence that has character-

ized continental geopolitics, but also in enjoying preconditions that allowed it to transform this bloodshed into modern political institutions. . . .

One of the most critical aspects of a modern state is its ability to create and enforce what Frederic Lane and later Charles Tilly have called a "protection racket."[24] From this vantage point, the state is often little more than the stereotypical Hollywood goon warning store owners of the potential disasters awaiting them should they fail to purchase his particular brand of insurance. For all its flags, anthems, and other symbolic paraphernalia, the state offers its citizens a simple proposal: in exchange for obedience to a set of laws, state institutions offer protection from both internal and external violence; the Weberian monopoly over legitimate use of violence.[25]

## Providing Protection

In order to maintain its racket, the state has to be able to defend preset frontiers and ensure obedience to its laws within those frontiers. It has to defend its right to exist and to demand internal recognition of its domination internally. The internal element involves two aspects (and they may be related, but it is important to keep them separate): (a) Only state officials may have access to means of violence; and (b) the central state institutions (those claiming national coverage) have priority over any other regional or local competitors. The first is about controlling lawless violence, for example, banditry; as well as the elimination of rival claimants to the national territory, for example, Indians in Latin America or the North American West. The second is about the number of governments inside the territory who are claiming the right or duty to stamp out the violence.

---

22 P. Anderson, *Lineages of the Absolutist State.*

23 Again, by this I do not mean to imply that such coalitions or alliances are either sufficient or necessary, but only that they increase the probability of being able to establish a successful central authority.

24 Tilly, "War Making and State Making as Organized Crime."

25 "[The state] is thus a compulsory organization with a territorial basis. . . . the use of force is regarded as legitimate only so far as it is either permitted by the state or prescribed by it" (M. Weber, *Economy and Society,* 56).

# 2: The Nation

*Walker Connor*

One of the most common manifestations of terminological license is the interutilization of the words *state* and *nation*. This tendency is perplexing because at one level of consciousness most scholars are clearly well aware of the vital distinctions between the two concepts. The state is the major political subdivision of the globe. As such, it is readily defined and, what is of greater moment to the present discussion, is easily conceptualized in quantitative terms. Peru, for illustration, can be defined in an easily conceptualized manner as the territorial-political unit consisting of the sixteen million inhabitants of the 514,060 square miles located on the west coast of South America between 69° and 80° West, and 2° and 18°, 21° South.

Defining and conceptualizing the nation is much more difficult because the essence of a nation is intangible. This essence is a psychological bond that joins a people and differentiates it, in the subconscious conviction of its members, from all other people in a most vital way. The nature of that bond and its wellspring remain shadowy and elusive, and the consequent difficulty of defining the nation is usually acknowledged by those who attempt this task. Thus, a popular dictionary of International Relations defines a nation as follows:

> A social group which shares a common ideology, common institutions and customs, and a *sense* of homogeneity. "Nation" is difficult to define so precisely as to differentiate the term from such other groups as religious sects, which exhibit some of the same characteristics. In the nation, however, there is also present a strong group *sense* of belonging associated with a particular territory considered to be peculiarly its own.[1]

Whereas the key word in this particular definition is *sense*, other authorities may substitute *feeling* or *intuition*, but proper appreciation of the abstract essence of the nation is customary *in definitions*. But after focusing attention upon that essential psychological bond, little probing of its nature follows. Indeed, having defined the nation as an essentially psychological phenomenon, authorities . . . then regularly proceed to treat it as fully synonymous with the very different and totally tangible concept of the state. . . .

With but very few exceptions, authorities have shied away from describing the nation as a kinship group and have usually explicitly denied that the notion of shared blood is a factor. Such denials are supported by data illustrating that most groups claiming nationhood do in fact incorporate several genetic strains. But such an approach ignores the wisdom of the old saw that when analysing sociopolitical situations, what ultimately matters is not *what is* but *what people believe is*. And a subconscious belief in the group's separate origin and evolution is an important ingredient of national psychology.

---

1   Jack C. Plano and Roy Olton, *The International Relations Dictionary* (New York: Holt, Rinehart and Winston, Inc., 1969), 119, emphasis added.

From *Ethnic and Racial Studies,* Volume 13, Number 1, pp. 92-100. Copyright 1990. Reprinted by permission of Routledge.

When one avers that he is Chinese, he is identifying himself not just with the Chinese people and culture of today, but with the Chinese people and their activities throughout time. The Chinese Communist Party was appealing to just such a sense of separate origin and evolution in 1937:

> [W]e know that in order to transform the glorious future into a new China, independent, free, and happy, all our fellow countrymen, every single, zealous descendant of Huang-ti [the legendary first emperor of China] must determinedly and relentlessly participate in the concerted struggle.
> . . . Our great Chinese nation, with its long history is inconquerable.[2]

Bismark's famous exhortation to the German people, over the heads of their particular political leaders, to "think with your blood" was a similar attempt to activate a mass psychological vibration predicated upon an intuitive sense of consanguinity. An unstated presumption of a Chinese (or German) nation is that there existed in some hazy, prerecorded era a Chinese (or German) Adam and Eve, and that the couple's progeny has evolved in essentially unadulterated form down to the present. It was recognition of this dimension of the nation that caused numerous writers of the nineteenth and early twentieth centuries to employ *race* as a synonym for *nation,* references to a German race or to the English race being quite common.

Since the nation is a self-defined rather than an other-defined grouping, the broadly held conviction concerning the group's singular origin need not and seldom will accord with factual data. Thus, the anthropologist may prove to his own satisfaction that there are several genetic strains within the Pushtun people who populate the Afghani-Pakistani border region and conclude therefrom that the group represents the variegated offspring of several peoples who have moved through the region. The important fact, however, is that the Pushtuns themselves are convinced that all Pushtuns are evolved from a single source and have remained essentially unadulterated. This is a matter which is known intuitively and unquestionably, a matter of attitude and not of fact. It is a matter, the underlying conviction of which is not apt to be disturbed substantially even by the rational acceptance of anthropological or other evidence to the contrary. Depending upon the sophistication of the treatise, this type of sensory knowledge may be described as "a priori," "an emotional rather than a rational conviction," "primordial," "thinking with the heart (or with the blood) rather than with the mind," or "a 'gut' or 'knee-jerk' response." Regardless of the nomenclature, it is an extremely important adjunct of the national idea.[3] It is the intuitive conviction which can give to nations a psychological dimension approximating that of the extended family, i.e., a feeling of common blood lineage.

The word *nation* comes from the Latin and, when first coined, clearly conveyed the idea of common blood ties. It was derived from the past participle of the verb *nasci,* meaning to be born. And hence the Latin noun, *nationem,* connoting *breed* or *race.* Unfortunately, terms used to describe human collectivities (terms such as race

---

2   Conrad Brandt, Benjamin Schwartz, and John Fairbank, *A Documentary History of Chinese Communism* (London: George Allen & Unwin Ltd., 1952), 245, parenthetic material added.

3   Max Weber, *Economy and Society,* ed. Guenther Roth and Claus Wittich (New York: Bedminster Press, 1968) 395, notes that "the concept of 'nationality' (or 'nation') shares with that of the 'people' *(Volk)*—in the 'ethnic' sense—the vague connotation that whatever is felt to be distinctively common must derive from common descent." An old European definition of a nation, though intended to be humorous and derisive and which Karl Deutsch cites as such, hit almost the same mark: "A nation is a group of people united by a common error about their ancestry and a common dislike of their neighbors" (*Nationalism and Its Alternatives* (New York: Alfred A. Knopf, 1969), 3).

and class) invite an unusual degree of literary license, and *nation* certainly proved to be no exception.[4] Thus, at some medieval universities, a student's *nationem* designated the sector of the country from whence he came. But when introduced into the English language in the late thirteenth century, it was with its primary connotation of a blood related group. . . .

Indeed, while proud of being "a nation of immigrants" with a "melting pot" tradition, the absence of a common origin may well make it more difficult, and conceivably impossible, for the American to appreciate instinctively the idea of the nation in the same dimension and with the same poignant clarity as do the Japanese, the Bengali, or the Kikuyu. It is difficult for an American to appreciate what it means for a German to be German or for a Frenchman to be French, because the psychological effect of being American is not precisely equatable. Some of the associations are missing and others may be quite different.

Far more detrimental to the study of nationalism, however, has been the propensity to employ the term nation as a substitute for that territorial juridical unit, the state. How this practice developed is unclear, though it seems to have become a relatively common practice in the late seventeenth century. Two possible explanations for this development present themselves. One involves the rapid spread of the doctrine of popular sovereignty that was precipitated about this time by the writings of men such as Locke.

In identifying *the people* as the font of all political power, this revolutionary doctrine made the people and the state almost synonymous. *L'état c'est moi* became *l'état c'est le peuple*. And therefore the nation and the state had become near synonyms. . . .

It is also probable that the habit of interutilizing *nation* and *state* developed as alternative abbreviations for the expression *nation-state*. The very coining of this hyphenate illustrated an appreciation of the vital differences between *nation* and *state*. It was designed to describe a territorialpolitical unit (a state) whose borders coincided or nearly coincided with the territorial distribution of a national group. More concisely, it described a situation in which a nation had its own state. Unfortunately, however, *nation-state* has come to be applied indiscriminately to all states. Thus one authority has stated that "a prime fact about the world is that it is largely composed of nation-states."[5] The statement should read that "a prime fact about the world is that it is *not* largely composed of nation-states." A survey of the 132 entities generally considered to be states as of 1971, produced the following breakdown:

1. Only 12 states (9.1%) can justifiably be described as nation-states.
2. Twenty-five (18.9%) contain a nation or potential nation accounting for more than 90% of the state's total population but also contain an important minority.[6]

---

4  A recent example of the loose manner in which "nation" may be used is a work, published in the United States, entitled *Lesbian Nation*.

5  Louis J. Halle, *Civilization and Foreign Policy* (New York: Harper & Row, 1952), 10. For another example of this practice of referring to states as nation-states, see Dankwart Rustow, *A World of Nations* (Washington, D.C.: Brookings, 1967), 30 for a reference to the United Kingdom and the Soviet Union as nation-states. Note also Rustow's concluding remarks (p. 282): "More than 130 *nations*, real or so-called, will each make its contribution to the history of the late twentieth century . . .". For other illustrations, see this writer's "Ethnonationalism in the First World: The present in historical perspective," in Milton Esman (ed.), *Ethnic Pluralism and Conflict in the Western World* (Ithaca, NY: Cornell University Press, 1977), particularly 201.

6  By a potential nation is meant a group of people who appear to have all of the necessary prerequisites for nationhood, but who have not as yet developed a consciousness of their sameness and commonality, nor a conviction that their destinies are interwound. They are usually referred to by anthropologists as ethnolinguistic groups. Such peoples' sense of fundamental identity is still restricted to the locale, extended family, clan, or tribe. The Andean states and South-western Asia offer several illustrations of such pre-national people.

3. Another 25 (18.9%) contain a nation or potential nation accounting for between 75% and 89% of the population.
4. In 31 (23.5%), the largest ethnic element accounts for 50% to 74% of the population.
5. In 39 (29.5%), the largest nation or potential nation accounts for less than half of the population.

Were all states nation-states, no great harm would result from referring to them as nations, and people who insisted that the distinction between *nation* and *state* be maintained could be dismissed as linguistic purists or semantic nitpickers. Where *nation* and *state* essentially coincide, their verbal interutilization is inconsequential because the two are indistinguishably merged in popular perception. The state is perceived as the political extension of the nation, and appeals to one trigger the identical, positive psychological responses as appeals to the other. To ask a Japanese *kamikaze* pilot or a banzai-charge participant whether he was about to die for *Nippon* or for the Nipponese people would be an incomprehensible query since the two blurred into an inseparable whole. Hitler could variously make his appeals to the German people in the name of state (Deutsches Reich), nation (Volksdeutsch), or homeland (Deutschland), because all triggered the same emotional associations. Similar responses can be elicited from members of a nation that is clearly predominant within a state. But the invoking of such symbols has quite a different impact upon minorities. Thus, "Mother Russia" evokes one type of response from a Russian and something quite different from a

Ukrainian. De Gaulle's emotional evocations of *La France* met quite different audiences within the Île de France and within Brittany or Corsica.

Whatever the original reason for the interutilization of *nation* and *state*, even the briefest reflection suffices to establish the all-pervasive effect that this careless use of terminology has had upon the intellectual-cultural milieu within which the study of nationalism is perforce conducted. The League of Nations and the United Nations are obvious misnomers. The discipline called International Relations should be designated *Interstate* Relations.[7] One listing of contemporary organizations contains sixty-six entries beginning with the word *International* (e.g. the International Court of Justice and the International Monetary Fund), none of which, either in its membership or in its function, reflects any relationship to nations. International Law and International Organization are still other significant illustrations of the common but improper tendency to equate state and nation. National income, national wealth, national interest, and the like, refer in fact to statal concerns. A recently coined malapropism, *transnational* (and even *transnationalism*) is used to describe interstate, extragovernmental relations. *Nationalization* is still another of the numerous misnomers that muddy understanding of the national phenomenon.

With the concepts of the nation and the state thus hopelessly confused, it is perhaps not too surprising that *nationalism* should come to mean identification with the state rather than loyalty to the nation. Even the same International Relations Dictionary whose definition of the *nation*

---

7 A random survey of books, published within the United States and designed for college courses in global politics, will provide ample documentation of the impact this misuse of terminology has exerted upon the discipline. In addition to the host of titles consisting of or containing the expressions *International Relations* or *International Politics* are such well-known examples as *Politics Among Nations, The Might of Nations, Nations and Men, The Insecurity of Nations, How Nations Behave*, and *Games Nations Play*. Another illustration is offered by the American professional organization called the International Studies Association. Its official *raison d'étre*, as set forth in the early issues of its Quarterly, notes that the organization "is devoted to the orderly growth of knowledge concerning the impact of nation upon nation."

we cited for its proper appreciation of the psychological essence of the nation, makes this error. After carefully noting that "a nation may comprise part of a state, or extend beyond the borders of a single state," it elsewhere says of *nationalism* that "it makes the state the ultimate focus of the individual's loyalty."[8] It also says of nationalism that "as a mass emotion it is the most powerful political force operative in the world."[9] Few would disagree with this assessment of the power of nationalism, *and this is precisely the problem. Impressed with the force of nationalism, and assuming it to be in the service of the state, the scholar of political development has been preprogrammed to assume that the new states of Africa and Asia would naturally become the foci of their inhabitants' loyalties.* Nationalism, here as elsewhere, would prove irresistible, and alternative foci of loyalty would therefore lose the competition to that political structure alternately called the nation, the state, or the nation-state. This syndrome of assumptions and terminological confusion which has generally characterized the political development school is reflected in the early self-description of its endeavors as "nation-building." Contrary to its nomenclature, the "nation-building" school has in fact been dedicated to building viable states. And with a very few exceptions, the greatest barrier to state unity has been the fact that the states each contain more than one nation, and sometimes hundreds. Yet, a review of the literature will uncover little reflection on how the psychological bonds that presently tie segments of the state's population are to be destroyed. One searches the literature in vain for techniques by which group-ties predicated upon such things as a sense of separate origin, development, and destiny are to be supplanted by loyalty to a

state-structure, whose population has never shared such common feelings. The nature and power of those abstract ties that identify the true nation remain almost unmentioned, to say nothing of unprobed. The assumption that the powerful force called nationalism is in the service of the state makes the difficult investigation of such abstractions unnecessary.

As in the case of substituting the word *nation* for *state,* it is difficult to pinpoint the origin of the tendency to equate *nationalism* with loyalty to the state. It is unquestionably a very recent development, for the word *nationalism* is itself of very recent creation. G. de Bertier de Sauvigny believes it first appeared in literature in 1798 and did not reappear until 1830. Moreover, its absence from lexicographies until the late nineteenth and early twentieth centuries suggests that its use was not extensive until much more recently. Furthermore, all of the examples of its early use convey the idea of identification *not* with the state, but with the nation as properly understood.[10] While unable to pinpoint nationalism's subsequent association with the state, it indubitably followed and flowed from the tendency to equate state and nation. It also unquestionably received a strong impetus from the great body of literature occasioned by the growth of militant nationalism in Germany and Japan during the 1930s and early 1940s.

As outstanding illustrations of the fanatical responses that nationalism can engender, German and Japanese nationalism of this period have come to occupy an important place in all subsequent scholarship on nationalism. And, unfortunately, these manifestations of extreme nationalism have been firmly identified with the loyalty to the state. The most common word applied to them has been *fascism,* a doctrine

8  Plano and Olton, op. cit. 119, 120.
9  Ibid. 120.
10  See G. de Bertier de Sauvigny, "Liberalism, nationalism, and socialism: The birth of three words," *Review of Politics,* 32 (Apr. 1970), particularly 155-61.

postulating unswerving obedience to an organic, corporate state. The most popular alternative descriptive phrase, *totalitarianism,* perhaps even more strongly conveys the idea of the complete (total) identification of the individual with the state.

The linking of the state to these examples *par excellence* of extreme nationalism suggests the likelihood that other states will also become the object of mass devotion. If some states could elicit such fanatical devotion, why not others? Granted, few would wish to see such extreme and perverted dedication to the state arise elsewhere. But if the concept of a Japanese state could, during World War II, motivate "banzai charges," kamikaze missions, and numerous decisions of suicide rather than surrender (as well as the many post-war illustrations of people enduring for years an animal-like existence in caves on Pacific islands) because of a loyalty to the Japanese state that was so unassailable as to place that state's defeat beyond comprehension, then surely the states of the Third World should at least be able to evoke a sufficiently strong loyalty from their inhabitants so as to prevail against any competing group-allegiances. If a loyalty to a German state could motivate Germans to carry on a war long after it became evident that the cause was hopeless and that perseverance could only entail more deprivation, destruction, and death, then surely other states could at least elicit a sense of common cause and identity from their populations that would prove more powerful than any counter-tendencies to draw distinctions among segments of the populace. If the German and Japanese experiences were pertinent elsewhere, then optimism concerning the stability of present state structures would be justified.

But what has been too readily ignored is the fact that Germany and Japan were among the handful of states that clearly qualify as nation-states. As earlier noted, in such cases the state and the nation are indistinguishably linked in popular perception. Japan to the Japanese, just as Germany to the Germans, was something far more personal and profound than a territorial-political structure termed a state; it was an embodiment of the nation-idea and therefore an extension of self. As postulated by fascist doctrine, these states were indeed popularly conceived as corporate organisms, for they were equated with the Japanese and German nations. As Hitler wrote in *Mein Kampf:* "We as Aryans, are therefore able to imagine a State only to be the living organism of a nationality which not only safeguards the preservation of that nationality, but which, by further training of its spiritual and ideal abilities, leads it to its highest freedom."[11]

But could such an emotion-laden conception of the state take root where the nation and the state were not popularly equated? The single rubric of fascism was applied to Hitler's Germany, Tojo's Japan, Mussolini's Italy, Franco's Spain, and Peron's Argentina. It is evident, however, that appeals in the name of Spain have not elicited any great emotion from the Basques, Catalans, and Galicians. In polygenetic Argentina, Peron's message was not a unifying appeal to all Argentinians, but was in fact a divisive call in the name of socioeconomic class. Within Italy, a sense of loyalty to the state proved woefully and surprisingly inadequate in the face of its first major test, the invasion by Allied forces. The reason appears to be that the concept of a single people (national awareness) has not yet permeated the subconsciousness of the Italians to the same measure as a similar concept had permeated the German and Japanese people.[12] In equating nationalism with loyalty to the

---

11  A. Hitler, *Mein Kampf* (New York: Reynal and Hitchcock, 1940), 595.

12  For details, see this writer's "The Political Significance of Ethnonationalism within Western Europe," in Abdul Said and Luiz Simmons (eds.), *Ethnicity in an International Context* (Edison, NJ: Transaction Books, Inc., 1976), particularly 126-30.

state, scholars had failed to inquire how many cases there have been where fanatical devotion to a state has arisen in the absence of a popular conception of the state as the state of one's particular nation. Rather than suggesting certain victory on the part of new states in the competition for loyalty, the experiences of Germany and Japan exemplify the potential strength of those emotional ties to one's nation with which the multiethnic state must contend. German and Japanese nationalism were more prophetic auguries of the growth of concepts such as, *inter alia,* Ibo, Bengali, Kikuyu, Naga, Karen, Lao, Bahutu, Kurd, and Baganda, than they were auguries of the growth of concepts such as Nigeria, Pakistan, Kenya, India, Burma, Thailand, Rwanda, Iraq and Uganda.

Mistakenly equating nationalism with loyalty to the state has further contributed to terminological confusion by leading to the introduction of still other confusing terms. With nationalism preempted, authorities have had difficulty agreeing on a term to describe the loyalty of segments of a state's population to their particular nation. Ethnicity, primordialism, pluralism, tribalism, regionalism, communalism, and parochialism are among the most commonly encountered. This varied vocabulary further impedes an understanding of nationalism by creating the impression that each is describing a separate phenomenon. Moreover, reserving nationalism to convey loyalty to the state (or, more commonly, to the word *nation* when the latter is improperly substituted for state), while using words with different roots and fundamentally different connotations to refer to loyalty to the nation, adds immeasurably to the confusion.

# 3: The Development of Nations

*Walker Connor*

A little more than a decade ago Eugene Weber wrote a study with the intriguing title *Peasants into Frenchmen: The Modernization of Rural France, 1870-1914*. The book's convincingly documented thesis was that most rural and small-town dwellers within France did not conceive of themselves as members of a French nation as recently as 1870 and that many still failed to do so as late as World War I. With the partial exception of the regions to the north and east of Paris, the integration of the countryside into the French social and political system was largely fanciful. The typical village was a physical, political, and cultural isolate. The famed road network was in essence a skeleton connecting the major cities to Paris but offering no access roads to the villages. The school system was still inadequate to effect the Jacobin dream of a single and unilingual French nation.[1] *To the mass of peasants—and therefore to most inhabitants of France—the* meaningful world and identity seldom extended beyond the village. This is how one mid-nineteenth century French observer described life in the countryside: "Every valley is still a little world that differs from the neighbouring world as Mercury does from Uranus. Every village is a clan, a sort of state with its own patriotism."[2]

Weber's findings were the more astonishing because conventional scholarship had treated the French nation as one of the very oldest, to many *the* oldest, of Europe's contemporary nations. Many distinguished historians had written that the French nation had crystallized during the Middle Ages. The French historian Marc Bloch, for example, had asserted: "that the texts make it plain that so far as France and Germany were concerned this national consciousness was already highly developed about the year 1100."[3] The Dutch scholar Johann Huizinga considered French and English nationalism "to be in full flower" by the fourteenth century.[4] To the British scholar Sydney Herbert, "if the Hundred Years War [1337-1453] between France and England is as far as possible from being a national war in its origins, yet toward its close genuine nationality appears, splendid and triumphant, with Jeanne d'Arc."[5] Still other historians have perceived the emergence of national consciousness among the French as a post-Medieval development, crediting the Bourbons (1589-1793) with its development, although usually considering the process completed by the reign of Louis XIV (1643-1715). This is how one group of scholars described the situation at the time of his accession.[6]

---

1   Eugene Weber cites a 1911 observer as noting that "for peasants and workers, the mother tongue is patois, the foreign speech is French" (*Peasants into Frenchmen: The Modernization of Rural France, 1870-1914* (London: Chatto & Windus, 1979), 73). Earlier (p. 67), he offers data demonstrating that at least 25 per cent of the population could speak no French and that French was considered a foreign language by approximately half of the population who achieved adulthood between 1875 and 1900.
2   Ibid., 47.
3   Marc Bloch, *Feudal Society,* trans. L. A. Manyon (Chicago: University of Chicago, 1964), 436.
4   Johann Huizinga, *Men and Ideas: History, the Middle Ages, the Renaissance* (New York: Free Press, 1959), 21.
5   Sydney Herbert, *Nationality and its Problems* (New York: Dutton, 1919), 66-7.
6   This work was the coordinated effort of six of the United States' most distinguished scholars.

*From Ethnic and Racial Studies, Volume 1, Number 4*, pp 379-388.  Copyright © 1978 by Routledge. Reprinted by permission of Routledge.

France, at the middle of the seventeenth century, held the first rank among the powers of Europe . . . For a time France alone in Europe was a consolidated unit of race and institutions, showing the spirit of nationality and employing the agencies and methods of a great modern state.[7]

To stress the obvious, Weber's disclosure that a French identity had still not penetrated the rural masses hundreds—in some cases several hundreds—of years later than scholars had presumed French nationalism to be in full flower, holds potentially immense ramifications for the study of nationalism. Is the French experience unique or has there been a general tendency to assume that national consciousness had rather thoroughly permeated this or that people long before such an assumption was justifiable? Unfortunately, I am unaware of any studies, similar to Weber's, dealing with other national groups. However, there is one source of such data that covers a broad sampling of peoples. Between 1840 and 1915, there occurred a massive migration of peoples from Europe to the United States. For the most part, these migrants were from rural areas, and their education had been either minimal or non-existent. The few intellectuals and those who came from major cities were often aware of their membership in one of the European groupings that are recognized today as nations. Yet the peasants, who were far more typical of the overall population of the countries from which they had migrated, certainly were not. They regularly identified themselves in terms of some other identity or identities. . . .

The peasants, who predominated throughout most of Europe, were not until quite recently cognizant of membership in the nations to which

nationalist writers and outsiders assigned them. Given that nationalism is a mass, not an élite phenomenon, the contemporary nations of Europe emerged far more recently than has generally been recognized. Indeed, even today Europe is not devoid of peoples whose sense of national consciousness is shrouded in ambiguity. Yugoslavia alone offers three cases: the Montenegrins, Macedonians, and Bosnians. There are Montenegrins, as well as Serbs, who consider Montenegrins part of the Serbian nation. Even more complex is the case of the Macedonians. Bulgaria has traditionally maintained that the Macedonians are Bulgars; Greece has claimed that at least a significant portion of them are Greeks; they have also historically been claimed by the Serbs; since World War II, the Yugoslavian government has insisted that they constitute a separate nation. At least until quite recently, Macedonian opinion has been divided. Majority opinion agreed with Sofia that Macedonians were a branch of the Bulgar nation, while others considered themselves to be either Serb or Greek. There was scant indication of any conviction that Macedonians considered themselves a separate nation. There is little reason to question Belgrade's recent success in encouraging a sense of separate nationhood among the Macedonians, although the 1981 census data, which indicated a total absence of people within Macedonia who claimed either Bulgar or Greek identity, are extremely suspect, particularly given the fact that most Macedonians in the United States continue to feel that they are of Bulgarian stock.[8] As to the Moslems of Bosnia-Hercegovina, they are claimed by both Croats and Serbs, while the government has been promoting a separate Bosnian identity among these people. . . .

---

7   Albert Bushnell Hart (ed.), "France: Historical outline," in *A Reference History of the World From the Earliest Times to the Present* (Springfield, Mass.: Merriam, 1934), 131.

8   While the Yugoslav census recorded no people claiming Bulgarian descent within Macedonia, it did report the presence of such people immediately across the Macedonian border in Serbia, further feeding a suspicion that those within Macedonia claiming a Bulgarian descent were simply not recorded.

As we noted earlier, national consciousness is a mass, not an élite phenomenon, and the masses' view of group-self has often been indiscernible. Scholars have therefore been over-reliant upon the musings of élites whose generalizations concerning the existence of national consciousness are highly suspect. Indeed, until quite recent times it is doubtful whether ostensibly nationalistic élites even considered the masses to be part of their nation. The Polish and Hungarian gentry, for example, manifested national consciousness and aspirations for generations, while simultaneously imposing a system of serfdom on the masses of their ostensible co-nationals. Perceiving themselves quite correctly as a pariah group, rather than as co-members of a national family, the ostensibly Polish serfs sided against the Polish landlords in 1846, although the latter were fighting for Polish national (read: élite) liberation. A sense of common nationhood is not compatible with a cross-cutting class-cleavage as deep and unremitting as that between slave and landowner.[9] To quote the late Rupert Emerson, the nation is "the largest community which, when the chips are down, effectively commands men's loyalty, overriding the claims of both lesser communities within it and those which cut across it or potentially enfold it within a still greater society."[10]

The nation is therefore incompatible with those "lesser" cross-cutting cleavages that an appeal to common nationhood does not or cannot transcend. The institution of serfdom in Eastern Europe prior to the mid-nineteenth century can therefore be treated as *prima facie* evidence of the absence therein of nations, as contrasted with élite group-identities.[11]

In some societies the history of the voting franchise also offers hints of when a nation came into existence. As we are reminded by the history of the rise of national consciousness in, *inter alia*, Japan and Germany, democratic institutions are certainly no prerequisite for nation-formation. However, if a society describes itself as a democracy, then the refusal to permit large sections of the populace to participate in the political process may be viewed as tantamount to declaring that those who are disenfranchised are not members of the nation. If the rights of Englishmen include the right to vote, then what can one say concerning a so-called English nation in which most Englishmen were prohibited from exercising that right? Before 1832, when landlords alone were allowed to vote, it is estimated that only one in sixty adult English males could vote. Following the so-called Reform Bill of that year, one in every thirty male adults would be permitted to do so. In 1867, the franchise was further extended to cover some 80 per cent of all adult males, and in 1918 to cover the remaining 20 per cent of males and all women over thirty years of age.

---

9   The magnitude of the cleavage is suggested by the following citation (*Nationalism: A Report by a Study Group of Members of the Royal Institute of International Affairs* (1939), 96): "It was said of a Croat landowner of the 19th century that he would sooner have regarded his horse than his peasant as a member of the Croat nation. The same was true of most Polish and Magyar landowners of the period." From this perspective, the so-called "Polish Question" that occupied Europe's leaders from the late eighteenth century until the First World War could more accurately be described as an élite rather than a national question.

10  Rupert Emerson, *From Empire to Nation* (Boston: Beacon, 1960), 95-6.

11  An interesting illustration of the incompatibility between outcast group and nation is offered by the *burakumin* of Japan. Although these people are physically indistinguishable from the Japanese, the Japanese treat them as contaminated inferiors with whom all social intercourse is to be avoided. This treatment is justified by the popularly held conviction—all biological and historical evidence to the contrary notwithstanding—that *burakumin* are not of Japanese descent. A number of quite fanciful theories of the *burakumin*'s separate descent have been periodically promoted, because upon such myths depends the justification for perpetuating the social ostracism of these people, that is, for denying them membership of an extended family.

Reflecting on such nineteenth-century limitations on the franchise in Britain and elsewhere,[12] E. H. Carr observed:

> Property, sometimes described as "a stake in the country," was a condition of political rights—and it might be said without much exaggeration—of full membership of the nation . . . The rise of new social strata to full membership of the nation marked the last three decades of the 19th century throughout western and central Europe . . . National policy was henceforth founded on the support of the masses; and the counterpart was the loyalty of the masses to a nation which had become the instrument of their collective interests and ambitions.[13]

The delay—in some cases stretching into centuries—between the appearance of national consciousness among sectors of the élite and its extension to the masses reminds us of the obvious but all-too-often ignored fact that nation-formation is a process, not an occurrence or event.[14] And this, in turn, further thwarts the attempt to answer the question, "When is a nation?" Events are easily dated; stages in a process are not. At what point did a sufficient number/percentage of a given people acquire national consciousness so that the group merited the title of nation? There is no formula. We want to know the point in the process at which a sufficient portion of the population has internalized the national identity in order to cause appeals in its name to become an effective force for mobilizing the masses. While this does not require that 100 per cent of the people have acquired such national consciousness, the point at which a quantitative addition in the number sharing a sense of common nationhood has triggered the qualitative transformation into a nation resists arithmetic definition. In most cases we shall probably have to be satisfied with assigning dates after the fact (after an effective illustration of mass mobilization in the name of the nation), although the sophisticated analysis of well-designed polling instruments can be very helpful in probing the breadth of national consciousness.[15] What we can say is that the presence of even substantial numbers of intellectuals proclaiming the existence of a new nation is not sufficient. Nearly a century ago, the Levant produced a bevy of writers proclaiming the reality of the Arab nation; yet even today Arab national consciousness remains anomalously weak.

Although numerous authorities over the decades have addressed the question, "What is a

---

12  The case of France is somewhat different, since the system was much less stable, with non-democratic political regimes in power during much of the late eighteenth and early nineteenth centuries. However, the franchise was still extremely limited more than half a century after the French Revolution. According to Hall and Albion (*A History of England and the British Empire,* 2nd ed. (Boston: Ginn, 1946), 613) the Revolution of 1830 only extended the vote to one in every 200 adult males. Palmer and Cotton (*A History of the Modern World,* 4th ed. (New York: Knopf, 1971), 498) place the post-1830 French figure at one voter in every thirty adult males, as contrasted with a pre-1830 figure of one in every sixty male adults. Whatever the correct figure, it is evident that a highly élitist view of the nation prevailed at least until the upheavals of 1848.

13  E. H. Carr, *Nationalism and After* (London: Macmillan, 1967), 10, 18, 20.

14  For a contemporary case of such confusion by a Soviet author, see S. Dumin, "Shlyakham ab'ektyunaga vyvuchennya," *Litaratura i mastatstva* (8 July 1988), as reported by Kathleen Mihalisko, "Historian outlines revisionist view of Belorussia's past," *Radio Liberty, RL, 415/88* (8 September 1988), 2. As reported by Kathleen Mihalisko, Dumin avers that Belorussian nationhood dates to the medieval era, although we have seen from the United States' migrant data that this sense of nationhood had probably not infected the masses as recently as the First World War.

15  For references to several such polls, see W. Connor, "From a theory of relative economic deprivation toward a theory of relative political deprivation," paper presented at the *Conference of the International Sociological Association's Research Committee on Ethnic, Race and Minority Relations,* Amsterdam, 8-10 December 1988.

nation?", far less attention has been paid to the question, "At what point in its development does a nation come into being?" There is ample evidence that Europe's currently recognized nations emerged only very recently, in many cases centuries later than the dates customarily assigned for their emergence. In the matter of nation-formation, there has been far less difference in the timetables of Western and Eastern Europe than is customarily acknowledged, and the lag time between Europe and the Third World has also been greatly exaggerated. Indeed, in the case of a number of putative nations within Europe, it is problematic whether nationhood has even yet been achieved.

A key problem faced by scholars when dating the emergence of nations is that national consciousness is a mass, not an élite phenomenon, and the masses, until quite recently isolated in rural pockets and being semi- or totally illiterate, were quite mute with regard to their sense of group identity(ies). Scholars have been necessarily largely dependent upon the written word for their evidence, yet it has been élites who have chronicled history. Seldom have their generalities about national consciousness been applicable to the masses, and very often the élites' conception of the nation did not even extend to the masses.

Another vexing problem is that nation-formation is a process, not an occurrence. The point in the process at which a sufficient portion of a people has internalized the national identity in order to cause nationalism to become an effective force for mobilizing the masses does not lend itself to precise calculation. In any event, claims that a particular nation existed prior to the late-nineteenth century should be treated cautiously.

# 4: Anarchy

*Kenneth N. Waltz*

### Violence at Home and Abroad

The state among states, it is often said, conducts its affairs in the brooding shadow of violence. Because some states may at any time use force, all states must be prepared to do so—or live at the mercy of their militarily more vigorous neighbors. Among states, the state of nature is a state of war. This is meant not in the sense that war constantly occurs but in the sense that, with each state deciding for itself whether or not to use force, war may at any time break out. Whether in the family, the community, or the world at large, contact without at least occasional conflict is inconceivable; and the hope that in the absence of an agent to manage or to manipulate conflicting parties the use of force will always be avoided cannot be realistically entertained. Among men as among states, anarchy, or the absence of government, is associated with the occurrence of violence.

The threat of violence and the recurrent use of force are said to distinguish international from national affairs. But in the history of the world surely most rulers have had to bear in mind that their subjects might use force to resist or overthrow them. If the absence of government is associated with the threat of violence, so also is its presence. A haphazard list of national tragedies illustrates the point all too well. The most destructive wars of the hundred years following the defeat of Napoleon took place not among states but *within* them. Estimates of deaths in China's Taiping Rebellion, which began in 1851 and lasted 13 years, range as high as 20 million. In the American Civil War some 600 thousand people lost their lives. In more recent history, forced collectivization and Stalin's purges eliminated five million Russians, and Hitler exterminated six million Jews. In some Latin American countries, coups d'états and rebellions have been normal features of national life. Between 1948 and 1957, for example, 200 thousand Colombians were killed in civil strife. In the middle 1970s most inhabitants of Idi Amin's Uganda must have felt their lives becoming nasty, brutish, and short, quite as in Thomas Hobbes's state of nature. If such cases constitute aberrations, they are uncomfortably common ones. We easily lose sight of the fact that struggles to achieve and maintain power, to establish order, and to contrive a kind of justice within states, may be bloodier than wars among them.

If anarchy is identified with chaos, destruction, and death, then the distinction between anarchy and government does not tell us much. Which is more precarious: the life of a state among states, or of a government in relation to its subjects? The answer varies with time and place. Among some states at some times, the actual or expected occurrence of violence is low. Within some states at some times, the actual or expected occurrence of violence is high. The use of force, or the constant fear of its use, are not

"Theory of International Politics" by Kenneth N. Waltz. © 1979 by McGraw-Hill, Inc. pp. 102-114. Reprinted by permission of McGraw-Hill, Inc

sufficient grounds for distinguishing international from domestic affairs. If the possible and the actual use of force mark both national and international orders, then no durable distinction between the two realms can be drawn in terms of the use or the nonuse of force. No human order is proof against violence.

To discover qualitative differences between internal and external affairs one must look for a criterion other than the occurrence of violence. The distinction between international and national realms of politics is not found in the use or the nonuse of force but in their different structures. But if the dangers of being violently attacked are greater, say, in taking an evening stroll through downtown Detroit than they are in picnicking along the French and German border, what practical difference does the difference of structure make? Nationally as internationally, contact generates conflict and at times issues in violence. The difference between national and international politics lies not in the use of force but in the different modes of organization for doing something about it. A government, ruling by some standard of legitimacy, arrogates to itself the right to use force—that is, to apply a variety of sanctions to control the use of force by its subjects. If some use private force, others may appeal to the government. A government has no monopoly on the use of force, as is all too evident. An effective government, however, has a monopoly on the *legitimate* use of force, and legitimate here means that public agents are organized to prevent and to counter the private use of force. Citizens need not prepare to defend themselves. Public agencies do that. A national system is not one of self-help. The international system is.

### Interdependence and Integration

The political significance of interdependence varies depending on whether a realm is organized, with relations of authority specified and established, or remains formally unorganized.

Insofar as a realm is formally organized, its units are free to specialize, to pursue their own interests without concern for developing the means of maintaining their identity and preserving their security in the presence of others. They are free to specialize because they have no reason to fear the increased interdependence that goes with specialization. If those who specialize most benefit most, then competition in specialization ensues. Goods are manufactured, grain is produced, law and order are maintained, commerce is conducted, and financial services are provided by people who ever more narrowly specialize. In simple economic terms, the cobbler depends on the tailor for his pants and the tailor on the cobbler for his shoes, and each would be ill-clad without the services of the other. In simple political terms, Kansas depends on Washington for protection and regulation and Washington depends on Kansas for beef and wheat. In saying that in such situations interdependence is close, one need not maintain that the one part could not learn to live without the other. One need only say that the cost of breaking the interdependent relation would be high. Persons and institutions depend heavily on one another because of the different tasks they perform and the different goods they produce and exchange. The parts of a polity bind themselves together by their differences (cf. Durkheim 1893, p. 212).

Differences between national and international structures are reflected in the ways the units of each system define their ends and develop the means for reaching them. In anarchic realms, like units coact. In hierarchic realms, unlike units interact. In an anarchic realm, the units are functionally similar and tend to remain so. Like units work to maintain a measure of independence and may even strive for autarchy. In a hierarchic realm, the units are differentiated, and they tend to increase the extent of their specialization. Differentiated units become closely interdependent, the more closely so as their specialization proceeds. Because of the difference of structure, interdependence within and interdependence among nations are two distinct concepts. So as to follow the logicians' admonition to keep a single meaning for a given term throughout one's discourse, I shall use "integration" to describe the condition within nations and "interdependence" to describe the condition among them.

Although states are like units functionally, they differ vastly in their capabilities. Out of such differences something of a division of labor develops. . . . The division of labor across nations, however, is slight in comparison with the highly articulated division of labor within them. Integration draws the parts of a nation closely together. Interdependence among nations leaves them loosely connected. Although the integration of nations is often talked about, it seldom takes place. Nations could mutually enrich themselves by further dividing not just the labor that goes into the production of goods but also some of the other tasks they perform, such as political management and military defense. Why does their integration not take place? The structure of international politics limits the cooperation of states in two ways.

In a self-help system each of the units spends a portion of its effort, not in forwarding its own good, but in providing the means of protecting itself against others. Specialization in a system of divided labor works to everyone's advantage, though not equally so. Inequality in the expected distribution of the increased product works strongly against extension of the division of labor internationally. When faced with the possibility of cooperating for mutual gain, states that feel insecure must ask how the gain will be divided. They are compelled to ask not "Will both of us gain?" but "Who will gain more?" If an expected gain is to be divided, say, in the ratio of two to one, one state may use its disproportionate gain to implement a policy intended to damage or destroy the other. Even the prospect of large absolute gains for both parties does not elicit their cooperation so long as each fears how the other will use its increased capabilities.

Notice that the impediments to collaboration may not lie in the character and the immediate intention of either party. Instead, the condition of insecurity—at the least, the uncertainty of each about the other's future intentions and actions—works against their cooperation.

In any self-help system, units worry about their survival, and the worry conditions their behavior. Oligopolistic markets limit the cooperation of firms in much the way that international- political structures limit the cooperation of states. Within rules laid down by governments, whether firms survive and prosper depends on their own efforts. Firms need not protect themselves physically against assaults from other firms. They are free to concentrate on their economic interests. As economic entities, however, they live in a self-help world. All want to increase profits. If they run undue risks in the effort to do so, they must expect to suffer the consequences. As William Fellner says, it is "impossible to maximize joint gains without the collusive handling of all relevant variables." And this can be accomplished only by "complete disarmament of the firms in relation to each other." But firms cannot sensibly disarm even to increase their profits. This statement qualifies, rather than contradicts, the assumption that firms aim at maximum profits. To maximize profits tomorrow as well as today, firms first have to survive. Pooling all resources implies, again as Fellner puts it, "discounting the future possibilities of all participating firms" (1949, p. 35). But the future cannot be discounted. The relative strength of firms changes over time in ways that cannot be foreseen. Firms are constrained to strike a compromise between maximizing their profits and minimizing the danger of their own demise. Each of two firms may be better off if one of them accepts compensation from the other in return for withdrawing from some part of the market. But a firm that accepts smaller markets in exchange for larger profits will be gravely disadvantaged if, for example, a price war should break out as part of a renewed struggle for markets. If possible, one must resist accepting smaller markets in return for larger profits (pp. 132, 217-18). "It is," Fellner insists, "not advisable to disarm in relation to one's rivals" (p. 199). Why not? Because "the potentiality of renewed warfare always exists" (p. 177). Fellner's reasoning is much like the reasoning that led Lenin to believe that capitalist countries would never be able to cooperate for their mutual enrichment in one vast imperialist enterprise. Like nations, oligopolistic firms must be more concerned with relative strength than with absolute advantage.

A state worries about a division of possible gains that may favor others more than itself. That is the first way in which the structure of international politics limits the cooperation of states. A state also worries lest it become dependent on others through cooperative endeavors and exchanges of goods and services. That is the second way in which the structure of international politics limits the cooperation of states. The more a state specializes, the more it relies on others to supply the materials and goods that it is not producing. The larger a state's imports and exports, the more it depends on others. The world's well-being would be increased if an ever more elaborate division of labor were developed, but states would thereby place themselves in situations of ever closer interdependence. Some states may not resist that. For small and ill-endowed states the costs of doing so are excessively high. But states that can resist becoming ever more enmeshed with others ordinarily do so in either or both of two ways. States that are heavily dependent, or closely interdependent, worry about securing that which they depend on. The high interdependence of states means that the states in question experience, or are subject to, the common vulnerability that high interdependence entails. Like other organizations, states seek to control what they depend on or to lessen the extent of their dependency. This simple thought explains quite a bit of the behavior of states: their imperial thrusts to widen the scope

of their control and their autarchic strivings toward greater self-sufficiency.

Structures encourage certain behaviors and penalize those who do not respond to the encouragement. Nationally, many lament the extreme development of the division of labor, a development that results in the allocation of ever narrower tasks to individuals. And yet specialization proceeds, and its extent is a measure of the development of societies. In a formally organized realm a premium is put on each unit's being able to specialize in order to increase its value to others in a system of divided labor. The domestic imperative is "specialize"! Internationally, many lament the resources states spend unproductively for their own defense and the opportunities they miss to enhance the welfare of their people through cooperation with other states. And yet the ways of states change little. In an unorganized realm each unit's incentive is to put itself in a position to be able to take care of itself since no one else can be counted on to do so. The international imperative is "take care of yourself"! Some leaders of nations may understand that the well-being of all of them would increase through their participation in a fuller division of labor. But to act on the idea would be to act on a domestic imperative, an imperative that does not run internationally. What one might want to do in the absence of structural constraints is different from what one is encouraged to do in their presence. States do not willingly place themselves in situations of increased dependence. In a self-help system, considerations of security subordinate economic gain to political interest.

What each state does for itself is much like what all of the others are doing. They are denied the advantages that a full division of labor, political as well as economic, would provide. Defense spending, moreover, is unproductive for all and unavoidable for most. Rather than increased well-being, their reward is in the maintenance of their autonomy. States compete, but not by contributing their individual efforts to the joint production of goods for their mutual benefit. Here is a second big difference between international-political and economic systems. . . .

### Structures and Strategies

That motives and outcomes may well be disjoined should now be easily seen. Structures cause actions to have consequences they were not intended to have. Surely most of the actors will notice that, and at least some of them will be able to figure out why. They may develop a pretty good sense of just how structures work their effects. Will they not then be able to achieve their original ends by appropriately adjusting their strategies? Unfortunately, they often cannot. To show why this is so I shall give only a few examples; once the point is made, the reader will easily think of others.

If shortage of a commodity is expected, all are collectively better off if they buy less of it in order to moderate price increases and to distribute shortages equitably. But because some will be better off if they lay in extra supplies quickly, all have a strong incentive to do so. If one expects others to make a run on a bank, one's prudent course is to run faster than they do even while knowing that if few others run, the bank will remain solvent, and if many run, it will fail. In such cases, pursuit of individual interest produces collective results that nobody wants, yet individuals by behaving differently will hurt themselves without altering outcomes. These two much used examples establish the main point. Some courses of action I cannot sensibly follow unless you do too, and you and I cannot sensibly follow them unless we are pretty sure that many others will as well. Let us go more deeply into the problem by considering two further examples in some detail.

Each of many persons may choose to drive a private car rather than take a train. Cars offer flexibility in scheduling and in choice of destination; yet at times, in bad weather for example, railway passenger service is a much wanted convenience. Each of many persons may shop in supermarkets rather than at corner grocery stores. The stocks of supermarkets are larger, and their prices lower; yet at times the corner grocery store, offering, say, credit and delivery service, is a much wanted convenience. The result of most people usually driving their own cars and shopping at supermarkets is to reduce passenger service and to decrease the number of corner grocery stores. These results may not be what most people want. They may be willing to pay to prevent services from disappearing. And yet individuals can do nothing to affect the outcomes. Increased patronage would do it, but not increased patronage by me and the few others I might persuade to follow my example.

We may well notice that our behavior produces unwanted outcomes, but we are also likely to see that such instances as these are examples of what Alfred E. Kahn describes as "large" changes that are brought about by the accumulation of "small" decisions. In such situations people are victims of the "tyranny of small decisions," a phrase suggesting that "if one hundred consumers choose option $x$, and this causes the market to make decision X (where X equals 100 $x$), it is not necessarily true that those same consumers would have voted for that outcome if that large decision had ever been presented for their explicit consideration" (Kahn 1966, p. 523). If the market does not present the large question for decision, then individuals are doomed to making decisions that are sensible within their narrow contexts even though they know all the while that in making such decisions they are bringing about a result that most of them do not want. Either that or they organize to overcome some of the effects of the market by changing its structure—for example, by bringing consumer units roughly up to the size of the units that are making producers' decisions. This nicely makes the point: So long as one leaves the structure unaffected it is not possible for changes in the intentions and the actions of particular actors to produce desirable outcomes or to avoid undesirable ones. Structures may be changed, as just mentioned, by changing the distribution of capabilities across units. Structures may also be changed by imposing requirements where previously people had to decide for themselves. If some merchants sell on Sunday, others may have to do so in order to remain competitive even though most prefer a six-day week. Most are able to do as they please only if all are required to keep comparable hours. The only remedies for strong structural effects are structural changes.

Structural constraints cannot be wished away, although many fail to understand this. In every age and place, the units of self-help systems—nations, corporations, or whatever—are told that the greater good, along with their own, requires them to act for the sake of the system and not for their own narrowly defined advantage. In the 1950s, as fear of the world's destruction in nuclear war grew, some concluded that the alternative to world destruction was world disarmament. In the 1970s, with the rapid growth of population, poverty, and pollution, some concluded, as one political scientist put it, that "states must meet the needs of the political ecosystem in its global dimensions or court annihilation" (Sterling 1974, p. 336). The international interest must be served; and if that means anything at all, it means that national interests are subordinate to it. The problems are found at the global level. Solutions to the problems continue to depend on national policies. What are the conditions that would make nations more or less willing to obey the injunctions that are so often laid on them? How can they resolve the tension between pursuing their own interests and acting for the sake of the system? No one has shown how that can be done, although many wring their hands and plead for rational behavior. The very problem, however, is that rational behavior, given structural constraints, does not

lead to the wanted results. With each country constrained to take care of itself, no one can take care of the system.[1]

A strong sense of peril and doom may lead to a clear definition of ends that must be achieved. Their achievement is not thereby made possible. The possibility of effective action depends on the ability to provide necessary means. It depends even more so on the existence of conditions that permit nations and other organizations to follow appropriate policies and strategies. World-shaking problems cry for global solutions, but there is no global agency to provide them. Necessities do not create possibilities. Wishing that final causes were efficient ones does not make them so.

Great tasks can be accomplished only by agents of great capability. That is why states, and especially the major ones, are called on to do what is necessary for the world's survival. But states have to do whatever they think necessary for their own preservation, since no one can be relied on to do it for them. Why the advice to place the international interest above national interests is meaningless can be explained precisely in terms of the distinction between micro- and macrotheories. Among economists the distinction is well understood. Among political scientists it is not. As I have explained, a microeconomic theory is a theory of the market built up from assumptions about the behavior of individuals. The theory shows how the actions and interactions of the units form and affect the market and how the market in turn affects them. A macrotheory is a theory about the national economy built on supply, income, and demand as systemwide aggregates. The theory shows how these and other aggregates are interconnected and indicates how changes in one or some of them affect others and the performance of the

---

1  Put differently, states face a "prisoners' dilemma." If each of two parties follows his own interest, both end up worse off than if each acted to achieve joint interests. For thorough examination of the logic of such situations, see Snyder and Diesing 1977; for brief and suggestive international applications, see Jervis, January 1978.

economy. In economics, both micro- and macrotheories deal with large realms. The difference between them is found not in the size of the objects of study, but in the way the objects of study are approached and the theory to explain them is constructed. A macrotheory of international politics would show how the international system is moved by system-wide aggregates. One can imagine what some of them might be— amount of world GNP, amount of world imports and exports, of deaths in war, of everybody's defense spending, and of migration, for example. The theory would look something like a macroeconomic theory in the style of John Maynard Keynes, although it is hard to see how the international aggregates would make much sense and how changes in one or some of them would produce changes in others. I am not saying that such a theory cannot be constructed, but only that I cannot see how to do it in any way that might be useful. The decisive point, anyway, is that a macrotheory of international politics would lack the practical implications of macroeconomic theory. National governments can manipulate system-wide economic variables. No agencies with comparable capabilities exist internationally. Who would act on the possibilities of adjustment that a macrotheory of international politics might reveal? Even were such a theory available, we would still be stuck with nations as the only agents capable of acting to solve global problems. We would still have to revert to a micropolitical approach in order to examine the conditions that make benign and effective action by states separately and collectively more or less likely.

Some have hoped that changes in the awareness and purpose, in the organization and ideology, of states would change the quality of international life. Over the centuries states have changed in many ways, but the quality of international life has remained much the same. States may seek reasonable and worthy ends, but they cannot figure out how to reach them. The problem is not in their stupidity or ill will, although one does not want to claim that those qualities are lacking. The depth of the difficulty is not understood until one realizes that intelligence and goodwill cannot discover and act on adequate programs. Early in this century Winston Churchill observed that the British-German naval race promised disaster and that Britain had no realistic choice other than to run it. States facing global problems are like individual consumers trapped by the "tyranny of small decisions." States, like consumers, can get out of the trap only by changing the structure of their field of activity. The message bears repeating: The only remedy for a strong structural effect is a structural change.

## The Virtues of Anarchy

To achieve their objectives and maintain their security, units in a condition of anarchy—be they people, corporations, states, or whatever— must rely on the means they can generate and the arrangements they can make for themselves. Self-help is necessarily the principle of action in an anarchic order. A self-help situation is one of high risk—of bankruptcy in the economic realm and of war in a world of free states. It is also one in which organizational costs are low. Within an economy or within an international order, risks may be avoided or lessened by moving from a situation of coordinate action to one of super- and subordination, that is, by erecting agencies with effective authority and extending a system of rules. Government emerges where the functions of regulation and management themselves become distinct and specialized tasks. The costs of maintaining a hierarchic order are frequently ignored by those who deplore its absence. Organizations have at least two aims: to get something done and to maintain themselves as organizations. Many of their activities are directed toward the second purpose. The leaders of organizations, and political leaders preeminently, are not masters of the matters their organizations deal with. They have become leaders not by being experts on one thing or another but by excelling in the organizational arts—in maintaining control of a group's members, in eliciting predictable and satisfactory efforts from them, in holding a group together. In making political decisions, the first and most important concern is not to achieve the aims the members of an organization may have but to secure the continuity and health of the organization itself (cf. Diesing 1962, pp. 198-204; Downs 1967, pp. 262-70).

Along with the advantages of hierarchic orders go the costs. In hierarchic orders, moreover, the means of control become an object of struggle. Substantive issues become entwined with efforts to influence or control the controllers. The hierarchic ordering of politics adds one to the already numerous objects of struggle, and the object added is at a new order of magnitude.

If the risks of war are unbearably high, can they be reduced by organizing to manage the affairs of nations? At a minimum, management requires controlling the military forces that are at the disposal of states. Within nations, organizations have to work to maintain themselves. As organizations, nations, in working to maintain themselves, sometimes have to use force against dissident elements and areas. As hierarchical systems, governments nationally or globally are disrupted by the defection of major parts. In a society of states with little coherence, attempts at world government would founder on the inability of an emerging central authority to mobilize the resources needed to create and maintain the unity of the system by regulating and managing its parts. The prospect of world government would be an invitation to prepare for world civil war. This calls to mind Milovan Djilas's reminiscence of World War II. According to him, he and many Russian soldiers in their wartime discussions came to believe that human struggles would acquire their ultimate bitterness if all men were subject to the same social system, "for the system would be untenable as such and various sects would undertake the reckless destruction of the human race for the sake of its greater 'happiness'"

(1962, p. 50). States cannot entrust managerial powers to a central agency unless that agency is able to protect its client states. The more powerful the clients and the more the power of each of them appears as a threat to the others, the greater the power lodged in the center must be. The greater the power of the center, the stronger the incentive for states to engage in a struggle to control it.

States, like people, are insecure in proportion to the extent of their freedom. If freedom is wanted, insecurity must be accepted. Organizations that establish relations of authority and control may increase security as they decrease freedom. If might does not make right, whether among people or states, then some institution or agency has intervened to lift them out of nature's realm. The more influential the agency, the stronger the desire to control it becomes. In contrast, units in an anarchic order act for their own sakes and not for the sake of preserving an organization and furthering their fortunes within it. Force is used for one's own interest. In the absence of organization, people or states are free to leave one another alone. Even when they do not do so, they are better able, in the absence of the politics of the organization, to concentrate on the politics of the problem and to aim for a minimum agreement that will permit their separate existence rather than a maximum agreement for the sake of maintaining unity. If might decides, then bloody struggles over right can more easily be avoided.

Nationally, the force of a government is exercised in the name of right and justice. Internationally, the force of a state is employed for the sake of its own protection and advantage. Rebels challenge a government's claim to authority; they question the rightfulness of its rule. Wars among states cannot settle questions of authority and right; they can only determine the allocation of gains and losses among contenders and settle for a time the question of who is the stronger. Nationally, relations of authority are established. Internationally, only relations of strength result.

Nationally, private force used against a government threatens the political system. Force used by a state—a public body—is, from the international perspective, the private use of force; but there is no government to overthrow and no governmental apparatus to capture. Short of a drive toward world hegemony, the private use of force does not threaten the system of international politics, only some of its members. War pits some states against others in a struggle among similarly constituted entities. The power of the strong may deter the weak from asserting their claims, not because the weak recognize a kind of rightfulness of rule on the part of the strong, but simply because it is not sensible to tangle with them. Conversely, the weak may enjoy considerable freedom of action if they are so far removed in their capabilities from the strong that the latter are not much bothered by their actions or much concerned by marginal increases in their capabilities.

National politics is the realm of authority, of administration, and of law. International politics is the realm of power, of struggle, and of accommodation. The international realm is preeminently a political one. The national realm is variously described as being hierarchic, vertical, centralized, heterogeneous, directed, and contrived; the international realm, as being anarchic, horizontal, decentralized, homogeneous, undirected, and mutually adaptive. The more centralized the order, the nearer to the top the locus of decisions ascends. Internationally, decisions are made at the bottom level, there being scarcely any other. In the vertical horizontal dichotomy, international structures assume the prone position. Adjustments are made internationally, but they are made without a formal or authoritative adjuster. Adjustment and accommodation proceed by mutual adaptation (cf. Barnard 1948, pp. 148-52; Polanyi 1941, pp. 428-56). Action and reaction, and reaction to the reaction, proceed by a piecemeal process. The parties feel each other out, so to speak, and define a situation simultaneously with its development. Among coordinate units, adjustment is achieved and accommodations arrived at by the exchange of "considerations," in a condition, as Chester Barnard put it, "in which the duty of command and the desire to obey are essentially absent" (pp. 150-51). Where the contest is over considerations, the parties seek to maintain or improve their positions by maneuvering, by bargaining, or by fighting. The manner and intensity of the competition is determined by the desires and the abilities of parties that are at once separate and interacting.

Whether or not by force, each state plots the course it thinks will best serve its interests. If force is used by one state or its use is expected, the recourse of other states is to use force or be prepared to use it singly or in combination. No appeal can be made to a higher entity clothed with the authority and equipped with the ability to act on its own initiative. Under such conditions the possibility that force will be used by one or another of the parties looms always as a threat in the background. In politics force is said to be the *ultima ratio*. In international politics force serves, not only as the *ultima ratio,* but indeed as the first and constant one. To limit force to being the *ultima ratio* of politics implies, in the words of Ortega y Gasset, "the previous submission of force to methods of reason" (quoted in Johnson 1966, p. 13). The constant possibility that force will be used limits manipulations, moderates demands, and serves as an incentive for the settlement of disputes. One who knows that pressing too hard may lead to war has strong reason to consider whether possible gains are worth the risks entailed. The threat of force internationally is comparable to the role of the strike in labor and management bargaining. "The few strikes that take place are in a sense," as Livernash has said, "the cost of the strike option which produces settlements in the large mass of negotiations" (1963, p. 430). Even if workers seldom strike, their doing so is always a possibility. The possibility of industrial disputes leading to long and costly strikes encourages labor and management to face difficult issues, to try to understand each other's problems, and to work hard to find accommodations. The possibility that conflicts among nations may lead to long and costly wars has similarly sobering effects.

## References

Barnard, Chester I. (1944). "On planning for world government." In Barnard (ed.), *Organization and Management*. Cambridge: Harvard University Press, 1948.

Diesing, Paul (1962). *Reason in Society*. Urbana: University of Illinois Press.

Djilas, Milovan (1962). *Conversations with Stalin*. Translated by Michael B. Petrovich. New York: Harcourt, Brace and World.

Downs, Anthony (1967). *Inside Bureaucracy*. Boston: Little, Brown.

Durkheim, Emile (1893). *The Division of Labor in Society*. Translated by George Simpson, 1933. New York: Free Press, 1964.

Fellner, William (1949). *Competition among the Few*. New York: Knopf.

Jervis, Robert (1976). *Perception and Misperception in International Politics*. Princeton: Princeton University Press

_____ (January 1978). "Cooperation under the security dilemma." *World Politics,* vol. 30.

Johnson, Chalmers A. (1966). *Revolutionary Change*. Boston: Little, Brown.

Kahn, Alfred E. (1966). "The tyranny of small decisions: market failures, imperfection, and the limits of econometrics." In Bruce M. Russett (ed.), *Economic Theories of International Relations*. Chicago: Markham, 1968.

Livernash, E. R. (1963). "The relation of power to the structure and process of collective bargaining." In Bruce M. Russett (ed.), *Economic Theories of International Politics*. Chicago: Markham, 1968.

Polanyi, Michael (November 1941). "The growth of thought in society." *Economica*, vol. 8.

Snyder, Glenn H. and Paul Diesing (1977). *Conflict among Nations*. Princeton: Princeton University Press.

Sterling, Richard W. (1974). *Macropolitics: International Relations in a Global Society*. New York: Knopf.

# 5: Power

*Joseph S. Nye, Jr.*

Power in international politics is like the weather. Everyone talks about it, but few understand it. Just as farmers and meteorologists try to forecast storms, so do statesmen and analysts try to understand the dynamics of major changes in the distribution of power among nations.

Power, like love, is easier to experience than to define or measure. Power is the ability to achieve one's purposes or goals. The dictionary tells us that it is the ability to do things and to control others. Robert Dahl, a leading political scientist, defines power as the ability to get others to do what they otherwise would not do.[1] But when we measure power in terms of the changed behavior of others, we have to know their preferences. Otherwise, we may be as mistaken about our power as was the fox who thought he was hurting Brer Rabbit when he threw him into the briar patch. Knowing in advance how other people or nations would behave in the absence of our efforts is often difficult.

The behavioral definition of power may be useful to analysts and historians who devote considerable time to reconstructing the past, but to practical politicians and leaders it often seems too ephemeral. Because the ability to control others is often associated with the possession of certain resources, political leaders commonly define power as the possession of resources. These resources include population, territory, natural resources, economic size, military forces, and political stability among others.[2] The virtue of this definition is that it makes power appear more concrete, measurable, and predictable than does the behavioral definition. Power in this sense means holding the high cards in the international poker game. A basic rule of poker is that if your opponent is showing cards that can beat anything you hold, fold your hand. If you know you will lose a war, don't start it.

Some wars, however, have been started by the eventual losers, which suggests that political leaders sometimes take risks or make mistakes. Often the opponent's cards are not all showing in the game of international politics. As in poker, playing skills, such as bluff and deception, can make a big difference. Even when there is no deception, mistakes can be made about which power resources are most relevant in particular situations (for example, France and Britain had more tanks than Hitler in 1940, but Hitler had greater maneuverability and a better military strategy). On the other hand, in long wars when there is time to mobilize, depth of territory and the size of an economy become more important, as the Soviet Union and the United States demonstrated in World War II.

---

1  Robert A. Dahl, *Who Governs? Democracy and Power in an American City* (New Haven, Conn.: Yale University Press, 1961). See also James March, "The Power of Power," in *Varieties of Political Theory*, ed. David Easton (New York: Prentice Hall, 1966), pp. 39-70; Herbert Simon, *Models of Man* (New York: John Wiley, 1957); and David Baldwin. "Power Analysis and World Politics." *World Politics* 31 (January 1979): 161-94.

2  See Ray S. Cline, *World Power Assessment* (Boulder, Colo.: Westview Press, 1977); Hans J. Morgenthau, *Politics among Nations* (New York: Alfred Knopf, 1955), chap. 9; and Klaus Knorr, *The Power of Nations* (New York: Basic Books, 1975), chaps. 3, 4.

*From Bound to Lead: The Changing Nature of American Power* by Joseph S. Nye, Jr. (ISBN: 0465007449).
Copyright © 1990 by Basic Books, Inc. Preface to the paperback edition Copyright ©. Reprinted by permission of Basic Books, a member of Perseus Books, L.L.C.

Power conversion is a basic problem that arises when we think of power in terms of resources. Some countries are better than others at converting their resources into effective influence, just as some skilled card players win despite being dealt weak hands. Power conversion is the capacity to convert potential power, as measured by resources, to realized power, as measured by the changed behavior of others. Thus, one has to know about a country's skill at power conversion as well as its possession of power resources to predict outcomes correctly.

Another problem is determining which resources provide the best basis for power in any particular context. In earlier periods, power resources were easier to judge. According to historian A. J. P. Taylor, traditionally "the test of a Great Power is . . . the test of strength for war."[3] For example, in the agrarian economies of eighteenth-century Europe, population was a critical power resource because it provided a base for taxes and recruitment of infantry. In population, France dominated Western Europe. Thus, at the end of the Napoleonic Wars, Prussia presented its fellow victors at the Congress of Vienna with a precise plan for its own reconstruction in order to maintain the balance of power. Its plan listed the territories and populations it had lost since 1805, and the territories and populations it would need to regain equivalent numbers.[4] In the pre-nationalist period, it did not much matter that many of the people in those provinces did not speak German or feel themselves to be German. However, within half a century, nationalist sentiments mattered very much. Germany's seizure of Alsace-Lorraine from France in 1870, for example, made hope of any future alliance with France impossible.

Another change that occurred during the nineteenth century was the growing importance of industry and rail systems that made rapid mobilization possible. In the 1860s, Bismarck's Germany pioneered the use of railways to transport armies for quick victories. Although Russia had always had greater population resources than the rest of Europe, they were difficult to mobilize. The growth of the rail system in Western Russia at the beginning of the twentieth century was one of the reasons the Germans feared rising Russian power in 1914. Further, the spread of rail systems on the Continent helped deprive Britain of the luxury of concentrating on naval power. There was no longer time, should it prove necessary, to insert an army to prevent another great power from dominating the Continent.

The application of industrial technology to warfare has long had a powerful impact. Advanced science and technology have been particularly critical power resources since the beginning of the nuclear age in 1945. But the power derived from nuclear weapons has proven to be so awesome and destructive that its actual application is muscle-bound. Nuclear war is simply too costly. More generally, there are many situations where any use of force may be inappropriate or too costly. In 1853, for example, Commodore Perry could threaten to bombard Japan if it did not open its ports for supplies and trade, but it is hard to imagine that the United States could effectively threaten force to open Japanese markets today.

### The Changing Sources of Power

Some observers have argued that the sources of power are, in general, moving away from the emphasis on military force and conquest that marked earlier eras. In assessing international power today, factors such as technology, education, and economic growth are becoming more important, whereas geography, population, and raw materials are becoming less important.

---

3  A. J. P. Taylor, *The Struggle for Mastery in Europe, 1848-1918* (Oxford: Oxford University Press, 1954), p. xxix.
4  Edward V. Gulick, *Europe's Classical Balance of Power* (New York: W. W. Norton, 1955), pp. 248-51.

Kenneth Waltz argues that a 5-percent rate of economic growth in the United States for three years would add more to American strength than does our alliance with Britain.[5] Richard Rosecrance argues that since 1945, the world has been poised between a territorial system composed of states that view power in terms of land mass, and a trading system "based in states which recognize that self-sufficiency is an illusion." In the past, says Rosecrance, "it was cheaper to seize another state's territory by force than to develop the sophisticated economic and trading apparatus needed to derive benefit from commercial exchange with it."[6]

If so, perhaps we are in a "Japanese period" in world politics. Japan has certainly done far better with its strategy as a trading state after 1945 than it did with its military strategy to create a Greater East Asian Co-Prosperity Sphere in the 1930s. But Japan's security vis-à-vis its large military neighbors—China and the Soviet Union—depends heavily on U.S. protection. In short, even if we can define power clearly, it still has become more difficult to be clear about the relationship of particular resources to it. Thus, we cannot leap too quickly to the conclusion that all trends favor economic power or countries like Japan.

Like other forms of power, economic power cannot be measured simply in terms of tangible resources. Intangible aspects also matter. For example, outcomes generally depend on bargaining, and bargaining depends on relative costs in particular situations and skill in converting potential power into effects. Relative costs are determined not only by the total amount of measurable economic resources of a country but also by the degree of its interdependence in a relationship. If, for example, the United States and Japan depend on each other but one is less dependent than the other, that asymmetry is a source of power. The United States may be less vulnerable than Japan if the relationship breaks down, and it may use that threat as a source of power.[7] . . .

Another consideration is that most large countries today find military force more costly to apply than in previous centuries. This has resulted from the dangers of nuclear escalation, the difficulty of ruling nationalistically awakened populations in otherwise weak states, the danger of rupturing profitable relations on other issues, and the public opposition in Western democracies to prolonged and expensive military conflicts. Even so, the increased cost of military force does not mean that it will be ruled out. To the contrary, in an anarchic system of states where there is no higher government to settle conflicts and where the ultimate recourse is self-help, this could never happen. In some cases, the stakes may justify a costly use of force.[8]

Even if the direct use of force were banned among a group of countries, military force would still play an important political role. For example, the American military role in deterring threats to allies, or of assuring access to a crucial resource such as oil in the Persian Gulf, means that the provision of protective force can be used in bargaining situations. Sometimes the linkage may be direct; more often it is a factor not mentioned openly but present in the back of statesmen's minds.

In addition, there is the consideration that is sometimes called "the second face of power."[9] . . .

5   Kenneth N. Waltz, *Theory of International Politics* (Reading, Mass.: Addison-Wesley, 1979), p. 172.

6   Richard N. Rosecrance, *The Rise of the Trading State* (New York: Basic Books, 1986), pp. 16, 160.

7   Robert O. Keohane and Joseph S. Nye, Jr., *Power and Interdependence* (Boston: Little, Brown, 1977), chap. 1. See also R. Harrison Wagner, "Economic Interdependence, Bargaining Power and Political Influence," *International Organization* 41 (Summer 1988): 461-84.

9   Peter Bachrach and Morton S. Baratz, "Decisions and Nondecisions: An Analytical Framework," *American Political Science Review* 57 (September 1963): 632-42. See also Richard Mansbach and John Vasquez, *In Search of Theory: A New Paradigm for Global Politics* (Englewood Cliffs, N.J.: Prentice Hall, 1981).

A country may achieve the outcomes it prefers in world politics because other countries want to follow it or have agreed to a system that produces such effects. In this sense, it is just as important to set the agenda and structure the situations in world politics as it is to get others to change in particular situations. This aspect of power—that is, getting others to want what you want—might be called indirect or co-optive power behavior. It is in contrast to the active command power behavior of getting others to do what you want.[10] Co-optive power can rest on the attraction of one's ideas or on the ability to set the political agenda in a way that shapes the preferences that others express. Parents of teenagers know that if they have structured their children's beliefs and preferences, their power will be greater and will last longer than if they had relied only on active control. Similarly, political leaders and philosophers have long understood the power that comes from setting the agenda and determining the framework of a debate. The ability to establish preferences tends to be associated with intangible power resources such as culture, ideology, and institutions. This dimension can be thought of as soft power, in contrast to the hard command power usually associated with tangible resources like military and economic strength.[11]

Robert Cox argues that the nineteenth-century *Pax Britannica* and the twentieth-century *Pax Americana* were effective because they created liberal international economic orders, in which certain types of economic relations were privileged over others and liberal international rules and institutions were broadly accepted. Following the insights of the Italian thinker Antonio Gramsci, Cox argues that the most critical feature for a dominant country is the ability to obtain a broad measure of consent on general principles—principles that ensure the supremacy of the leading state and dominant social classes—and at the same time to offer some prospect of satisfaction to the less powerful. Cox identifies Britain from 1845 to 1875 and the United States from 1945 to 1967 as such countries.[12] Although we may not agree with his terminology or dates, Cox has touched a major point: Soft co-optive power is just as important as hard command power. If a state can make its power legitimate in the eyes of others, it will encounter less resistance to its wishes. If its culture

---

10  Susan Strange uses the term *structural power*, which she defines as "power to shape and determine the structures of the global political economy" (*States and Markets* [New York: Basil Blackwell, 1988], p. 24). My term, *co-optive power*, is similar in its focus on preferences but is somewhat broader, encompassing all elements of international politics. The term *structural power*, in contrast, tends to be associated with the neo-realist theories of Kenneth Waltz.

11  The distinction between hard and soft power resources is one of degree, both in the nature of the behavior and in the tangibility of the resources. Both types are aspects of the ability to achieve one's purposes by controlling the behavior of others. Command power—the ability to change what others *do*—can rest on coercion or inducement. Co-optive power— the ability to shape what others *want*—can rest on the attractiveness of one's culture and ideology or the ability to manipulate the agenda of political choices in a manner that makes actors fail to express some preferences because they seem to be too unrealistic. The forms of behavior between command and co-optive power range along this continuum:

| Command | coercion | inducement | agenda setting | attraction | Co-optive |
| power | | | | | power |

Further, soft power resources tend to be associated with co-optive power behavior, whereas hard power resources are usually associated with command behavior. But the relationship is imperfect. For example, countries may be attracted to others with command power by myths of invincibility, and command power may sometimes be used to establish institutions that later become regarded as legitimate. But the general association is strong enough to allow the useful shorthand reference to hard and soft power resources.

12  Robert W. Cox, *Production, Power, and World Order* (New York: Columbia University Press, 1987), chaps. 6, 7.

**Table 5-1**

**Leading States and Major Power Resources, 1500s-1900s**

| Period | Leading State | Major Resources |
|---|---|---|
| Sixteenth century | Spain | Gold bullion, colonial trade, mercenary armies, dynastic ties |
| Seventeenth century | Netherlands | Trade, capital markets, navy |
| Eighteenth century | France | Population, rural industry, public administration, army |
| Nineteenth century | Britain | Industry, political cohesion, finance and credit, navy, liberal norms, island location (easy to defend) |
| Twentieth century | United States | Economic scale, scientific and technical leadership, universalistic culture, military forces and alliances, liberal international regimes, hub of transnational communications |

and ideology are attractive, others will more willingly follow. If it can establish international norms that are consistent with its society, it will be less likely to have to change. If it can help support institutions that encourage other states to channel or limit their activities in ways the dominant state prefers, it may not need as many costly exercises of coercive or hard power in bargaining situations. In short, the universalism of a country's culture and its ability to establish a set of favorable rules and institutions that govern areas of international activity are critical sources of power.[13] . . .

---

13 See Stephen D. Krasner, *International Regimes* (Ithaca, N.Y.: Cornell University Press. 1983).

# 6: Coercion

## Thomas C. Schelling

There is a difference between taking what you want and making someone give it to you, between fending off assault and making someone afraid to assault you, between holding what people are trying to take and making them afraid to take it, between losing what someone can forcibly take and giving it up to avoid risk or damage. It is the difference between defense and deterrence, between brute force and intimidation, between conquest and blackmail, between action and threats. It is the difference between the unilateral, "undiplomatic" recourse to strength, and coercive diplomacy based on the power to hurt.

The contrasts are several. The purely "military" or "undiplomatic" recourse to forcible action is concerned with enemy strength, not enemy interests; the coercive use of the power to hurt, though, is the very exploitation of enemy wants and fears. And brute strength is usually measured relative to enemy strength, the one directly opposing the other, while the power to hurt is typically not reduced by the enemy's power to hurt in return. Opposing strengths may cancel each other, pain and grief do not. The willingness to hurt, the credibility of a threat, and the ability to exploit the power to hurt will indeed depend on how much the adversary can hurt in return; but there is little or nothing about an adversary's pain or grief that directly reduces one's own. Two sides cannot both overcome each other with superior strength; they may both be able to hurt each other. With strength they can dispute objects of value; with sheer violence they can destroy them.

And brute force succeeds when it is used, whereas the power to hurt is most successful when held in reserve. It is the *threat* of damage, or of more damage to come, that can make someone yield or comply. It is *latent* violence that can influence someone's choice—violence that can still be withheld or inflicted, or that a victim believes can be withheld or inflicted. The threat of pain tries to structure someone's motives, while brute force tries to overcome his strength. Unhappily, the power to hurt is often communicated by some performance of it. Whether it is sheer terroristic violence to induce an irrational response, or cool premeditated violence to persuade somebody that you mean it and may do it again, it is not the pain and damage itself but its influence on somebody's behavior that matters. It is the expectation of *more* violence that gets the wanted behavior, if the power to hurt can get it at all.

To exploit a capacity for hurting and inflicting damage one needs to know what an adversary treasures and what scares him and one needs the adversary to understand what behavior of his will cause the violence to be inflicted and what will cause it to be withheld. The victim has to know what is wanted, and he may have to be assured of what is not wanted. The pain and suffering have to appear *contingent* on his behavior; it is not alone the threat that is effective—the threat of pain or loss if he fails to comply—but

Excerpt from *Arms and Influence* by Thomas C. Schelling. pp. 2-11. © 1966 by Yale University Press, New Haven, CT. Reprinted by permision of the publisher.

the corresponding assurance, possibly an implicit one, that he can avoid the pain or loss if he does comply. The prospect of certain death may stun him, but it gives him no choice.

Coercion by threat of damage also requires that our interests and our opponent's not be absolutely opposed. If his pain were our greatest delight and our satisfaction his greatest woe, we would just proceed to hurt and to frustrate each other. It is when his pain gives us little or no satisfaction compared with what he can do for us, and the action or inaction that satisfies us costs him less than the pain we can cause, that there is room for coercion. Coercion requires finding a bargain, arranging for him to be better off doing what we want—worse off not doing what we want—when he takes the threatened penalty into account.

It is this capacity for pure damage, pure violence, that is usually associated with the most vicious labor disputes, with racial disorders, with civil uprisings and their suppression, with racketeering. It is also the power to hurt rather than brute force that we use in dealing with criminals; we hurt them afterward, or threaten to, for their misdeeds rather than protect ourselves with cordons of electric wires, masonry walls, and armed guards. Jail, of course, can be either forcible restraint or threatened privation; if the object is to keep criminals out of mischief by confinement, success is measured by how many of them are gotten behind bars, but if the object is to *threaten* privation, success will be measured by how few have to be put behind bars and success then depends on the subject's understanding of the consequences. Pure damage is what a car threatens when it tries to hog the road or to keep its rightful share, or to go first through an intersection. A tank or a bulldozer can force its way regardless of others' wishes; the rest of us have to threaten damage, usually mutual damage, hoping the other driver values his car or his limbs enough to give way, hoping he sees us, and hoping he is in control of his own car. The threat of pure damage will not work against an unmanned vehicle.

This difference between coercion and brute force is as often in the intent as in the instrument. To hunt down Comanches and to exterminate them was brute force; to raid their villages to make them behave was coercive diplomacy, based on the power to hurt. The pain and loss to the Indians might have looked much the same one way as the other; the difference was one of purpose and effect. If Indians were killed because they were in the way, or somebody wanted their land, or the authorities despaired of making them behave and could not confine them and decided to exterminate them, that was pure unilateral force. If *some* Indians were killed to make *other* Indians behave, that was coercive violence—intended to be, whether or not it was effective. The Germans at Verdun perceived themselves to be chewing up hundreds of thousands of French soldiers in a gruesome "meatgrinder." If the purpose was to eliminate a military obstacle—the French infantryman, viewed as a military "asset" rather than as a warm human being—the offensive at Verdun was a unilateral exercise of military force. If instead the object was to make the loss of young men—not of impersonal "effectives," but of sons, husbands, fathers, and the pride of French manhood—so anguishing as to be unendurable, to make surrender a welcome relief and to spoil the foretaste of an Allied victory, then it was an exercise in coercion, in applied violence, intended to offer relief upon accommodation. And of course, since any use of force tends to be brutal, thoughtless, vengeful, or plain obstinate, the motives themselves can be mixed and confused. The fact that heroism and brutality can be either coercive diplomacy or a contest in pure strength does not promise that the distinction will be made, and the strategies enlightened by the distinction, every time some vicious enterprise gets launched.

The contrast between brute force and coercion is illustrated by two alternative strategies attributed to Genghis Khan. Early in his career he pursued the war creed of the Mongols: the vanquished can never be the friends of the victors, their death is necessary for the victor's safety. This was the unilateral extermination of a menace or a liability. The turning point of his career, according to Lynn Montross, came later when he discovered how to use his power to hurt for diplomatic ends. "The great Khan, who was not inhibited by the usual mercies, conceived the plan of forcing captives—women, children, aged fathers, favorite sons-to march ahead of his army as the first potential victims of resistance."[1] Live captives have often proved more valuable than enemy dead; and the technique discovered by the Khan in his maturity remains contemporary. North Koreans and Chinese were reported to have quartered prisoners of war near strategic targets to inhibit bombing attacks by United Nations aircraft. Hostages represent the power to hurt in its purest form.

### Coercive Violence in Warfare

This distinction between the power to hurt and the power to seize or hold forcibly is important in modern war, both big war and little war, hypothetical war and real war. For many years the Greeks and the Turks on Cyprus could hurt each other indefinitely but neither could quite take or hold forcibly what they wanted or protect themselves from violence by physical means. The Jews in Palestine could not expel the British in the late 1940s but they could cause pain and fear and frustration through terrorism, and eventually influence somebody's decision. The brutal war in Algeria was more a contest in pure violence than in military strength; the question was who would first find the pain and degradation unendurable. The French troops preferred—indeed they continually tried—to make it a contest of strength, to pit military force against the nationalists' capacity for terror, to exterminate or disable the nationalists and to screen off the nationalists from the victims of their violence. But because in civil war terrorists commonly have access to victims by sheer physical propinquity, the victims and their properties could not be forcibly defended and in the end the French troops themselves resorted, unsuccessfully, to a war of pain.

Nobody believes that the Russians can take Hawaii from us, or New York, or Chicago, but nobody doubts that they might destroy people and buildings in Hawaii, Chicago, or New York. Whether the Russians can conquer West Germany in any meaningful sense is questionable; whether they can hurt it terribly is not doubted. That the United States can destroy a large part of Russia is universally taken for granted; that the United States can keep from being badly hurt, even devastated, in return, or can keep Western Europe from being devastated while itself destroying Russia, is a best arguable; and it is virtually out of the question that we could conquer Russia territorially and use its economic assets unless it were by threatening disaster and inducing compliance. It is the power to hurt, not military strength in the traditional sense, that inheres in our most impressive military capabilities at the present time. We have a Department of *Defense* but emphasize *retaliation* — "return evil for evil" (synonyms: requital, reprisal, revenge, vengeance, retribution). And it is pain and violence, not force in the traditional sense, that inheres also in some of the least impressive military capabilities of the present time—the plastic bomb, the terrorist's bullet, the burnt crops, and the tortured farmer.

War appears to be, or threatens to be, not so much a contest of strength as one of endurance, nerve, obstinacy, and pain. It appears to be, and threatens to be, not so much a contest of military strength as a bargaining process—dirty, extortionate, and often quite reluctant bargaining on one side or both—nevertheless a bargaining process.

---

1  Lynn Montross, *War Through the Ages* (3d ed. New York, Harper and Brothers, 1960), p. 146.

The difference cannot quite be expressed as one between the *use* of force and the *threat* of force. The actions involved in forcible accomplishment, on the one hand, and in fulfilling a threat, on the other, can be quite different. Sometimes the most effective direct action inflicts enough cost or pain on the enemy to serve as a threat, sometimes not. The United States threatens the Soviet Union with virtual destruction of its society in the event of a surprise attack on the United States; a hundred million deaths are awesome as pure damage, but they are useless in stopping the Soviet attack—especially if the threat is to do it all afterward anyway. So it is worth while to keep the concepts distinct—to distinguish forcible action from the threat of pain—recognizing that some actions serve as both a means of forcible accomplishment and a means of inflicting pure damage, some do not. Hostages tend to entail almost pure pain and damage, as do all forms of reprisal after the fact. Some modes of self-defense may exact so little in blood or treasure as to entail negligible violence; and some forcible actions entail so much violence that their threat can be effective by itself.

The power to hurt, though it can usually accomplish nothing directly, is potentially more versatile than a straightforward capacity for forcible accomplishment. By force alone we cannot even lead a horse to water—we have to drag him—much less make him drink. Any affirmative action, any collaboration, almost anything but physical exclusion, expulsion, or extermination, requires that an opponent or a victim do something, even if only to stop or get out. The threat of pain and damage may make him want to do it, and anything he can do is potentially susceptible to inducement. Brute force can only accomplish what requires no collaboration. The principle is illustrated by a technique of unarmed combat: one can disable a man by various stunning, fracturing, or killing blows, but to take him to jail one has to exploit the man's own efforts. "Come-along" holds are those that threaten pain or disablement, giving relief as long as the victim complies, giving him the option of using his own legs to get to jail.

We have to keep in mind, though, that what is pure pain, or the threat of it, at one level of decision can be equivalent to brute force at another level. Churchill was worried, during the early bombing raids on London in 1940, that Londoners might panic. Against people the bombs were pure violence, to induce their undisciplined evasion; to Churchill and the government, the bombs were a cause of inefficiency, whether they spoiled transport and made people late to work or scared people and made them afraid to work. Churchill's decisions were not going to be coerced by the fear of a few casualties. Similarly on the battlefield: tactics that frighten soldiers so that they run, duck their heads, or lay down their arms and surrender represent coercion based on the power to hurt; to the top command, which is frustrated but not coerced, such tactics are part of the contest in military discipline and strength.

The fact that violence—pure pain and damage—can be used or threatened to coerce and to deter, to intimidate and to blackmail, to demoralize and to paralyze, in a conscious process of dirty bargaining, does not by any means imply that violence is not often wanton and meaningless or, even when purposive, in danger of getting out of hand. Ancient wars were often quite "total" for the loser, the men being put to death, the women sold as slaves, the boys castrated, the cattle slaughtered, and the buildings leveled, for the sake of revenge, justice, personal gain, or merely custom. If an enemy bombs a city, by design or by carelessness, we usually bomb his if we can. In the excitement and fatigue of warfare, revenge is one of the few satisfactions that can be savored; and justice can often be construed to demand the enemy's punishment, even if it is delivered with more enthusiasm than justice requires. When Jerusalem fell to the Crusaders in 1099 the ensuing slaughter was one of the bloodiest in military chronicles. "The men of the West literally waded in gore, their march to the church of the Holy Sepulcher being gruesomely likened to 'treading out the wine press' . . . ," reports Montross (p. 138), who observes that these excesses usually came at the climax of the capture of a fortified post or city. "For long the assailants have endured more punishment than they were able to inflict; then once the walls are breached, pent up emotions find an outlet in murder, rape and plunder, which discipline is powerless to prevent." The same occurred when Tyre fell to Alexander after a painful siege, and the phenomenon was not unknown on Pacific islands in the Second World War. Pure violence, like fire, can be harnessed to a purpose; that does not mean that behind every holocaust is a shrewd intention successfully fulfilled.

But if the occurrence of violence does not always bespeak a shrewd purpose, the absence of pain and destruction is no sign that violence was idle. Violence is most purposive and most successful when it is threatened and not used. Successful threats are those that do not have to be carried out. By European standards, Denmark was virtually unharmed in the Second World War; it was violence that made the Danes submit. Withheld violence—successfully threatened violence—can look clean, even merciful. The fact that a kidnap victim is returned unharmed, against receipt of ample ransom, does not make kidnapping a nonviolent enterprise. The American victory at Mexico City in 1847 was a great success; with a minimum of brutality we traded a capital city for everything we wanted from the war. We did not even have to say what we could do to Mexico City to make the Mexican government understand what they had at stake. (They had undoubtedly got the message a month earlier, when Vera Cruz was being pounded into submission. After forty-eight hours of shellfire, the foreign consuls in that city approached General Scott's headquarters to ask for a truce so that women, children, and neutrals could evacuate the city. General Scott, "counting on such internal pressure to help bring about the city's surrender," refused their request and added that anyone, soldier or noncombatant, who attempted to leave the city would be fired upon.)[2]

Whether spoken or not, the threat is usually there. In earlier eras the etiquette was more permissive. When the Persians wanted to induce some Ionian cities to surrender and join them, without having to fight them, they instructed their ambassadors to

> make your proposals to them and promise that, if they abandon their allies, there will be no disagreeable consequences for them; we will not set fire to their houses or temples, or threaten them with any greater harshness than before this trouble occurred. If, however, they refuse, and insist upon fighting, then you must resort to threats, and say exactly what we will do to them; tell them, that is, that when they are beaten they will be sold as slaves, their boys will be made eunuchs, their girls carried off to Bactria, and their land confiscated.[3]

---

2  Otis A. Singletary, *The Mexican War* (Chicago, University of Chicago Press, 1960), pp. 75-76. In a similar episode the Gauls, defending the town of Alesia in 52 B.C., "decided to send out of the town those whom age or infirmity incapacitated for fighting. . . . They came up to the Roman fortifications and with tears besought the soldiers to take them as slaves and relieve their hunger. But Caesar posted guards, on the ramparts with orders to refuse them admission." Caesar, The *Conquest of Gaul,* S. A. Handford, transl. (Baltimore, Penguin Books, 1951 ), p. 227.

3  Herodotus, *The Histories*, Aubrey de Selincourt, transl. (Baltimore Penguin Books, 1954), p. 362.

# 7: International Systems and Societies

## Hedley Bull

The starting point of international relations is the existence of *states,* or independent political communities, each of which possesses a government and asserts sovereignty in relation to a particular portion of the earth's surface and a particular segment of the human population. On the one hand, states assert, in relation to this territory and population, what may be called internal sovereignty, which means supremacy over all other authorities within that territory and population. On the other hand, they assert what may be called external sovereignty, by which is meant not supremacy but independence of outside authorities. The sovereignty of states, both internal and external, may be said to exist both at a normative level and at a factual level. On the one hand, states assert the right to supremacy over authorities within their territory and population and independence of authorities outside it; but, on the other hand, they also actually exercise, in varying degrees, such supremacy and independence in practice. An independent political community which merely claims a right to sovereignty (or is judged by others to have such a right), but cannot assert this right in practice, is not a state properly so-called.

The independent political communities that are states in this sense include city-states, such as those of ancient Greece or renaissance Italy, as well as modern nation-states. They include states in which government is based on dynastic principles of legitimacy, such as predominated in modern Europe up to the time of the French Revolution, as well as states in which government is based upon popular or national principles of legitimacy, such as have predominated in Europe since that time. They include multinational states, such as the European empires of the nineteenth century, as well as states of a single nationality. They include states whose territory is scattered in parts, such as the oceanic imperial states of Western Europe, as well as states whose territory is a single geographical entity.

There are, however, a great variety of independent political communities that have existed in history and yet are not states in this sense. The Germanic peoples of the Dark Ages, for example, were independent political communities, but while their rulers asserted supremacy over a population, they did not assert it over a distinct territory. The kingdoms and principalities of Western Christendom in the Middle Ages were not states: they did not possess internal sovereignty because they were not supreme over authorities within their territory and population; and at the same time they did not possess external sovereignty since they were not independent of the Pope or, in some cases, the Holy Roman Emperor. In parts of Africa, Australia and Oceania, before the European intrusion, there were independent political communities held together by ties of lineage or kinship, in which there was no such institution as government. Entities such as these fall outside the purview of

THE ANARCHICAL SOCIETY by Hedley Bull, pp. 8-11, 12-20. © 1977 by Columbia University Press, New York. Reprinted by permission of the publishers.

"international relations," if by this we mean (as we generally do) not the relations of nations but the relations of states in the strict sense. The relations of these independent political communities might be encompassed in a wider theory of the relations of *powers,* in which the relations of states would figure as a special case, but lie outside the domain of "international relations" in the strict sense.[1]

A *system of states* (or international system) is formed when two or more states have sufficient contact between them, and have sufficient impact on one another's decisions, to cause them to behave—at least in some measure—as parts of a whole. Two or more states can of course exist without forming an international system in this sense: for example, the independent political communities that existed in the Americas before the voyage of Columbus did not form an international system with those that existed in Europe; the independent political communities that existed in China during the Period of Warring States (*circa* 481-221 B.C.) did not form an international system with those that existed in Greece and the Mediterranean at the same time.

But where states are in regular contact with one another, and where in addition there is interaction between them sufficient to make the behaviour of each a necessary element in the calculations of the other, then we may speak of their forming a system. The interactions among states may be direct—as when two states are neighbours, or competitors for the same object, or partners in the same enterprise. Or their interactions may be indirect—the consequence of the dealings each of them has with a third party, or merely of the impact each of them makes on the system as a whole. Nepal and Bolivia are neither neighbours, nor competitors, nor partners in a common enterprise (except, perhaps, as members

of the United Nations). But they affect each other through the chain of links among states in which both participate. The interactions among states by which an international system is defined may take the form of cooperation, but also of conflict, or even of neutrality or indifference with regard to one another's objectives. The interactions may be present over a whole range of activities—political, strategic, economic, social—as they are today, or only in one or two; it may be enough, as Raymond Aron's definition of an international system implies, that the independent political communities in question "maintain regular relations with each other" and "are all capable of being implicated in a generalised war."[2]

Martin Wight, in classifying different kinds of states system, has distinguished what he calls an "international states system" from a "suzerain-state system."[3] The former is a system composed of states that are sovereign, in the sense in which the term has been defined here. The latter is a system in which one state asserts and maintains paramountcy or supremacy over the rest. The relations of the Roman Empire to its barbarian neighbours illustrate the concept of a suzerainstate system; so do the relations of Byzantium to its lesser neighbours, of the Abbasid Caliphate to surrounding lesser powers, or of Imperial China to its tributary states. In some of what Martin Wight would call "international states systems," it has been assumed that at any one time there is bound to be a dominant or hegemonial power: the classical Greek city-state system, for example, and the later system of Hellenistic kingdoms, witnessed a perpetual contest as to which state was to be *hegemon.* What distinguishes a "suzerain-state system" such as China-and-its-vassals from an "international states system," in which one or another

---

1  For an attempt to view international relations as a special case of the relations of powers, see Arthur Lee Burns, *Of Powers and their Politics: A Critique of Theoretical Approaches* (Englewood Cliffs, N.J.: Prentice-Hall, 1968).

2  Raymond Aron, *Peace and War: A Theory of International Relations* (London: Weidenfeld & Nicolson, 1966) p. 94.

3  See Martin Wight, *Systems of States* (Leicester University Press and London School of Economics, forthcoming) ch. 1.

state at any one time exerts hegemonial power, is that in the former one power exerts a hegemony that is permanent and for practical purposes unchallengeable, whereas in the latter, hegemony passes from one power to another and is constantly subject to dispute.

In terms of the approach being developed here, only what Wight calls an "international states system" is a states system at all. Among the independent political entities constituting a "suzerain-state system" such as China-and-its-vassals, only one state—the suzerain state itself—possesses sovereignty, and therefore one of the basic conditions of the existence of a states system, that there should be two or more sovereign states, is absent. . . .

The term "international system" has been a fashionable one among recent students of international relations, principally as a consequence of the writings of Morton A. Kaplan.[4] Kaplan's use of the term is not unlike that employed here, but what distinguishes Kaplan's work is the attempt to use the concept of a system to explain and predict international behaviour, especially by treating international systems as a particular kind of "system of action."[5] Here nothing of this sort is intended, and the term is employed simply to identify a particular kind of international constellation.

It should be recognised, however, that the term "system of states" had a long history, and embodied some rather different meanings, before it came to have its present one. It appears to have begun with Pufendorf, whose tract *De systematibus civitatum* was published in 1675.[6] Pufendorf, however, was referring not to the European states system as a whole, but to particular groups of states within that system, which were sovereign yet at the same time connected so as to form one body—like the German states after the peace of Westphalia. While the term "system" was applied to European states as a whole by eighteenth-century writers such as Rousseau and Nettelbladt, it was writers of the Napoleonic period, such as Gentz, Ancillon and Heeren, who were chiefly responsible for giving the term currency. At a time when the growth of French power threatened to destroy the states system and transform it into a universal empire, these writers sought to draw attention to the existence of the system, and also to show why it was worth preserving; they were not merely the analysts of the states system, but were also its apologists or protagonists. Of their works, the most important was A. H. L. Heeren's *Handbuch der Geschichte des Europaischen Staatensystems und seiner Kolonien*, first published in 1809. The term "states system" first appeared in English in the translation of this work that was published in 1834, the translator noting that it was "not strictly English."[7] For Heeren the states system was not simply a constellation of states having a certain degree of contact and interaction, as it is defined here. It involved much more than simply the causal connection of certain sets of variables to each other, which Kaplan takes to define a "system of action."[8] A states system for Heeren was "the union of several contiguous states, resembling each other in their manners, religion and degree of social improvement, and cemented together by a reciprocity of interests."[9] He saw a states system, in other words, as involving common interests and common values

---

4  See especially *System and Process in International Politics* (New York: Wiley, 1957).
5  Kaplan defines a system of action as "a set of variables so related in contradistinction to its environment, that describable behavioural regularities characterise the internal relationships of the variables to each other, and the external relationships of the set of individual variables to combinations of external variables": Ibid. p. 4.
6  I owe this point to Martin Wight, *System of States*.
7  See A. H. L. Heeren, *A Manual of the History of the Political System of Europe and its Colonies*, Göttingen, 1809, (Oxford: Talboys, 1834) vol. I. p. v.
8  See footnote 5.
9  Heeren, *Manual*, pp. vii-viii.

and as resting upon a common culture or civilisation. Moreover, Heeren had a sense of the fragility of the states system, the freedom of its members to act so as to maintain the system or allow it to be destroyed, as the Greek city-state system had been destroyed by Macedon, and as later the system of Hellenistic states that succeeded Alexander's empire had in turn been destroyed by Rome. Indeed, Heeren in the "Preface" to his first and second editions thought that Napoleon had in fact destroyed the European states system, and that he was writing its epitaph. Such a conception of the states system differs basically from what is called an international system in the present study, and is closer to what I call here an international society.

A *society of states* (or international society) exists when a group of states, conscious of certain common interests and common values, form a society in the sense that they conceive themselves to be bound by a common set of rules in their relations with one another, and share in the working of common institutions. If states today form an international society (to what extent they do is the subject of the next chapter), this is because, recognising certain common interests and perhaps some common values, they regard themselves as bound by certain rules in their dealings with one another, such as that they should respect one another's claims to independence, that they should honour agreements into which they enter, and that they should be subject to certain limitations in exercising force against one another. At the same time they cooperate in the working of institutions such as the forms of procedures of international law, the machinery of diplomacy and general international organisation, and the customs and conventions of war.

An international society in this sense presupposes an international system, but an international system may exist that is not an international society. Two or more states, in other words, may be in contact with each other and interact in such a way as to be necessary factors in each other's calculations without their being conscious of common interests or values, conceiving themselves to be bound by a common set of rules, or cooperating in the working of common institutions. Turkey, China, Japan, Korea and Siam, for example, were part of the European-dominated international system before they were part of the European-dominated international society. That is to say, they were in contact with European powers, and interacted significantly with them in war and commerce, before they and the European powers came to recognise common interests or values, to regard each other as subject to the same set of rules and as cooperating in the working of common institutions. Turkey formed part of the European-dominated international system from the time of its emergence in the sixteenth century, taking part in wars and alliances as a member of the system. Yet in the first three centuries of this relationship it was specifically denied on both sides that the European powers and Turkey possessed any common interests or values; it was held on both sides that agreements entered into with each other were not binding, and there were no common institutions, such as united the European powers, in whose working they cooperated. Turkey was not accepted by the European states as a member of international society until the Treaty of Paris of 1856, terminating the Crimean War, and perhaps did not achieve full equality of rights within international society until the Treaty of Lausanne in 1923.

In the same way Persia and Carthage formed part of a single international system with the classical Greek city-states, but were not part of the Greek international society. That is to say, Persia (and to a lesser extent Carthage) interacted with the Greek city-states, and was always an essential factor in the strategic equation, either as an outside threat against which the Greek city-states were ready to combine, or as a power able to intervene in the conflicts among them. But Persia was perceived by the Greeks as a barbarian power; it did not share the common values of the Greeks, expressed in the Greek language, the pan-Hellenic games or consultation of the Delphic oracle; it was not subject to the rules which required Greek city-states to limit their conflicts with one another; and it was not a participant in the *amphictyonae* in which institutional co-operation among the Greek states took place, or in the diplomatic institution of *proxenoi*.

When, as in the case of encounters between European and non-European states from the sixteenth century until the late nineteenth century, states are participants in a single international system, but not members of a single international society, there may be communication, exchanges of envoys or messengers and agreements—not only about trade but also about war, peace and alliances. But these forms of interaction do not in themselves demonstrate that there is an international society. Communication may take place, envoys may be exchanged and agreements entered into without there being a sense of common interests or values that gives such exchange substance and a prospect of permanence, without any sense that there are rules which lay down how the interaction should proceed, and without the attempt of the parties concerned to cooperate in institutions in whose survival they have a stake. When Cortes and Pizarro parleyed with the Aztec and Inca kings, when George III sent Lord Macartney to Peking, or when Queen Victoria's representatives entered into agreements with the Maori chieftains, the Sultan of Sokoto or the Kabaka of Buganda, this was outside the framework of any shared conception of an international society of which the parties on both sides were members with like rights and duties.

Whether or not these distinguishing features of an international society are present in an international system, it is not always easy to determine: as between an international system that is clearly also an international society, and a system that is clearly not a society, there lie cases where a sense of common interests is tentative and inchoate; where the common rules perceived are vague and ill-formed, and there is doubt as to whether they are worthy of the name of rules; or where common institutions—relating to diplomatic machinery or to limitations in war—are implicit or embryonic. If we ask of modern international society the questions "when did it begin?" or "what were its geographical limits?" we are at once involved in difficult problems of the tracing of boundaries.

But certain international systems have quite clearly been international societies also. The chief examples are the classical Greek city-state system; the international system formed by the Hellenistic kingdoms in the period between the disintegration of Alexander's empire and the Roman conquest; the international system of China during the Period of Warring States; the states system of ancient India; and the modern states system, which arose in Europe and is now worldwide.

A common feature of these historical international societies is that they were all founded upon a common culture or civilisation, or at least on some of the elements of such a civilisation: a common language, a common epistemology and understanding of the universe, a common religion, a common ethical code, a common aesthetic or artistic tradition. It is reasonable to suppose that where such elements of a common civilisation underlie an international society, they facilitate its working in two ways. On the one hand, they may make for easier communication and closer awareness and understanding between one state and another, and thus facilitate the definition of common rules and the evolution of common institutions. On the other hand, they may reinforce the sense of common interests that impels states to accept common rules and institutions with a sense of common values. This is a question to which we shall return when, later in this study, we consider the contention that the global international society of the twentieth century, unlike the Christian international society of the sixteenth and seventeenth centuries, or the European international society of the eighteenth and nineteenth centuries, is without any such common culture or civilisation. . . .

Having elaborated our conception of states, of a system of states, and of a society of states, we may return to the proposition with which this section began: that by international order is meant a pattern or disposition of international activity that sustains those goals of the society of states that are elementary, primary or universal. What goals, then, are these?

First, there is the goal of preservation of the system and society of states itself. Whatever the divisions among them, modern states have been united in the belief that they are the principal actors in world politics and the chief bearers of rights and duties within it. The society of states has sought to ensure that it will remain the prevailing form of universal political organisation, in fact and in right. Challenges to the continued existence of the society of states have sometimes come from a particular dominant state—the Habsburg Empire, the France of Louis XIV, the France of Napoleon, Hitler's Germany, perhaps post-1945 America—which seemed capable of overthrowing the system and society of states and transforming it into a universal empire. Challenges have also been delivered by actors other than states which threaten to deprive states of their position as the principal actors in world politics, or the principal bearers of rights and duties within it. "Supra-state" actors such as, in the sixteenth and seventeenth centuries, the Papacy and the Holy Roman Emperor, or, in the twentieth century, the United Nations (one thinks especially of its role as a violent actor in the 1960-1 Congo crisis) present such a threat. "Sub-state" actors which operate in world politics from within a particular state, or "transstate" actors which are groups cutting across the boundaries of states, may also challenge the privileged position of states in world politics, or their right to enjoy it; in the history of modern international society the revolutionary and counter-revolutionary manifestations of human solidarity engendered by the Reformation, the

French Revolution and the Russian Revolution are principal examples.

Second, there is the goal of maintaining the independence or external sovereignty of individual states. From the perspective of any particular state what it chiefly hopes to gain from participation in the society of states is recognition of its independence of outside authority, and in particular of its supreme jurisdiction over its subjects and territory. The chief price it has to pay for this is recognition of like rights to independence and sovereignty on the part of other states.

International society has in fact treated preservation of the independence of particular states as a goal that is subordinate to preservation of the society of states itself; this reflects the predominant role played in shaping international society by the great powers, which view themselves as its custodians . . . . Thus international society has often allowed the independence of individual states to be extinguished, as in the great process of partition and absorption of small powers by greater ones, in the name of principles such as "compensation" and the "balance of power" that produced a steady decline in the number of states in Europe from the Peace of Westphalia in 1648 until the Congress of Vienna in 1815. In the same way, international society, at least in the perspective of the great powers which see themselves as its guardians, treats the independence of particular states as subordinate to the preservation of the system as a whole when it tolerates or encourages limitation of the sovereignty or independence of small states through such devices as spheres-of-influence agreements, or agreements to create buffer or neutralised states.

Third, there is the goal of peace. By this is meant not the goal of establishing universal and permanent peace, such as has been the dream of irenists or theorists of peace, and stands in contrast to actual historical experience: this is not a goal which the society of states can be said to have pursued in any serious way. Rather what is meant is the maintenance of peace in the sense of the absence of war among member states of international society as the normal condition of their relationship, to be breached only in special circumstances and according to principles that are generally accepted.

Peace in this sense has been viewed by international society as a goal subordinate to that of the preservation of the states system itself, for which it has been widely held that it can be right to wage war; and as subordinate also to preservation of the sovereignty or independence of individual states, which have insisted on the right to wage war in self-defence, and to protect other rights also. The subordinate status of peace in relation to these other goals is reflected in the phrase "peace and security," which occurs in the United Nations Charter. Security in international politics means no more than safety: either objective safety, safety which actually exists, or subjective safety, that which is felt or experienced. What states seek to make secure or safe is not merely peace, but their independence and the continued existence of the society of states itself which that independence requires; and for these objectives, as we have noted, they are ready to resort to war and the threat of war. The coupling of the two terms together in the Charter reflects the judgement that the requirements of security may conflict with those of peace, and that in this event the latter will not necessarily take priority.

Fourth, it should be noted that among the elementary or primary goals of the society of states are those which . . . were said to be the common goals of all social life: limitation of violence resulting in death or bodily harm, the keeping of promises and the stabilisation of possession by rules of property.

The goal of limitation of violence is represented in international society in a number of ways. States cooperate in international society so as to maintain their monopoly of violence, and deny the right to employ it to other groups. States also accept limitations on their own right to use violence; at a minimum they accept that they shall not kill one another's envoys or messengers, since this would make communication impossible. Beyond this, they accept that war should be waged only for a "just" cause, or a cause the justice of which can be argued in terms of common rules. They have also constantly proclaimed adherence to rules requiring that wars be fought within certain limits, the *temperamenta belli*.

The goal of the keeping of promises is represented in the principle *pacta sunt servanda*. Among states as among individuals, cooperation can take place only on the basis of agreements, and agreements can fulfil their function in social life only on the basis of a presumption that once entered into they will be upheld. International society adjusts itself to the pressures for change that make for the breaking of treaties, and at the same time salvages the principle itself, through the doctrine of *rebus sic stantibus*.

The goal of stability of possession is reflected in international society not only by the recognition by states of one another's property, but more fundamentally in the compact of mutual recognition of sovereignty, in which states accept one another's spheres of jurisdiction: indeed, the idea of the sovereignty of the state derived historically from the idea that certain territories and peoples were the property or patrimony of the ruler.

The above are among the elementary or primary goals of modern international society, and of other international societies. It is not suggested here that this list is exhaustive, nor that it could not be formulated in some other way. Nor is it any part of my thesis that these goals should be accepted as a valid basis for action, as legislating right conduct in international relations. It should also be said that at this stage in the argument we are concerned only with what maybe called the "statics" of international order and not with its "dynamics"; we are concerned only to spell out what is involved in the idea of international order, not to trace how it is embodied in historical institutions subject to change.

# 8: Anarchical Society

## Hedley Bull

### The Idea of International Society

Throughout the history of the modern states system there have been three competing traditions of thought: the Hobbesian or realist tradition, which views international politics as a state of war; the Kantian or universalist tradition, which sees at work in international politics a potential community of mankind; and the Grotian or internationalist tradition, which views international politics as taking place within an international society.[1] Here I shall state what is essential to the Grotian or internationalist idea of international society, and what divides it from the Hobbesian or realist tradition on the one hand, and from the Kantian or universalist tradition on the other. Each of these traditional patterns of thought embodies a description of the nature of international politics and a set of prescriptions about international conduct.

The Hobbesian tradition describes international relations as a state of war of all against all, an arena of struggle in which each state is pitted against every other. International relations, on the Hobbesian view, represent pure conflict between states and resemble a game that is wholly distributive or zero-sum: the interests of each state exclude the interests of any other. The particular international activity that, on the Hobbesian view, is most typical of international activity as a whole, or best provides the clue to it, is war itself. Thus peace, on the Hobbesian view, is a period of recuperation from the last war and preparation for the next.

The Hobbesian prescription for international conduct is that the state is free to pursue its goals in relation to other states without moral or legal restrictions of any kind. Ideas of morality and law, on this view, are valid only in the context of a society, but international life is beyond the bounds of any society. If any moral or legal goals are to be pursued in international politics, these can only be the moral or legal goals of the state itself. Either it is held (as by Machiavelli) that the state conducts foreign policy in a kind of moral and legal vacuum, or it is held (as by Hegel and his successors) that moral behaviour for the state in foreign policy lies in its own self-assertion. The only rules or principles which, for those in the Hobbesian tradition, may be said to limit or circumscribe the behaviour of states in their relations with one another are rules of prudence or expediency. Thus agreements may be kept if it is expedient to keep them, but may be broken if it is not.

The Kantian or universalist tradition, at the other extreme, takes the essential nature of international politics to lie not in conflict among states, as on the Hobbesian view, but in the trans national social bonds that link the individual

---

1 This threefold division derives from Martin Wight. The best published account of it is his "Western Values in International Relations," in *Diplomatic Investigations*, ed. Herbert Butterfield and Martin Wight (London: Allen & Unwin, 1967). The division is further discussed in my "Martin Wight and The Theory of International Relations. The Second Martin Wight Memorial Lecture," *British Journal of International Studies*, vol. II, no. 2 (1976).

THE ANARCHICAL SOCIETY by Hedley Bull, pp. 24-27, 40-52, 65-74. ©1977 by Columbia University Press, New York. Reprinted by permission of the publishers.)

human beings who are the subjects or citizens of states. The dominant theme of international relations, on the Kantian view, is only apparently the relationship among states, and is really the relationship among all men in the community of mankind—which exists potentially, even if it does not exist actually, and which when it comes into being will sweep the system of states into limbo.[2]

Within the community of all mankind, on the universalist view, the interests of all men are one and the same; international politics, considered from this perspective, is not a purely distributive or zero-sum game, as the Hobbesians maintain, but a purely cooperative or non-zero-sum game. Conflicts of interest exist among the ruling cliques of states, but this is only at the superficial or transient level of the existing system of states; properly understood, the interests of all peoples are the same. The particular international activity which, on the Kantian view, most typifies international activity as a whole is the horizontal conflict of ideology that cuts across the boundaries of states and divides human society into two camps—the trustees of the immanent community of mankind and those who stand in its way, those who are of the true faith and the heretics, the liberators and the oppressed.

The Kantian or universalist view of international morality is that, in contrast to the Hobbesian conception, there are moral imperatives in the field of international relations limiting the action of states, but that these imperatives enjoin not coexistence and cooperation among states but rather the overthrow of the system of states and its replacement by a cosmopolitan society. The community of mankind, on the Kantian view, is not only the central reality in international politics, in the sense that the forces able to bring it into being are present; it is also the end or object of the highest moral endeavour. The rules that sustain coexistence and social intercourse among states should be ignored if the imperatives of this higher morality require it. Good faith with heretics has no meaning, except in terms of tactical convenience; between the elect and the damned, the liberators and the oppressed, the question of mutual acceptance of rights to sovereignty or independence does not arise.

What has been called the Grotian or internationalist tradition stands between the realist tradition and the universalist tradition. The Grotian tradition describes international politics in terms of a society of states or international society.[3] As against the Hobbesian tradition, the Grotians contend that states are not engaged in simple struggle, like gladiators in an arena, but are limited in their conflicts with one another by common rules and institutions. But as against the Kantian or universalist perspective the Grotians accept the Hobbesian premise that sovereigns or states are the principal reality in international politics; the immediate members of international society are states rather than individual human beings. International politics, in the Grotian understanding, expresses neither complete conflict of interest between states nor complete identity of interest; it resembles a game that is partly distributive but also partly productive. The particular international activity which, on the Grotian view, best typifies international activity as a whole is neither war between states, nor horizontal conflict cutting across the boundaries of

---

2   In Kant's own doctrine there is of course ambivalence as between the universalism of *The Idea of Universal History from a Cosmopolitical Point of View* (1784) and the position taken up in *Perpetual Peace* (1795), in which Kant accepts the substitute goal of a league of "republican" states.

3   I have myself used the term "Grotian" in two senses: (i) as here, to describe the broad doctrine that there is a society of states; (ii) to describe the solidarist form of this doctrine, which united Grotius himself and the twentieth-century neo-Grotians, in opposition to the pluralist conception of international society entertained by Vattel and later positivist writers. See "The Grotian Conception of International Society," in *Diplomatic Investigations*.

states, but trade—or, more generally, economic and social intercourse between one country and another.

The Grotian prescription for international conduct is that all states, in their dealings with one another, are bound by the rules and institutions of the society they form. As against the view of the Hobbesians, states in the Grotian view are bound not only by rules of prudence or expediency but also by imperatives of morality and law. But, as against the view of the universalists, what these imperatives enjoin is not the overthrow of the system of states and its replacement by a universal community of mankind, but rather acceptance of the requirements of coexistence and co-operation in a society of states. . . .

## The Reality of International Society

But does this idea of international society conform to reality? Do the theories of philosophers, international lawyers and historians in the Grotian tradition reflect the thought of statesmen? If statesmen pay lip-service to international society and its rules, does this mean that the latter affect their decisions? If the idea of international society played some real part during periods of relative international harmony, as in Europe for long stretches of the eighteenth and nineteenth centuries, was it not extinguished during the wars of religion, the wars of the French Revolution and Napoleon, and the World Wars of the present century? What meaning can it have, for example, to say that Hitler's Germany and Stalin's Russia, locked in a struggle to the death during the Second World War, regarded each other as bound by common rules and cooperated in the working of common institutions? If the Christian and, later, European international system that existed from the sixteenth century to the nineteenth was also an international society, were not the bonds of this society stretched and ultimately broken as the system expanded and became worldwide? Is not

the international politics of the present time best viewed as an international system that is not an international society?

## *The Element of Society*

My contention is that the element of a society has always been present, and remains present, in the modern international system, although only as one of the elements in it, whose survival is sometimes precarious. The modern international system in fact reflects all three of the elements singled out, respectively, by the Hobbesian, the Kantian and the Grotian traditions: the element of war and struggle for power among states, the element of transnational solidarity and conflict, cutting across the divisions among states, and the element of cooperation and regulated intercourse among states. In different historical phases of the states system, in different geographical theatres of its operation, and in the policies of different states and statesmen, one of these three elements may predominate over the others.

Thus one may say that in the trade and colonial wars fought in the late seventeenth and eighteenth centuries, chiefly by Holland, France and England, where the object was trading monopoly enforced by sea power and the political control of colonies, the element of a state of war was predominant. In the wars of religion that marked the first phase of the states system up till the Peace of Westphalia, in the European convulsion of the wars of the French Revolution and Napoleon, and in the ideological struggle of communist and anti-communist powers in our own times, the element of transnational solidarity and conflict has been uppermost—expressed not only in the revolutionist transnational solidarities of the Protestant parties, the democratic or republican forces favourable to the French Revolution, and the Communist Internationals, but also in the counter-revolutionist solidarities of the Society of Jesus, International Legitimism and Dullesian anticommunism. In nineteenth-century Europe, in the interval between the struggle of revolutionism and Legitimism that remained in the aftermath of the Napoleonic wars, and the reemergence, late in the century, of the patterns of great power conflict that led to the First World War, one may say that the element of international society was predominant.

The element of international society has always been present in the modern international system because at no stage can it be said that the conception of the common interests of states, of common rules accepted and common institutions worked by them, has ceased to exert an influence. Most states at most times pay some respect to the basic rules of coexistence in international society, such as mutual respect for sovereignty, the rule that agreements should be kept, and rules limiting resort to violence. In the same way most states at most times take part in the working of common institutions: the forms and procedures of international law, the system of diplomatic representation, acceptance of the special position of great powers, and universal international organizations such as the functional organizations that grew up in the nineteenth century, the League of Nations and the United Nations.

The idea of "international society" has a basis in reality that is sometimes precarious but has at no stage disappeared. Great wars that engulf the states system as a whole strain the capability of the idea, and cause thinkers and statesmen to turn to Hobbesian interpretations and solutions, but they are followed by periods of peace. Ideological conflicts in which states and factions within them are ranged on opposite sides sometimes lead to a denial of the idea of international society by both sides, and lend confirmation to Kantian interpretations, but they are followed by accommodations in which the idea reappears.

Even at the height of a great war or ideological conflict the idea of international society, while it may be denied by the pronouncements of the contending states—each side treating the other as outside the framework of any common society—does not disappear so much as go underground, where it continues to influence the practice of states. The Allied and Axis powers at the height of the Second World War did not accept each other as members of a common international society, and they did not cooperate with each other in the working of common institutions. But one could not say that the idea of international society ceased to affect the practice of international relations in that period. The Allied powers continued to respect the ordinary rules of international society in their relations among themselves and in their dealings with neutral countries; so did Germany, Italy and Japan. Within both groups of belligerent powers there were persons and movements who sought out the basis of a negotiated peace. The Allied and Axis states each insisted that the others were bound as members of international society to observe the Geneva conventions concerning prisoners of war, and in the case of the Western allies and Germany, in respect of one another's prisoners, in large measure actually did observe these conventions.

Similarly, when the Cold War was being prosecuted most vigorously, the United States and the Soviet Union were inclined to speak of each other as heretics or outcasts beyond the pale, rather than as member states of the same international society. However, they did not even then break off diplomatic relations, withdraw recognition of one another's sovereignty, repudiate the idea of a common international law or cause the break-up of the United Nations into rival organizations. In both the Western and communist blocs there were voices raised in favor of compromise, drawing attention to the common interests of the two sides in coexistence and restating, in secular form, the principle *cuijus regio, eijus religio* that had provided a basis for accommodation in the wars of religion. Thus, even in periods when international politics is best described in terms of a Hobbesian state of war or a Kantian condition of transnational solidarity, the idea of international society has survived as an important part of reality, and its survival in these times of stress lays the foundation for the reconstruction of international society when war gives place to peace or ideological conflict to *detente*.

It may help to make clear the persistent reality of the element of international society if we contrast the relations of states within that system with examples of relations between independent political communities in which the element of society is entirely absent. The relations of Chingis Khan's Mongol invaders, and the Asian and European peoples whom they subjugated, were not moderated by a belief on each side in common rules binding on both in their dealings with one another. Chingis Khan's conquests did have a basis in the moral ideas of the Mongols themselves: Chingis believed that he had the mandate of heaven to rule the world, that whatever peoples lay outside the *de facto* control of the Mongols were nevertheless *de jure* subjects of the Mongol empire, and that peoples who failed to submit to the Mongol court were therefore rebels against the divinely inspired order, against whom the waging of war was a right and a duty.[4] But these ideas formed no part of the thinking of the peoples who were subjugated and in some cases annihilated by the Mongols.

When the Spanish Conquistadors confronted the Aztecs and the Incas, this similarly took place in the absence of any common notion of rules and institutions. The Spaniards debated among themselves what duties they had towards the Indians—whether their right to invade derived from the claim of the Pope to *imperium mundi*, the duty of a Christian prince to spread the faith, the failure of the Indians to extend rights of hospitality, and so on.[5] But the rights which the Indians were acknowledged—by scholars such as Victoria—to have, were rights deriving from a system of rules recognised by the Spaniards; they did not derive from any system of rules acknowledged by the Indians also. The Spaniards and the Indians were able to recognize each other as human beings, to engage in negotiations and to conclude agreements. But these dealings took place in the absence of any common framework of rules and institutions.

The long history of relations between Europe and Islam provides a further illustration of this theme. As long as modern international society thought of itself as Christian or European, Islam in its successive embodiments was viewed as a barbarian power against which it was the duty of Christian princes to maintain a common front, even if they did not always do so in practice. Islamic thought reciprocated by dividing the world into *dar-al-Islam*, the region of submission to the will of God, and *dar-al-Harb*, the region of war which was yet to be converted. Coexistence with infidel states was possible; diplomatic exchanges, treaties and alliances could be and were concluded; and these relations were subject to rules—but only rules binding on Moslems. There was no conception of a common society in which Islamic and infidel states both had their place; the latter were regarded as having only a provisional existence, and coexistence with them as only a temporary phase in a process leading inexorably to their absorption.

It might be argued that while there is indeed a contrast between cases where a common idea of international society is shared by adversary communities, and cases where no such idea exists, this is of no practical consequence; the language of a common international society spoken by states in the modern international system is mere lip-service. Thus, as Grotius notes, for some states which claim that they have a just cause for going to war with one another, this just cause is often simply a pretext, their real motives being

---

4   See Igor de Rachewiltz, "Some Remarks on the Ideological Foundations of Chingis Khan's Empire," *Papers on Far Eastern History*, 7 (March 1973).

5   See, for example, Francisco de Victoria, "De Indis et de Jure Belli Relectiones," trans. J. P. Bate, in *The Classics of International Law*, ed. E. Nys (Washington: Carnegie Institute, 1917).

quite otherwise. Grotius distinguishes between causes of war that are "justifiable," that is to say which are undertaken in the belief that there is a just cause, from causes of war that are merely "persuasive," that is in which allegation of a just cause is simply a pretext.[6]

The question, however, is whether an international system in which it is necessary to have a pretext for beginning a war is not radically different from one in which it is not. The state which at least alleges a just cause, even where belief in the existence of a just cause has played no part in its decision, offers less of a threat to international order than one which does not. The state which alleges a just cause, even one it does not itself believe in, is at least acknowledging that it owes other states an explanation of its conduct, in terms of rules that they accept. There are, of course, differences of opinion as to the interpretation of the rules and their application to concrete situations; but such rules are not infinitely malleable and do circumscribe the range of choice of states which seek to give pretexts in terms of them. The giving of a pretext, moreover, means that the violence which the offending state does to the structure of commonly accepted rules by going to war in disregard of them is less than it would otherwise be; to make war without any explanation, or with an explanation stated only in terms of the recalcitrant state's own beliefs—such as the Mongols' belief in the Mandate of Heaven or the belief of the Conquistadors in the Pope's *imperium mundi*—is to hold all other states in contempt, and to place in jeopardy all the settled expectations that states have about one another's behaviour.

Grotius recognizes that while international society is threatened by states which wage war for merely "persuasive" causes, and not for "justifiable" ones, it is even more threatened by states which wage war without "persuasive" causes either; wars which lack causes of either sort he speaks of as "the wars of savages."[7] Vattel speaks of those who wage war without pretext of any kind as "monsters unworthy of the name of men," whom nations may unite to suppress.[8]

### The Anarchical Society

It is often maintained that the existence of international society is disproved by the fact of anarchy, in the sense of the absence of government or rule. It is obvious that sovereign states, unlike the individuals within them, are not subject to a common government, and that in this sense there is, in the phrase made famous by Goldsworthy Lowes Dickinson, an "international anarchy."[9] A persistent theme in the modern discussion of international relations has been that, as a consequence of this anarchy, states do not form together any kind of society; and that if they were to do so it could only be by subordinating themselves to a common authority.

A chief intellectual support of this doctrine is what I have called the domestic analogy, the argument from the experience of individual men in domestic society to the experience of states, according to which states, like individuals, are capable of orderly social life only if, as in Hobbes's phrase, they stand in awe of a common power.[10] In the case of Hobbes himself and his successors, the domestic analogy takes the form simply of the assertion that states or sovereign princes,

---

6   Grotius, *De Jure Belli ac Pacis*, trans. Francis W. Kelsey (Oxford: Clarendon Press, 1925) II, xxii, 2.

7   Ibid.

8   Vattel, *Law of Nations*, III, iii, 34.

9   See *The European Anarchy* (London: Allen & Unwin, 1916) and *The International Anarchy* (London: Allen & Unwin, 1926).

10  See my "Society and Anarchy in International Relations," in *Diplomatic Investigations*. The present section incorporates some material from this essay.

like individual men who live without government, are in a state of nature which is a state of war. It is not the view of Hobbes, or other thinkers of his school, that a social contract of states that would bring international anarchy to an end either should or can take place. By contrast, in the thinking of those who look forward—or backward—to a universal or world government, the domestic analogy is taken further, to embrace not only the conception of a state of nature but also that of a social contract among states that will reproduce the conditions of order within the state on a universal scale.

There are three weaknesses in the argument that states do not form a society because they are in a condition of international anarchy. The first is that the modern international system does not entirely resemble a Hobbesian state of nature. Hobbes's account of relations between sovereign princes is a subordinate part of his explanation and justification of government among individual men. As evidence for his speculations as to how men would live were they to find themselves in a situation of anarchy, Hobbes mentions the experience of civil war, the life of certain American tribes and the facts of international relations:

> But though there had never been any time wherein particular men were in a condition of warre one against another; yet in all times Kings, and Persons of Soveraigne authority, because of their Independency, are in continual jealousies, and in the state and posture of Gladiators; having their weapons pointing, and their eyes fixed on one another; that is, their Forts, Garrisons and Guns, upon the Frontiers of their Kingdomes; and continual Spyes upon their neighbours; which is a posture of warre.[11]

In Hobbes's account the situation in which men live without a common power to keep them in awe has three principal characteristics. In this situation there can be no industry, agriculture, navigation, trade or other refinements of living because the strength and invention of men is absorbed in providing security against one another. There are no legal or moral rules: "The notions of Right and Wrong, Justice and Injustice have there no place. . . . It is consequent also to the same condition, that there can be no Propriety, no Dominion, no *Mine* and *Thine* distinct; but only that to be every mans, that he can get; and for so long as he can keep it."[12] Finally, the state of nature is a state of war: war understood to consist "not in actual fighting; but in the known disposition thereto, during all the time there is no assurance to the contrary"; and to be "such a warre, as is of every man, against every man."[13]

The first of these characteristics clearly does not obtain in international anarchy. The absence of a world government is no necessary bar to industry, trade and other refinements of living. States do not in fact so exhaust their strength and invention in providing security against one another that the lives of their inhabitants are solitary, poor, nasty, brutish and short; they do not as a rule invest resources in war and military preparations to such an extent that their economic fabric is ruined. On the contrary, the armed forces of states, by providing security against external attack and internal disorder, establish the conditions under which economic improvements may take place within their borders. The absence of a universal government has not been incompatible with international economic interdependence.

It is also clear that the second feature of Hobbes's state of nature, the absence in it of notions of right and wrong, including notions of property, does not apply to modern international relations. Within the system of states that grew up in Europe and spread around the world, notions

---

11   Thomas Hobbes, *Leviathan* (Everyman's Library, 1953) ch. 13, p. 65.
12   Ibid. p. 66.
13   Ibid. p. 64.

of right and wrong in international behaviour have always held a central place.

Of the three principal features of Hobbes's state of nature the only one that might be held to apply to modern international relations is the third—the existence in it of a state of war, in the sense of a disposition on the part of every state to war with every other state. Sovereign states, even while they are at peace, nevertheless display a disposition to go to war with one another, inasmuch as they prepare for war and treat war as one of the options open to them.

The second weakness of the argument from international anarchy is that it is based on false premises about the conditions of order among individuals and groups other than the state. It is not, of course, the case that fear of a supreme government is the only source of order within a modern state: no account of the reasons why men are capable of orderly social coexistence within a modern state can be complete which does not give due weight to factors such as reciprocal interest, a sense of community or general will, and habit or inertia.

If, then, we are to compare international relations with an imagined, pre-contractual state of nature among individual men, we may well choose not Hobbes's description of that condition but Locke's. Locke's conception of the state of nature as a society without government does in fact provide us with a close analogy with the society of states. In modern international society, as in Locke's state of nature, there is no central authority able to interpret and enforce the law, and thus individual members of the society must themselves judge and enforce it. Because in such a society each member of it is a judge in his own cause, and because those who seek to enforce the law do not always prevail, justice in such a society is crude and uncertain. But there is

nevertheless a great difference between such a rudimentary form of social life and none at all.

The third weakness of the argument from international anarchy is that it overlooks the limitations of the domestic analogy. States, after all, are very unlike human individuals. Even if it could be contended that government is a necessary condition of order among individual men, there are good reasons for holding that anarchy among states is tolerable to a degree to which among individuals it is not.

We have already noted that, unlike the individual in Hobbes's state of nature, the state does not find its energies so absorbed in the pursuit of security that the life of its members is that of mere brutes. Hobbes himself recognizes this when, having observed that persons in sovereign authority are in "a posture of war," he goes on to say that "because they uphold thereby the industry of their subjects, there does not follow from it that misery which accompanies the liberty of particular men."[14] The same sovereigns that find themselves in a state of nature in relation to one another have provided, within their territories, the conditions in which refinements of life can flourish.

Moreover, states are not vulnerable to violent attack to the same degree that individuals are. Spinoza, echoing Hobbes in his assertion that "two states are in the same relation to one another as two men in the condition of nature," goes on to add, "with this exception, that a commonwealth can guard itself against being subjugated by another, as a man in the state of nature cannot do. For, of course, a man is overcome by sleep every day, is often afflicted by disease of body or mind, and is finally prostrated by old age; in addition, he is subject to troubles against which a commonwealth can make itself secure."[15] One human being in the state of nature

---

14   Ibid. p. 65.
15   Spinoza, *Tractatus Politicus*, III, ii, in *The Political Works of Spinoza*, ed. A. G. Wernham (Oxford: Clarendon Press, 1958) p. 293.

cannot make himself secure against violent attack; and this attack carries with it the prospect of sudden death. Groups of human beings organised as states, however, may provide themselves with a means of defense that exists independently of the frailties of any one of them. And armed attack by one state upon another has not brought with it a prospect comparable to the killing of one individual by another. For one man's death may be brought about suddenly in a single act; and once it has occurred it cannot be undone. But war has only occasionally resulted in the physical extinction of the vanquished people.

In modern history it has been possible to take Clausewitz's view that "war is never absolute in its results," and that defeat in it may be "a passing evil which can be remedied."[16] Moreover, war in the past, even if it could in principle lead to the physical extermination of one or both of the belligerent peoples, could not be thought capable of doing so at once in the course of a single act. Clausewitz, in holding that war does not consist of a single instantaneous blow, but always of a succession of separate actions, was drawing attention to something that in the past has always held true and has rendered violence among independent political communities different from violence between individual persons.[17] It is only in the context of nuclear weapons and other recent military technology that it has become pertinent to ask whether war could not now both be "absolute in its results" and "take the form of a single, instantaneous blow," in Clausewitz's understanding of these terms; and whether, therefore, violence does not now confront the state with the same sort of prospect it has always held for the individual.

This difference, that states have been less vulnerable to violent attack by one another than individual men is reinforced by a further one: that

in so far as states have been vulnerable to physical attack, they have not been equally so. Hobbes builds his account of the state of nature on the proposition that "Nature hath made men so equal, in the faculties of body and mind, [that] the weakest has strength enough to kill the strongest."[18] It is this equal vulnerability of every man to every other that, in Hobbes's view, renders the condition of anarchy intolerable. But in modern international society there has been a persistent distinction between great powers and small. Great powers have not been vulnerable to violent attack by small powers to the same extent that small powers have been vulnerable to attack by great ones. Once again it is only the spread of nuclear weapons to small states and the possibility of a world of many nuclear powers, that raises the question whether in international relations, also, a situation may come about in which "the weakest has strength enough to kill the strongest."

The argument, then, that because men cannot form a society without government, sovereign princes or states cannot, breaks down not only because some degree of order can in fact be achieved among individuals in the absence of government, but also because states are unlike individuals, and are more capable of forming an anarchical society. The domestic analogy is no more than an analogy; the fact that states form a society without government reflects features of their situation that are unique.

## The Limitations of International Society

We have shown that the modern international system is also an international society, at least in the sense that international society has been one of the elements permanently at work in it; and that the existence of this international society is

---

16  Carl von Clausewitz, *On War*, trans. Jolles (Modern Library Edition, 1943) pt I, ch. 1, p. 8.
17  Ibid. pp. 7-8.
18  Hobbes, *Leviathan*, p. 63.

not as such disproved by the fact of international anarchy. It is important, however, to retain a sense of the limitations of the anarchical international society.

Because international society is no more than one of the basic elements at work in modern international politics, and is always in competition with the elements of a state of war and of transnational solidarity or conflict, it is always erroneous to interpret international events as if international society were the sole or the dominant element. This is the error committed by those who speak or write as if the Concert of Europe, the League of Nations or the United Nations were the principal factors in international politics in their respective time; as if international law were to be assessed only in relation to the function it has of binding states together, and not also in relation to its function as an instrument of state interest and as a vehicle of transnational purposes; as if attempts to maintain a balance of power were to be interpreted only as endeavours to preserve the system of states, and not also as manoeuvres on the part of particular powers to gain ascendancy; as if great powers were to be viewed only as "great responsibles" or "great indispensables," and not also as great predators; as if wars were to be construed only as attempts to violate the law or to uphold it, and not also simply as attempts to advance the interests of particular states or of transnational groups. The element of international society is real, but the elements of a state of war and of transnational loyalties and divisions are real also, and to reify the first element, or to speak as if it annulled the second and third, is an illusion.

Moreover, the fact that international society provides some element of order in international politics should not be taken as justifying an attitude of complacency about it, or as showing that the arguments of those who are dissatisfied with the order provided by international society are without foundation. The order provided within modern international society is precarious and imperfect. To show that modern international society has provided some degree of order is not to have shown that order in world politics could not be provided more effectively by structures of a quite different kind. . . .

## Order in International Society

The maintenance of order in world politics depends, in the first instance, on certain contingent facts which would make for order even if states were without any conception of common interests, common rules or common institutions—even if, in other words, they formed an international system only, and not also an international society. A balance of power, for example, may arise in an international system quite fortuitously, in the absence of any belief that it serves common interests, or any attempt to regulate or institutionalise it. If it does arise, it may help to limit violence, to render undertakings credible or to safeguard governments from challenges to their local supremacy. Within international society, however, as in other societies, order is the consequence not merely of contingent facts such as this, but of a sense of common interests in the elementary goals of social life; rules prescribing behaviour that sustains these goals; and institutions that help to make these rules effective.

### Common Interests

To say that $x$ is in someone's interest is merely to say that it serves as a means to some end that he is pursuing. Whether or not $x$ does serve as a means to any particular end is a matter of objective fact. But whether or not $x$ is in his interest will depend not only on this but also on what ends he is actually pursuing. It follows from this that the conception of interest is an empty or vacuous guide, both as to what a person does do and as to what he should do. To provide such a guide we need to know what ends he does or should pursue, and the conception of interest in itself tells us nothing about either.

Thus the criterion of "national interest," or "interest of state," in itself provides us with no specific guidance either in interpreting the behaviour of states or in prescribing how they should behave—unless we are told what concrete ends or objectives states do or should pursue: security, prosperity, ideological objectives or whatever. Still less does it provide us with a criterion that is objective, in the sense of being independent of the way state ends or purposes are perceived by particular decision-makers. It does not even provide a basis for distinguishing moral or ideological considerations in a country's foreign policy from non-moral or non-ideological ones: for *x* can be in a country's interest if it serves as a means to a moral or ideological objective that the country has.

However, the conception of national interest or interest of state does have some meaning in a situation in which national or state ends are defined and agreed, and the question at issue is by what means they can be promoted. To say that a state's foreign policy should be based on pursuit of the national interest is to insist that whatever steps are taken should be part of some rational plan of action; an approach to foreign policy based on the national interest may thus be contrasted with one consisting simply of the uncritical pursuit of some established policy, or one consisting simply of unconsidered reactions to events. A policy based on the idea of the national interest, moreover, may be contrasted with one based on a sectional interest, or one based on the interests of some group wider than the state, such as an alliance or international organization to which it belongs. To speak of the national interest as the criterion at least directs our attention to the ends or objectives of the nation or state, as against those of some other group, narrower or wider.

The maintenance of order in international society has as its starting-point the development among states of a sense of common interests in the elementary goals of social life. However different and conflicting their objectives may be,

they are united in viewing these goals as instrumental to them. Their sense of common interests may derive from fear of unrestricted violence, of the instability of agreements or of the insecurity of their independence or sovereignty. It may have its origins in rational calculation that the willingness of states to accept restrictions on their freedom of action is reciprocal. Or it may be based also on the treatment of these goals as valuable in themselves and not merely as a means to an end—it may express a sense of common values as well as of common interests.

### Rules

In international society, as in other societies, the sense of common interests in elementary goals of social life does not in itself provide precise guidance as to what behaviour is consistent with these goals; to do this is the function of *rules*. These rules may have the status of international law, of moral rules, of custom or established practice, or they may be merely operational rules or "rules of the game" worked out without formal agreement or even without verbal communication. It is not uncommon for a rule to emerge first as an operational rule, then to become established practice, then to attain the status of a moral principle and finally to be incorporated in a legal convention; this appears to have been the genesis, for example, of many of the rules now embodied in multilateral treaties or conventions concerning the laws of war, diplomatic and consular status, and the law of the sea.

The range of these rules is vast, and over much of this range they are in a state of flux. Here we shall mention only three complexes of rules that play a part in the maintenance of international order.

First, there is the complex of rules that states what may be called the fundamental or constitutional normative principle of world politics in the present era. This is the principle that identifies the idea of a society of states, as opposed to such alternative ideas as that of a universal empire, a cosmopolitan community of individual human beings, or a Hobbesian state of nature or state of war, as the supreme normative principle of the political organization of mankind. It is emphasized elsewhere in this study that there is nothing historically inevitable or morally sacrosanct about the idea of a society of states. Nor does this idea in fact monopolize human thought and action, even in the present phase; on the contrary, it has always had to do battle with competing principles, and does so now. Order on a world scale, however, does require that one or another of these basic ideas should be clearly in the ascendancy; what is incompatible with order on a world scale is a discord of competing principles of universal political organization.

On the one hand, the idea of international society identifies states as members of this society and the units competent to carry out political tasks within it, including the tasks necessary to make its basic rules effective; it thus excludes conceptions which assign this political competence to groups other than the state, such as universal authorities above it or sectional groups within it. On the other hand, the idea of international society identifies the relationship between the states as that of members of a society bound by common rules and committed to common institutions; it thus excludes the conception of world politics as a mere arena or state of war.

This fundamental or constitutional principle of international order is presupposed in ordinary state conduct. The daily actions of states—in arrogating to themselves the rights or competences of principal actors in world politics, and in combining with each other to this end, in resisting the claims of supra-state or sub-state groups to wrest these rights and competences from them—display this principle and provide evidence of its central role. The principle is contained in a number of basic rules of international law. Thus it has been the predominant doctrine that states are the only or the principal bearers of rights and duties in international law; that they alone have the right to use force to uphold it; and that its source lies in the consent of states, expressed in custom or treaty. The principle, however, is prior to international law, or to any particular formulation of international law; it is manifest in a whole complex of rules—legal, moral, customary and operational. It is not a static principle, but is subject to constant development. In the formative stages of international society, it had to meet the challenge of doctrines which proclaimed the right of individuals and of groups other than the state to a place in universal political organization; and at the present time it faces a similar challenge.

Second, there are what may be called "the rules of coexistence." Given the guidance supplied by the constitutional principle as to who are the members of international society, these rules set out the minimum conditions of their coexistence. They include, first of all, the complex of rules which restrict the place of violence in world politics. These rules seek to confine the legitimate use of violence to sovereign states and to deny it to other agents by confining legitimate violence to a particular kind of violence called "war," and by treating war as violence that is waged on the authority of a sovereign state. Furthermore, the rules seek to limit the causes or purposes for which a sovereign state can legitimately begin a war, for example by requiring that it be begun for a just cause, as maintained by the natural-law doctrines of the formative era of the states system, or by requiring that it be begun only after certain other procedures had been tried first, as insisted by the Covenant of the League of Nations. The rules also have sought to restrict the manner in which sovereign states conduct war, for example by insisting that war be conducted in a way proportionate to the end pursued, or in such a way as to spare noncombatants, or so as to employ no more violence than necessary. In addition, the rules have sought to restrict the geographical spread of a war, by establishing the rights and duties of neutrals and belligerents in relation to one another.

There is a further complex of rules of coexistence which prescribes the behaviour appropriate to sustain the goal of the carrying out of undertakings. The basic rule *pacta sunt servanda*, sometimes seen as a presupposition of the law of nations, and sometimes as a first principle of it, established the presumption on which alone there can be point in entering into agreements at all. Subordinate or qualifying rules concern whether or not good faith need be kept with heretics or infidels, whether or not agreements remain valid in changing circumstances and who is the judge as to whether or not they have changed, whether or not and in what sense agreements are valid that are imposed by force, what the circumstances are in which a party to an agreement can be released from it, what are the principles according to which agreements should be interpreted, whether or not and to what extent a new government succeeds to the obligations of its predecessors, and so on.

The rules of coexistence also include those which prescribe behaviour that sustains the goal of the stabilisation of each state's control or jurisdiction over its own persons and territory. At the heart of this complex of rules is the principle that each state accepts the duty to respect the sovereignty or supreme jurisdiction of every other state over its own citizens and domain, in return for the right to expect similar respect for its own sovereignty from other states. A corollary or near-corollary of this central rule is the rule that states will not intervene forcibly or dictatorially in one another's internal affairs. Another is the rule establishing the "equality" of all states in the sense of their like enjoyment of like rights of sovereignty.

Third, there is the complex of rules concerned to regulate cooperation among states—whether on universal or on a more limited scale—above and beyond what is necessary for mere coexistence. This includes the rules that facilitate cooperation, not merely of a political and strategic, but also of a social and economic nature. The growth in this century of legal rules concerned with cooperation between states in economic, social, communications and environmental matters exemplifies the place of rules of cooperation and will be considered later. . . .

Rules of this kind prescribe behaviour that is appropriate not to the elementary or primary goals of international life, but rather to those more advanced or secondary goals that are a feature of an international society in which a consensus has been reached about a wider range of objectives than mere coexistence. Nevertheless, these rules may be said to play a role in relation to international order, inasmuch as the development of cooperation and consensus among states about these wider goals may be expected to strengthen the framework of coexistence.

This is not the place to expound these three complexes of rules in full, or to examine the problems of interpreting them or reconciling the conflicts between them. Nor is it appropriate here to consider which of them has the status of law, which the status of moral rules, which should be seen as customary or as operational rules, nor to trace the historical evolution through which these rules have passed from one of these embodiments to another, and sometimes back again. It is sufficient to note that the vast and changing corpus of rules and quasi-rules, of which those cited are part of the central core, provide the means whereby international society moves from the vague perception of a common interest to a clear conception of the kind of conduct it requires.

### Institutions

In international society it is the members of the society themselves—sovereign states—which are chiefly responsible for performing the functions of helping to make the rules effective; they do so in the absence of either a supreme government, which is able to undertake these functions in the modern state, or the degree of solidarity among themselves that characterizes the performance of these functions by politically competent groups in primitive stateless societies.

In this sense it is states themselves that are the principal institutions of the society of states.

Thus states undertake the function of making the rules, or legislating, by signifying their consent to them. Rules of general application, like the rules of coexistence, arise out of custom and established practice, and are in some cases confirmed by multilateral conventions. Rules that apply only to particular groups of states may also arise out of custom and established practice—as do the operational rules of crisis avoidance and management now being evolved by the great powers—but they may also be the subject of explicit agreements or treaties.

States communicate the rules through their official words, as when they state that they respect the legal principle of the sovereignty of states, or the moral principle of national self-determination, or the operational rule that great powers should not interfere in each other's spheres of influence. But they also communicate the rules through their actions, when they behave in such a way as to indicate that they accept or do not accept that a particular rule is valid. Because the communication of the rules is in the hands of states themselves, and not of an authority independent of them, the advertisement of the rules is commonly distorted in favor of the interests of particular states.

States administer the rules of international society inasmuch as executive acts ancillary to the rules themselves are performed either by themselves (as when particular states are designated as the depository states for a treaty, or the guarantors of a neutralization arrangement, or the arbiters of a dispute) or by international organizations which are responsible to them (as when organizations are set up to implement agreements concerning international post and telecommunications, or a host of other matters).

Each state provides its own interpretation of the rules—legal, moral or operational. Even in the case of legal rules, a state relies on its own legal advisers, and there is no conclusive way in which disagreements about interpretation can be settled by an independent authority. The interpretation of moral or of operational rules is even more uncertain.

The enforcement of the rules, in the absence of a central authority, is carried out by states, which may resort to acts of self-help, including acts of force, in defense of their rights under operational, moral or legal rules. Because states are frequently not in a position to carry out effective action in defense of their rights, the enforcement of the rules is uncertain. Because of the low degree of consensus or solidarity among states, actions which the state committing them sees as self-help or rule-enforcement are frequently not viewed as such by international society at large.

States undertake the task of legitimizing the rules, in the sense of promoting the acceptance of them as valuable in their own right, by employing their powers of persuasion and propaganda to mobilize support for them in world politics as a whole. At the present time an important means to the legitimization of rules is to have them endorsed by international assemblies and international organizations.

States undertake the task of changing or adapting operational, moral and legal rules to hanging circumstances, but have to do so in the absence of a universal legislative authority competent to rescind old rules and devise new ones, and with the handicap that there is often no consensus as to whether or not, or how, the rules should be changed. States change the rules by demonstrating, through their words or their actions, that they are withdrawing their consent from old rules and bestowing it upon new ones, and thus altering the content of custom or established practice. The operational rules observed by great powers, whereby they respect one another's spheres of influence in particular parts of the world, are rescinded or changed when these powers show by what they do or say that they no longer accept them, or regard their boundaries or limiting conditions as having changed. The moral principle of national self-determination— the rule that states should be nation-states— came to displace that of dynastic legitimacy not by enactment of any legislative authority, but by war and revolution. In the changing of legal rules a part is sometimes played by multilateral conventions or treaties, but here also states change the old rules by violating or ignoring them systematically enough to demonstrate that they have withdrawn their consent to them. In other words, while the adaptation of the rules to changed circumstances is part of the process whereby order is maintained, it is itself often accompanied by disorder.

Finally, states undertake the task which, for want of a better term, has been called "protection" of the rules. The rules which sustain order in international society can operate only if conditions obtain in the international political system that enable them to do so. In particular, they can operate only if that sense of common interests among states, which they seek to translate into a precise guide to conduct, continues to exist. The function of "protection" of the rules comprises all those things which states may do to create or maintain that state or condition of the system in which respect for the rules can flourish.

The "protection" of the rules encompasses, first and foremost, those classical acts of diplomacy and war whereby states seek to preserve a general balance of power in the international system (and today a relationship of mutual nuclear deterrence among contending nuclear powers); to accommodate or contain conflicts of ideology; to resolve or moderate conflicts of state interest; to limit or control armaments and armed forces in relation to interests perceived in international security; to appease the demands of dissatisfied states for what they regard as just change; and to secure and maintain the acquiescence of the smaller powers in the assumption by great powers of special rights and responsibilities.

These measures of "protection" of the rules are not prescribed by the rules of coexistence, or by international law, in which some of the rules of coexistence are stated. Indeed, some of the measures which states take in the course of "protecting" the rules may bring them into conflict with international law. The activities that go to make up "protection" of the rules of coexistence are themselves the subject of further bodies of rules, such as those which regulate the balance of power, diplomacy and the special position of the great powers.

In carrying out these functions, states collaborate with one another, in varying degrees, in what may be called the institutions of international society: the balance of power, international law, the diplomatic mechanism, the managerial system of the great powers, and war. By an institution we do not necessarily imply an organization or administrative machinery, but rather a set of habits and practices shaped towards the realization of common goals. These institutions do not deprive states of their central role in carrying out the political functions of international society, or serve as a surrogate central authority in the international system. They are rather an expression of the element of collaboration among states in discharging their political functions—and at the same time a means of sustaining this collaboration. These institutions serve to symbolize the existence of an international society that is more than the sum of its members, to give substance and permanence to their collaboration in carrying out the political functions of international society, and to moderate their tendency to lose sight of common interests.

# 9: International Regimes

*Robert O. Keohane*

## Harmony, Cooperation, and Discord

Cooperation must be distinguished from harmony. Harmony refers to a situation in which actors' policies (pursued in their own self-interest without regard for others) *automatically* facilitate the attainment of others' goals. The classic example of harmony is the hypothetical competitive market world of the classical economists, in which the Invisible Hand ensures that the pursuit of self-interest by each contributes to the interest of all. In this idealized, unreal world, no one's actions damage anyone else; there are no "negative externalities," in the economists' jargon. Where harmony reigns, cooperation is unnecessary. It may even be injurious, if it means that certain individuals conspire to exploit others. Adam Smith, for one, was very critical of guilds and other conspiracies against freedom of trade (1776/1976). Cooperation and harmony are by no means identical and ought not to be confused with one another.

Cooperation requires that the actions of separate individuals or organizations—which are not in preexistent harmony—be brought into conformity with one another through a process of negotiation, which is often referred to as "policy coordination." Charles E. Lindblom has defined policy coordination as follows (1965, p. 227):

> A set of decisions is coordinated if adjustments have been made in them, such that the adverse consequences of any one decision for other decisions are to a degree and in some frequency avoided, reduced, or counterbalanced or overweighed.

Cooperation occurs when actors adjust their behavior to the actual or anticipated preferences of others, through a process of policy coordination. To summarize more formally, *intergovernmental cooperation takes place when the policies actually followed by one government are regarded by its partners as facilitating realization of their own objectives, as the result of a process of policy coordination.*

With this definition in mind, we can differentiate among cooperation, harmony, and discord. . . . First, we ask whether actors' policies automatically facilitate the attainment of others' goals. If so, there is harmony: no adjustments need to take place. Yet harmony is rare in world politics. Rousseau sought to account for this rarity when he declared that even two countries guided by the General Will in their internal affairs would come into conflict if they had extensive contact with one another, since the General Will of each would not be general for both. Each would have a partial, self-interested perspective on their mutual interactions. Even for Adam Smith, efforts to ensure state security took precedence over measures to increase national prosperity. In defending the Navigation Acts, Smith declared: "As defense is of much more importance than opulence, the act of navigation is, perhaps, the wisest of all the commercial

Keohane, Robert O.; AFTER HEGEMONY, pp. 51-55, 56-57, 58-59, 61-63. © 1984 by Princeton University Press. Reprinted by permission of Princeton University Press.

regulations of England" (1776/1976, p. 487). Waltz summarizes the point by saying that "In anarchy there is no automatic harmony" (1959, p. 182).

Yet this insight tells us nothing definitive about the prospects for cooperation. For this we need to ask a further question about situations in which harmony does not exist. Are attempts made by actors (governmental or nongovernmental) to adjust their policies to each others' objectives? If no such attempts are made, the result is discord: a situation in which governments regard each others' policies as hindering the attainment of their goals, and hold each other responsible for these constraints.

Discord often leads to efforts to induce others to change their policies; when these attempts meet resistance, policy conflict results. Insofar as these attempts at policy adjustment succeed in making policies more compatible, however, cooperation ensues. The policy coordination that leads to cooperation need not involve bargaining or negotiation at all. What Lindblom calls "adaptive" as opposed to "manipulative" adjustment can take place: one country may shift its policy in the direction of another's preferences without regard for the effect of its action on the other state, defer to the other country, or partially shift its policy in order to avoid adverse consequences for its partner. Or nonbargained manipulation—such as one actor confronting another with a *fait accompli*—may occur (Lindblom, 1965, pp. 33-34 and ch. 4). Frequently, of course, negotiation and bargaining indeed take place, often accompanied by other actions that are designed to induce others to adjust their policies to one's own. Each government pursues what it perceives as its self-interest, but looks for bargains that can benefit all parties to the deal, though not necessarily equally.

Harmony and cooperation are not usually distinguished from one another so clearly. Yet, in the study of world politics, they should be. Harmony is apolitical. No communication is necessary, and no influence need be exercised.

Cooperation, by contrast, is highly political: somehow, patterns of behavior must be altered. This change may be accomplished through negative as well as positive inducements. Indeed, studies of international crises, as well as game-theoretic experiments and simulations, have shown that under a variety of conditions strategies that involve threats and punishments as well as promises and rewards are more effective in attaining cooperative outcomes than those that rely entirely on persuasion and the force of good example (Axelrod, 1981, 1984; Lebow, 1981; Snyder and Diesing, 1977).

Cooperation therefore does not imply an absence of conflict. On the contrary, it is typically mixed with conflict and reflects partially successful efforts to overcome conflict, real or potential. Cooperation takes place only in situations in which actors perceive that their policies are actually or potentially in conflict, not where there is harmony. Cooperation should not be viewed as the absence of conflict, but rather as a reaction to conflict or potential conflict. Without the specter of conflict, there is no need to cooperate.

The example of trade relations among friendly countries in a liberal international political economy may help to illustrate this crucial point. A naive observer, trained only to appreciate the overall welfare benefits of trade, might assume that trade relations would be harmonious: consumers in importing countries benefit from cheap foreign goods and increased competition, and producers can increasingly take advantage of the division of labor as their export markets expand. But harmony does not normally ensue. Discord on trade issues may prevail because governments do not even seek to reduce the adverse consequences of their own policies for others, but rather strive in certain respects to increase the severity of those effects. Mercantilist governments have sought in the twentieth century as well as the seventeenth to manipulate foreign trade, in conjunction with warfare, to damage each other economically and to gain productive resources themselves (Wilson, 1957; Hirschman, 1945/1980). Governments may desire "positional goods," such as high status (Hirsch, 1976), and may therefore resist even mutually beneficial cooperation if it helps others more than themselves. Yet even when neither power nor positional motivations are present, and when all participants would benefit in the aggregate from liberal trade, discord tends to predominate over harmony as the initial result of independent governmental action.

This occurs even under otherwise benign conditions because some groups or industries are forced to incur adjustment costs as changes in comparative advantage take place. Governments often respond to the ensuing demands for protection by attempting, more or less effectively, to cushion the burdens of adjustment for groups and industries that are politically influential at home. Yet unilateral measures to this effect almost always impose adjustment costs abroad, and discord continually threatens. Governments enter into international negotiations in order to reduce the conflict that would otherwise result. Even substantial potential common benefits do not create harmony when state power can be exercised on behalf of certain interests and against others. In world politics, harmony tends to vanish: attainment of the gains from pursuing complementary policies depends on cooperation.

Observers of world politics who take power and conflict seriously should be attracted to this way of defining cooperation, since my definition does not relegate cooperation to the mythological world of relations among equals in power. Hegemonic cooperation is not a contradiction in terms. Defining cooperation in contrast to harmony should, I hope, lead readers with a Realist orientation to take cooperation in world politics seriously rather than to dismiss it out of hand. . . .

The concept of international regime not only enables us to describe patterns of cooperation; it also helps to account for both cooperation and discord. Although regimes themselves depend on conditions that are conducive to interstate agreements, they may also facilitate further efforts to coordinate policies. . . . To understand international cooperation, it is necessary to comprehend how institutions and rules not only reflect, but also affect, the facts of world politics.

### Defining and Identifying Regimes

When John Ruggie introduced the concept of international regimes into the international politics literature in 1975, he defined a regime as "a set of mutual expectations, rules and regulations, plans, organizational energies and financial commitments, which have been accepted by a group of states" (p. 570). More recently, a collective definition, worked out at a conference on the subject, defined international regimes as "sets of implicit or explicit principles, norms, rules and decision-making procedures around which actors' expectations converge in a given area of international relations. Principles are beliefs of fact, causation, and rectitude. Norms are standards of behavior defined in terms of rights and obligations. Rules are specific prescriptions or proscriptions for action. Decision-making procedures are prevailing practices for making and implementing collective choice" (Krasner, 1983, p. 2). . . .

The principles of regimes define, in general, the purposes that their members are expected to pursue. For instance, the principles of the postwar trade and monetary regimes have emphasized the value of open, nondiscriminatory patterns of international economic transactions; the fundamental principle of the nonproliferation regime is that the spread of nuclear weapons is dangerous. Norms contain somewhat clearer injunctions to members about legitimate and illegitimate behavior, still defining responsibilities and obligations in relatively general terms. For instance, the norms of the General Agreement on Tariffs and Trade (GATT) do not require that members resort to free trade immediately, but incorporate injunctions to members to practice nondiscrimination and reciprocity and to move toward increased liberalization. Fundamental to the nonproliferation regime is the norm that members of the regime should not act in ways that facilitate nuclear proliferation.

The rules of a regime are difficult to distinguish from its norms; at the margin, they merge into one another. Rules are, however, more specific: they indicate in more detail the specific rights and obligations of members. Rules can be altered more easily than principles or norms, since there may be more than one set of rules that can attain a given set of purposes. Finally, at the same level of specificity as rules, but referring to procedures rather than substances, the decision-making procedures of regimes provide ways of implementing their principles and altering their rules.

An example from the field of international monetary relations may be helpful. The most important principle of the international balance-of-payments regime since the end of World War II has been that of liberalization of trade and payments. A key norm of the regime has been the injunction to states not to manipulate their exchange rates unilaterally for national advantage. Between 1958 and 1971 this norm was realized through pegged exchange rates and procedures for consultation in the event of change, supplemented with a variety of devices to help governments avoid exchange-rate changes through a combination of borrowing and internal adjustment. After 1973 governments have subscribed to the same norm, although it has been implemented more informally and probably less effectively under a system of floating exchange rates. Ruggie (1983b) has argued that the abstract principle of liberalization, subject to constraints imposed by the acceptance of the welfare state, has been maintained throughout the postwar period: "embedded liberalism" continues, reflecting a fundamental element of continuity in the international balance-of-payments regime. The norm of nonmanipulation has also been maintained, even though the specific rules of the 1958-71 system having to do with adjustment have been swept away.

The concept of international regime is complex because it is defined in terms of four distinct components: principles, norms, rules, and decisionmaking procedures. It is tempting to select one of these levels of specificity—particularly, principles and norms or rules and procedures—as *the* defining characteristic of regimes (Krasner, 1983; Ruggie, 1983b). Such an approach, however, creates a false dichotomy between principles on the one hand and rules and procedures on the other. As we have noted, at the margin norms and rules cannot be sharply distinguished from each other. It is difficult if not impossible to tell the difference between an "implicit rule" of broad significance and a well-understood, relatively specific operating principle. Both rules and principles may affect expectations and even values. In a strong international regime, the linkages between principles and rules are likely to be tight. Indeed, it is precisely the linkages among principles, norms, and rules that give regimes their legitimacy. Since rules, norms, and principles are so closely intertwined, judgments about whether changes in rules constitute changes *of* regime or merely changes *within* regimes necessarily contain arbitrary elements.

Principles, norms, rules, and procedures all contain injunctions about behavior: they prescribe certain actions and proscribe others. They imply obligations, even though these obligations are not enforceable through a hierarchical legal system. It clarifies the definition of regime, therefore, to think of it in terms of injunctions of greater or lesser specificity. Some are far-reaching and extremely important. They may change only rarely. At the other extreme, injunctions may be merely technical, matters of convenience that can be altered without great political or economic impact. In-between are injunctions that are both specific enough that violations of them are in principle identifiable and that changes in them can be observed, and sufficiently significant that changes in them make a difference for the behavior of actors and the nature of the international political economy. It is these intermediate injunctions—politically consequential but specific enough that violations and changes can be identified—that I take as the essence of international regimes.[1] . . .

### Self-Help and International Regimes

The injunctions of international regimes rarely affect economic transactions directly: state institutions, rather than international organizations, impose tariffs and quotas, intervene in foreign exchange markets, and manipulate oil prices through taxes and subsidies. If we think about the impact of the principles, norms, rules, and decision-making procedures of regimes, it becomes clear that insofar as they have any effect at all, it must be exerted on national controls, and especially on the specific interstate agreements that affect the exercise of national controls (Aggarwal, 1981). International regimes must be distinguished from these specific agreements . . . a major function of regimes is to facilitate the making of specific cooperative agreements among governments.

Superficially, it could seem that since international regimes affect national controls, the regimes are of superior importance—just as federal laws in the United States frequently override state and local legislation. Yet this would be a fundamentally misleading conclusion. In a well-ordered society, the units of action—individuals in classic liberal thought—live together within a framework of constitutional principles that define property rights, establish who may control the state, and specify the conditions under which

subjects must obey governmental regulations. In the United States, these principles establish the supremacy of the federal government in a number of policy areas, though not in all. But world politics is decentralized rather than hierarchic: the prevailing principle of sovereignty means that states are subject to no superior government (Ruggie, 1983a). The resulting system is sometimes referred to as one of "self-help" (Waltz, 1979).

Sovereignty and self-help mean that the principles and rules of international regimes will necessarily be weaker than in domestic society. In a civil society, these rules "specify terms of exchange" within the framework of constitutional principles (North, 1981, p. 203). In world politics, the principles, norms, and rules of regimes are necessarily fragile because they risk coming into conflict with the principle of sovereignty and the associated norm of self-help. They may promote cooperation, but the fundamental basis of order on which they would rest in a well-ordered society does not exist. They drift around without being tied to the solid anchor of the state.

Yet even if the principles of sovereignty and self-help limit the degree of confidence to be placed in international agreements, they do not render cooperation impossible. Orthodox theory itself relies on mutual interests to explain forms of cooperation that are used by states as instruments of competition. According to balance-of-power theory, cooperative endeavors such as political-military alliances necessarily form in self-help systems (Waltz, 1979). Acts of cooperation are

---

1   Some authors have defined "regime" as equivalent to the conventional concept of international system. For instance, Puchala and Hopkins (1983) claim that "a regime exists in every substantive issue-area in international relations where there is discernibly patterned behavior." To adopt this definition would be to make either "system" or "regime" a redundant term. At the opposite extreme, the concept of regime could be limited to situations with genuine normative content, in which governments followed regime rules *instead of* pursuing their own self-interests when the two conflicted. If this course were chosen, the concept of regime would be just another way of expressing ancient "idealist" sentiments in international relations. The category of regime would become virtually empty. This dichotomy poses a false choice between using "regime" as a new label for old patterns and defining regimes as utopias. Either strategy would make the term irrelevant.

accounted for on the grounds that mutual interests are sufficient to enable states to over come their suspicions of one another. But since even orthodox theory relies on mutual interests, its advocates are on weak ground in objecting to interpretations of system-wide cooperation along these lines. There is no logical or empirical reason why mutual interests in world politics should be limited to interests in combining forces against adversaries. As economists emphasize, there can also be mutual interests in securing efficiency gains from voluntary exchange or oligopolistic rewards from the creation and division of rents resulting from the control and manipulation of markets.

International regimes should not be interpreted as elements of a new international order "beyond the nation-state." They should be comprehended chiefly as arrangements motivated by self-interest: as components of systems in which sovereignty remains a constitutive principle. This means that, as Realists emphasize, they will be shaped largely by their most powerful members, pursuing their own interests. But regimes can also affect state interests, for the notion of self-interest is itself elastic and largely subjective. Perceptions of self-interest depend both on actors' expectations of the likely consequences that will follow from particular actions and on their fundamental values. Regimes can certainly affect expectations and may affect values as well. Far from being contradicted by the view that international behavior is shaped largely by power and interests, the concept of international regime is consistent both with the importance of differential power and with a sophisticated view of self-interest. Theories of regimes can incorporate Realist insights about the role of power and interest, while also indicating the inadequacy of theories that define interests so narrowly that they fail to take the role of institutions into account.

Regimes not only are consistent with self-interest but may under some conditions even be necessary to its effective pursuit. They facilitate the smooth operation of decentralized international political systems and therefore perform an important function for states. In a world political economy characterized by growing interdependence, they may become increasingly useful for governments that wish to solve common problems and pursue complementary purposes without subordinating themselves to hierarchical systems of control.

## Bibliography

Aggarwal, Vinod, 1981. Hanging by a Thread: International Regime Change in the Textile/Apparel System, 1950-1979 (Ph.D. dissertation. Stanford University).

Axelrod, Robert, 1981. The emergence of cooperation among egoists. *American Political Science Review*, vol. 75, no. 2 (June), pp. 306-18.

Axelrod, Robert, 1984. *The Evolution of Cooperation* (New York: Basic Books).

Hirsch, Fred, 1976. *Social Limits to Growth* (Cambridge: Harvard University Press).

Hirschman, Albert O., 1945/1980. *National Power and the Structure of Foreign Trade* (Berkeley: University of California Press).

Krasner, Stephen D., 1983. Structural causes and regime consequences: regimes as intervening variables. In Krasner, 1983, pp. 1-22. Krasner, Stephen D., ed., 1983. *International Regimes* (Ithaca: Cornell University Press).

Lebow, Richard Ned, 1981. *Between Peace and War: The Nature of International Crisis* (Baltimore: The Johns Hopkins University Press).

Lindblom, Charles E., 1965. *The Intelligence of Democracy* (New York: The Free Press).

North, Douglass C., 1981. *Structure and Change in Economic History* (New York: W. W. Norton).

Ruggie, John Gerard, 1975. International responses to technology: concepts and trends. *International Organization*, vol. 29, no. 3 (Summer), pp. 557-84.

Ruggie, John Gerard, 1983a. Continuity and transformation in the world polity: toward a neorealist synthesis. *World Politics*, vol. 35, no. 2 (January), pp. 261-86.

Ruggie, John Gerard, 1983b. International regimes, transactions, and change: embedded liberalism in the postwar economic order. In Krasner, 1983, pp. 195-232.

Smith, Adam, 1776/1976. *The Wealth of Nations* (Chicago: University of Chicago Press).

Snyder, Glenn H., and Paul Diesing, 1977. *Conflict among Nations: Bargaining, Decision making, and System Structure in International Crises* (Princeton: Princeton University Press).

Waltz, Kenneth, 1959. *Man, the State and War* (New York: Columbia University Press).

Waltz, Kenneth, 1979. *Theory of World Politics* (Reading, Mass.: Addison-Wesley).

Wilson, Charles, 1957. *Profit and Power. A Study of England and the Dutch Wars* (Cambridge: Cambridge University Press).

# 10: International Law

*Hedley Bull*

International law . . . is taken to be a body of rules which is considered to have *the status of law*. That there are rules which states and other agents in international politics regard as binding on one another, there can be no doubt. It is by virtue of this fact that we may speak of the existence of an international society. But whether or not these rules, or some of them, have the status of law, is a matter of controversy.

Throughout modern history there has been a tradition of thought which has sought to deny that international law is "law" properly so-called, on the grounds that an essential feature of law is that it is the product of sanctions, force or coercion. The origins of this tradition lie in the view of Hobbes that, "where there is no common power, there is no law."[1] It received its most celebrated statement in the doctrine of John Austin that law is "the command of the sovereign," and that since there exists no sovereign in international society (no "determinate human persons, to whom the bulk of society pay habitual obedience, and who do not habitually obey any other person"), international law is not "law" properly so-called but is merely "positive international morality."[2] The Austinian view of law is powerfully maintained, although with important modifications, in the contemporary doctrine of Hans Kelsen that law is distinguished from other kinds of social order (for example, from religious orders based on supernatural sanctions, and from moral orders based on voluntary obedience) by its character as a "coercive order."[3] The essential feature of a rule of law, in Kelsen's view, is that it stipulates that a delict (or violation of a norm) ought to be followed by a sanction (or threatened evil).

Whatever the difficulties of the Austinian view, it does help to bring out the fact that international law, whether or not it is "law" properly so-called, differs from municipal law in one central respect: whereas law within the modern state is backed up by the authority of a government, including its power to use or threaten force, international law is without this kind of prop. . . .

## The Efficacy of International Law

Having defined international law we have now to consider what bearing it has on the actual behaviour of states. Rules by themselves are mere intellectual constructs. If we are to speak of the rules of international law as a factor seriously affecting the life of international society, we must establish that they have a degree of efficacy; that is to say, that there is some degree of resemblance as between the behaviour prescribed by the rules, and the actual behaviour of states and other actors in international politics.

In order to establish the efficacy of the rules of international law, it is not necessary to establish

---

1   Hobbes, *Leviathan* (London: Blackwell, 1946) ch. 13, p. 83.
2   John Austin, *The Province of Jurisprudence Determined* (originally published in 1832, and London: Weidenfeld & Nicholson, 1954) lecture VI.
3   Hans Kelsen, *The General Theory of the Law and State*, trans. A. Wedburg (Harvard University Press, 1946).

THE ANARCHICAL SOCIETY by Hedley Bull, pp. 129-30, 136-45. © 1977 by Columbia University Press, New York. (Reprinted by permission of the publishers.)

an *identity* as between actual and prescribed behaviour; that is to say, that there are no cases in which the rules are disregarded. It is not true of any system of legal rules that it is never disregarded; indeed, in cases where conformity between actual and prescribed behaviour can be regarded as a forgone conclusion, there can be no point in having rules at all. It is for this reason that societies do not develop rules requiring their members to breathe, eat and sleep, which they can be relied upon to do, but do develop rules requiring them not to kill, steal or lie, which some of them are likely to do, whether there are rules prohibiting this kind of behaviour or not.

The question is whether the rules of international law are observed to a sufficient degree (it is not possible to specify precisely to what degree) to justify our treating them as a substantial factor at work in international politics, and, in particular, as a means of preserving international order. There has always been a school of thought which, whether or not it rejects the claims of international law to the term "law," regards these rules as a non-existent or at most a negligible factor in the actual conduct of international relations.

There is no doubt that there exists a substantial degree of coincidence as between actual international behaviour and the behaviour prescribed by the rules of international law. If it were possible or meaningful to conduct a quantitative study of obedience to the rules of international law, it might be expected to show that most states obey most agreed rules of international law most of the time. Any state which lives at peace with at least one other state, which is involved in diplomatic relations with it, which exchanges money, goods and visitors with it, or which enters into agreements with it, is involved constantly in obedience to rules of international law.

In particular cases, rules of law are violated or disregarded; but these cases do not in themselves provide evidence that international law as such is without efficacy. In the first place, violation of a particular rule usually takes place against the background of conformity to other rules of international law, and indeed of conformity even to the rule that is being violated, in instances other than the present one. When, for example, Germany in 1914 invaded Belgium, in violation of the treaty of 1839 (neutralising Belgium) and of the rule of international law that treaties should be honoured, it continued to respect other principles of international law and to base its relations with other countries upon them. Moreover, in cases other than that of the treaty providing for the neutrality of Belgium, it continued to proclaim and to practise the rule of the sanctity of treaties.

In the second place, the violation is sometimes in itself of such a nature as to embody some element of conformity to the rule that is being violated. The distinction between violation of a rule and conformity to it is not always a sharp one; the decision of an authority as to whether or not a violation has occurred is always, in the end, yea or nay, but the processes of argument whereby this decision is arrived at may contain uncertain and arbitrary elements, both in the interpretation of the rule and in the construction of the facts. In reality the behaviour of a state in relation to the particular rule of international law is best thought of as finding its place in a spectrum of positions stretching from clear-cut conformity at one extreme to a clear-cut violation at the other. The violation of an agreement may be a measured response to some action of another party, designed to preserve some part of the agreement or to keep alive the possibility of restoring it.

In the third place, where a violation takes place the offending state usually goes out of its way to demonstrate that it still considers itself (and other states) bound by the rule in question. In some cases the state in question may deny that any violation has taken place, arguing, for example, as Nazi Germany did in remilitarising the Rhineland in 1936, that the agreement being disregarded had already lapsed because of previous violations by other parties, or that it was invalid in the first place. In other cases, such as Germany in violating Belgian neutrality in 1914, or the United

States in admitting violation of Soviet air space by the U2 aircraft in 1960, the offending state may admit that a rule has been broken but appeal to some conflicting principle of overriding importance. Even when the appeal is to a principle such as "necessity" or "vital interests," at least there is acceptance of the need to provide an explanation.

What is a clearer sign of the inefficacy of a set of rules is the case where there is not merely a lack of conformity as between actual and prescribed behaviour, but a failure to accept the validity or binding quality of the obligations themselves—as indicated by a reasoned appeal to different and conflicting principles, or by an unreasoning disregard of the rules. An unreasoning disregard of the rules—a failure to respond to them because of lack of knowledge of what they are, lack of understanding of them or lack of acceptance of the premises from which they derive—is characteristic of the behaviour of groups not recognising any common international society; for historical examples of it we have to look to encounters between member states of international society and political entities outside it. . . . What does from time to time occur in the history of modern international society is a reasoned rejection of its legal rules, or of certain of them, by states committed to revolutionary change, such as Bolshevik Russia (for example, in relation to the law of succession) or certain contemporary African and Asian states (for example, in relation to the legitimacy of colonial sovereignty and foreign property rights). But these examples of reasoned rejection of rules of international law have represented the temporary and local breakdown of these rules, not the general breakdown of the international legal system as a whole.

The denigrators of international law, however, while they are wrong when they claim that international law is without efficacy, are right to insist that respect for the law is not in itself the principal motive that accounts for conformity to law. International law is a social reality to the extent that there is a very substantial degree of conformity to its rules; but it does not follow from this that international law is a powerful agent or motive force in world politics.

States obey international law in part because of habit or inertia; they are, as it were, programmed to operate within the framework of established principles. In so far as their conformity to law derives from deliberation or calculation, it results from motives of three sorts. First, obedience may be the consequence of the fact that the action enjoined by the law is thought to be valuable, mandatory or obligatory, apart from its being legally required, either as an end in itself or as part of, or a means to, some wider set of values. Rules that are carried out primarily for this sort of reason are sometimes spoken of as "the international law of community." Second, obedience may result from coercion, or the threat of it, by some superior power bent on enforcing the agreement. Agreements that are observed chiefly for reasons of this sort are sometimes spoken of as "the international law of power," and are exemplified by the acceptance of peace treaties by vanquished states at the time of their defeat and for as long a period thereafter as they remain too weak to challenge the verdict of war. Third, obedience may result from the interest a state perceives in reciprocal action by another state or states. Agreements and principles resting on this sense of mutual interest are sometimes called "the international law of reciprocity." These are exemplified by the most central principles of international law, such as mutual respect for sovereignty, the keeping of promises and the laws of war.[4]

The argument that states obey the law only for ulterior motives, or that they do so only when

---

4  For a discussion of this threefold division, see Georg Schwarzenberger, *The Frontiers of International Law* (London: Stevens & Son, 1962) ch. I.

they consider it is in their interests to do so, is sometimes put forward as if it somehow disposed of the claims of international law to be taken seriously. Of course, it does not. The importance of international law does not rest on the willingness of states to abide by its principles to the detriment of their interests, but in the fact that they so often judge it in their interests to conform to it.

### The Contribution of International Law to International Order

What is the role of law in relation to international order? The first function of international law has been to identify, as the supreme normative principle of the political organisation of mankind, the idea of a society of sovereign states. This is what was called . . . the fundamental or constitutional principle of world politics in the present era. Order in the great society of all mankind has been attained, during the present phase of the modern states system, through general acceptance of the principle that men and territory are divided into states, each with its own proper sphere of authority, but linked together by a common set of rules. International law, by stating and elaborating this principle and by excluding alternative principles—such as the Hobbesian notion that international politics is an arena in which there are no rules restricting states in their relations with one another, or the notion that mankind is properly organised as a universal state based on cosmopolitan rights, or as a universal empire founded on the supremacy of a particular nation or race—establishes this particular realm of ideas as the determining one for human thought and action in the present phase, and so precludes the opening of questions without end and the eruption of conflicts without limit.

It is emphasised elsewhere in this study that order in the great society of all mankind might in principle be attained in many other ways than through a society of sovereign states

which is neither historically inevitable nor morally sacrosanct. If in fact mankind were organised as a cosmopolitan state, or a universal empire, or according to some other principle, law might play a part in identifying this other principle as the supreme and seminal one. What, however, is incompatible with order on a global scale is a welter of competing principles of universal political organisation, such as existed in Europe during the period of the wars of religion. The first function of law in relation to order in world politics is thus to identify one of these principles of universal political organisation and proclaim its supremacy over all competitors.

The second function of international law in relation to international order has been to state the basic rules of coexistence among states and other actors in international society. These rules, which have been discussed above, relate to three core areas: there are rules relating to the restriction of violence among states and other actors; rules relating to agreements among them; and rules relating to sovereignty or independence. . . .

The third function of international law is to help mobilise compliance with the rules of international society—both the basic rules of coexistence . . . the rules of co-operation . . . and others. We have seen that while the actual behaviour of states does in some measure conform to the prescriptions of international law, respect for international law is not the principal motive force accounting for this conformity. It follows from this that it is erroneous to view the principal contribution of international law to international order as lying in its imposition of restraints on international behaviour. Governments have a degree of respect for legal obligations; they are reluctant to acquire a reputation for disregarding them, and, in relation to most of the agreements into which they enter, they calculate that their interests lie in fulfilling them. But when their legal obligations and the interest they perceive in being known as governments that fulfil them come into conflict with their major interests and objectives, instead of being confirmed by them, these obligations are often disregarded.

However, it is not only through imposing restraints on international behaviour that international law helps to secure compliance with the basic rules of international society; the basic factors making for compliance with international law—acceptance by the parties of the ends or values underlying the agreement, coercion by a superior power, and reciprocal interest—exist independently of legal commitments, and without their operation legal commitments are ineffective. But the framework of international law serves to mobilise and channel these factors in the direction of compliance with agreements. In particular, international law provides a means by which states can advertise their intentions with regard to the matter in question; provide one another with reassurance about their future policies in relation to it; specify precisely what the nature of the agreement is, including its boundaries and limiting conditions; and solemnise the agreement in such a way as to create an expectation of permanence.

## The Limitations of International Law

While the above functions are those which international law fulfils in relation to international order, it is important to take account of the limitations within which they are carried out. First, it is not the case that international law is a necessary or essential condition of international order. The functions which international law fulfils are essential to international order, but these functions might in principle be carried out in other ways. The idea of a society of states might be identified and its centrality proclaimed, the basic rules of coexistence might be stated, and a means provided for facilitating compliance with agreements, by a body of rules which has the status of moral rules or supernatural rules. Some past international societies—the Greek city-state system, the system of Hellenistic kingdoms that arose after the death of Alexander, the ancient

Indian system of states—were without the institution of international law. That modern international society includes international law as one of its institutions is a consequence of the historical accident that it evolved out of a previous unitary system, Western Christendom, and that in this system notions of law—embodied in Roman law, divine law, canon law and natural law—were preeminent. The place of international law in our present international society gives it a distinctive stamp. Because the central rules of this society are considered to have the status of law, and not merely of morality, the sense of their binding force is an especially strong one, and the notion that there does exist in principle a single authoritative definition of the meaning of the rules (however difficult it may be, owing to the lack of authoritative "rules of adjudication" to discover what they are) is a deeply entrenched one.

Second, international law is not by itself sufficient to bring about international order. International law cannot fulfil any of the functions that have been ascribed to it unless other conditions, not guaranteed by international law itself, are present. International law cannot identify the idea of international society as the supreme normative principle unless an international society in some measure already exists, and is receptive to the treatment of this principle as the supreme one. International law can contribute to international order by stating the basic rules of coexistence among states only if these rules have some basis in the actual dealings of states with one another. International law can mobilise the factors making for compliance with rules and agreements in international society only if these factors are present. Still less is it the case that international law by itself can be an instrument for the strengthening of order or peace, as is implied by programmes for "world peace through law," or "world peace through world law." The multiplication or "strengthening" of international legal restraints and prohibitions may play a part in strengthening international order in cases where it serves to mobilise or dramatise other factors at work in the situation, but attempts to legislate order or peace in the absence of these factors serve only to bring international law into discredit without advancing the prospects of peace.

In the third place, international law, or some particular interpretation of international law, is sometimes found actually to hinder measures to maintain international order. A classic case is the clash between international law and measures deemed necessary to maintain a balance of power. The clash between imperatives deriving from international law, and imperatives deriving from the principle that a balance of power should be maintained, can be traced at several points. One point is the question of preventive war. Most expositions of international law contend that preventive war is illegal; in cases where no legal injury has been done by one state to another, the latter cannot legally make war. The imperatives of the balance of power, however . . . point to the possible need to make war against a state which has not done legal injury to any other, but whose relative power is growing in such a way as to threaten the balance.

Another point of clash between these two sets of imperatives is the question of sanctions against aggressive war. At the time of the Italian invasion of Ethiopia, it was widely held by international lawyers that Italy had gone to war in disregard of its obligations under the League Covenant, and that, the League having called for sanctions against Italy, Britain, France and other member states should apply them. From the point of view of the balance of power, however, the effect of sanctions against Italy was simply that Italy would be driven into the arms of Germany, and the efforts of Britain and France to maintain a balance in relation to Germany placed in jeopardy. The same clash of imperatives was repeated at the time of the Russian invasion of Finland in 1939, when Britain and France again had to choose between taking action against Russia as an "aggressor," and preserving the option of cooperation with Russia against Germany.

A final point of clash between the imperatives of international law and of the balance of power concerns the question of intervention. Most expositions of international law contend that states are bound to refrain from forcible or dictatorial intervention in one another's internal affairs (though on some views they may intervene on the invitation of a local government in order to resist intervention by another power). It is often argued, however, that considerations of the balance of power require intervention in the internal affairs of a state in order to establish a great power's influence in it, or resist the influence of another great power, because of wider considerations of the distribution of power in international society at large.

There have been various attempts to resolve this clash of imperatives between international law and the balance of power. One is to seek to absorb the principle of the balance into international law itself. Another is to adopt a restrictive view of the sphere of validity of international law, and assign the question of the balance of power, along with other imperatives deriving from devices for the maintenance of order, to a sphere of "power politics" that law does not attempt to regulate. Here I do not seek to consider whether or not, or how, this clash could be resolved, but only to, draw attention to it as a basic limitation of the contribution of international law to international order.

Fourth, it should be noted that international law is a vehicle or instrumentality of purposes other than international order, and which may indeed be opposed to it. Legal instrumentalities are sometimes used for example, to promote justice in world politics—international justice, human justice or cosmopolitan justice—and this is an objective which can be disruptive of international order. . . . Law is an instrumentality of political purposes of all kinds, and the promotion of order is only one of them.

# 11: Complex Interdependence

## Robert O. Keohane and Joseph S. Nye, Jr.

We live in an era of interdependence. This vague phrase expresses a poorly understood but widespread feeling that the very nature of world politics is changing. The power of nations—that age-old touchstone of analysts and statesmen—has become more elusive: "calculations of power are even more delicate and deceptive than in previous ages."[1] Henry Kissinger, though deeply rooted in the classical tradition, has stated that "the traditional agenda of international affairs—the balance among major powers, the security of nations—no longer defines our perils or our possibilities. . . . Now we are entering a new era. Old international patterns are crumbling; old slogans are uninstructive; old solutions are unavailing. The world has become interdependent in economics, in communications, in human aspirations."[2]

How profound are the changes? A modernist school sees telecommunications and jet travel as creating a "global village" and believes that burgeoning social and economic transactions are creating a "world without borders."[3] To greater or lesser extent, a number of scholars see our era as one in which the territorial state, which has been dominant in world politics for the four

centuries since feudal times ended, is being eclipsed by nonterritorial actors such as multinational corporations, transnational social movements, and international organizations. As one economist put it, "the state is about through as an economic unit."[4]

Traditionalists call these assertions unfounded "globaloney." They point to the continuity in world politics. Military interdependence has always existed, and military power is still important in world politics—witness nuclear deterrence; the Vietnam, Middle East, and India-Pakistan wars; and . . . American influence in the Caribbean. Moreover . . . authoritarian states can, to a considerable extent, control telecommunications and social transactions that they consider disruptive. Even poor and weak countries have been able to nationalize multinational corporations, and the prevalence of nationalism casts doubt on the proposition that the nation-state is fading away.

Neither the modernists nor the traditionalists have an adequate framework for understanding the politics of global interdependence.[5] Modernists point correctly to the fundamental changes now taking place, but they often assume

---

1 Stanley Hoffmann, "Notes on the Elusiveness of Modern Power," *International Journal* 30: (Spring 1975) 184.
2 "A New National Partnership," speech by Secretary of State Henry A. Kissinger at Los Angeles, January 24, 1975. News release, Department of State, Bureau of Public Affairs, Office of Media Services, p. 1.
3 See, for example, Lester R. Brown, *World Without Borders: The Interdependence of Nations* (New York: Foreign Policy Association, Headline Series, 1972).
4 Charles Kindleberger, *American Business Abroad* (New Haven: Yale University Press, 1969), p. 207.
5 The terms are derived from Stanley Hoffmann, "Choices," *Foreign Policy* 12 (Fall 1973): 6.

without sufficient analysis that advances in technology and increases in social and economic transactions will lead to a new world in which states, and their control of force, will no longer be important.[6] Traditionalists are adept at showing flaws in the modernist vision by pointing out how military interdependence continues, but find it very difficult accurately to interpret today's multidimensional economic, social, and ecological interdependence. . . .

Our task . . . is not to argue either the modernist or traditionalist position. Because our era is marked by both continuity and change, this would be fruitless. Rather, our task is to provide a means of distilling and blending the wisdom in both positions by developing a coherent theoretical framework for the political analysis of interdependence. . . .

We are not suggesting that international conflict disappears when interdependence prevails. On the contrary, conflict will take new forms, and may even increase. But the traditional approaches to understanding conflict in world politics will not explain interdependence conflict particularly well. Applying the wrong image and the wrong rhetoric to problems will lead to erroneous analysis and bad policy.

## Interdependence as an Analytic Concept

In common parlance, *dependence* means a state of being determined or significantly affected by external forces. *Interdependence,* most simply defined, means *mutual* dependence. Interdependence in world politics refers to situations characterized by reciprocal effects among countries or among actors in different countries.

These effects often result from international transactions—flows of money, goods, people, and messages across international boundaries. Such transactions have increased dramatically since World War II: "Recent decades reveal a general tendency for many forms of human interconnectedness across national boundaries to be doubling every ten years."[7] Yet this interconnectedness is not the same as interdependence. The effects of transactions on interdependence will depend on the constraints, or costs, associated with them. A country that imports all of its oil is likely to be more dependent on a continual flow of petroleum than a country importing furs, jewelry, and perfume (even of equivalent monetary value) will be on uninterrupted access to these luxury goods. Where there are reciprocal (although not necessarily symmetrical) costly effects of transactions, there is interdependence. Where interactions do not have significant costly effects, there is simply interconnectedness. The distinction is vital if we are to understand the politics of interdependence.

Costly effects may be imposed directly and intentionally by another actor—as in Soviet-American strategic interdependence, which derives from the mutual threat of nuclear destruction. But some costly effects do not come directly or intentionally from other actors. For example, collective action may be necessary to prevent disaster for an alliance (the members of which are interdependent), for an international economic system (which may face chaos because of the absence of coordination, rather than through the malevolence of any actor), or for an ecological system threatened by a gradual increase of industrial effluents.

We do not limit the term *interdependence* to situations of mutual benefit. Such a definition would assume that the concept is only useful analytically where the modernist view of the world prevails: where threats of military force are few and levels of conflict are low. It would exclude from interdependence cases of mutual dependence, such as the strategic interdependence

---

6  For instance, see Robert Angell, *Peace on the March: Transnational Participation* (New York: Van Nostrand, 1969).

7  Alex Inkeles, "The Emerging Social Structure of the World," *World Politics* 27 (July 1975): 479.

between the United States and the Soviet Union. Furthermore, it would make it very ambiguous whether relations between industrialized countries and less developed countries should be considered interdependent or not. Their inclusion would depend on an inherently subjective judgment about whether the relationships were "mutually beneficial." . . .

We must also be careful not to define interdependence entirely in terms of situations of *evenly balanced* mutual dependence. It is *asymmetries* in dependence that are most likely to provide sources of influence for actors in their dealings with one another. Less dependent actors can often use the interdependent relationship as a source of power in bargaining over an issue and perhaps to affect other issues. At the other extreme from pure symmetry is pure dependence (sometimes disguised by calling the situation interdependence); but it too is rare. Most cases lie between these two extremes. And that is where the heart of the political bargaining process of interdependence lies.

### Power and Interdependence

Power has always been an elusive concept for statesmen and analysts of international politics; now it is even more slippery. The traditional view was that military power dominated other forms, and that states with the most military power controlled world affairs. But the resources that produce power capabilities have become more complex. In the eyes of one astute observer, "the postwar era has witnessed radical transformations in the elements, the uses, and the achievements of power."[8] . . .

Power can be thought of as the ability of an actor to get others to do something they otherwise would not do (and at an acceptable cost to the actor). Power can also be conceived in terms of control over outcomes. In either case, measurement is not simple.[9] We can look at the initial power resources that give an actor a potential ability; or we can look at that actor's actual influence over patterns of outcomes. When we say that asymmetrical interdependence can be a source of power we are thinking of power as control over resources, or the *potential* to affect outcomes. A less dependent actor in a relationship often has a significant political resource, because changes in the relationship (which the actor may be able to initiate or threaten) will be less costly to that actor than to its partners. This advantage does not guarantee, however, that the political resources provided by favorable asymmetries in interdependence will lead to similar patterns of control over outcomes. There is rarely a one-to-one relationship between power measured by any type of resources and power measured by effects on outcomes. Political bargaining is the usual means of translating potential into effects, and a lot is often lost in the translation. . . .

### Realism and Complex Interdependence

For political realists, international politics, like all other politics, is a struggle for power but, unlike domestic politics, a struggle dominated by organized violence. In the words of the most influential postwar textbook, "All history shows that nations active in international politics are continuously preparing for, actively involved in, or recovering from organized violence in the form of war."[10] Three assumptions are integral to the realist vision. First, states as coherent units are the dominant actors in world politics. This is a double assumption: states are predominant; and they act as coherent units. Second, realists

---

8   Hoffman, "Notes on the Elusiveness of Modern Power," p. 183.

9   See Jeffrey Hart, "Dominance in International Politics," *International Organization* 30 (Spring 1976).

10  Hans J. Morgenthau, *Politics Among Nations: The Struggle for Power and Peace,* 4th ed. (New York: Knopf, 1967), p. 36.

assume that force is a usable and effective instrument of policy. Other instruments may also be employed, but using or threatening force is the most effective means of wielding power. Third, partly because of their second assumption, realists assume a hierarchy of issues in world politics, headed by questions of military security: the "high politics" of military security dominates the "low politics" of economic and social affairs.

These realist assumptions define an ideal type of world politics. They allow us to imagine a world in which politics is continually characterized by active or potential conflict among states, with the use of force possible at any time. Each state attempts to defend its territory and interests from real or perceived threats. Political integration among states is slight and lasts only as long as it serves the national interests of the most powerful states. Transnational actors either do not exist or are politically unimportant. Only the adept exercise of force or the threat of force permits states to survive, and only while statesmen succeed in adjusting their interests, as in a well-functioning balance of power, is the system stable.

Each of the realist assumptions can be challenged. If we challenge them all simultaneously, we can imagine a world in which actors other than states participate directly in world politics, in which a clear hierarchy of issues does not exist, and in which force is an ineffective instrument of policy. Under these conditions—which we call the characteristics of complex interdependence—one would expect world politics to be very different than under realist conditions. . . .

We do not argue . . . that complex interdependence faithfully reflects world political reality. Quite the contrary: both it and the realist portrait are ideal types. Most situations will fall somewhere between these two extremes. Sometimes, realist assumptions will be accurate, or largely accurate, but frequently complex interdependence will provide a better portrayal of reality. Before one decides what explanatory model to apply to a situation or problem, one will need to understand the degree to which realist or complex interdependence assumptions correspond to the situation.

## The Characteristics of Complex Interdependence

Complex interdependence has three main characteristics:

1. *Multiple channels* connect societies, including: informal ties between governmental elites as well as formal foreign office arrangements; informal ties among nongovernmental elites (face-to-face and through telecommunications); and transnational organizations (such as multinational banks or corporations). These channels can be summarized as interstate, transgovernmental, and transnational relations. *Interstate* relations are the normal channels assumed by realists. *Transgovernmental* applies when we relax the realist assumption that states act coherently as units; *transnational* applies when we relax the assumption that states are the only units.

2. The agenda of interstate relationships consists of multiple issues that are not arranged in a clear or consistent hierarchy. This *absence of hierarchy among issues* means, among other things, that military security does not consistently dominate the agenda. Many issues arise from what used to be considered domestic policy, and the distinction between domestic and foreign issues becomes blurred. These issues are considered in several government departments (not just foreign offices), and at several levels. Inadequate policy coordination on these issues involves significant costs. Different issues generate different coalitions, both within governments and across them, and involve different degrees of conflict. Politics does not stop at the water's edge.

3. Military force is not used by governments toward other governments within the region, or on the issues, when complex interdependence prevails. It may, however, be important in these governments' relations with governments outside that region, or on other issues. Military force could, for instance, be irrelevant to resolving disagreements on economic issues among members of an alliance, yet at the same time be very important for that alliance's political and military relations with a rival bloc. For the former relationships this condition of complex interdependence would be met; for the latter, it would not.

Traditional theories of international politics implicitly or explicitly deny the accuracy of these three assumptions. Traditionalists are therefore tempted also to deny the relevance of criticisms based on the complex interdependence ideal type. We believe, however, that our three conditions are fairly well approximated on some global issues of economic and ecological interdependence and that they come close to characterizing the entire relationship between some countries. . . .

### *Multiple Channels*

A visit to any major airport is a dramatic way to confirm the existence of multiple channels of contact among advanced industrial countries; there is a voluminous literature to prove it.[11] Bureaucrats from different countries deal directly with one another at meetings and on the telephone as well as in writing. Similarly, nongovernmental elites frequently get together in the normal course of business, in organizations such as the Trilateral Commission, and in conferences sponsored by private foundations.

In addition, multinational firms and banks affect both domestic and interstate relations. The limits

on private firms, or the closeness of ties between government and business, vary considerably from one society to another; but the participation of large and dynamic organizations, not controlled entirely by governments, has become a normal part of foreign as well as domestic relations.

These actors are important not only because of their activities in pursuit of their own interests, but also because they act as transmission belts, making government policies in various countries more sensitive to one another. As the scope of governments' domestic activities has broadened, and as corporations, banks, and (to a lesser extent) trade unions have made decisions that transcend national boundaries, the domestic policies of different countries impinge on one another more and more. Transnational communications reinforce these effects. Thus, foreign economic policies touch more domestic economic activity than in the past, blurring the lines between domestic and foreign policy and increasing the number of issues relevant to foreign policy. Parallel developments in issues of environmental regulation and control over technology reinforce this trend.

### *Absence of Hierarchy among Issues*

Foreign affairs agendas—that is, sets of issues relevant to foreign policy with which governments are concerned—have become larger and more diverse. No longer can all issues be subordinated to military security. As Secretary of State Kissinger described the situation in 1975:

> Progress in dealing with the traditional agenda is no longer enough. A new and unprecedented kind of issue has emerged. The problems of energy, resources, environment, population, the uses of space and the seas now rank with questions of military security, ideology and territorial rivalry which have traditionally made up the diplomatic agenda.[12]

---

11  See . . . Edward L. Morse, "Transnational Economic Processes," in Robert O. Keohane and Joseph S. Nye, Jr. (eds.), *Transnational Relations and World Politics* (Cambridge, Mass.: Harvard University Press, 1972).

12  Henry A. Kissinger, "A New National Partnership," *Department of State Bulletin,* February 17, 1975, p. 199.

Kissinger's list, which could be expanded, illustrates how governments' policies, even those previously considered merely domestic, impinge on one another. The extensive consultative arrangements developed by the OECD, as well as the GATT, IMF, and the European Community indicate how characteristic the overlap of domestic and foreign policy is among developed pluralist countries. The organization within nine major departments of the United States government (Agriculture, Commerce, Defense, Health, Education and Welfare, Interior, Justice, Labor, State, and Treasury) and many other agencies reflects their extensive international commitments. The multiple, overlapping issues that result make a nightmare of governmental organization.[13]

When there are multiple issues on the agenda, many of which threaten the interests of domestic groups but do not clearly threaten the nation as a whole, the problems of formulating a coherent and consistent foreign policy increase. . . . Opportunities for delay, for special protection, for inconsistency and incoherence abound when international politics requires aligning the domestic policies of pluralist democratic countries.

### *Minor Role of Military Force*

Political scientists have traditionally emphasized the role of military force in international politics. . . . Survival is the primary goal of all states, and in the worst situations, force is ultimately necessary to guarantee survival. Thus military force is always a central component of national power.

Yet particularly among industrialized, pluralist countries, the perceived margin of safety has widened: fears of attack in general have declined, and fears of attacks *by one another* are virtually nonexistent. France has abandoned the *tous azimuts* (defense in all directions) strategy that President de Gaulle advocated (it was not taken entirely seriously even at the time). Canada's last war plans for fighting the United States were abandoned half a century ago. Britain and Germany no longer feel threatened by each other. Intense relationships of mutual influence exist between these countries, but in most of them force is irrelevant or unimportant as an instrument of policy.

Moreover, force is often not an appropriate way of achieving other goals (such as economic and ecological welfare) that are becoming more important. It is not impossible to imagine dramatic conflict or revolutionary change in which the use or threat of military force over an economic issue or among advanced industrial countries might become plausible. Then realist assumptions would again be a reliable guide to events. But in most situations, the effects of military force are both costly and uncertain.[14]

Even when the direct use of force is barred among a group of countries, however, military power can still be used politically. Each superpower continues to use the threat of force to deter attacks by other superpowers on itself or its allies; its deterrence ability thus serves an indirect, protective role, which it can use in bargaining on other issues with its allies. . . . The United States has, accordingly, taken advantage of the Europeans' (particularly the Germans') desire for its protection and linked the issue of troop levels in Europe to trade and monetary negotiations. Thus, although the first-order effect of deterrent force is essentially negative—to

---

13  See the report of the Commission on the Organization of the Government for the Conduct of Foreign Policy (Murphy Commission) (Washington, D.C.: U.S. Government Printing Office, 1975), and the studies prepared for that report. See also Raymond Hopkins, "The International Role of 'Domestic' Bureaucracy," *International Organization* 30, no. 3 (Summer 1976).

14  For a valuable discussion, see Klaus Knorr, *The Power of Nations: The Political Economy of International Relations* (New York: Basic Books, 1975).

deny effective offensive power to a superpower opponent—a state can use that force positively—to gain political influence.

Thus, even for countries whose relations approximate complex interdependence, two serious qualifications remain: (1) drastic social and political change could cause force again to become an important direct instrument of policy; and (2) even when elites' interests are complementary, a country that uses military force to protect another may have significant political influence over the other country.

In North-South relations, or relations among Third World countries . . . force is often important. . . . The threat of open or covert American military intervention has helped to limit revolutionary changes in the Caribbean, especially in Guatemala in 1954 and in the Dominican Republic in 1965. Secretary of State Kissinger, in January 1975, issued a veiled warning to members of the Organization of Petroleum Exporting Countries (OPEC) that the United States might use force against them "where there is some actual strangulation of the industrialized world."[15]

Even in these rather conflictual situations, however, the recourse to force seems less likely now than at most times during the century before 1945. The destructiveness of nuclear weapons makes attack against a nuclear power dangerous. Nuclear weapons are mostly used as a deterrent. Threats of nuclear action against much weaker countries may occasionally be efficacious, but they are equally or more likely to solidify relations between one's adversaries. The limited usefulness of conventional force to control socially mobilized populations has been shown by the United States failure in Vietnam as well as by the rapid decline of colonialism in Africa. Furthermore, employing force on one issue against an independent state with which one has a variety of relationships is likely to rupture mutually profitable relations on other issues. In other words, the use of force often has costly effects on non-security goals. And finally, in Western democracies, popular opposition to prolonged military conflicts is very high.[16]

It is clear that these constraints bear unequally on various countries, or on the same countries in different situations. Risks of nuclear escalation affect everyone, but domestic opinion is far less constraining . . . for authoritarian regional powers than for the United States, Europe, or Japan. Even authoritarian countries may be reluctant to use force to obtain economic objectives when such use might be ineffective and disrupt other relationships. Both the difficulty of controlling socially mobilized populations with foreign troops and the changing technology of weaponry may actually enhance the ability of certain countries, or nonstate groups, to use terrorism as a political weapon without effective fear of reprisal.

The fact that the changing role of force has uneven effects does not make the change less important, but it does make matters more complex. This complexity is compounded by differences in the usability of force among issue areas. When an issue arouses little interest or passion, force may be unthinkable. In such instances, complex interdependence may be a valuable concept for analyzing the political process. But if that issue becomes a matter of life and death—as some people thought oil might become—the use or threat of force could become decisive again. Realist assumptions would then be more relevant.

It is thus important to determine the applicability of realism or of complex interdependence to each situation. Without this determination, further analysis is likely to be confused. Our

---

15  *Business Week,* January 13, 1975.
16  Stanley Hoffmann, "The Acceptability of Military Force," and Laurence Martin, "The Utility of Military Force," in *Force in Modern Societies: Its Place in International Politics* (Adelphi Paper, International Institute for Strategic Studies, 1973). See also Knorr, *The Power of Nations.*

purpose in developing an alternative to the realist description of world politics is to encourage a differentiated approach that distinguishes among dimensions and areas of world politics—not (as some modernist observers do) to replace one over-simplification with another.

## The Political Processes of Complex Interdependence

The three main characteristics of complex interdependence give rise to distinctive political processes, which translate power resources into power as control of outcomes. As we argued earlier, something is usually lost or added in the translation. Under conditions of complex interdependence the translation will be different than under realist conditions, and our predictions about outcomes will need to be adjusted accordingly.

In the realist world, military security will be the dominant goal of states. It will even affect issues that are not directly involved with military power or territorial defense. Nonmilitary problems will not only be subordinated to military ones; they will be studied for their politico-military implications. Balance of payments issues, for instance, will be considered at least as much in the light of their implications for world power generally as for their purely financial ramifications. McGeorge Bundy conformed to realist expectations when he argued in 1964 that devaluation of the dollar should be seriously considered if necessary to fight the war in Vietnam.[17] To some extent, so did former Treasury Secretary Henry Fowler when he contended in 1971 that the United States needed a trade surplus of $4 billion to $6 billion in order to lead in Western defense.[18]

In a world of complex interdependence, however, one expects some officials, particularly at lower levels, to emphasize the *variety* of state goals that must be pursued. In the absence of a clear hierarchy of issues, goals will vary by issue, and may not be closely related. Each bureaucracy will pursue its own concerns; and although several agencies may reach compromises on issues that affect them all, they will find that a consistent pattern of policy is difficult to maintain. Moreover, transnational actors will introduce different goals into various groups of issues.

### Linkage Strategies

Goals will therefore vary by issue area under complex interdependence, but so will the distribution of power and the typical political processes. Traditional analysis focuses on *the* international system, and leads us to anticipate similar political processes on a variety of issues. Militarily and economically strong states will dominate a variety of organizations and a variety of issues, by linking their own policies on some issues to other states' policies on other issues. By using their overall dominance to prevail on their weak issues, the strongest states will, in the traditional model, ensure a congruence between the overall structure of military and economic power and the pattern of outcomes on any one issue area. Thus world politics can be treated as a seamless web.

Under complex interdependence, such congruence is less likely to occur. As military force is devalued, militarily strong states will find it more difficult to use their overall dominance to control outcomes on issues in which they are weak. And since the distribution of power resources in trade, shipping, or oil, for example, may be quite different, patterns of outcomes and distinctive political processes are likely to vary from one set of issues to another. If force were readily applicable, and military security were the highest foreign policy goal, these variations in the issue structures of power would not matter

---

17 Henry Brandon, *The Retreat of American Power* (New York: Doubleday, 1974), p. 218.

18 *International Implications of the New Economic Policy,* U.S. Congress, House of Representatives, Committee on Foreign Affairs, Subcommittee on Foreign Economic Policy, Hearings, September 16, 1971.

very much. The linkages drawn from them to military issues would ensure consistent dominance by the overall strongest states. But when military force is largely immobilized, strong states will find that linkage is less effective. They may still attempt such links, but in the absence of a hierarchy of issues, their success will be problematic.

Dominant states may try to secure much the same result by using overall economic power to affect results on other issues. If only economic objectives are at stake, they may succeed: money, after all, is fungible. But economic objectives have political implications, and economic linkage by the strong is limited by domestic, transnational, and transgovernmental actors who resist having their interests traded off. Furthermore, the international actors may be different on different issues, and the international organizations in which negotiations take place are often quite separate. Thus it is difficult, for example, to imagine a militarily or economically strong state linking concessions on monetary policy to reciprocal concessions in oceans policy. On the other hand, poor weak states are not similarly inhibited from linking unrelated issues, partly because their domestic interests are less complex. Linkage of unrelated issues is often a means of extracting concessions or side payments from rich and powerful states. And unlike powerful states whose instrument for linkage (military force) is often too costly to use, the linkage instrument used by poor, weak states—international organization—is available and inexpensive.

Thus as the utility of force declines, and as issues become more equal in importance, the distribution of power within each issue will become more important. If linkages become less effective on the whole, outcomes of political bargaining will increasingly vary by issue area. . . .

### Agenda Setting

Our second assumption of complex interdependence, the lack of clear hierarchy among multiple issues, leads us to expect that the politics of agenda formation and control will become more important. Traditional analyses lead statesmen to focus on politico-military issues and to pay little attention to the broader politics of agenda formation. Statesmen assume that the agenda will be set by shifts in the balance of power, actual or anticipated, and by perceived threats to the security of states. Other issues will only be very important when they seem to affect security and military power. In these cases, agendas will be influenced strongly by considerations of the overall balance of power. . . .

Under complex interdependence we can expect the agenda to be affected by the international and domestic problems created by economic growth and increasing sensitivity interdependence. . . . Discontented domestic groups will politicize issues and force more issues once considered domestic onto the interstate agenda. Shifts in the distribution of power resources within sets of issues will also affect agendas. During the early 1970s the increased power of oil-producing governments over the transnational corporations and the consumer countries dramatically altered the policy agenda. . . . Even if capabilities among states do not change, agendas may be affected by shifts in the importance of transnational actors. The publicity surrounding multinational corporations in the early 1970s, coupled with their rapid growth over the past twenty years, put the regulation of such corporations higher on both the United Nations agenda and national agendas. . . .

The technical characteristics and institutional setting in which issues are raised will strongly affect politicization patterns. In the United States, congressional attention is an effective instrument of politicization. Generally, we expect transnational economic organizations and transgovernmental networks of bureaucrats to seek to avoid politicization. Domestically based groups (such as trade unions) and domestically oriented bureaucracies will tend to use politicization (particularly congressional attention) against their transnationally mobile competitors. At the international level, we expect states and actors to "shop among forums" and struggle to get issues raised in international organizations that will maximize their advantage by broadening or narrowing the agenda.

### Transnational and Transgovernmental Relations

Our third condition of complex interdependence, multiple channels of contact among societies, further blurs the distinction between domestic and international politics. The availability of partners in political coalitions is not necessarily limited by national boundaries as traditional analysis assumes. The nearer a situation is to complex interdependence, the more we expect the outcomes of political bargaining to be affected by transnational relations. Multinational corporations may be significant both as independent actors and as instruments manipulated by governments. The attitudes and policy stands of domestic groups are likely to be affected by communications, organized or not, between them and their counterparts abroad. . . .

The multiple channels of contact found in complex interdependence are not limited to nongovernmental actors. Contacts between governmental bureaucracies charged with similar tasks may not only alter their perspectives but lead to transgovernmental coalitions on particular policy questions. To improve their chances of success, government agencies attempt to bring actors from other governments into their own decision-making processes as allies. Agencies of powerful states such as the United States have used such coalitions to penetrate weaker governments in such countries as Turkey and Chile. They have also been used to help agencies of

other governments penetrate the United States bureaucracy.[19] . . .

The existence of transgovernmental policy networks leads to a different interpretation of one of the standard propositions about international politics—that states act in their own interest. Under complex interdependence, this conventional wisdom begs two important questions: which self and which interest? A government agency may pursue its own interests under the guise of the national interest; and recurrent interactions can change official perceptions of their interests. As a careful study of the politics of United States trade policy has documented, concentrating only on pressures of various interests for decisions leads to an overly mechanistic view of a continuous process and neglects the important role of communications in slowly changing perceptions of self-interest.[20]

The ambiguity of the national interest raises serious problems for the top political leaders of governments. As bureaucracies contact each other directly across national borders (without going through foreign offices), centralized control becomes more difficult. There is less assurance that the state will be united when dealing with foreign governments or that its components will interpret national interests similarly when negotiating with foreigners. The state may prove to be multifaceted, even schizophrenic. National interests will be defined differently on different issues, at different times, and by different governmental units. . . .

### Role of International Organizations

Finally, the existence of multiple channels leads one to predict a different and significant role for international organizations in world politics. Realists in the tradition of Hans J. Morgenthau

---

19 For a more detailed discussion, see Robert O. Keohane and Joseph S. Nye, Jr., "Transgovernmental Relations and International Organizations," *World Politics* 27, no. 1 (October 1974): 39-62.

20 Raymond Bauer, Ithiel de Sola Pool, and Lewis Dexter, *American Business and Foreign Policy* (New York: Atherton, 1963), chap. 35, esp. pp. 472-75.

have portrayed a world in which states, acting from self-interest, struggle for "power and peace." Security issues are dominant; war threatens. In such a world, one may assume that international institutions will have a minor role, limited by the rare congruence of such interests. International organizations are then clearly peripheral to world politics. But in a world of multiple issues imperfectly linked, in which coalitions are formed transnationally and transgovernmentally, the potential role of international institutions in political bargaining is greatly increased. In particular, they help set the international agenda, and act as catalysts for coalition-formation and as arenas for political initiatives and linkage by weak states.

Governments must organize themselves to cope with the flow of business generated by international organizations. By defining the salient issues, and deciding which issues can be grouped together, organizations may help to determine governmental priorities and the nature of interdepartmental committees and other arrangements within governments. The 1972 Stockholm Environment Conference strengthened the position of environmental agencies in various governments. The 1974 World Food Conference focused the attention of important parts of the United States government on prevention of food shortages. The September 1975 United Nations special session on proposals for a New International Economic Order generated an intragovernmental debate about policies toward the Third World in general. The International Monetary Fund and the General Agreement on Tariffs and Trade have focused governmental activity on money and trade instead of on private direct investment, which has no comparable international organization.

By bringing officials together, international organizations help to activate potential coalitions in world politics. It is quite obvious that international organizations have been very important in bringing together representatives of less developed countries, most of which do not maintain embassies in one another's capitals. Third World strategies of solidarity among poor countries have been developed in and for a series of international conferences, mostly under the auspices of the United Nations.[21] International organizations also allow agencies of governments, which might not otherwise come into contact, to turn potential or tacit coalitions into explicit transgovernmental coalitions characterized by direct communications. In some cases, international secretariats deliberately promote this process by forming coalitions with groups of governments, or with units of governments, as well as with nongovernmental organizations having similar interests.[22]

International organizations are frequently congenial institutions for weak states. The onestate-one-vote norm of the United Nations system favors coalitions of the small and powerless. Secretariats are often responsive to Third World demands. Furthermore, the substantive norms of most international organizations, as they have developed over the years, stress social and economic equity as well as the equality of states. Past resolutions expressing Third World positions, sometimes agreed to with reservations by industrialized countries, are used to legitimize other demands. These agreements are rarely binding, but up to a point the norms of the institution make opposition look more harshly self-interested and less defensible.

International organizations also allow small and weak states to pursue linkage strategies. In the discussions on a New International Economic Order, Third World states insisted on linking oil price and availability to other questions on which they had traditionally been unable to achieve their objectives. . . .

---

21  Branislav Gosovic and John Gerard Ruggie, "On the Creation of a New International Economic Order: Issue Linkage and the Seventh Special Session of the U.N. General Assembly," *International Organization* 30, no. 2 (Spring 1976): 309-46.

22  Robert W. Cox, "The Executive Head," *International Organization* 23, no. 2 (Spring 1969): 205-30.

Complex interdependence therefore yields different political patterns than does the realist conception of the world. (Table 11-1 summarizes these differences.) Thus, one would expect traditional theories to fail to explain international regime change in situations of complex interdependence. But, for a situation that approximates realist conditions, traditional theories should be appropriate. . . .

## Table 11-1

### Political Processes under Conditions of Realism and Complex Interdependence

| | Realism | Complex Interdependence |
|---|---|---|
| Goals of actors | Military security will be the dominant goal. | Goals of states will vary by issue area. Transgovernmental politics will make goals difficult to define. Transnational actors will pursue their own goals. |
| Instruments of state policy | Military force will be most effective, although economic and other instruments will also be used. | Power resources specific to issue areas will be most relevant. Manipulation of interdependence, international organizations, and transnational actors will be major instruments. |
| Agenda formation | Potential shifts in the balance of power and security threats will set the agenda in high politics and will strongly influence other agendas. | Agenda will be affected by changes in the distribution of power resources within issue areas; the status of international regimes; changes in the importance of transnational actors; linkages from other issues and politicization as a result of rising sensitivity interdependence. |
| Linkages of issues | Linkages will reduce differences in outcomes among issue areas and reinforce international hierarchy. | Linkages by strong states will be more difficult to make since force will be ineffective. Linkages by weak states through international organizations will erode rather than reinforce hierarchy. |
| Roles of international organizations | Roles are minor, limited by state power and the importance of military force. | Organizations will set agendas, induce coalition-formation |

# 12: A Realist Theory of International Politics

*Greg Russell*

## A Realist Political Philosophy

. . . [Hans] Morgenthau's intellectual perspective attempted to provide a foundation for systematic political inquiry as well as a normative guide for the practicing statesman. A realist political philosophy, he believed, is distinguished by several important principles. First, the realist believes that politics forms an "autonomous" field of behavior and inquiry. Against those who would apply natural-science methods to the study of political behavior, the realist holds that the historic arena—the human universe—is essentially different from the natural universe. The political theorist is one who thinks in terms of interest defined as power, as the economist thinks in terms of interest defined as wealth; the lawyer, of the conformity of action with legal rules; the moralist, of the conformity of action with ethical principles. The concept of power allows the observer "to distinguish politics from other social spheres, to orient himself in the maze of empirical phenomena which make up the field, and to establish a measure of rational order within it."[1]

Second, a realist theory of politics evolves from certain philosophical conceptions about the human condition and political society. Perhaps with some oversimplification, Morgenthau reduces the history of Western political thought to the story of a contest between two schools that differ in their conception of man, society, and politics. One— the horizon of political idealism—assumes the essential goodness and infinite malleability of human nature; it blames the failure of the social order to measure up to the rational standards of a progressive society on lack of knowledge and antiquated institutions. The idealist in politics is inclined to place his optimistic faith in education, reform, and a minimum reliance on the instrumentalities of power and coercion. By contrast, the tradition of political realism acknowledges that forces inherent in human nature prevent man from achieving a thoroughly rational or moral political order.[2] The realist views man as a self-interested creature whose ego is inevitably contaminated by the propensity for sin and evil. In seeking fundamental political changes, the statesmen must work with those forces, not against them. Integral to the realist world view is the primary assumption that power conflicts are an ineradicable feature of all political relationships— more so perhaps among nation-states than any other level of political intercourse.

Morgenthau's pessimism was a function of his beliefs concerning the omnipresence of the lust for power of the universal desire of the self to dominate others. To the extent that politics can be defined as the exercise of power over man, politics is rooted in evil in that it degrades and relegates man to a means for other men. Yet Morgenthau did distinguish between human selfishness and the ubiquitous impulse to power. The typical goals of human selfishness (*e.g.*, food, shelter, and existence) have an objective relation

---

1 Morgenthau, *Dilemmas of Politics*, (Chicago, 1958) 39.
2 Morgenthau, *Politics Among Nations* 5th ed. (New York, 1973), 3-4.

to the survival needs of the individual; their acquisition represents the prerequisites for survival under the particular natural and social conditions in which man lives. On the other hand, the desire for power concerns itself mainly with man's position among his fellows once survival has been achieved. Whereas the selfishness of man has objective limits, his will to power has none. "For here," as Morgenthau insisted, "the *animus dominandi* is not merely blended with dominant aims of a different kind but is the . . . essence of the intention . . . the constitutive principle of politics as a distinct sphere of activity."[3]

Third, the realist believes that politics is governed by objective laws that have their roots in human nature. For realists the possibility exists, therefore, of developing a rational theory of politics that reflects, however imperfectly, these objective laws. Moreover, any theory of politics must be submitted to the dual tests of reason and experience. For Morgenthau, the concept of power "provides a kind of rational outline of politics, a map of the political scene." In commenting on the rational requirements of any political theory, he observed: "Such a map does not provide a complete description of the political landscape as it is in any particular period of history. It . . . provides the timeless features of its geography distinct from their ever-changing historic setting. . . . A theory of politics, by the . . . fact of painting a rational picture of the political scene, points to the contrast between what the political scene actually is and what it tends to be, but can never completely become."[4]

The struggle for power by both men and nations in a wide variety of historic settings supplies the nexus between reason trying to understand politics and the facts to be understood. In expounding his theory of international politics, Morgenthau exhorted the student to assume the position of the statesman who is called upon to meet a certain problem of foreign policy under specific circumstances. In so doing, "we ask ourselves what the rational alternatives are from which a statesman may choose who must meet this problem under these circumstances . . . and which of these rational alternatives this particular statesman . . . is likely to choose."[5] It is the testing of this rational hypothesis against the actual facts and their consequences that imparts meaning to the patterns of international political behavior. The validity of a realist theory, Morgenthau believed, does not hinge on its strict conformity to preestablished methodological criteria; rather, it is subject only to the "pragmatic" requirement that it broaden our knowledge and deepen our understanding of what is worth knowing.

Fourth, Morgenthau's theory of international politics also contains a normative element. The political realist values the rational elements of political action for practical reasons: Political realism assumes that a rational foreign policy is, of necessity, *good* foreign policy. It minimizes risks and maximizes benefits and, hence, complies with the moral precept of prudence and the political requirement of success.[6] In short, a realist theory of international politics offers not only a guide to understanding but an ideal for action.

Fifth, realism treats the concept of interest defined as power as an objective category that is universally valid, but it does not endow the concept with a meaning that is fixed once and for all. Morgenthau observed that the significance of interest in state relations is surpassed by the variety of configurations through which man transforms the abstract concept of the national interest into foreign policy. Taken in isolation,

---

3  Morgenthau, *Dilemmas of Politics*, 247; *Scientific Man vs. Power Politics* (Chicago, 1960), 192-93.
4  Morgenthau, *Dilemmas of Politics*, 39; *The Decline of Democratic Politics* (Chicago, 1962), 48; "International Relations: Common Sense and Theories," *Journal of International Affairs*, XXI (1967), 207-14.
5  Morgenthau, *Politics Among Nations*, 5.
6  *Ibid.*, 8.

the determination of a nation's interest in a concrete situation is relatively simple: it encompasses the integrity of a nation's territory and political institutions, and of its culture. However, an objective determination of a foreign policy designed to ensure national survival in a particular period depends on the specific mix of political and cultural factors impacting on the decision-making process. Morgenthau repeatedly warned: "While the realist . . . believes that interest is the perennial standard by which political action must be directed, the contemporary connection between interest and the nation state is a product of history, and is . . . bound to disappear. Nothing in the realist position militates against the assumption that the present division of the . . . world into nation states will be replaced by larger units . . . more in keeping with the . . . potentialities and the moral prerequisites of the contemporary world."[7]

Sixth, political realism holds that multiple factors affect moral reasoning and that "universal principles cannot be applied to the actions of states in their abstract . . . formulation, but . . . must be filtered through the concrete circumstances of time and place." Therefore, in a hostile world arena, moral principles can never be fully realized, but can only be approximated through the temporary balancing of interests and the precarious settlement of conflicts.[8] As will be discussed at some length in the pages that follow, Morgenthau avoided a conception of ethical dualism segregating the morality of man from that of the state. Yet, and in giving expression to perhaps the high paradox in the history of political ethics, he acknowledged that the standard (or criterion) of judgment for moral man is different from the requirements of political morality governing state behavior. Whereas the individual may justly claim that right to self-sacrifice in defense of moral low, the state has no right to let its moral disapprobation get in the way of successful political action. The operative moral strategy for politics, then, is to choose the lesser evil and minimize the intrinsic immorality of the political act.

Finally, political realism does not identity "the moral aspirations of a particular nation with the moral laws that govern the universe." Morgenthau held that crusading and pretentious idealism contains two principal defects. On the one hand, the idealist falls victim to world-embracing ideals which, because of their vagueness and generality, can provide no national guidance for resolving concrete political problems. On the other, the idealist dresses parochial interest in the garb of universal moral principles and then presumes that the rest of the world, in refusing to grant his policy cosmic righteousness, is *ipso facto* less moral (or national) than he.[9] Alternatively, Morgenthau stipulated that the national interest itself commands a certain moral dignity, because it functions as the protector of minimal world values in a world lacking order and moral consensus beyond the bounds of the national state. . . .

In a more pessimistic assessment, Morgenthau once wrote: "There is a profound and neglected truth hidden in Hobbes' extreme dictum that the state creates morality as well as law and that there is neither morality nor law outside the state." Universal moral principles, such as justice and equality, apply to concrete situations only in the measure in which they are given content by a particular society. Specifically, Morgenthau doubted the existence of acceptable standards of justice and human rights in the

---

7   Kenneth W. Thompson, "Moral Reasoning in American Thought on War and Peace," *Review of Politics*, XLIX (July, 1977), 392. See also Morgenthau, *Dilemmas of Politics*, 68-69; *Politics Among Nations*, 10.

8   See also Hans J. Morgenthau, "National Interest and Moral Principles in Foreign Policy," *American Scholar*, XVIII (Spring, 1949), 210-12.

9   Morgenthau, *Politics Among Nations*, 10-11; "National Interest and Moral Principles in Foreign Policy," 207, 211; *In Defense of the National Interest* (New York, 1951), 35.

absence of a politically and morally integrated international society. Reflecting on what has euphemistically been termed the "society of nations," Morgenthau remarked: "Not only are there no supranational moral principles concrete enough to give guidance to the political actions of . . . nations; there is also no agency on the international scene to promote the interests of the individual nations themselves. . . . If a nation is . . . to escape the Scylla of national suicide, the threat of which is ever present in the emphasis on moral principles to the neglect of the national interest, it is likely to fall into the Charybdis of the crusading spirit which is the great destroyer of morality among nations."[10] . . .

## A Realist Theory of International Politics

For Morgenthau, the calculus of the national interest functions as the central concept for a theory of international politics. "All successful statesmen of modern times from Richelieu to Churchill," he wrote, "have made the national interest the ultimate standard of their policies, and none of the great moralists in international affairs has attained his goals." In international politics, the national interest is shaped by the "struggle for power . . . for national advantage."[11] Idealistic detractors of the national interest jeopardize the welfare and security of the nation by failing to act on the fundamental lesson of all diplomatic-history: a foreign policy based upon moral abstractions without consideration of the national interest is bound to fail, for it accepts a standard of conduct alien to the nature of the action. Self-preservation for individuals and societies is both a biological and psychological necessity; in the international realm, the attainment of a modicum of order and the realization of a minimum of moral principles are contingent upon the existence of national communities capable of preserving order and realizing moral values within the limits of their power. . . .

Morgenthau refused to consider the national interest as a static, self-evident principle of state-craft whose formulation is immune from the complex interaction of domestic and external influences on the decision-making process in foreign policy. Like the "great generalities" in the United States Constitution (*e.g.*, due process and general welfare), the concept of the national interest "contains residual meaning . . . inherent in the concept itself, but beyond these minimum requirements its content can run the whole gamut of meanings that are logically compatible with it."[12] Therefore, the meaning of the national interest is affected by the political traditions and the overall cultural context within which a nation formulates its foreign policy.

Morgenthau clearly emphasized that the concept of national interest contains two elements: one that is logically necessary and relatively permanent, and one that is variable according to changing circumstances.[13] The permanent "hard core" of the national interest stems from three criteria: (1) the nature of the interests to be defended; (2) the international milieu within which the interests operate; and (3) the rational necessities limiting the choice of means and ends by all foreign-policy actors. The survival of the political identity of the nation is the irreducible minimum, the necessary element of its interests vis-à-vis other nations. In a global setting where a number of sovereign nations compete for power, the foreign policies of all nations strive to protect their physical, political, and cultural

---

10  Morgenthau, *Dilemmas of Politics*, 80–81; "National Interest and Moral Principles in Foreign Policy," 211. For an early refutation of Morgenthau's position, see A. H. Feller, "In Defense of International Law and Morality," *Annals of the American Academy of Political and Social Science*, No. 282 (July, 1952), 80.
11  Morgenthau, *In Defense of the National Interest*, 34.
12  Morgenthau, *Dilemmas of Politics*, 65.
13  *Ibid.*, 66.

identity against the aggressive designs of rival forces. Moreover, Morgenthau stipulated that the nature of the threat to which the hard core is exposed remains relatively constant over long periods of time. For example, the chief threat to Great Britain has resided in hegemonic aspirations of one or more European nations. Russian security has been threatened by a great power having uncontested access to the plains of eastern Europe. The successful defense of American national interest has encompassed such goals as unrivaled American superiority in the Western Hemisphere and preserving a balance of power in both Europe and Asia.[14] Bipartisanship in foreign policy, especially in times of war, has been most easily achieved in the promotion of these minimum requirements of the national interest.

The rational character of the national interest derives from the reasoning by which the statesman translates abstract goals into concrete foreign-policy options. Governments throughout history attempted to uphold a nation's core interests by pursuing such policies as competitive armaments, balance-of-power tactics, defensive alliances, and subversion. In commenting on the relation between rational necessities of foreign policy (*i.e.*, selecting one of a limited number of alternatives through which to bring the nation's power to bear upon the power of other nations) and the universal character of the national interest, Morgenthau remarked: "It is this assumption of universality of the national interest in time and space which enables us to understand the foreign policies of Demosthenes and Caesar, Kautilya and Henry VIII, of the contemporary statesmen of Russia and China. Regardless of all the differences in personality . . . and environment, their thinking was predetermined . . . when they were faced with . . . protecting . . . the rational core of the national interest." In brief,

Morgenthau calculated that the rational character of the national interest could be detected and understood by thinking as the statesman must have thought and by theorists "putting their thoughts into the context of their personalities and social environment."[15]

With regard to the variable elements of the national interest, identifying the content and range of a nation's goals becomes more problematic. Morgenthau pointed to the difficulty of measuring accurately all the crosscurrents of personalities, public opinion, sectional interests, partisan politics, moral folkways, and transnational loyalties that impact on the formulation of a nation's interest at any one time. The national interest can function as a meaningful standard in foreign policy only if nations and statesmen impose some hierarchical and rational order upon the values that make up the national interest and among the limited resources committed to them. Against those critics who claim that he treated the national interest as a purely self-evident diplomatic norm, Morgenthau's position was clear: "While the interests which a nation may pursue in its relation with other nations are of infinite variety and magnitude, the resources which are available for the pursuit of such interests are necessarily limited in quantity and kind." In fact, Morgenthau's position parallels the essence of Walter Lippmann's classic observation that a workable foreign policy "consists in bringing into balance, with a comfortable surplus of power in reserve, the nation's commitments and the nation's power."[16]

The precondition for this rational assessment, according to Morgenthau, "is a clear understanding of the distinction between the necessary and variable elements of the national interest." Especially in democratic countries, where the variable elements of the national interest tend to

---

14 Hans J. Morgenthau, *The Impasse of American Foreign Policy* (Chicago, 1962), 56-58. Vol. II of Morgenthau, *Politics in the Twentieth Century*; Morgenthau, *Dilemmas of Politics*, 69.

15 Morgenthau, *The Decline of Democratic Politics*, 92.

16 Morgenthau, *Dilemmas of Politics*, 69; Walter Lippmann, *U.S. Foreign Policy: Shield of the Republic* (Boston, 1943), 8.

be the subject of contentious debate, those advocating an extensive conception of the national interest often present certain variable elements as though their attainment were necessary for a nation's survival and well-being. For example, a nation's security may be invoked to rationalize unqualified support for such variable foreign-policy aims as the rearmament of Germany, the rollback of communism, or the defense of Nationalist China. In making a distinction between the necessary and the desirable in foreign policy, a rational conception of the national interest requires that all external objectives (actual or potential) be subjected to scrutiny and assigned an approximate place in the scale of national values.[17] . . . .

Morgenthau focused upon opposing realist and idealist conceptions of international politics in American experience. For example, the idea that "a nation can escape . . . from power politics into a realm where action is guided by moral principles rather than by considerations of power is deeply rooted in the American mind."[18] Standing for moral purposes beyond the state (*e.g.*, freedom and order, liberty and justice, economic growth and social equality), Americans have typically regarded the struggle for power as a social aberration—the result of ignorance, faulty institutional arrangements, or the suppression of the public voice. From Washington's warning against "inveterate antipathies against particular nations and passionate attachments to others" to Wilson's Fourteen Points, the nation's identity was deeply involved with the assertion of universal human rights and political liberties. For well over a century of relative isolation from world politics, Americans resorted to that mixture of self-righteousness and genuine moral fervor in the expectation that their lofty moral example would shed enlightenment abroad. Commenting on the American inclination to invoke abstract moral principles to justify concrete national interests, Morgenthau wrote: "Wherever American foreign policy has operated, political thought has been divorced from political action. Even where our long range policies reflect . . . the true interests of the United States, we think about them in terms that have . . . a tenuous connection with the policies pursued. We have acted on the international scene, as all nations must, in power-political terms; but we have tended to conceive of our actions in non-political, moralistic terms."[19]

---

17  Morgenthau, *Dilemmas of Politics*, 74.

18  Morgenthau, *In Defense of the National Interest*, 23; "Outline and Notes for Contemporary Diplomatic Problems," 1950 (TS in Morgenthau Papers, Box 76), 1-10.

19  *Ibid.*, 7.

# 13: Realism

## *Thucydides*

The Athenians next made an expedition against the island of Melos. . . .

The Melians are colonists of the Lacedaemonians who would not submit to Athens like the other islanders. At first they were neutral and took no part. But when the Athenians tried to coerce them by ravaging their lands, they were driven into open hostilities. The generals, Cleomedes the son of Lycomedes and Tisias the son of Tisimachus, encamped with the Athenian forces on the island. But before they did the country any harm they sent envoys to negotiate with the Melians. Instead of bringing these envoys before the people, the Melians desired them to explain their errand to the magistrates and to the dominant class. They spoke as follows:

"Since we are not allowed to speak to the people, lest, forsooth, a multitude should be deceived by seductive and unanswerable arguments which they would hear set forth in a single uninterrupted oration (for we are perfectly aware that this is what you mean in bringing us before a select few), you who are sitting here may as well make assurance yet surer. Let us have no set speeches at all, but do you reply to each several statement of which you disapprove, and criticise it at once. Say first of all how you like this mode of proceeding."

The Melian representatives answered: "The quiet interchanging of explanations is a reasonable thing, and we do not object to that. But your warlike movements, which are present not only to our fears but to our eyes, seem to belie your words. We see that, although you may reason with us, you mean to be our judges; and that at the end of the discussion, if the justice of our cause prevail and we therefore refuse to yield, we may expect war; if we are convinced by you, slavery."

Ath. "Nay, but if you are only going to argue from fancies about the future, or if you meet us with any other purpose than that of looking your circumstances in the face and saving your city, we have done; but if this is your intention we will proceed."

Mel. "It is an excusable and natural thing that men in our position should neglect no argument and no view which may avail. But we admit that this conference has met to consider the question of our preservation; and therefore let the argument proceed in the manner which you propose."

Ath. "Well, then, we Athenians will use no fine words; we will not go out of our way to prove at length that we have a right to rule, because we overthrew the Persians; or that we attack you now because we are suffering any injury at your hands. We should not convince you if we did; nor must you expect to convince us by arguing that, although a colony of the Lacedaemonians, you have taken no part in their expeditions, or that you have never done us any wrong. But you and we should say what we really think, and aim only at what is possible, for we both alike know that into the discussion of

From *The History of Thucydides, Volume II*, translated from the Ancient Greek by Benjamin Jowett. © 1909 by The Tandy-Thomas Company, New York.

human affairs the question of justice only enters where there is equal power to enforce it, and that the powerful exact what they can, and the weak grant what they must."

Mel. "Well, then, since you set aside justice and invite us to speak of expediency, in our judgment it is certainly expedient that you should respect a principle which is for the common good; that to every man when in peril a reasonable claim should be accounted a claim of right, and that any plea which he is disposed to urge, even if failing of the point a little, should help his cause. Your interest in this principle is quite as great as ours, inasmuch as you, if you fall, will incur the heaviest vengeance, and will be the most terrible example to mankind."

Ath. "The fall of our empire, if it should fall, is not an event to which we look forward with dismay; for ruling states such as Lacedaemon are not cruel to their vanquished enemies. With the Lacedaemonians, however, we are not now contending; the real danger is from our many subject states, who may of their own motion rise up and overcome their masters. But this is a danger which you may leave to us. And we will now endeavour to show that we have come in the interest of our empire, and that in what we are about to say we are only seeking the preservation of your city. For we want to make you ours with the least trouble to ourselves, and it is for the interest of us both that you should not be destroyed."

Mel. "It may be your interest to be our masters, but how can it be ours to be your slaves?"

Ath. "To you the gain will be that by submission you will avert the worst; and we shall be all the richer for your preservation."

Mel. "But must we be your enemies? Will you not receive us as friends if we are neutral and remain at peace with you?"

Ath. "No, your enmity is not half so mischievous to us as your friendship; for the one is in the eyes of our subjects an argument of our power, the other of our weakness."

Mel. "But are your subjects really unable to distinguish between states in which you have no concern, and those which are chiefly your own colonies, and in some cases have revolted and been subdued by you?"

Ath. "Why, they do not doubt that both of them have a good deal to say for themselves on the score of justice, but they think that states like yours are left free because they are able to defend themselves, and that we do not attack them because we dare not. So that your subjection will give us an increase of security, as well as an extension of empire. For we are masters of the sea, and you who are islanders, and insignificant islanders too, must not be allowed to escape us."

Mel. "But do you not recognise another danger? For once more, since you drive us from the plea of justice and press upon us your doctrine of expediency, we must show you what is for our interest, and, if it be for yours also, may hope to convince you: Will you not be making enemies of all who are now neutrals? When they see how you are treating us they will expect you some day to turn against them; and if so, are you not strengthening the enemies whom you already have, and bringing upon you others who, if they could help, would never dream of being your enemies at all?"

Ath. "We do not consider our really dangerous enemies to be any of the peoples inhabiting the mainland who, secure in their freedom, may defer indefinitely any measures of precaution which they take against us, but islanders who, like you, happen to be under no control, and all who may be already irritated by the necessity of submission to our empire—these are our real enemies, for they are the most reckless and most likely to bring themselves as well as us into a danger which they cannot but foresee."

Mel. "Surely then, it you and your subjects will brave all this risk, you to preserve your empire and they to be quit of it, how base and cowardly would it be in us who retain our freedom, not to do and suffer anything rather than be your slaves."

Ath. "Not so, if you calmly reflect: for you are not fighting against equals to whom you cannot yield without disgrace, but you are taking counsel whether or no you shall resist an overwhelming force. The question is not only of honour but of prudence."

Mel. "But we know that the fortune of war is sometimes impartial; and not always on the side of numbers. If we yield now, all is over; but if we fight, there is yet a hope that we may stand upright."

Ath. "Hope is a good comforter in the hour of danger, and when men have something else to depend upon, although hurtful, she is not ruinous. But when her spendthrift nature has induced them to stake their all, they see her as she is in the moment of their fall, and not till then. While the knowledge of her might enable them to be aware of her, she never fails. You are weak and a single turn of the scale might be your ruin. Do not you be thus deluded; avoid the error of which so many are guilty, who, although they might still be saved if they would take the natural means, when visible grounds of confidence forsake them, have recourse to the invisible, to prophecies and oracles and the like, which ruin men by the hopes which they inspire in them."

Mel. "We know only too well now hard the struggle must be against your power, and against fortune, if she does not mean to be impartial. Nevertheless we do not despair of fortune; for we hope to stand as high as you in the favour of heaven, because we are righteous, and you against whom we contend are unrighteous; and we are satisfied that our deficiency in power will be compensated by the aid of our allies the Lacedaemonians; they cannot refuse to help us, if only because we are their kinsmen, and for the sake of their own honour. And therefore our confidence is not so utterly blind as you suppose."

Ath. "As for the gods, we expect to have quite as much of their favour as you: for we are not doing or claiming anything which goes beyond common opinion about divine or men's desires about human things. For of the gods we believe, and of men we know, that by a law of their nature wherever they can rule they will. This law was not made by us, and we are not the first who have acted upon it; we did but inherit it, and shall bequeath it to all time, and we know that you and all mankind, if you were as strong as we are, would do as we do. So much for the gods; we have told you why we expect to stand as high in their opinion as you. And then as to the Lacedaemonians—when you imagine that out of very shame they will assist you, we admire the innocence of your idea, but we do not envy you the folly of it. The Lacedaemonians are exceedingly virtuous among themselves, and according to their national standard of morality. But, in respect of their dealings with others, although many things might be said, they can be described in few words—of all men whom we know they are the most notorious for identifying what is pleasant with what is honourable, and what is expedient with what is just. But how inconsistent is such a character with your present blind hope of deliverance!"

Mel. "That is the very reason why we trust them; they will look to their interest, and therefore will not be willing to betray the Melians, who are their own colonists, lest they should be distrusted by their friends in Hellas and play into the hands of their enemies."

Ath. "But do you not see that the path of expediency is safe, whereas justice and honour involve danger in practice, and such dangers the Lacedaemonians seldom care to face?"

Mel. "On the other hand, we think that whatever perils there may be, they will be ready to face them for our sakes, and will consider danger less dangerous where we are concerned. For if they need our aid we are close at hand, and they can better trust our loyal feeling because we are their kinsmen."

Ath. "Yes, but what encourages men who are invited to join in a conflict is clearly not the good-will of those who summon them to their side, but a decided superiority in real power. To this no men look more keenly than the Lacedaemonians; so little confidence have they in their own resources, that they only attack their neighbors when they have numerous allies, and therefore they are not likely to find their way by themselves to an island, when we are masters of the sea."

Mel. "But they may send their allies: the Cretan sea is a large place; and the masters of the sea will have more difficulty in overtaking vessels which want to escape than the pursued in escaping. If the attempt should fail they may invade Attica itself, and find their way to allies of yours whom Brasidas did not reach: and then you will have to fight, not for the conquest of a land in which you have no concern, but nearer home, for the preservation of your confederacy and of your own territory."

Ath. "Help may come from Lacedaemon to you as it has come to others, and should you ever have actual experience of it, then you will know that never once have the Athenians retired from a siege through fear of a foe elsewhere. You told us that the safety of your city would be your first care, but we remark that, in this long discussion, not a word has been uttered by you which would give a reasonable man expectation of deliverance. Your strongest grounds are hopes deferred, and what power you have is not to be compared with that which is already arrayed against you. Unless after we have withdrawn you mean to come, as even now you may, to a wiser conclusion, you are showing a great want of sense. For surely you cannot dream of flying to that false sense of honour which has been the ruin of so many when danger and dishonour were staring them in the face. Many men with their eyes still open to the consequences have found the word 'honour' too much for them, and have suffered a mere name to lure them on, until it has drawn down upon them real and irretrievable calamities; through their own folly they have incurred a worse dishonour than fortune would have inflicted upon them. If you are wise you will not run this risk; you ought to see that there can be no disgrace in yielding to a great city which invites you to become her ally on reasonable terms, keeping your own land, and merely paying tribute; and that you will certainly gain no honour if, having to choose between two alternatives, safety and war, you obstinately prefer the worse. To maintain our rights against equals, to be politic with superiors, and to be moderate towards inferiors is the path of safety. Reflect once more when we have withdrawn, and say to yourselves over and over again that you are deliberating about your one and only country, which may be saved or may be destroyed by a single decision."

The Athenians left the conference; the Melians, after consulting among themselves, resolved to persevere in their refusal, and made answer as follows: "Men of Athens, our resolution is unchanged; and we will not in a moment surrender that liberty which our city, founded seven hundred years ago, still enjoys; we will trust to the good fortune which, by the favour of the gods, has hitherto preserved us, and for human help to the Lacedaemonians, and endeavour to save ourselves. We are ready however to be your friends, and the enemies neither of you nor of the Lacedaemonians, and we ask you to leave our country when you have made such a peace as may appear to be in the interest of both parties."

Such was the answer of the Melians; the Athenians, as they quitted the conference, spoke as follows: "Well, we must say, judging from the decision at which you have arrived, that you are the only men who deem the future to be more certain than the present, and regard things unseen as already realised in your fond anticipation, and that the more you cast yourselves upon the Lacedaemonians and fortune and hope, and trust them, the more complete will be your ruin."

The Athenian envoys returned to the army; and the generals, when they found that the Melians would not yield, immediately commenced hostilities. They surrounded the town of Melos with a wall, dividing the work among the several contingents. They then left troops of their own and of their allies to keep guard both by land and by sea, and retired with the greater part of their army; the remainder carried on the blockade. . . .

The Melians took that part of the Athenian wall which looked towards the agora by a night assault, killed a few men, and brought in as much corn and other necessaries as they could; they then retreated and remained inactive. After this the Athenians set a better watch. So the summer ended.

In the following winter the Lacedaemonians had intended to make an expedition into the Argive territory, but finding that the sacrifices which they offered at the frontier were unfavourable they returned home. The Argives, suspecting that the threatened invasion was instigated by citizens of their own, apprehended some of them; others however escaped.

About the same time the Melians took another part of the Athenian wall; for the fortifications were insufficiently guarded. Whereupon the Athenians sent fresh troops, under the command of Philocrates the son of Demeas. The place was now closely invested, and there was treachery among the citizens themselves. So the Melians were induced to surrender at discretion. The Athenians thereupon put to death all who were of military age, and made slaves of the women and children. They then colonized the island, sending thither five hundred settlers of their own.

# 14: Just and Unjust Wars

## Michael Walzer

For as long as men and women have talked about war, they have talked about it in terms of right and wrong. And for almost as long, some among them have derided such talk, called it a charade, insisted that war lies beyond (or beneath) moral judgment. War is a world apart, where life itself is at stake, where human nature is reduced to its elemental forms, where self-interest and necessity prevail. Here men and women do what they must to save themselves and their communities, and morality and law have no place. *Inter arma silent leges*: in time of war the law is silent.

Sometimes this silence is extended to other forms of competitive activity, as in the popular proverb, "All's fair in love and war." That means that anything goes—any kind of deceit in love, any kind of violence in war. We can neither praise nor blame; there is nothing to say. And yet we are rarely silent. The language we use to talk about love and war is so rich with moral meaning that it could hardly have been developed except through centuries of argument. Faithfulness, devotion, chastity, shame, adultery, seduction, betrayal; aggression, self-defense, appeasement, cruelty, ruthlessness, atrocity, massacre—all these words are judgments, and judging is as common a human activity as loving or fighting.

It is true, however, that we often lack the courage of our judgments, and especially so in the case of military conflict. The moral posture of mankind is not well represented by that popular proverb about love and war. We would do better to mark a contrast rather than a similarity: before Venus, censorious; before Mars, timid. Not that we don't justify or condemn particular attacks, but we do so hesitantly and uncertainly (or loudly and recklessly), as if we were not sure that our judgments reach to the reality of war.

### The Realist Argument

Realism is the issue. The defenders of *silent leges* claim to have discovered an awful truth: what we conventionally call inhumanity is simply humanity under pressure. War strips away our civilized adornments and reveals our nakedness. They describe that nakedness for us, not without a certain relish: fearful, self-concerned, driven, murderous. They aren't wrong in any simple sense. The words are sometimes descriptive. Paradoxically, the description is often a kind of apology: yes, our soldiers committed atrocities in the course of the battle, but that's what war does to people, that's what war is like. The proverb, all's fair, is invoked in defense of conduct that appears to be unfair. And one urges silence on the law when one is engaged in activities that would otherwise be called unlawful. So there are arguments here that will enter into my own argument: justifications and excuses, references to necessity and duress, that we can recognize as forms of moral discourse and that have or don't have force in particular cases. But there is also a general account of war as a realm of necessity and duress, the purpose of which is to make discourse about particular cases appear to be idle chatter, a mask of noise with which we conceal, even from ourselves, the awful truth. It is that general account that I have to challenge before I can begin my own work, and I want to challenge it at its source

From *Just and Unjust Wars* by Michael Walzer (ISBN: 04650374046). Copyright © 1977 by Basic Books. Reprinted by permission of Basic Books, a member of Perseus Books, L. L. C.

and in its most compelling form, as it is put forward by the historian Thucydides and the philosopher Thomas Hobbes. These two men, separated by 2,000 years, are collaborators of a kind, for Hobbes translated Thucydides' *History of the Peloponnesian War* and then generalized its argument in his own *Leviathan*. It is not my purpose here to write a full philosophical response to Thucydides and Hobbes. I wish only to suggest, first by argument and then by example, that the judgment of war and of wartime conduct is a serious enterprise.

### The Melian Dialogue

The dialogue between the Athenian generals Cleomedes and Tisias and the magistrates of the island state of Melos is one of the high points of Thucydides' *History* and the climax of his realism. Melos was a Spartan colony, and its people had "therefore refused to be subject, as the rest of the islands were, unto the Athenians; but rested at first neutral; and afterwards, when the Athenians put them to it by wasting of their lands, they entered into open war."[1] This is a classic account of aggression, for to commit aggression is simply to "put people to it" as Thucydides describes. But such a description, he seems to say, is merely external; he wants to show us the inner meaning of war. His spokesmen are the two Athenian generals, who demand a parley and then speak as generals have rarely done in military history. Let us have no fine words about justice, they say. We for our part will not pretend that, having defeated the Persians, our empire is deserved; you must not claim that having done no injury to the Athenian people, you have a right to be let alone. We will talk instead of what is feasible and what is necessary. For this is what war is really like: "they that have odds of power exact as much as they can, and the weak yield to such conditions as they can get."

It is not only the Melians here who bear the burdens of necessity. The Athenians are driven, too; they must expand their empire, Cleomedes and Tisias believe, or lose what they already have. The neutrality of Melos "will be an argument of our weakness, and your hatred of our power, among those we have rule over." It will inspire rebellion throughout the islands, wherever men and women are "offended with the necessity of subjection"—and what subject is not offended, eager for freedom, resentful of his conquerors? When the Athenian generals say that men "will everywhere reign over such as they be too strong for," they are not only describing the desire for glory and command, but also the more narrow necessity of inter-state politics: reign or be subject. If they do not conquer when they can, they only reveal weakness and invite attack; and so, "by a necessity of nature" (a phrase Hobbes later made his own), they conquer when they can.

The Melians, on the other hand, are too weak to conquer. They face a harsher necessity: yield or be destroyed. "For you have not in hand a match of valor upon equal terms . . . but rather a consultation upon your safety . . ." The rulers of Melos, however, value freedom above safety: "If you then to retain your command, and your vassals to get loose from you, will undergo the utmost danger: would it not in us, that be already free, be great baseness and cowardice, if we should not encounter anything whatsoever rather than suffer ourselves to be brought into bondage?" Though they know that it will be a "hard matter" to stand against the power and fortune of Athens, "nevertheless we believe that, for fortune, we shall be nothing inferior, as having the gods on our side, because we stand innocent against men unjust." And as for power, they hope for assistance from the Spartans, "who are of necessity obliged, if for no other cause, yet for

---

1   This and subsequent quotations are from *Hobbes' Thucydides*, ed. Richard Schlatter (New Brunswick, N.J., 1975), pp. 377-85 (*The History of The Peloponnesian War*, 5:84-116).

consanguinity's sake and for their own honor to defend us." But the gods, too, reign where they can, reply the Athenian generals, and consanguinity and honor have nothing to do with necessity. The Spartans will (necessarily) think only of themselves: "most apparently of all men, they hold for honorable that which pleaseth and for just that which profiteth."

So the argument ended. The magistrates refused to surrender; the Athenians laid siege to their city; the Spartans sent no help. Finally, after some months of fighting, in the winter of 416 B.C., Melos was betrayed by several of its citizens. When further resistance seemed impossible, the Melians "yielded themselves to the discretion of the Athenians: who slew all the men of military age, made slaves of the women and children; and inhabited the place with a colony sent thither afterwards of 500 men of their own."

The dialogue between the generals and the magistrates is a literary and philosophical construction of Thucydides. . . . Thucydides has given us a morality play in the Greek style. We can glimpse his meaning in Euripides' *The Trojan Women*, written in the immediate aftermath of the conquest of Melos and undoubtedly intended to suggest the human significance of slaughter and slavery—and to predict a divine retribution:[2]

> How ye are blind

> Ye treaders down of cities, ye that cast
> Temples to desolation, and lay waste
> Tombs, the untrodden sanctuaries where lie
> The ancient dead; yourselves so soon to die!

But Thucydides seems in fact to be making a rather different, and a more secular, statement than this quotation suggests, and not about Athens so much as about war itself. He probably did not mean the harshness of the Athenian generals to be taken as a sign of depravity, but rather as a sign of impatience, toughmindedness, honesty—qualities of mind not inappropriate in military commanders. He is arguing, as Werner Jaeger has said, that "the principle of force forms a realm of its own, with laws of its own," distinct and separate from the laws of moral life.[3] This is certainly the way Hobbes read Thucydides, and it is the reading with which we must come to grips. For if the realm of force is indeed distinct and if this is an accurate account of its laws, then one could no more criticize the Athenians for their wartime policies than one could criticize a stone for falling downwards. The slaughter of the Melians is explained by reference to the circumstances of war and the necessities of nature; and again, there is nothing to say. Or rather, one can *say* anything, call necessity cruel and war hellish; but while these statements may be true in their own terms, they do not touch the political realities of the case or help us understand the Athenian decision.

It is important to stress, however, that Thucydides has told us nothing at all about the Athenian decision. And if we place ourselves, not in the council room at Melos where a cruel policy was being expounded, but in the assembly at Athens where that policy was first adopted, the argument of the generals has a very different ring. In the Greek as in the English language, the word *necessity* "doubles the parts of indispensable and inevitable."[4] At Melos, Cleomedes and Tisias mixed the two of these, stressing the last. In the assembly they could have argued only about the first, claiming, I suppose, that the destruction of Melos was necessary (indispensable) for the preservation of the empire. But this claim is rhetorical in two senses. First, it evades

---

2  *The Trojan Women*, trans. Gilbert Murray (London, 1905), p. 16.

3  Werner Jaeger, *Paideia: the Ideals of Greek Culture*, trans. Gilbert Highet (New York, 1939), I, 402.

4  H. W. Fowler, *A Dictionary of Modern English Usage*, second ed., rev. Sir Ernest Gowers (New York, 1965), p. 168; cf. Jaeger, I, 397.

the moral question of whether the preservation of the empire was itself necessary. There were some Athenians, at least, who had doubts about that, and more who doubted that the empire had to be a uniform system of domination and subjection (as the policy adopted for Melos suggested). Secondly, it exaggerates the knowledge and foresight of the generals. They are not saying with certainty that Athens will fall unless Melos is destroyed; their argument has to do with probabilities and risks. And such arguments are always arguable. Would the destruction of Melos really reduce Athenian risks? Are there alternative policies? What are the likely costs of this one? Would it be right? What would other people think of Athens if it were carried out?

Once the debate begins, all sorts of moral and strategic questions are likely to come up. And for the participants in the debate, the outcome is not going to be determined "by a necessity of nature," but by the opinions they hold or come to hold as a result of the arguments they hear and then by the decisions they freely make, individually and collectively. Afterwards, the generals claim that a certain decision was inevitable; and that, presumably, is what Thucydides wants us to believe. But the claim can only be made afterwards, for inevitability here is mediated by a process of political deliberation, and Thucydides could not know what was inevitable until that process had been completed. Judgments of necessity in this sense are always retrospective in character—the work of historians, not historical actors.

Now, the moral point of view derives its legitimacy from the perspective of the actor. When we make moral judgments, we try to recapture that perspective. We reiterate the decision-making process, or we rehearse our own future decisions, asking what we would have done (or what we would do) in similar circumstances. The Athenian

generals recognize the importance of such questions, for they defend their policy certain "that you likewise, and others that should have the same power which we have, would do the same." But that is a dubious knowledge, especially so once we realize that the "Melian decree" was sharply opposed in the Athenian assembly. Our standpoint is that of citizens debating the decree. What *should* we do?

We have no account of the Athenian decision to attack Melos or of the decision (which may have been taken at the same time) to kill and enslave its people. Plutarch claims that it was Alcibiades, chief architect of the Sicilian expedition, who was "the principal cause of the slaughter . . . having spoken in favor of the decree."[5] He played the part of Cleon in the debate that Thucydides does record, that occurred some years earlier, over the fate of Mytilene. It is worth glancing back at that earlier argument. Mytilene had been an ally of Athens from the time of the Persian War; it was never a subject city in any formal way, but bound by treaty to the Athenian cause. In 428, it rebelled and formed an alliance with the Spartans. After considerable fighting, the city was captured by Athenian forces, and the assembly determined "to put to death . . . all the men of Mytilene that were of age, and to make slaves of the women and children: laying to their charge the revolt itself, in that they revolted not being in subjection as others were . . ."[6] But the following day the citizens "felt a kind of repentance . . . and began to consider what a great and cruel decree it was, that not the authors only, but that the whole city should be destroyed." It is this second debate that Thucydides has recorded, or some part of it, giving us two speeches, that of Cleon upholding the original decree and that of Diodotus urging its revocation. Cleon argues largely in terms of collective guilt and retributive justice; Diodotus

5  *Plutarch's Lives*, trans. John Dryden, rev. Arthur Ilugh Clough (London, 1910), I, 303. Alcibiades also "selected for himself one of the captive Melian women . . ."
6  *Hobbes' Thucydides*, pp. 194-204 (*The History of the Peloponnesian War*, 3:36-49).

offers a critique of the deterrent effects of capital punishment. The assembly accepts Diodotus' position, convinced apparently that the destruction of Mytilene would not uphold the force of treaties or ensure the stability of the empire. It is the appeal to interest that triumphs—as has often been pointed out—though it should be remembered that the occasion for the appeal was the repentance of the citizens. Moral anxiety, not political calculation, leads them to worry about the effectiveness of their decree.

In the debate over Melos, the positions must have been reversed. Now there was no retributivist argument to make, for the Melians had done Athens no injury. Aleibiades probably talked like Thucydides' generals, though with the all-important difference I have already noted. When he told his fellow citizens that the decree was necessary, he didn't mean that it was ordained by the laws that govern the realm of force; he meant merely that it was needed (in his view) to reduce the risks of rebellion among the subject cities of the Athenian empire. And his opponents probably argued, like the Melians, that the decree was dishonorable and unjust and would more likely excite resentment than fear throughout the islands, that Melos did not threaten Athens in any way, and that other policies would serve Athenian interests and Athenian self-esteem. Perhaps they also reminded the citizens of their repentance in the case of Mytilene and urged them once again to avoid the cruelty of massacre and enslavement. How Alcibiades won out, and how close the vote was, we don't know. But there is no reason to think that the decision was predetermined and debate of no avail: no more with Melos than with Mytilene. Stand in imagination in the Athenian assembly, and one can still feel a sense of freedom.

But the realism of the Athenian generals has a further thrust. It is not only a denial of the freedom that makes moral decision possible; it is a denial also of the meaningfulness of moral argument. The second claim is closely related to the first. If we must act in accordance with our interests, driven by our fears of one another, then talk about justice cannot possibly be anything more than talk. It refers to no purposes that we can make our own and to no goals that we can share with others. That is why the Athenian generals could have woven "fair pretenses" as easily as the Melian magistrates; in discourse of this sort anything can be said. The words have no clear references, no certain definitions, no logical entailments. They are, as Hobbes writes in *Leviathan*, "ever used with relation to the person that useth them," and they express that person's appetites and fears and nothing else. It is only "most apparent" in the Spartans, but true for everyone, that "they hold for honorable that which pleaseth them and for just that which profiteth." Or, as Hobbes later explained, the names of the virtues and vices are of "uncertain signification."[7]

> For one calleth wisdom, what another calleth fear; and one cruelty what another justice; one prodigality what another magnanimity . . . etc. And therefore such names can never be true grounds of any ratiocination.

*"Never"*—until the sovereign, who is also the supreme linguistic authority, fixes the meaning of the moral vocabulary; but in the state of war, *"never"* without qualification, because in that state, by definition, no sovereign rules. In fact, even in civil society, the sovereign does not entirely succeed in bringing certainty into the world of virtue and vice. Hence moral discourse is always suspect, and war is only an extreme case of the anarchy of moral meanings. It is generally true, but especially so in time of violent conflict, that we can understand what other people are saying only if we see through their "fair pretenses" and translate moral talk into the harder currency of interest talk. When the Melians insist

---

7 Thomas Hobbes, *Leviathan*, ch. IV.

that their cause is just, they are saying only that they don't want to be subject: and had the generals claimed that Athens deserved its empire, they would simply have been expressing the lust for conquest or the fear of overthrow.

This is a powerful argument because it plays upon the common experience of moral disagreement—painful, sustained, exasperating, and endless. For all its realism, however, it fails to get at the realities of that experience or to explain its character. We can see this clearly, I think, if we look again at the argument over the Mytilene decree. Hobbes may well have had this debate in mind when he wrote, "and one [calleth] cruelty what another justice . . ." The Athenians repented of their cruelty, writes Thucydides, while Cleon told them that they had not been cruel at all but justly severe. Yet this was in no sense a disagreement over the meaning of words. Had there been no common meanings, there could have been no debate at all. The cruelty of the Athenians consisted in seeking to punish not only the authors of the rebellion but others as well, and Cleon agreed that that would indeed be cruel. He then went on to argue, as he had to do given his position, that in Mytilene there were no "others." "Let not the fault be laid upon a few, and the people absolved. For they have all alike taken arms against us . . .".

I cannot pursue the argument further, since Thucydides doesn't, but there is an obvious rejoinder to Cleon, having to do with the status of the women and children of Mytilene. This might involve the deployment of additional moral terms (innocence, for example); but it would not hang—any more than the argument about cruelty and justice hangs—on idiosyncratic definitions. In fact, definitions are not at issue here, but descriptions and interpretations. The Athenians shared a moral vocabulary, shared it with the people of Mytilene and Melos; and allowing for cultural differences, they share it with us too. They had no difficulty, and we have none, in understanding the claim of the Melian magistrates that the invasion of their island was unjust. It is in applying the agreed-upon words to actual cases that we come to disagree. These disagreements are in part generated and always compounded by antagonistic interests and mutual fears. But they have other causes, too, which help to explain the complex and disparate ways in which men and women (even when they have similar interests and no reason to fear one another) position themselves in the moral world. There are, first of all, serious difficulties of perception and information (in war and politics generally), and so controversies arise over "the facts of the case." There are sharp disparities in the weight we attach even to values we share, as there are in the actions we are ready to condone when these values are threatened. There are conflicting commitments and obligations that force us into violent antagonism even when we see the point of one another's positions. All this is real enough, and common enough: it makes morality into a world of good-faith quarrels as well as a world of ideology and verbal manipulation. . . .

It is important to stress that the moral reality of war is not fixed by the actual activities of soldiers but by the opinions of mankind. That means, in part, that it is fixed by the activity of philosophers, lawyers, publicists of all sorts. But these people don't work in isolation from the experience of combat, and their views have value only insofar as they give shape and structure to that experience in ways that are plausible to the rest of us. We often say, for example, that in time of war soldiers and statesmen must make agonizing decisions. The pain is real enough, but it is not one of the natural effects of combat. Agony is not like Hobbist fear; it is entirely the product of our moral views, and it is common in war only insofar as those views are common. It was not some unusual Athenian who "repented" of the decision to kill the men of Mytilene, but the citizens generally. They repented, and they were able to understand one another's repentance, because they shared a sense of what cruelty meant. It is by the assignment of such meanings that we make war what it is—which is to say that it could be (and it probably has been) something different.

What of a soldier or statesman who does not feel the agony? We say of him that he is morally ignorant or morally insensitive, much as we might say of a general who experienced no difficulty making a (really) difficult decision that he did not understand the strategic realities of his own position or that he was reckless and insensible of danger. And we might go on to argue, in the case of the general, that such a man has no business fighting or leading others in battle, that he ought to know that his army's right flank, say, is vulnerable, and ought to worry about the danger and take steps to avoid it. Once again, the case is the same with moral decisions: soldiers and statesmen ought to know the dangers of cruelty and injustice and worry about them and take steps to avoid them.

### The Crime of War

The moral reality of war is divided into two parts. War is always judged twice, first with reference to the reasons states have for fighting, secondly with reference to the means they adopt. The first kind of judgment is adjectival in character: we say that a particular war is just or unjust. The second is adverbial: we say that the war is being fought justly or unjustly. Medieval writers made the difference a matter of prepositions, distinguishing *jus ad bellum,* the justice of war, from *jus in bello,* justice in war. These grammatical distinctions point to deep issues. *Jus ad bellum* requires us to make judgments about aggression and self-defense; *jus in bello* about the observance or violation of the customary and positive rules of engagement. The two sorts of judgment are logically independent. It is perfectly possible for a just war to be fought unjustly and for an unjust war to be fought in strict accordance with the rules. But this independence, though our views of particular wars often conform to its terms, is nevertheless puzzling. It is a crime to commit aggression, but aggressive war is a rule-governed activity. It is right to resist aggression, but the resistance is subject to moral (and legal) restraint. The dualism of *jus ad bellum* and *jus in bello* is at the heart of all that is most problematic in the moral reality of war.

# 15: Just War Theory

*James Turner Johnson*

During the first part of the fifth century of the Christian era, Augustine of Hippo, revered today as a saint in the Catholic faith and yet also deeply influential on Protestant theology, set down in writing certain ideas on the use of violence that have had a decisive impact on thought about war in Western culture. Augustine wrote as a Christian theologian, dealing with a problem that clearly for him was profoundly painful: how to reconcile traditional Christian teaching against the use of violence with the need to defend the Roman Empire—Christian for more than a century by Augustine's time—from the invading Vandals. The solution he reached—a justification of war under certain prescribed circumstances, yet with genuine limits on the harm that could be done even in a justified war—is generally regarded as the beginning of just war doctrine in Christian teaching, as well as a major contribution to the development of consensual Western thought on the restraint of war.

That there exists a consensual tradition in Western culture on the justification and limitation of war will be a surprise to persons who think of war as inherently incapable of restraint and of justifying reasons for war as being convenient rationalizations of state power. Yet every culture has some such tradition, and ours has remained remarkably consistent (though going through considerable development) right up into the contemporary period, where it finds expression in international law, in military manuals of the laws and customs of war, in moral debate over nuclear arms and strategic doctrines like Mutual Assured Destruction, in the concept of conscientious objection to military service. In a

fundamental sense we in the West cannot think about war without using the terms of this broad tradition, even if we disagree with what it teaches. And for this reason if for no other, it is important to understand what is implied by this dual theme of permission to engage in violence accompanied by clearly enunciated restraints on that violence. For my own part, I would have us understand this tradition for another, perhaps more pressing, reason: the experience of all-out war in the two global conflicts of this century has led a great many people to think that the use of military force must inevitably be total and unrestrained, and the problem is not simply that by thinking this way we are being unfaithful to our roots. Rather, given the destructive power of modern weaponry, to conceive of the use of force in this totalistic, unlimited way is to put the world in enormous danger. Having largely forgotten the lessons on the good of restraint in war discovered when weapons themselves imposed some limits, we have the greater responsibility to recover those lessons in a time when the only restraints on the destructiveness of war can be those set by purposeful human choice. . . .

In classic terminology the whole range of issues on the management of force is covered by the phrase *jus in bello*, meaning literally what it is right or just to do in war, while the issues pertaining to whether to resort to war are collectively grouped under the heading *jus ad bellum*. . . . The *jus ad bellum* includes such concepts as just cause, right authority, right intention, that the resort to war be a last resort, and proportionality in a larger, overall sense weighing the total evil a war would cause against whatever good it can be

Excerpt from *Can Modern War Be Just?* by James Turner Johnson, pp. 1-2, 3-5, 12-16, 18-19, 25-29. © 1984 by Yale University Press, New Haven, CT. Reprinted by permission of the publisher.

expected to achieve. In this connection, a further idea is generally added as part of the *jus ad bellum* criteria: that the goal of a war be peace, or at least a more secure peace than that which obtained beforehand. Such, at least, is the *jus ad bellum* in *moral* terms. In contemporary international law these ideas tend to be collapsed into regulations defining aggression and the proper limits of defense.

Augustine treated defense by means of a paradigmatic situation involving three persons: a criminal who is attacking or about to attack a second person, the innocent victim, and a third person, an onlooker, on whose behalf Augustine offers his thoughts. What should this third person do in such a situation? We must recall that Augustine wrote within a Christian context in which the use of violence had been generally deplored: in telling his disciple Peter to sheath his sword, so the argument went, Jesus had in principle disarmed all Christians. But Augustine was not convinced by this, and his argument advanced toward a quite different conclusion. The onlooker, as Christian, must be motivated by love toward both those individuals before him, the criminal as well as the victim. Yet the criminal, who is armed, is unjustly aggressing against the innocent weaponless victim. The proper action for the Christian, reasoned Augustine, is to intervene between criminal and victim, defending the latter even at the risk of his own life against attack or threat of attack by the former. Such defense of the victim, argued Augustine, is mandated by the onlooker's love for him as someone for whom Christ died; yet Christ also died for the criminal, and this limits what may be done toward him in defending the innocent victim. Briefly stated, Augustine argued for a proportionate response to the threat represented by the criminal: the onlooker should seek to prevent the criminal from carrying out his evil intention by defensive measures designed to thwart whatever the criminal may try. Escalation here is made the attacker's responsibility, not the defender's. The latter may meet force with proportionately effective force right up to and including the possibility of killing the criminal, if he does not relent before that. Meanwhile, the Christian onlooker, now become his innocent neighbor's defender, is not in any sense guilty for doing what he must, for he is acting the only way he can when motivated by love: opposing the doing of evil, yet separating his hatred for evil from his love for the person of the evildoer.

Though couched in centrally Christian terminology and forms of thought, Augustine's argument here introduces in sharp definition the two moral principles that have historically defined the *jus in bello*: the ideas of proportionality and discrimination or noncombatant immunity. Augustine's criminal stands for any soldier who menaces an unarmed noncombatant peacefully going about his business. Transferred to the context of war, the criminal and the defender who opposes him become enemy soldiers on the battlefield, and the purpose of war is defined in terms of the defense of peaceful life and resistance to evil actions. But opposition to the enemy's evil should not imply hatred for the enemy soldiers. Augustine's reason for this was a theological one: Christ died for the evildoers as well as for the just. But in its later development this idea was radically secularized into what is known today as the principle of humanity. Its meaning was well stated by the eighteenth-century Swiss theorist of international law, Emmerich de Vattel: "Let us never forget," he wrote, "that our enemies are men." Augustine could not have put this idea more pungently. The principle of humanity underlies the modern law of war, providing its own moral underpinning to the ideas of proportion and noncombatant immunity, though these concepts are rooted as well in the idea of justice. From their roots in Christian theorizing about violence, then, the essential concepts of restraint in war have over the centuries become secularized, and the values undergirding them have ceased to be specifically those of Christian religion but have become perceived as generic to Western culture. . . .

## What Is Just War Tradition?

What is before us is not a doctrine, as it is often called, especially in religious circles, but a *tradition* including many individual doctrines from various sources within the culture and various periods of historical development and representing variations in content. If we would speak of "just war doctrine," we are immediately confronted by a bewildering multiplicity. We must ask, "Whose doctrine?" and end up favoring one or the other lifted up out of the whole. This approach often results in historical positivism about morals: so-and-so said this is what to think or do, so that's what I must think or do. A Catholic who depends too heavily on the (comparatively minimal) just war theory of Thomas Aquinas would provide one example of this wrong way of thinking about just war tradition as a single doctrine; other examples would include Protestants who overuse Augustine, Luther, or even the Bible in this way and international lawyers who attempt to lift the modern law of war as a unit out of its historical context. By contrast with such approaches, thinking of just war tradition requires entering the circle of continuing development of that tradition, regarding each of its various historical contributors as coparticipants worthy to be heard and necessary to be taken seriously, but not as prophets to be followed blindly. Just war tradition as a guide to moral analysis requires active moral judgment within a historical context that includes not only the contemporary world but the significantly remembered past. It cannot properly be a basis for historical positivism in ethics.

Another widespread misconception is to think of just war ideas as being the more or less exclusive property of Christian—and more specifically, Catholic—moral thought. On this view the just war tradition is first and foremost a product of specifically theological wisdom and a repository of narrowly Christian ethical principles having some bearing on relations among states. There are several things wrong with this way of conceiving the nature of just war tradition. Admittedly, Christian theologians have had an important impact on the development of this historical moral tradition; otherwise it would not represent, as I have asserted above, a culture-wide moral consensus on the justification and limitation of war. But in the first place, these specifically Christian contributions have not come only or even principally from the theologians; canon law and the traditions of the confessional, both sources closer to the dirtiness and moral ambiguity of ordinary life than is theology as a discipline of thought, have contributed as much or more fundamentally to shaping the peculiarly Christian inputs into the developing historical tradition on just war. Indeed, in the twelfth and thirteenth centuries, when the just war tradition as a coherent body of ideas and practices began to coalesce, it was not the theologians but the canonists within the European ecclesiastical establishment who dealt most forcefully, sustainedly, and thoroughly with matters of morality relating to warfare.[1] Second, the Christian contributors are not properly thought of as Catholics in the modern denominational sense. There was no Catholic Church, in this sense, before the events of the Reformation and the Counter-Reformation. Earlier there is only Christendom, the common heritage of modern Protestants and Catholics alike, and, because of the commonality of Christian faith in the West in this era, the heritage as well of modern secular culture. Again, what we confront in just war tradition is a multifaceted and various unity of moral insights and practices reflecting the experience and judgments of historical persons

---

1   For further discussion of this point, see my *Just War Tradition and the Restraint of War* (Princeton: Princeton University Press, 1981), chap. 5; cf. Frederick H. Russell, *The Just War in the Middle Ages* (Cambridge: Cambridge University Press, 1971), passim.

across the whole breadth of cultural institutions. The relegation of just war ideas to a narrow sphere of peculiarly Christian (or Catholic, in the modern sense) theological reflection is wrong not only because it is bad history, but because it incorrectly attempts to separate our own identity from a portion of our common cultural past.

One of the most astonishing aspects of the historical development of just war tradition is how much it owes to secular sources, some of them, like the military, thought by many people not to have anything to do with morality at all. This is a poor understanding of morality which relegates it to the cloisters of ecclesiastical life. In fact the historical origin and much of the early development of the ideas defining the limits of permissible violence in war was in the military sphere.[2] Medieval Christianity produced a *jus ad bellum,* but the *jus in bello* came out of the customs and sensibilities of the knightly class, who provided the professional soldiers of their time. Similarly it is necessary to credit later *jus in bello* developments importantly to the early modern manuals of military conduct, such as Gustavus Adolphus's *Swedish Discipline* in the Thirty Years War, to later military practice like that of the sovereigns' wars of the eighteenth century, still later to developments within military professional self-consciousness like the Union Army's *General Orders No. 100* in the American Civil War and, finally, to the contemporary discussion on professionalism within the United States military. All of these are the subject of a chapter below; at this point what is necessary is to note that they properly belong to the continuing historical development of just war tradition, right alongside its other component parts, including Christian religion and secular law.

I have already alluded in passing to the mistaken conception that Western moral tradition on war can be reduced to what is contained in international law on war. Modern international law is one of the bearers of this tradition—one among others. It is, moreover, a continuation of the line of effort begun by nonecclesiastical lawyers in the Middle Ages who were concerned to identify the implications of the natural law and the "law of nations," as they conceived these in the terminology of classical Rome, to the conduct of war in their day. Modern international law as a discrete discipline of thought rose out of the broader consensual just war tradition at the birth of the modern era by means of the combined work of neo-scholastic theologians like Franciscus de Victoria and Francisco Suarez and early publicists like Alberico Gentili and Hugo Grotius. But even as this discipline of thought arose, it defined its own parameters, thereby ruling out some kinds of concerns while including and magnifying others. Thus it is a misconception to think of the international law of war as it has developed down to our own time as containing all that there is to say about the justification and limitation of war. At least two other major lines of development have to be laid alongside it for the outlines of the whole to emerge: military professionalism in theory and practice, as noted above, and moral concerns both secular and religious, newly defined in the modern period as distinguishable disciplines of thought by themselves.

Implicit in all that I have been saying thus far is a rejection of yet another wrong conception: that just war tradition has only to do with ideas and thus is abstractedly remote from real-life circumstances, which require not ideas but actions. This is far from the truth. Just war tradition represents above all a fund of *practical* moral wisdom, based not in abstract speculation or theorization but in reflection on actual problems encountered in war as these have presented

---

2  *Just War Tradition and the Restraint of War;* see also my *Ideology, Reason, and the Limitation of War* (Princeton: Princeton University Press, 1976), chap. 1.

themselves in different historical circumstances. Thus, for example, I have taken pains to note that military *practice* has functioned in the development and bearing of the tradition. Indeed, without such a fundamental rooting in practical concerns, it is hard to see what would be the point of asking about the meaning of just war tradition in the context of contemporary war. While I, like other writers, often use terms like "moral thought" and "ideas," they function as a kind of shorthand to indicate the practice and product of reflection on practical realities. As I have argued above, thinking about war in terms of just war tradition means allowing one's own individual reflections to be guided by the experience and reflections of others in a rich cultural history who have attempted to deal with practical problems both similar and dissimilar to our own. This requires that we look at the practices of war as well as at moral theorizing about war to "keep faith" with this tradition.

Still, though, it is necessary to hold that critical and constructive moral thought provides an indispensable balance to the purely practical side of just war tradition. Only the theorist can take the long view; only the theorist can analyze, summarize, cut through deadwood, identify wrong turns, and draw out the implications of positive elements in the developing tradition. The need for moral theoretical input into the process of development was substantially forgotten through much of the nineteenth century, and I believe this is one reason why in world wars I and II Western culture came to accept the rightness of unlimited means of war—the shelling of cities and gas warfare in World War I, and in World War II the obliteration of population centers by conventional explosives, napalm, and finally by atomic weapons. That our culture has come to accept such an intentionality as this concept of "total war" is directly counter to the meaning of the entire tradition that treats warfare as sometimes justifiable, yet always to be practiced within limits, with restraint. A significant portion of the role of the contemporary moral theorist dealing with war is to remind the larger culture that, in terms of its own highest values as they have taken shape and been expressed over history, the turn toward total war has been a wrong turn: war does not have to be total; it is possible to think again, as in the past, of justified force that may be employed with restraint. . . .

## Major Just War Concepts

In the classic terminology, the component parts of just war theory are grouped under two headings, as follows:

*jus ad bellum*

(whether resort to force is justified)
- just cause
- right authority
- right intent
- proportionality (in the sense of total good and evil anticipated)
- the end of peace
- last resort

*jus in bello*

(whether a particular form of the use of force is justified)
- proportionality (in the sense of proximate good over evil)
- discrimination, or noncombatant protection

The *jus ad bellum* is, in other words, that portion of the tradition that deals with the justification of force, while the *jus in bello* addresses restraints or limits on how force may be used. . . .

*Proportionality* as a moral principle applied to the restraint of war has two faces, having to do both with the original decision whether to use forceful means and with the multifold later decisions as to what levels or means of force are proper. Here I wish to speak about both of these ideas.

In *jus ad bellum* terms, the aim of the idea of proportionality is to ensure that the overall damage to human values that will result from the resort to force will be at least balanced evenly by the degree to which the same or other important values are preserved or protected. This "counting the costs" requires thinking into the future, and while such projection is notoriously risky, it must be done.

When we reflect on the proportionality or disproportionality of contemporary warfare in this sense of the idea, it is important to differentiate between the *destructive capability* of modern weapons and the *intentionality* that determines whether the most destructive means available will be used and, if so, how and in what context(s). These are distinct questions, and it is necessary for a genuinely moral weighing of the issue to divide them. World War II offers numerous examples of an intentionality aimed at producing indiscriminate mass destruction: the death camps and conventional countercity bombing long predated the atomic bomb. Without the precedents of London, Dresden, Hamburg, and Tokyo the obliteration of Hiroshima and Nagasaki would not have been thinkable. The kind of intentionality that led Vattel and others to question bombardment of cities with red-hot cannon balls and other incendiary means was emphatically lost in the total-war idea present in World War II, and it is this latter kind of intentionality that must morally be challenged no matter what sorts of weapons are available. Thus when we think of contemporary occasions when the use of force might be justified, the idea of proportionality requires that we think not only of the foreseeable results of the unlimited use of whatever weapons are available—whether nuclear, chemical, biological, or conventional. It requires also that we consider how workable and responsible limits may be imposed to make it possible to use forceful means to protect values that otherwise could not be preserved.

Modern-war pacifists generally overlook this distinction that must be made between intentionality and the destructive potential of weapons. This allows them to appeal to the "disproportionality" of modern weapons (and hence of modern war) as compared with any values that might be served by their employment. The most common form of this claim today is nuclear pacifism. Nuclear pacifists argue that whatever might have been said about the possibility of justice in war during earlier eras, today the use of nuclear weapons would necessarily result in a holocaust of unimaginable fury and horrifying impact. Their distortion of this moral concept of proportionality is that they deny the possibility of moral controls over the employment of forceful means. The tragic irony of this position is that it tends to remove nuclear weapons altogether from the sphere of human moral intentionality, so that the very end that is so dreadfully feared becomes the more possible: the holocaust that would result from an unlimited exchange of strategic nuclear weapons.

The purpose of thinking in just war terms, including the idea of proportionality as one of these terms, is to attempt to make rational moral decisions among possibilities that are available. Unless nuclear weapons, among all the others that are now available, are subordinated like all the others to a searching examination of the proper limits to human intentionality, we will have made a grave and potentially disastrous mistake.

This consideration leads naturally into the *jus in bello* meaning of the traditional concept of proportionality. At the very least, I would suggest, those persons are right who have advocated counterforce targeting of strategic nuclear weapons. This is one example of how human moral intentionality may be applied to define a restrained yet possibly rational use of such weaponry. The presumption against chemical and biological weapons is also rightly directed, for reasons having to do with discrimination or non-combatant protection as well as with proportionality, since such weapons tend both to be indiscriminate in use and to produce, more perhaps than nuclear weapons, long-term damage to human lives and values. In general, considerations of proportionality point us toward utilization of conventional weapons, whose effects can be predictably known and moderated; beyond that, such considerations point to the need to develop weapons of war that may be employed more proportionately than those now available. A moral obligation to use restraint in the protection of values implies developing means of war that can be employed with restraint, in the service of human intentionality. Thus the just war concept of proportionality drives toward two conclusions: that we forget the past intentionality that has conceived war as necessarily total and has nourished means of war that serve that conception, and further that we establish an intentionality of restraint and control over the weapons of war while fostering the development of new weapons that lend themselves to use in the service of such intentionality.

I have kept till last the wisdom preserved in the just war idea that noncombatants should be protected from the ravages of war. This idea of *noncombatant immunity,* also called the moral principle of *discrimination,* has been one of the strongest and most regular themes in just war tradition throughout its development, though it has not always been understood the same way. As stated forcefully by Paul Ramsey, for example, this idea is that noncombatants enjoy an absolute moral immunity from direct, intentional attack; but in the limited-war practice of the eighteenth century an equally powerful effort to protect noncombatants emerged, centered not on the immunity from harm of the individual but rather on restricting the theater of military operations so as not directly to threaten most of the inhabitants of belligerent nations. Here absolute immunity was defined geographically. The latter concept has again surfaced in some contemporary limited-war thought (that aimed at restricting the geographic scope of war), while contemporary humanitarian international law, like Ramsey, holds that certain classes of persons must be protected no matter where they are found. We are charged with remembering that noncombatants are indeed morally different from combatants, and that our behavior toward them in wartime must accordingly be different. Warfare in which combatants and noncombatants are perceived and treated as essentially alike is fundamentally against the major moral tradition of war in Western culture.

Yet powerful forces in the modern world have tended to suppress the memory of this moral obligation to protect noncombatants. Nowhere is the result of this suppression more obvious than in a strategic nuclear policy that threatens population centers rather than military forces that (I should think presumably) represent the real enemy in wartime. But the evil is not limited to such strategic targeting or to the actions of nation-states; when terrorists choose as their preferred targets persons who have no perceptible connection to the exercise of power or to the military use of force—and the more disconnected from power the victims are, the more successful the terrorism—we have an equally glaring case of the immorality of a conception of the use of force that does not recognize the moral duty not to harm noncombatants.

The moral requirement to protect noncombatants implies the development of weapons usable in ways that satisfy legitimate military functions without corollary damage to the lives, livelihoods, and property of noncombatants. In the fourteenth century the noble monk Honoré Bonet, writing of the law of war in his own time, put this in homely terms: warriors were not to use their arms on peaceful peasants, merchants, or others as they went about their business, nor on the ox of the peasant nor the ass that carried the merchant's wares. These were neither of the knightly class (that is, they were not socialized as soldiers), nor were they functioning in warlike ways; they ought as a moral duty to be left alone, not only in their lives but in their property. Such a moral consideration has important implications for future weapons development, as well as for the debate over such new weapons as the neutron bomb, the cruise missile, MX, and other components of contemporary military policy.

## Conclusion

I have been arguing in this chapter for the contemporary relevance of the moral ideas developed and preserved in just war tradition and known by reflection on that tradition. These ideas represent, I have argued, the only way actually open for persons in our culture to think about morality and war. At the very least they represent formal criteria for our thinking, questions that we must ask whenever we begin to think seriously about the possibility of using forceful means to protect important values. But beyond this purely formal set of questions, I have suggested further that there is wisdom present in the content given to these ideas in our historical tradition of moral judgment on war, and that reflection on that wisdom will help to keep us from making mistakes in our contemporary efforts to answer the questions of whether and how we might justifiably employ force in the protection of important values. In sum, I have been arguing that just war tradition provides us with three fundamental moral reminders: first, that sometimes the use of force may be necessary to protect or preserve values that would otherwise be damaged or lost; second, that both the resort to force and the application of forceful means must be subjected to a searching intentionality of justification and restraint; and third, that means and methods of war should be developed so as to serve the legitimate moral purposes of the employment of force in international affairs.

Part II

The Roots of War

# Introduction

Given the historical constancy, frequency, and destructiveness of war, the question why war occurs occupies a central place in the study of international relations. Three general types of explanations have been suggested. In the first place, war may be the logical result of the nature of the international system, particularly its anarchic, self-help character. Second, war may be the consequence of the nature of particular states or nations. In this view, the blame for war rightly lies not on the international environment in which states interact but on individual states or nations that have some inherent flaw that makes them desire or tolerate war. The third explanation points the accusing finger at man. It suggests that war is the natural product of man's aggressiveness, ignorance, or irrationality. These three "levels of analysis" characterize different theories about why states behave as they do: perhaps, as Realists argue, this behavior is dictated by imperatives imposed by the international environment (a systemic-level explanation); perhaps it reflects the domestic politics of presidential or bureaucratic decision-making (a state-level explanation); or perhaps it stems from decision-makers' peculiar psychology, from large national cultural forces, or from particular ways or paradigms of understanding the world (individual-level explanations).

Chapters 16 through 18 explore a few of the ways in which the structure of the international system and society can lead to conflict. Robert Jervis, in chapter 16, examines the logic of the *security dilemma*—the fact that, in a self-help system, steps one state takes to make itself feel more secure may have the unfortunate consequence

of making its neighbors feel less secure. Jervis considers the conditions that make the security dilemma more or less likely and more or less severe. In chapter 17, Edward Gulick discusses why states tend to engage in *balance-of-power* behavior and the logical consequences of this balancing. In theory, balancing preserves a stable equilibrium and prevents the emergence of a preponderant power capable of dominating the system. In practice, a preponderant power occasionally emerges to become a hegemon, a leader in international society capable of creating international regimes that facilitate cooperation among states. A Realist alternative to balance of power theories emphasizes the stabilizing role of hegemony (although competition for the role of hegemon occasionally destabilizes the system and risks major war). In Chapter 18, Robert Keohane examines the possibilities for cooperation within the international system in the absence of a hegemon.

The following six chapters question the assumption that all states are basically the same except for the amount of power they possess and suggest some of the ways in which the characteristics of particular nations or states might affect state behavior, making them more or less warprone. In chapter 19, Stephen Krasner discusses two very different explanations for why states behave as they do. Marxist accounts argue that states serve the interests of dominant economic classes; liberal explanations contend that state behavior is the outcome of competitive pressures from a range of special interest groups. In either case, we would expect state behavior—including willingness to go to war—to depend on power relationships within the state's domestic society. In the following chapter, Jack Levy explores the relationship between a variety of state and national attributes and the occurrence of war. V.P. Gagnon in chapter 21 expands on one of those attributes—ethnic nationalism—and examines the relationship between ethnic nationalism and armed conflict. In chapter 22, we rejoin Jack Levy for a discussion of government structures and processes; in particular, he focuses on a particular, hotly-debated and now much-studied relationship: the one that may exist between democracy and peace. Levy reviews three important explanations for this apparent relationship, as well as the policy implications of a "democratic peace."

Chapters 23 and 24 turn to the individual as a cause of war. In chapter 23, Azar Gat articulates an evolutionary explanation for human aggressiveness. In the following chapter, Richard Ned Lebow considers humans' limited potential for rational decision-making and explores the impact of psychological stress on leaders' capacity to choose policies that would avoid war.

# 16: The Security Dilemma

## Robert Jervis

### Anarchy and the Security Dilemma

The lack of an international sovereign not only permits wars to occur, but also makes it difficult for states that are satisfied with the status quo to arrive at goals that they recognize as being in their common interest. Because there are no institutions or authorities that can make and enforce international laws, the policies of cooperation that will bring mutual rewards if others cooperate may bring disaster if they do not. Because states are aware of this, anarchy encourages behavior that leaves all concerned worse off than they could be, even in the extreme case in which all states would like to freeze the status quo. This is true of the men in Rousseau's "Stag Hunt." If they cooperate to trap the stag, they will all eat well. But if one person defects to chase a rabbit,—which he likes less than stag—none of the others will get anything. Thus, all actors have the same preference order, and there is a solution that gives each his first choice: (1) cooperate and trap the stag (the international analogue being cooperation and disarmament); (2) chase a rabbit while others remain at their posts (maintain a high level of arms while others are disarmed); (3) all chase rabbits (arms competition and high risk of war); and (4) stay at the original position while another chases a rabbit (being disarmed while others are armed).[1] Unless each person thinks that the others will cooperate, he himself will not. And why might he fear that any other person would do something that would sacrifice his own first choice? The other might not understand the situation, or might not be able to control his impulses if he saw a rabbit, or might fear that some other member of the group is unreliable. If the person voices any of these suspicions, others are more likely to fear that he will defect, thus making them more likely to defect, thus making it more rational for him to defect. Of course in this simple case—and in many that are more realistic—there are a number of arrangements that could permit cooperation. But the main point remains: although actors

---

1 This kind of rank-ordering is not entirely an analyst's invention, as is shown by the following section of a British army memo of 1903 dealing with British and Russian railroad construction near the Persia-Afghanistan border:
The conditions of the problem may . . . be briefly summarized as follows:
    a) If we make a railway to Seistan while Russia remains inactive, we gain a considerable defensive advantage at considerable financial cost;
    b) If Russia makes a railway to Seistan, while we remain inactive, she gains a considerable offensive advantage at considerable financial cost;
    c) If both we and Russia make railways to Seistan, the defensive and offensive advantages may be held to neutralize each other; in other words, we shall have spent a good deal of money and be no better off than we are at present. On the other hand, we shall be no worse off, whereas under alternative (b) we shall be much worse off. Consequently, the theoretical balance of advantage lies with the proposed railway extension from Quetta to Seistan.
W. G. Nicholson, "Memorandum on Seistan and Other Points Raised in the Discussion on the Defence of India,"
(Committee of Imperial Defence, March 20, 1903). It should be noted that the possibility of neither side building railways was not mentioned, thus strongly biasing the analysis.

Robert Jervis, "Cooperation Under the Security Dilemma," *World Politics* (1978), pp. 167-74, 176-80, 182-92, 194-214. Reprinted by permission of the author and The Johns Hopkins University Press.

may know that they seek a common goal, they may not be able to reach it.

Even when there is a solution that is everyone's first choice, the international case is characterized by three difficulties not present in the Stag Hunt. First, to the incentives to defect given above must be added the potent fear that even if the other state now supports the status quo, it may become dissatisfied later. No matter how much decision makers are committed to the status quo, they cannot bind themselves and their successors to the same path. Minds can be changed, new leaders can come to power, values can shift, new opportunities and dangers can arise.

The second problem arises from a possible solution. In order to protect their possessions, states often seek to control resources or land outside their own territory. Countries that are not self-sufficient must try to assure that the necessary supplies will continue to flow in wartime. This was part of the explanation for Japan's drive into China and Southeast Asia before World War II. If there were an international authority that could guarantee access, this motive for control would disappear. But since there is not, even a state that would prefer the status quo to increasing its area of control may pursue the latter policy.

When there are believed to be tight linkages between domestic and foreign policy or between the domestic politics of two states, the quest for security may drive states to interfere preemptively in the domestic politics of others in order to provide an ideological buffer zone. Thus, Metternich's justification for supervising the politics of the Italian states has been summarized as follows:

> Every state is absolutely sovereign in its internal affairs. But this implies that every state must do nothing to interfere in the internal affairs of any other. However, any false or pernicious step taken by any state in its internal affairs may disturb the repose of another state, and this consequent disturbance of another state's repose constitutes an interference in that state's internal affairs. Therefore, every state—or rather, every sovereign of a great power—has the duty, in the name of the sacred right of independence of every state, to supervise the governments of smaller states and to prevent them from taking false and pernicious steps in their internal affairs.[2]

More frequently, the concern is with direct attack. In order to protect themselves, states seek to control, or at least to neutralize, areas on their borders. But attempts to establish buffer zones can alarm others who have stakes there, who fear that undesirable precedents will be set, or who believe that their own vulnerability will be increased. When buffers are sought in areas empty of great powers, expansion tends to feed on itself in order to protect what is acquired, as was often noted by those who opposed colonial expansion. Balfour's complaint was typical: "Every time I come to a discussion—at intervals of, say, five years—I find there is a new sphere which we have got to guard, which is supposed to protect the gateways of India. Those gateways are getting further and further away from India, and I do not know how far west they are going to be brought by the General Staff."[3]

Though this process is most clearly visible when it involves territorial expansion, it often operates with the increase of less tangible power and influence. The expansion of power usually brings with it an expansion of responsibilities and commitments; to meet them, still greater power is required. The state will take many positions that are subject to challenge. It will be involved with a wide range of controversial issues unrelated to its core values. And retreats

---

2   Paul Schroeder, *Metternich's Diplomacy at its Zenith, 1820-1823* (Westport, Conn.: Greenwood Press 1969), 126.
3   Quoted in Michael Howard, *The Continental Commitment* (Harmondsworth, England: Penguin 1974), 67.

that would be seen as normal if made by a small power would be taken as an index of weakness inviting predation if made by a large one.

The third problem present in international politics but not in the Stag Hunt is the security dilemma: many of the means by which a state tries to increase its security decrease the security of others. In domestic society, there are several ways to increase the safety of one's person and property without endangering others. One can move to a safer neighborhood, put bars on the windows, avoid dark streets, and keep a distance from suspicious-looking characters. Of course these measures are not convenient, cheap, or certain of success. But no one save criminals need be alarmed if a person takes them. In international politics, however, one state's gain in security often inadvertently threatens others. In explaining British policy on naval disarmament in the interwar period to the Japanese, Ramsey MacDonald said that "Nobody wanted Japan to be insecure."[4] But the problem was not with British desires, but with the consequences of her policy. In earlier periods, too, Britain had needed a navy large enough to keep the shipping lanes open. But such a navy could not avoid being a menace to any other state with a coast that could be raided, trade that could be interdicted, or colonies that could be isolated. When Germany started building a powerful navy before World War I, Britain objected that it could only be an offensive weapon aimed at her. As Sir Edward Grey, the Foreign Secretary, put it to King Edward VII: "If the German Fleet ever becomes superior to ours, the German Army can conquer this country. There is no correspon-

ding risk of this kind to Germany; for however superior our Fleet was, no naval victory could bring us any nearer to Berlin." The English position was half correct: Germany's navy was an anti-British instrument. But the British often overlooked what the Germans knew full well: "in every quarrel with England, German colonies and trade were . . . hostages for England to take." Thus, whether she intended it or not, the British Navy constituted an important instrument of coercion.[5]

## What Makes Cooperation More Likely?

Given this gloomy picture, the obvious question is, why are we not all dead? Or, to put it less starkly, what kinds of variables ameliorate the impact of anarchy and the security dilemma? The workings of several can be seen in terms of the Stag Hunt or repeated plays of the Prisoner's Dilemma. The Prisoner's Dilemma differs from the Stag Hunt in that there is no solution that is in the best interests of all the participants; there are offensive as well as defensive incentives to defect from the coalition with the others; and, if the game is to be played only once, the only rational response is to defect. But if the game is repeated indefinitely, the latter characteristic no longer holds and we can analyze the game in terms similar to those applied to the Stag Hunt. It would be in the interest of each actor to have others deprived of the power to defect; each would be willing to sacrifice this ability if others were similarly restrained. But if the others are not, then it is in the actor's interest to retain the power to defect.[6] The game theory matrices for

---

4  Quoted in Gerald Wheeler, *Prelude to Pearl Harbor* (Columbia: University of Missouri Press 1963), 67.

5  Quoted in Leonard Wainstein, "The Dreadnought Gap," in Robert Art and Kenneth Waltz, eds., *The Use of Force* (Boston: Little, Brown 1971), 155; Raymond Sontag, *European Diplomatic History, 1871-1932* (New York: Appleton-Century-Crofts 1933), 147. The French had made a similar argument 50 years earlier; see James Phinney Baxter III, *The Introduction of the Ironclad Warship* (Cambridge: Harvard University Press 1933), 149. For a more detailed discussion of the security dilemma, see Jervis, *Perception and Misperception in International Politics* (Princeton: Princeton University Press 1976), 62-76.

6  Experimental evidence for this proposition is summarized in James Tedeschi, Barry Schlenker, and Thomas Bonoma, *Conflict, Power, and Games* (Chicago: Aldine 1973), 135-41.

**Stag Hunt**

| B \ A | Cooperate | Defect |
|---|---|---|
| **Cooperate** | 1 / 1 | 2 / 4 |
| **Defect** | 4 / 2 | 3 / 3 |

**Prisoner's Dilemma**

| B \ A | Cooperate | Defect |
|---|---|---|
| **Cooperate** | 2 / 2 | 1 / 4 |
| **Defect** | 4 / 1 | 3 / 3 |

these two situations are given above, with the numbers in the boxes being the order of the actors' preferences.

We can see the logical possibilities by re-phrasing our question: "Given either of the above situations, what makes it more or less likely that the players will cooperate and arrive at CC?" The chances of achieving this outcome will be increased by: (1) anything that increases incentives to cooperate by increasing the gains of mutual cooperation (CC) and/or decreasing the costs the actor will pay if he cooperates and the other does not (CD); (2) anything that decreases the incentives for defecting by decreasing the gains of taking advantage of the other (DC) and/or increasing the costs of mutual noncooperation (DD); (3) anything that increases each side's expectation that the other will cooperate.[7]

### The Costs of Being Exploited (CD)

The fear of being exploited (that is, the cost of CD) most strongly drives the security dilemma; one of the main reasons why international life is not more nasty, brutish, and short is that states are not as vulnerable as men are in a state of nature. People are easy to kill, but as Adam Smith replied to a friend who feared that the Napoleonic Wars would ruin England, "Sir, there is a great deal of ruin in a nation."[8] The easier it is to destroy a state, the greater the reason for it either

to join a larger and more secure unit, or else to be especially suspicious of others, to require a large army, and, if conditions are favorable, to attack at the slightest provocation rather than wait to be attacked. If the failure to eat that day—be it venison or rabbit—means that he will starve, a person is likely to defect in the Stag Hunt even if be really likes venison and has a high level of trust in his colleagues. (Defection is especially likely if the others are also starving or if they know that he is.) By contrast, if the costs of CD are lower, if people are well-fed or states are resilient, they can afford to take a more relaxed view of threats.

A relatively low cost of CD has the effect of transforming the game from one in which both players make their choices simultaneously to one in which an actor can make his choice after the other has moved. He will not have to defect out of fear that the other will, but can wait to see what the other will do. States that can afford to be cheated in a bargain or that cannot be destroyed by a surprise attack can more easily trust others and need not act at the first, and ambiguous, sign of menace. Because they have a margin of time and error, they need not match, or more than match, any others' arms in peacetime. They can mobilize in the prewar period or even at the start of the war itself, and still survive. For example, those who opposed a crash program to develop the H-bomb felt that the U.S. margin of safety was large enough so that even if Russia

---

7 The results of Prisoner's Dilemma games played in the laboratory support this argument. See Anatol Rapoport and Albert Chammah, *Prisoner's Dilemma* (Ann Arbor: University of Michigan Press 1965), 33-50. Also see Robert Axelrod, *Conflict of Interest* (Chicago: Markham 1970), 60-70.

8 Quoted in Bernard Brodie, *Strategy in the Missile Age* (Princeton: Princeton University Press 1959), 6.

managed to gain a lead in the race, America would not be endangered. The program's advocates disagreed: "If we let the Russians get the super first, catastrophe becomes all but certain."[9]

When the costs of CD are tolerable, not only is security easier to attain but, what is even more important here, the relatively low level of arms and relatively passive foreign policy that a status-quo power will be able to adopt are less likely to threaten others. Thus it is easier for status-quo states to act on their common interests if they are hard to conquer. All other things being equal, a world of small states will feel the effects of anarchy much more than a world of large ones. Defensible borders, large size, and protection against sudden attack not only aid the state, but facilitate cooperation that can benefit all states.

Of course, if one state gains invulnerability by being more powerful than most others, the problem will remain because its security provides a base from which it can exploit others. When the price a state will pay for DD is low, it leaves others with few hostages for its good behavior. Others who are more vulnerable will grow apprehensive, which will lead them to acquire more arms and will reduce the chances of cooperation. The best situation is one in which a state will not suffer greatly if others exploit it, for example, by cheating on an arms control agreement (that is, the costs of CD are low); but it will pay a high long-run price if cooperation with the others breaks down—for example, if agreements cease functioning or if there is a long war (that is, the costs of DD are high). The state's invulnerability is then mostly passive; it provides some protection, but it cannot be used to menace others. As we will discuss below, this situation is approximated when it is easier for states to defend themselves than to attack others, or when mutual deterrence obtains because neither side can protect itself.

The differences between highly vulnerable and less vulnerable states are illustrated by the contrasting policies of Britain and Austria after the Napoleonic Wars. Britain's geographic isolation and political stability allowed her to take a fairly relaxed view of disturbances on the Continent. Minor wars and small changes in territory or in the distribution of power did not affect her vital interests. An adversary who was out to overthrow the system could be stopped after he had made his intentions clear. And revolutions within other states were no menace, since they would not set off unrest within England. Austria, surrounded by strong powers, was not so fortunate; her policy had to be more closely attuned to all conflicts. By the time an aggressor-state had clearly shown its colors, Austria would be gravely threatened. And foreign revolutions, be they democratic or nationalistic, would encourage groups in Austria to upset the existing order. So it is not surprising that Metternich propounded the doctrine summarized earlier, which defended Austria's right to interfere in the internal affairs of others, and that British leaders rejected this view. Similarly, Austria wanted the Congress system to be a relatively tight one, regulating most disputes. The British favored a less centralized system. In other words, in order to protect herself, Austria had either to threaten or to harm others, whereas Britain did not. For Austria and her neighbors the security dilemma was acute; for Britain it was not.

The ultimate cost of CD is of course loss of sovereignty. This cost can vary from situation to situation. The lower it is (for instance, because the two states have compatible ideologies, are similar ethnically, have a common culture, or because the citizens of the losing state expect economic benefits), the less the impact of the security dilemma; the greater the costs, the greater the impact of the dilemma. Here is another reason why extreme differences in values and ideologies exacerbate international conflict. . . .

9  Herbert York, *The Advisors: Oppenheimer, Teller, and the Superbomb* (San Francisco: Freeman 1976), 56-60.

### Gains from Cooperation and Costs of a Breakdown (CC and DD)

The main costs of a policy of reacting quickly and severely to increases in the other's arms are not the price of one's own arms, but rather the sacrifice of the potential gains from cooperation (CC) and the increase in the dangers of needless arms races and wars (DD). The greater these costs, the greater the incentives to try cooperation and wait for fairly unambiguous evidence before assuming that the other must be checked by force. Wars would be much more frequent—even if the first choice of all states was the status quo—if they were less risky and costly, and if peaceful intercourse did not provide rich benefits. Ethiopia recently asked for guarantees that the Territory of Afars and Issas would not join a hostile alliance against it when it gained independence. A spokesman for the Territory replied that this was not necessary: Ethiopia "already had the best possible guarantee in the railroad" that links the two countries and provides indispensable revenue for the Territory.[10]

The basic points are well known and so we can move to elaboration. First, most statesmen know that to enter a war is to set off a chain of unpredictable and uncontrollable events. Even if everything they see points to a quick victory, they are likely to hesitate before all the uncertainties. And if the battlefield often produces startling results, so do the council chambers. The state may be deserted by allies or attacked by neutrals. Or the postwar alignment may rob it of the fruits of victory, as happened to Japan in 1895. Second, the domestic costs of wars must be weighed. Even strong states can be undermined by dissatisfaction with the way the war is run and by the necessary mobilization of men and ideas. Memories of such disruptions were one of the main reasons for the era of relative peace that followed the Napoleonic Wars. Liberal statesmen feared that large armies would lead to despotism; conservative leaders feared that wars would lead to revolution. (The other side of this coin is that when there are domestic consequences of foreign conflict that are positively valued, the net cost of conflict is lowered and cooperation becomes more difficult.) Third—turning to the advantages of cooperation—for states with large and diverse economies the gains from economic exchange are rarely if ever sufficient to prevent war. Norman Angell was wrong about World War I being impossible because of economic ties among the powers; and before World War II, the U.S. was Japan's most important trading partner. Fourth, the gains from cooperation can be increased, not only if each side gets more of the traditional values such as wealth, but also if each comes to value the other's well-being positively. Mutual cooperation will then have a double payoff: in addition to the direct gains, there will be the satisfaction of seeing the other prosper.[11]

While high costs of war and gains from cooperation will ameliorate the impact of the security dilemma, they can create a different problem. If the costs are high enough so that DD is the last choice for both sides, the game will shift to "Chicken." This game differs from the Stag Hunt in that each actor seeks to exploit the other; it differs from Prisoner's Dilemma in that both actors share an interest in avoiding mutual noncooperation. In Chicken, if you think the other side is going to defect, you have to cooperate because, although being exploited (CD) is bad, it is not as bad as a total breakdown (DD). As the familiar logic of deterrence shows, the actor must then try to convince his adversary that he is going to stand firm (defect) and that the only way the other can avoid disaster is to back down

---

10  Michael Kaufman, "Tension Increases in French Colony," *New York Times,* July 11, 1976.

11  Experimental support for this argument is summarized in Morton Deutsch, *The Resolution of Conflict* (New Haven: Yale University Press 1973), 181-95.

(cooperate). Commitment, the rationality of irrationality, manipulating the communications system, and pretending not to understand the situation, are among the tactics used to reach this goal. The same logic applies when both sides are enjoying great benefits from cooperation. The side that can credibly threaten to disrupt the relationship unless its demands are met can exploit the other. This situation may not be stable, since the frequent use of threats may be incompatible with the maintenance of a cooperative relationship. Still, de Gaulle's successful threats to break up the Common Market unless his partners acceded to his wishes remind us that the shared benefits of cooperation as well as the shared costs of defection can provide the basis for exploitation. Similarly, one reason for the collapse of the Franco-British entente more than a hundred years earlier was that decision makers on both sides felt confident that their own country could safely pursue a policy that was against the other's interest because the other could not afford to destroy the highly valued relationship.[12] Because statesmen realize that the growth of positive interdependence can provide others with new levers of influence over them, they may resist such developments more than would be expected from the theories that stress the advantages of cooperation.

### Gains from Exploitation (DC)

Defecting not only avoids the danger that a state will be exploited (CD), but brings positive advantages by exploiting the other (DC). The lower these possible gains, the greater the chances of cooperation. Even a relatively satisfied state can be tempted to expand by the hope of gaining major values. The temptation will be less when the state sees other ways of reaching its goals, and/or places a low value on what exploitation could bring. The gains may be low either because the immediate advantage provided by DC (for example, having more arms than the other side) cannot be translated into a political advantage (for example, gains in territory), or because the political advantage itself is not highly valued. For instance, a state may not seek to annex additional territory because the latter lacks raw materials, is inhabited by people of a different ethnic group, would be costly to garrison, or would be hard to assimilate without disturbing domestic politics and values. A state can reduce the incentives that another state has to attack it, by not being a threat to the latter and by providing goods and services that would be lost were the other to attempt exploitation.

Even where the direct advantages of DC are great, other considerations can reduce the net gain. Victory as well as defeat can set off undesired domestic changes within the state. Exploitation has at times been frowned upon by the international community, thus reducing the prestige of a state that engages in it. Or others might in the future be quicker to see the state as a menace to them, making them more likely to arm, and to oppose it later. Thus, Bismarck's attempts to get other powers to cooperate with him in maintaining the status quo after 1871 were made more difficult by the widely-held mistrust of him that grew out of his earlier aggressions.[13]

### The Probability That the Other Will Cooperate

The variables discussed so far influence the payoffs for each of the four possible outcomes.

---

12 Roger Bullen, *Palmerston, Guizot, and the Collapse of the Entente Cordiale* (London: Athlone Press 1974), 81, 88, 93, 212. For a different view of this case, see Stanley Mellon, "Entente, Diplomacy, and Fantasy," *Reviews in European History*, II (September 1976), 376-80.

13 Similarly, a French diplomat has argued that "the worst result of Louis XIV's abandonment of our traditional policy was the distrust it aroused towards us abroad." Jules Cambon, "The Permanent Bases of French Foreign Policy," *Foreign Affairs*, VIII (January 1930), 179.

To decide what to do, the state has to go further and calculate the expected value of cooperating or defecting. Because such calculations involve estimating the probability that the other will cooperate, the state will have to judge how the variables discussed so far act on the other. To encourage the other to cooperate, a state may try to manipulate these variables. It can lower the other's incentives to defect by decreasing what it could gain by exploiting the state (DC)—the details would be similar to those discussed in the previous paragraph—and it can raise the costs of deadlock (DD). But if the state cannot make DD the worst outcome for the other, coercion is likely to be ineffective in the short run because the other can respond by refusing to cooperate, and dangerous in the long run because the other is likely to become convinced that the state is aggressive. So the state will have to concentrate on making cooperation more attractive. One way to do this is to decrease the costs the other will pay if it cooperates and the state defects (CD). Thus, the state could try to make the other less vulnerable. It was for this reason that in the late 1950's and early 1960's some American defense analysts argued that it would be good for both sides if the Russians developed hardened missiles. Of course decreasing the other's vulnerability also decreases the state's ability to coerce it, and opens the possibility that the other will use this protection as a shield behind which to engage in actions inimical to the state. But by sacrificing some ability to harm the other, the state can increase the chances of mutually beneficial cooperation. . . .

Statesmen who do not understand the security dilemma will think that the money spent is the only cost of building up their arms. This belief removes one important restraint on arms spending. Furthermore, it is also likely to lead states to set their security requirements too high. Since they do not understand that trying to increase one's security can actually decrease it, they will overestimate the amount of security that is attainable; they will think that when in doubt they can "play it safe" by increasing their arms. Thus it is very likely that two states which support the status quo but do not understand the security dilemma will end up, if not in a war, then at least in a relationship of higher conflict than is required by the objective situation.

The belief that an increase in military strength always leads to an increase in security is often linked to the belief that the only route to security is through military strength. As a consequence, a whole range of meliorative policies will be downgraded. Decision makers who do not believe that adopting a more conciliatory posture, meeting the other's legitimate grievances, or developing mutual gains from cooperation can increase their state's security, will not devote much attention or effort to these possibilities.

On the other hand, a heightened sensitivity to the security dilemma makes it more likely that the state will treat an aggressor as though it were an insecure defender of the status quo. Partly because of their views about the causes of World War I, the British were predisposed to believe that Hitler sought only the rectification of legitimate and limited grievances and that security could best be gained by constructing an equitable international system. As a result they pursued a policy which, although well designed to avoid the danger of creating unnecessary conflict with a status-quo Germany, helped destroy Europe.

### *Geography, Commitments, Beliefs, and Security Through Expansion*

A final consideration does not easily fit in the matrix we have been using, although it can be seen as an aspect of vulnerability and of the costs of CD. Situations vary in the ease or difficulty with which all states can simultaneously achieve a high degree of security. The influence of military technology on this variable is the subject of the next section. Here we want to treat the impact of beliefs, geography, and commitments (many of which can be considered to be modifications of geography, since they bind states to defend areas outside their homelands). In the crowded continent of Europe, security requirements were hard to mesh. Being surrounded by powerful states, Germany's problem—or the problem created by Germany—was always great and was even worse when her relations with both France and Russia were bad, such as before World War I. In that case, even a status-quo Germany, if she could not change the political situation, would almost have been forced to adopt something like the Schlieffen Plan. Because she could not hold off both of her enemies, she had to be prepared to defeat one quickly and then deal with the other in a more leisurely fashion. If France or Russia stayed out of a war between the other state and Germany, they would allow Germany to dominate the Continent (even if that was not Germany's aim). They therefore had to deny Germany this ability, thus making Germany less secure. Although Germany's arrogant and erratic behavior, coupled with the desire for an unreasonably high level of security (which amounted to the desire to escape from her geographic plight), compounded the problem, even wise German statesmen would have been hard put to gain a high degree of security without alarming their neighbors.

A similar situation arose for France after World War I. She was committed to protecting her allies in Eastern Europe, a commitment she could meet only by taking the offensive against Germany. But since there was no way to guarantee that France might not later seek expansion, a France that could successfully launch an attack in response to a German move into Eastern Europe would constitute a potential danger to German core values. Similarly, a United States credibly able to threaten retaliation with strategic nuclear weapons if the Soviet Union attacks Western Europe also constitutes a menace, albeit a reduced one, to the Soviet ability to maintain the status quo. The incompatibility of these security requirements is not complete. Herman Kahn is correct in arguing that the United States could have Type II deterrence (the ability to deter a major Soviet provocation) without gaining first-strike capability because the expected Soviet retaliation following an American strike could be great enough to deter the U.S. from attacking unless the U.S. believed it would suffer enormous deprivation (for instance, the loss of Europe) if it did not strike.[14] Similarly, the Franco-German military balance could have been such that France could successfully attack Germany if the latter's armies were embroiled in Eastern Europe, but could not defeat a Germany that was free to devote all her resources to defending herself. But this delicate balance is very hard to achieve, especially because states usually calculate conservatively. Therefore, such a solution is not likely to be available.

For the United States, the problem posed by the need to protect Europe is an exception. Throughout most of its history, this country has been in a much more favorable position: relatively self-sufficient and secure from invasion, it has not only been able to get security relatively cheaply, but by doing so, did not menace others.[15] But ambitions and commitments have changed this situation. After the American conquest of the Philippines, "neither the United States nor Japan could assure protection for their territories by military and naval means without compromising the defenses of the other. This problem would plague American and Japanese statesmen down to 1941."[16] Furthermore, to the extent that Japan could protect herself, she could

---

14 Kahn, *On Thermonuclear War* (Princeton: Princeton University Press 1960), 138-60. It should be noted that the French example is largely hypothetical because France had no intention of fulfilling her obligations once Germany became strong.

15 Wolfers, chap. 15; C. Vann Woodward, "The Age of Reinterpretation," *American Historical Review,* Vol. 67 (October 1960), 1-19.

16 William Braisted, *The United States Navy in the Pacific, 1897-1909* (Austin: University of Texas Press 1958), 240.

resist American threats to go to war if Japan did not respect China's independence. These complications were minor compared to those that followed World War II. A world power cannot help but have the ability to harm many others that is out of proportion to the others' ability to harm it.

Britain had been able to gain security without menacing others to a greater degree than the Continental powers, though to a lesser one than the United States. But the acquisition of colonies and a dependence on foreign trade sacrificed her relative invulnerability of being an island. Once she took India, she had to consider Russia as a neighbor; the latter was expanding in Central Asia, thus making it much more difficult for both countries to feel secure. The need to maintain reliable sea lanes to India meant that no state could be allowed to menace South Africa and, later, Egypt. But the need to protect these two areas brought new fears, new obligations, and new security requirements that conflicted with those of other European nations. Furthermore, once Britain needed a flow of imports during both peace and wartime, she required a navy that could prevent a blockade. A navy sufficient for that task could not help but be a threat to any other state that had valuable trade.

A related problem is raised by the fact that defending the status quo often means protecting more than territory. Nonterritorial interests, norms, and the structure of the international system must be maintained. If all status-quo powers agree on these values and interpret them in compatible ways, problems will be minimized. But the potential for conflict is great, and the policies followed are likely to exacerbate the security dilemma. The greater the range of interests that have to be protected, the more likely it is that national efforts to maintain the status quo will clash. As a French spokesman put it in 1930: "Security! The term signifies more indeed than the maintenance of a people's homeland, or even of their territories beyond the seas. It also means the maintenance of the world's respect for them, the maintenance of their economic interests, everything in a word, which goes to make up the grandeur, the life itself, of the nation."[17] When security is thought of in this sense, it almost automatically has a competitive connotation. It involves asserting one state's will over others, showing a high degree of leadership if not dominance, and displaying a prickly demeanor. The resulting behavior will almost surely clash with that of others who define their security in the same way.

The problem will be almost insoluble if statesmen believe that their security requires the threatening or attacking of others. "That which stops growing begins to rot," declared a minister to Catherine the Great.[18] More common is the belief that if the other is secure, it will be emboldened to act against one's own state's interests, and the belief that in a war it will not be enough for the state to protect itself: it must be able to take the war to the other's homeland. These convictions make it very difficult for status-quo states to develop compatible security policies, for they lead the state to conclude that its security requires that others be rendered insecure.

In other cases, "A country engaged in a war of defense might be obliged for strategic reasons to assume the offensive," as a French delegate to an interwar disarmament conference put it.[19] That was the case for France in 1799:

> The Directory's political objectives were essentially defensive, for the French wanted only

---

17 Cambon, 185.

18 Quoted in Adam Ulam, *Expansion and Co-Existence* (New York: Praeger 1968), 5. In 1920 the U.S. Navy's General Board similarly declared "A nation must advance or retrocede in world position." Quoted in William Braisted, *The United States Navy in the Pacific, 1909-1922* (Austin: University of Texas Press 1971), 488.

19 Quoted in Marion Boggs, *Attempts to Define and Limit "Aggressive" Armament in Diplomacy and Strategy* (Columbia: University of Missouri Studies, XVI, No. 1, 1941), 41.

to protect the Republic from invasion and pre-serve the security and territory of the satellite regimes in Holland, Switzerland, and Italy. French leaders sought no new conquests; they wanted only to preserve the earlier gains of the Revolution. The Directory believed, however, that only a military offensive could enable the nation to achieve its defensive political objective. By inflicting rapid and decisive defeats upon one or more members of the coalition, the directors hoped to rupture allied unity and force individual powers to seek a separate peace.[20]

It did not matter to the surrounding states that France was not attacking because she was greedy, but because she wanted to be left in peace. Unless there was some way her neighbors could provide France with an alternate route to her goal, France had to go to war.

## Offense, Defense, and the Security Dilemma

Another approach starts with the central point of the security dilemma—that an increase in one state's security decreases the security of others—and examines the conditions under which this proposition holds. Two crucial variables are involved: whether defensive weapons and policies can be distinguished from offensive ones, and whether the defense or the offense has the advantage. The definitions are not always clear, and many cases are difficult to judge, but these two variables shed a great deal of light on the question of whether status-quo powers will adopt compatible security policies. All the variables discussed so far leave the heart of the problem untouched. But when defensive weapons differ from offensive ones, it is possible for a state to make itself more secure without making

others less secure. And when the defense has the advantage over the offense, a large increase in one state's security only slightly decreases the security of the others, and status-quo powers can all enjoy a high level of security and largely escape from the state of nature.

### Offense-Defense Balance

When we say that the offense has the advantage, we simply mean that it is easier to destroy the other's army and take its territory than it is to defend one's own. When the defense has the advantage, it is easier to protect and to hold than it is to move forward, destroy, and take. If effective defenses can be erected quickly, an attacker may be able to keep territory he has taken in an initial victory. Thus, the dominance of the defense made it very hard for Britain and France to push Germany out of France in World War I. But when superior defenses are difficult for an aggressor to improvise on the battlefield and must be constructed during peacetime, they provide no direct assistance to him.

The security dilemma is at its most vicious when commitments, strategy, or technology dictate that the only route to security lies through expansion. Status-quo powers must then act like aggressors; the fact that they would gladly agree to forego the opportunity for expansion in return for guarantees for their security has no implications for their behavior. Even if expansion is not sought as a goal in itself, there will be quick and drastic changes in the distribution of territory and influence. Conversely, when the defense has the advantage, status-quo states can make themselves more secure without gravely endangering others.[21] Indeed, if the defense has enough of an advantage and if the states are of roughly equal size, not only will the security dilemma cease to

---

20 Steven Ross, *European Diplomatic History, 1789-1815* (Garden City, N.Y.: Doubleday 1969), 194.

21 Thus, when Wolfers, 126, argues that a status-quo state that settles for rough equality of power with its adversary, rather than seeking preponderance, may be able to convince the other to reciprocate by showing that it wants only to protect itself, not menace the other, he assumes that the defense has an advantage.

inhibit status-quo states from cooperating, but aggression will be next to impossible, thus rendering international anarchy relatively unimportant. If states cannot conquer each other, then the lack of sovereignty, although it presents problems of collective goods in a number of areas, no longer forces states to devote their primary attention to self-preservation. Although, if force were not usable, there would be fewer restraints on the use of nonmilitary instruments, these are rarely powerful enough to threaten the vital interests of a major state.

Two questions of the offense-defense balance can be separated. First, does the state have to spend more or less than one dollar on defensive forces to offset each dollar spent by the other side on forces that could be used to attack? If the state has one dollar to spend on increasing its security, should it put it into offensive or defensive forces? Second, with a given inventory of forces, is it better to attack or to defend? Is there an incentive to strike first or to absorb the other's blow? These two aspects are often linked: if each dollar spent on offense can overcome each dollar spent on defense, and if both sides have the same defense budgets, then both are likely to build offensive forces and find it attractive to attack rather than to wait for the adversary to strike.

These aspects affect the security dilemma in different ways. The first has its greatest impact on arms races. If the defense has the advantage, and if the status-quo powers have reasonable subjective security requirements, they can probably avoid an arms race. Although an increase in one side's arms and security will still decrease the other's security, the former's increase will be larger than the latter's decrease. So if one side increases its arms, the other can bring its security back up to its previous level by adding a smaller amount to its forces. And if the first side reacts to this change, its increase will also be smaller than

the stimulus that produced it. Thus a stable equilibrium will be reached. Shifting from dynamics to statics, each side can be quite secure with forces roughly equal to those of the other. Indeed, if the defense is much more potent than the offense, each side can be willing to have forces much smaller than the other's, and can be indifferent to a wide range of the other's defense policies.

The second aspect—whether it is better to attack or to defend—influences short-run stability. When the offense has the advantage, a state's reaction to international tension will increase the chances of war. The incentives for preemption and the "reciprocal fear of surprise attack" in this situation have been made clear by analyses of the dangers that exist when two countries have first-strike capabilities.[22] There is no way for the state to increase its security without menacing, or even attacking, the other. Even Bismarck, who once called preventive war "committing suicide from fear of death," said that "no government, if it regards war as inevitable even if it does not want it, would be so foolish as to leave to the enemy the choice of time and occasion and to wait for the moment which is most convenient for the enemy."[23] In another arena, the same dilemma applies to the policeman in a dark alley confronting a suspected criminal who appears to be holding a weapon. Though racism may indeed be present, the security dilemma can account for many of the tragic shootings of innocent people in the ghettos.

Beliefs about the course of a war in which the offense has the advantage further deepen the security dilemma. When there are incentives to strike first, a successful attack will usually so weaken the other side that victory will be relatively quick, bloodless, and decisive. It is in these periods when conquest is possible and attractive that states consolidate power by

---

22 Thomas Schelling, *The Strategy of Conflict* (New York: Oxford University Press 1963), chap. 9.
23 Quoted in Fritz Fischer, *War of Illusions* (New York: Norton 1975), 377, 461.

destroying the feudal barons—and expand externally. There are several consequences that decrease the chance of cooperation among status-quo states. First, war will be profitable for the winner. The costs will be low and the benefits high. Of course, losers will suffer; the fear of losing could induce states to try to form stable cooperative arrangements, but the temptation of victory will make this particularly difficult. Second, because wars are expected to be both frequent and short, there will be incentives for high levels of arms, and quick and strong reaction to the other's increases in arms. The state cannot afford to wait until there is unambiguous evidence that the other is building new weapons. Even large states that have faith in their economic strength cannot wait, because the war will be over before their products can reach the army. Third, when wars are quick, states will have to recruit allies in advance.[24] Without the opportunity for bargaining and realignments during the opening stages of hostilities, peacetime diplomacy loses a degree of the fluidity that facilitates balance-of-power policies. Because alliances must be secured during peacetime, the international system is more likely to become bipolar. It is hard to say whether war therefore becomes more or less likely, but this bipolarity increases tension between the two camps and makes it harder for status-quo states to gain the benefits of cooperation. Fourth, if wars are frequent, statesmen's perceptual thresholds will be adjusted accordingly and they will be quick to perceive ambiguous evidence as indicating that others are aggressive. Thus, there will be more cases of status-quo powers arming against each other in the incorrect belief that the other is hostile.

When the defense has the advantage, all the foregoing is reversed. The state that fears attack does not pre-empt—since that would be a wasteful use of its military resources—but rather prepares to receive an attack. Doing so does not decrease the security of others, and several states can do it simultaneously; the situation will therefore be stable, and status-quo powers will be able to cooperate. When Herman Kahn argues that ultimatums "are vastly too dangerous to give because . . . they are quite likely to touch off a preemptive strike,"[25] he incorrectly assumes that it is always advantageous to strike first.

More is involved than short-run dynamics. When the defense is dominant, wars are likely to become stalemates and can be won only at enormous cost. Relatively small and weak states can hold off larger and stronger ones, or can deter attack by raising the costs of conquest to an unacceptable level. States then approach equality in what they can do to each other. Like the .45-caliber pistol in the American West, fortifications were the "great equalizer" in some periods. Changes in the status quo are less frequent and cooperation is more common wherever the security dilemma is thereby reduced.

Many of these arguments can be illustrated by the major powers' policies in the periods preceding the two world wars. Bismarck's wars surprised statesmen by showing that the offense had the advantage, and by being quick, relatively cheap, and quite decisive. Falling into a common error, observers projected this pattern into the future.[26] The resulting expectations had several effects. First, states sought semi-permanent allies. In the early stages of the Franco-Prussian War,

---

24 George Quester, *Offense and Defense in the International System* (New York: John Wiley 1977), 105-6; Sontag, 4-5.

25 Kahn, 211 (also see 144).

26 For a general discussion of such mistaken learning from the past, see Jervis, chap. 6. The important and still not completely understood question of why this belief formed and was maintained throughout the war is examined in Bernard Brodie, *War and Politics* (New York: Macmillan 1973), 262-70; Brodie, "Technological Change, Strategic Doctrine, and Political Outcomes," in Klaus Knorr, ed., *Historical Dimensions of National Security Problems* (Lawrence: University Press of Kansas 1976), 290-92; and Douglas Porch, "The French Army and the Spirit of the Offensive, 1900-14," in Brian Bond and Ian Roy, eds., *War and Society* (New York: Holmes & Meier 1975), 117-43.

Napoleon III had thought that there would be plenty of time to recruit Austria to his side. Now, others were not going to repeat this mistake. Second, defense budgets were high and reacted quite sharply to increases on the other side. It is not surprising that Richardson's theory of arms races fits this period well. Third, most decision makers thought that the next European war would not cost much blood and treasure.[27] That is one reason why war was generally seen as inevitable and why mass opinion was so bellicose. Fourth, once war seemed likely, there were strong pressures to preempt. Both sides believed that whoever moved first could penetrate the other deep enough to disrupt mobilization and thus gain an insurmountable advantage. (There was no such belief about the use of naval forces. Although Churchill made an ill-advised speech saying that if German ships "do not come out and fight in time of war they will be dug out like rats in a hole,"[28] everyone knew that submarines, mines, and coastal fortifications made this impossible. So at the start of the war each navy prepared to defend itself rather than attack, and the short-run destabilizing forces that launched the armies toward each other did not operate.)[29] Furthermore each side knew that the other saw the situation the same way, thus increasing the perceived danger that the other would attack, and giving each added reasons to precipitate a war if conditions seemed favorable. In the long and the short run, there were thus both offensive and defensive incentives to strike. This situation casts light on the common question about German motives in 1914: "Did Germany unleash the war

deliberately to become a world power or did she support Austria merely to defend a weakening ally," thereby protecting her own position?[30] To some extent, this question is misleading. Because of the perceived advantage of the offense, war was seen as the best route both to gaining expansion and to avoiding drastic loss of influence. There seemed to be no way for Germany merely to retain and safeguard her existing position.

Of course the war showed these beliefs to have been wrong on all points. Trenches and machine guns gave the defense an overwhelming advantage. The fighting became deadlocked and produced horrendous casualties. It made no sense for the combatants to bleed themselves to death. If they had known the power of the defense beforehand, they would have rushed for their own trenches rather than for the enemy's territory. Each side could have done this without increasing the other's incentives to strike. War might have broken out anyway, just as DD is a possible outcome of Chicken, but at least the pressures of time and the fear of allowing the other to get the first blow would not have contributed to this end. And, had both sides known the costs of the war, they would have negotiated much more seriously. . . .

*Technology and Geography.* Technology and geography are the two main factors that determine whether the offense or the defense has the advantage. As Brodie notes, "On the tactical level, as a rule, few physical factors favor the attacker but many favor the defender. The defender usually has the advantage of cover. He characteristically fires from behind some form

---

27  Some were not so optimistic. Gray's remark is well-known: "The lamps are going out all over Europe; we shall not see them lit again in our life-time." The German Prime Minister, Bethmann Hollweg, also feared the consequences of the war. But the controlling view was that it would certainly pay for the winner.

28  Quoted in Martin Gilbert, *Winston S. Churchill*, III, *The Challenge of War, 1914-1916* (Boston: Houghton Mifflin 1971), 84.

29  Quester, 98-99. Robert Art, *The Influence of Foreign Policy on Seapower*, II (Beverly Hills: Sage Professional Papers in International Studies Series, 1973), 14-18, 26-28.

30  Konrad Jarausch, "The Illusion of Limited War: Chancellor Bethmann Hollweg's Calculated Risk, July 1914," *Central European History*, II (March 1969), 50.

of shelter while his opponent crosses open ground."[31] Anything that increases the amount of ground the attacker has to cross, or impedes his progress across it, or makes him more vulnerable while crossing, increases the advantage accruing to the defense. When states are separated by barriers that produce these effects, the security dilemma is eased, since both can have forces adequate for defense without being able to attack. Impenetrable barriers would actually prevent war; in reality, decision makers have to settle for a good deal less. Buffer zones slow the attacker's progress; they thereby give the defender time to prepare, increase problems of logistics, and reduce the number of soldiers available for the final assault. At the end of the 19th century, Arthur Balfour noted Afghanistan's "non-conducting" qualities. "So long as it possesses few roads, and no railroads, it will be impossible for Russia to make effective use of her great numerical superiority at any point immediately vital to the Empire." The Russians valued buffers for the same reasons; it is not surprising that when Persia was being divided into Russian and British spheres of influence some years later, the Russians sought assurances that the British would refrain from building potentially menacing railroads in their sphere. Indeed, since railroad construction radically altered the abilities of countries to defend themselves and to attack others, many diplomatic notes and much intelligence activity in the late 19th century centered on this subject.[32]

Oceans, large rivers, and mountain ranges serve the same function as buffer zones. Being hard to cross, they allow defense against superior numbers. The defender has merely to stay on his side of the barrier and so can utilize all the men he can bring up to it. The attacker's men, however, can cross only a few at a time, and they are very vulnerable when doing so. If all states were self-sufficient islands, anarchy would be much less of a problem. A small investment in shore defenses and a small army would be sufficient to repel invasion. Only very weak states would be vulnerable, and only very large ones could menace others. As noted above, the United States, and to a lesser extent Great Britain, have partly been able to escape from the state of nature because their geographical positions approximated this ideal.

Although geography cannot be changed to conform to borders, borders can and do change to conform to geography. Borders across which an attack is easy tend to be unstable. States living within them are likely to expand or be absorbed. Frequent wars are almost inevitable since attacking will often seem the best way to protect what one has. This process will at least slow down, when the state's borders reach—by expansion or contraction—a line of natural obstacles. Security without attack will then be possible. Furthermore, these lines constitute salient solutions to bargaining problems and, to the extent that they are barriers to migration, are likely to divide ethnic groups, thereby raising the costs and lowering the incentives for conquest.

Attachment to one's state and its land reinforce one quasi-geographical aid to the defense. Conquest usually becomes more difficult the deeper the attacker pushes into the other's territory. Nationalism spurs the defenders to fight harder; advancing not only lengthens the attacker's supply lines, but takes him through unfamiliar and often devastated lands that require troops for garrison duty. These stabilizing

---

31 Brodie, 179.

32 Arthur Balfour, "Memorandum," Committee on Imperial Defence, April 30, 1903, pp. 2-3; see the telegrams by Sir Arthur Nicolson, in G. P. Gooch and Harold Temperley, eds., *British Documents on the Origins of the War*, Vol. 4 (London: H.M.S.O. 1929), 429, 524. These barriers do not prevent the passage of long-range aircraft; but even in the air, distance usually aids the defender.

dynamics will not operate, however, if the defender's war material is situated near its borders, or if the people do not care about their state, but only about being on the winning side. In such cases, positive feedback will be at work and initial defeats will be insurmountable.[33]

Imitating geography, men have tried to create barriers. Treaties may provide for demilitarized zones on both sides of the border, although such zones will rarely be deep enough to provide more than warning. Even this was not possible in Europe, but the Russians adopted a gauge for their railroads that was broader than that of the neighboring states, thereby complicating the logistics problems of any attacker—including Russia.

Perhaps the most ambitious and at least temporarily successful attempts to construct a system that would aid the defenses of both sides were the interwar naval treaties, as they affected Japanese-American relations. As mentioned earlier, the problem was that the United States could not defend the Philippines without denying Japan the ability to protect her home islands.[34] (In 1941 this dilemma became insoluble when Japan sought to extend her control to Malaya and the Dutch East Indies. If the Philippines had been invulnerable, they could have provided a secure base from which the U.S. could interdict Japanese shipping between the homeland and the areas she was trying to conquer.) In the 1920's and early 1930's each side would have been willing to grant the other security for its possessions in return for a reciprocal grant, and the Washington Naval Conference agreements were designed to approach this goal. As a Japanese diplomat later put it, their country's "fundamental principle" was to have "a strength insufficient for attack and adequate for defense."[35] Thus, Japan agreed in 1922 to accept a navy only three-fifths as large as that of the United States, and the U.S. agreed not to fortify its Pacific islands.[36] (Japan had earlier been forced to agree not to fortify the islands she had taken from Germany in World War I.) Japan's navy would not be large enough to defeat America's anywhere other than close to the home islands. Although the Japanese could still take the Philippines, not only would they be unable to move farther, but they might be weakened enough by their efforts to be vulnerable to counterattack. Japan, however, gained security. An American attack was rendered more difficult because the American bases were unprotected and because, until 1930, Japan was allowed unlimited numbers of cruisers, destroyers, and submarines that could weaken the American fleet as it made its way across the ocean.[37]

The other major determinant of the offense-defense balance is technology. When weapons are highly vulnerable, they must be employed before they are attacked. Others can remain quite invulnerable in their bases. The former characteristics are embodied in unprotected missiles and many kinds of bombers. (It should be noted that it is not vulnerability *per se* that is crucial, but the location of the vulnerability. Bombers and missiles that are easy to destroy only after having been launched toward their targets do not create destabilizing dynamics.) Incentives to

---

33 See, for example, the discussion of warfare among Chinese warlords in Hsi-Sheng Chi, "The Chinese Warlord System as an International System," in Morton Kaplan, ed., *New Approaches to International Relations* (New York: St. Martin's 1968), 405-25.

34 Some American decision makers, including military officers, thought that the best way out of the dilemma was to abandon the Philippines.

35 Quoted in Elting Morrison, *Turmoil and Tradition: A Study of the Life and Times of Henry L. Stimson* (Boston: Houghton Mifflin 1960), 326.

36 The U.S. "refused to consider limitations on Hawaiian defenses, since these works posed no threat to Japan." Braisted, 612.

37 That is part of the reason why the Japanese admirals strongly objected when the civilian leaders decided to accept a seven-to-ten ratio in lighter craft in 1930. Stephen Pelz, *Race to Pearl Harbor* (Cambridge: Harvard University Press 1974), 3.

strike first are usually absent for naval forces that are threatened by a naval attack. Like missiles in hardened silos, they are usually well protected when in their bases. Both sides can then simultaneously be prepared to defend themselves successfully.

In ground warfare under some conditions, forts, trenches, and small groups of men in prepared positions can hold off large numbers of attackers. Less frequently, a few attackers can storm the defenses. By and large, it is a contest between fortifications and supporting light weapons on the one hand, and mobility and heavier weapons that clear the way for the attack on the other. As the erroneous views held before the two world wars show, there is no simple way to determine which is dominant. "[T]hese oscillations are not smooth and predictable like those of a swinging pendulum. They are uneven in both extent and time. Some occur in the course of a single battle or campaign, others in the course of a war, still others during a series of wars." Longer-term oscillations can also be detected:

The early Gothic age, from the twelfth to the late thirteenth century, with its wonderful cathedrals and fortified places, was a period during which the attackers in Europe generally met serious and increasing difficulties, because the improvement in the strength of fortresses outran the advance in the power of destruction. Later, with the spread of firearms at the end of the fifteenth century, old fortresses lost their power to resist. An age ensued during which the offense possessed, apart from short-term setbacks, new advantages. Then, during the seventeenth century, especially after about 1660, and until at least the outbreak of the War of the Austrian Succession in 1740, the defense regained much of the ground it had lost since the great medieval fortresses had proved unable to meet the bombardment of the new and more numerous artillery.[38]

Another scholar has continued the argument: "The offensive gained an advantage with new forms of heavy mobile artillery in the nineteenth century, but the stalemate of World War I created the impression that the defense again had an advantage; the German invasion in World War II, however, indicated the offensive superiority of highly mechanized armies in the field."[39]

The situation today with respect to conventional weapons is unclear. Until recently it was believed that tanks and tactical air power gave the attacker an advantage. The initial analyses of the 1973 Arab-Israeli war indicated that new anti-tank and anti-aircraft weapons have restored the primacy of the defense. These weapons are cheap, easy to use, and can destroy a high proportion of the attacking vehicles and planes that are sighted. It then would make sense for a status-quo power to buy lots of $20,000 missiles rather than buy a few half-million dollar tanks and multi-million dollar fighter-bombers. Defense would be possible even against a large and well-equipped force; states that care primarily about self-protection would not need to engage in arms races. But further examinations of the new technologies and the history of the October War cast doubt on these optimistic conclusions and leave us unable to render any firm judgment.[40]

---

38 John Nef, *War and Human Progress* (New York: Norton 1963), 185. Also see *ibid.*, 237, 242-43, and 323; C. W. Oman, *The Art of War in the Middle Ages* (Ithaca, N.Y.: Cornell University Press 1953), 70-72; John Beeler, *Warfare in Feudal Europe, 730-1200* (Ithaca, N.Y.: Cornell University Press 1971), 212-14; Michael Howard, *War in European History* (London: Oxford University Press 1976), 33-37.

39 Quincy Wright, *A Study of War* (abridged ed.; Chicago: University of Chicago Press 1964), 142. Also see 63-70, 74-75. There are important exceptions to these generalizations—the American Civil War, for instance, falls in the middle of the period Wright says is dominated by the offense.

40 Geoffrey Kemp, Robert Pfaltzgraff, and Uri Ra'anan, eds., *The Other Arms Race* (Lexington, Mass.: D.C. Heath 1975); James Foster, "The Future of Conventional Arms Control," *Policy Sciences,* No. 8 (Spring 1977), 1-19.

Concerning nuclear weapons, it is generally agreed that defense is impossible—a triumph not of the offense, but of deterrence. Attack makes no sense, not because it can be beaten off, but because the attacker will be destroyed in turn. In terms of the questions under consideration here, the result is the equivalent of the primacy of the defense. First, security is relatively cheap. Less than one percent of the G.N.P. is devoted to deterring a direct attack on the United States; most of it is spent on acquiring redundant systems to provide a lot of insurance against the worst conceivable contingencies. Second, both sides can simultaneously gain security in the form of second-strike capability. Third, and related to the foregoing, second-strike capability can be maintained in the face of wide variations in the other side's military posture. There is no purely military reason why each side has to react quickly and strongly to the other's increases in arms. Any spending that the other devotes to trying to achieve first-strike capability can be neutralized by the state's spending much smaller sums on protecting its second-strike capability. Fourth, there are no incentives to strike first in a crisis.

Important problems remain, of course. Both sides have interests that go well beyond defense of the homeland. The protection of these interests creates conflicts even if neither side desires expansion. Furthermore, the shift from defense to deterrence has greatly increased the importance and perceptions of resolve. Security now rests on each side's belief that the other would prefer to run high risks of total destruction rather than sacrifice its vital interests. Aspects of the security dilemma thus appear in a new form. Are weapons procurements used as an index of resolve? Must they be so used? If one side fails to respond to the other's buildup, will it appear weak and thereby invite predation? Can both sides simultaneously have images of high resolve or is there a zero-sum element involved? Although these problems are real, they are not as severe as those in the prenuclear era: there are many indices of resolve, and states do not so

much judge images of resolve in the abstract as ask how likely it is that the other will stand firm in a particular dispute. Since states are most likely to stand firm on matters which concern them most, it is quite possible for both to demonstrate their resolve to protect their own security simultaneously.

### Offense-Defense Differentiation

The other major variable that affects how strongly the security dilemma operates is whether weapons and policies that protect the state also provide the capability for attack. If they do not, the basic postulate of the security dilemma no longer applies. A state can increase its own security without decreasing that of others. The advantage of the defense can only ameliorate the security dilemma. A differentiation between offensive and defensive stances comes close to abolishing it. Such differentiation does not mean, however, that all security problems will be abolished. If the offense has the advantage, conquest and aggression will still be possible. And if the offense's advantage is great enough, status-quo powers may find it too expensive to protect themselves by defensive forces and decide to procure offensive weapons even though this will menace others. Furthermore, states will still have to worry that even if the other's military posture shows that it is peaceful now, it may develop aggressive intentions in the future.

Assuming that the defense is at least as potent as offense, the differentiation between them allows status-quo states to behave in ways that are clearly different from those of aggressors. Three beneficial consequences follow. First, status-quo powers can identify each other, thus laying the foundations for cooperation. Conflicts growing out of the mistaken belief that the other side is expansionist will be less frequent. Second, status-quo states will obtain advance warning when others plan aggression. Before a state can attack, it has to develop and deploy offensive weapons. If procurement of these weapons cannot be disguised and takes a fair amount of time, as it almost always does, a status-quo state will have the time to take countermeasures. It need not maintain a high level of defensive arms as long as its potential adversaries are adopting a peaceful posture. (Although being so armed should not, with the one important exception noted below, alarm other status-quo powers.) States do, in fact, pay special attention to actions that they believe would not be taken by a status-quo state because they feel that states exhibiting such behavior are aggressive. Thus the seizure or development of transportation facilities will alarm others more if these facilities have no commercial value, and therefore can only be wanted for military reasons. In 1906, the British rejected a Russian protest about their activities in a district of Persia by claiming that this area was "only of [strategic] importance [to the Russians] if they wished to attack the Indian frontier, or to put pressure upon us by making us think that they intend to attack it."[41]

The same inferences are drawn when a state acquires more weapons than observers feel are needed for defense. Thus, the Japanese spokesman at the 1930 London naval conference said that his country was alarmed by the American refusal to give Japan a 70 percent ratio (in place of a 60 percent ratio) in heavy cruisers: "As long as America held that ten percent advantage, it was possible for her to attack. So when America insisted on sixty percent instead of seventy percent, the idea would exist that they were trying to keep that possibility, and the Japanese people could not accept that."[42] Similarly, when Mussolini told Chamberlain in January 1939 that Hitler's

arms program was motivated by defensive considerations, the Prime Minister replied that "German military forces were now so strong as to make it impossible for any Power or combination of Powers to attack her successfully. She could not want any further armaments for defensive purposes; what then did she want them for?"[43]

Of course these inferences can be wrong—as they are especially likely to be because states underestimate the degree to which they menace others.[44] And when they are wrong, the security dilemma is deepened. Because the state thinks it has received notice that the other is aggressive, its own arms building will be less restrained and the chances of cooperation will be decreased. But the dangers of incorrect inferences should not obscure the main point: when offensive and defensive postures are different, much of the uncertainty about the other's intentions that contributes to the security dilemma is removed.

The third beneficial consequence of a difference between offensive and defensive weapons is that if all states support the status quo, an obvious arms control agreement is a ban on weapons that are useful for attacking. As President Roosevelt put it in his message to the Geneva Disarmament Conference in 1933: "If all nations will agree wholly to eliminate from possession and use the weapons which make possible a successful attack, defenses automatically will become impregnable, and the frontiers and independence of every nation will become secure."[45] The fact that such treaties have been rare—the Washington naval agreements discussed above and the anti-ABM treaty can be

---

41 Richard Challener, *Admirals, Generals, and American Foreign Policy, 1898-1914* (Princeton: Princeton University Press 1973), 273; Grey to Nicolson, in Gooch and Temperley, 414.

42 Quoted in James Crowley, *Japan's Quest for Autonomy* (Princeton: Princeton University Press 1966), 49. American naval officers agreed with the Japanese that a ten-to-six ratio would endanger Japan's supremacy in her home waters.

43 E. L. Woodward and R. Butler, eds., *Documents on British Foreign Policy, 1919-1939,* Third series, III (London: H.M.S.O. 1950), 526.

44 Jervis, 69-72, 352-55.

45 Quoted in Merze Tate, *The United States and Armaments* (Cambridge: Harvard University Press 1948), 108.

cited as examples—shows either that states are not always willing to guarantee the security of others, or that it is hard to distinguish offensive from defensive weapons.

Is such a distinction possible? Salvador de Madariaga, the Spanish statesman active in the disarmament negotiations of the interwar years, thought not: "A weapon is either offensive or defensive according to which end of it you are looking at." The French Foreign Minister agreed (although French policy did not always follow this view): "Every arm can be employed offensively or defensively in turn. . . . The only way to discover whether arms are intended for purely defensive purposes or are held in a spirit of aggression is in all cases to enquire into the intentions of the country concerned." Some evidence for the validity of this argument is provided by the fact that much time in these unsuccessful negotiations was devoted to separating offensive from defensive weapons. Indeed, no simple and unambiguous definition is possible and in many cases no judgment can be reached. Before the American entry into World War I, Woodrow Wilson wanted to arm merchantmen only with guns in the back of the ship so they could not initiate a fight, but this expedient cannot be applied to more common forms of armaments.[46]

There are several problems. Even when a differentiation is possible, a status-quo power will want offensive arms under any of three conditions. (1) If the offense has a great advantage over the defense, protection through defensive forces will be too expensive. (2) Status-quo states may need offensive weapons to regain territory lost in the opening stages of a war. It might be possible, however, for a state to wait to procure these weapons until war

seems likely, and they might be needed only in relatively small numbers, unless the aggressor was able to construct strong defenses quickly in the occupied areas. (3) The state may feel that it must be prepared to take the offensive either because the other side will make peace only if it loses territory or because the state has commitments to attack if the other makes war on a third party. As noted above, status-quo states with extensive commitments are often forced to behave like aggressors. Even when they lack such commitments, status-quo states must worry about the possibility that if they are able to hold off an attack, they will still not be able to end the war unless they move into the other's territory to damage its military forces and inflict pain. Many American naval officers after the Civil War, for example, believed that "only by destroying the commerce of the opponent could the United States bring him to terms."[47]

A further complication is introduced by the fact that aggressors as well as status-quo powers require defensive forces as a prelude to acquiring offensive ones, to protect one frontier while attacking another, or for insurance in case the war goes badly. Criminals as well as policemen can use bulletproof vests. Hitler as well as Maginot built a line of forts. Indeed, Churchill reports that in 1936 the German Foreign Minister said: "As soon as our fortifications are constructed [on our western borders] and the countries in Central Europe realize that France cannot enter German territory, all these countries will begin to feel very differently about their foreign policies, and a new constellation will develop."[48] So a state may not necessarily be reassured if its neighbor constructs strong defenses.

---

46  Boggs, 15, 40.

47  Kenneth Hagan, *American Gunboat Diplomacy and the Old Navy. 1877-1889* (Westport, Conn.: Greenwood Press 1973), 20.

48  Winston Churchill, *The Gathering Storm* (Boston: Houghton 1948), 206.

More central difficulties are created by the fact that whether a weapon is offensive or defensive often depends on the particular situation—for instance, the geographical setting and the way in which the weapon is used. "Tanks . . . spearheaded the fateful German thrust through the Ardennes in 1940, but if the French had disposed of a properly concentrated armored reserve, it would have provided the best means for their cutting off the penetration and turning into a disaster for the Germans what became instead an overwhelming victory."[49] Anti-aircraft weapons seem obviously defensive—to be used, they must wait for the other side to come to them. But the Egyptian attack on Israel in 1973 would have been impossible without effective air defenses that covered the battlefield. Nevertheless, some distinctions are possible. Sir John Simon, then the British Foreign Secretary, in response to the views cited earlier, stated that just because a fine line could not be drawn, "that was no reason for saying that there were not stretches of territory on either side which all practical men and women knew to be well on this or that side of the line." Although there are almost no weapons and strategies that are useful only for attacking, there are some that are almost exclusively defensive. Aggressors could want them for protection, but a state that relied mostly on them could not menace others. More frequently, we cannot "determine the absolute character of a weapon, but [we can] make a comparison . . . [and] discover whether or not the offensive potentialities predominate, whether a weapon is more useful in attack or in defense."[50]

The essence of defense is keeping the other side out of your territory. A purely defensive weapon is one that can do this without being able to penetrate the enemy's land. Thus a committee of military experts in an interwar disarmament conference declared that armaments "incapable of mobility by means of self-contained power," or movable only after long delay, were "only capable of being used for the defense of a State's territory."[51] The most obvious examples are fortifications. They can shelter attacking forces, especially when they are built right along the frontier,[52] but they cannot occupy enemy territory. A state with only a strong line of forts, fixed guns, and a small army to man them would not be much of a menace. Anything else that can serve only as a barrier against attacking troops is similarly defensive. In this category are systems that provide warning of an attack, the Russian's adoption of a different railroad gauge, and nuclear land mines that can seal off invasion routes.

If total immobility clearly defines a system that is defensive only, limited mobility is unfortunately ambiguous. As noted above, short-range fighter aircraft and anti-aircraft missiles can be used to cover an attack. And, unlike forts, they can advance with the troops. Still, their inability to reach deep into enemy territory does make them more useful for the defense than for the offense. Thus, the United States and Israel would have been more harmed in the early 1970's had the Russians provided the Egyptians with long-range instead of short-range aircraft. Naval forces are particularly difficult to classify in these terms but those that are very short-legged can be used only for coastal defense.

Any forces that for various reasons fight well only when on their own soil in effect lack mobility and therefore are defensive. The most

---

49 Brodie, *War and Politics, 325.*

50 Boggs, 42, 83. For a good argument about the possible differentiation between offensive and defensive weapons in the 1930's, see Basil Liddell Hart, "Aggression and the Problem of Weapons," *English Review,* Vol. 55 (July 1932), 71-78.

51 Quoted in Boggs, 39.

52 On these grounds, the Germans claimed in 1932 that the French forts were offensive *(ibid.,* 49). Similarly, fortified forward naval bases can be necessary for launching an attack; see Braisted, 643.

extreme example would be passive resistance. Noncooperation can thwart an aggressor, but it is very hard for large numbers of people to cross the border and stage a sit-in on another's territory. Morocco's recent march on the Spanish Sahara approached this tactic, but its success depended on special circumstances. Similarly, guerrilla warfare is defensive to the extent to which it requires civilian support that is likely to be forthcoming only in opposition to a foreign invasion. Indeed, if guerrilla warfare were easily exportable and if it took ten defenders to destroy each guerrilla, then this weapon would not only be one which could be used as easily to attack the other's territory as to defend one's own, but one in which the offense had the advantage: so the security dilemma would operate especially strongly.

If guerrillas are unable to fight on foreign soil, other kinds of armies may be unwilling to do so. An army imbued with the idea that only defensive wars were just would fight less effectively, if at all, if the goal were conquest. Citizen militias may lack both the ability and the will for aggression. The weapons employed, the short term of service, the time required for mobilization, and the spirit of repelling attacks on the homeland, all lend themselves much more to defense than to attacks on foreign territory.[53]

Less idealistic motives can produce the same result. A leading student of medieval warfare has described the armies of that period as follows: "Assembled with difficulty, insubordinate, unable to maneuver, ready to melt away from its standard the moment that its short period of service was over, a feudal force presented an assemblage of unsoldierlike qualities such as have seldom been known to coexist. Primarily intended to defend its own borders from the Magyar, the Northman, or the Saracen . . ., the institution was utterly unadapted to take the offensive."[54] Some political groupings can be similarly described. International coalitions are more readily held together by fear than by hope of gain. Thus Castlereagh was not being entirely self-serving when in 1816 be argued that the Quadruple Alliance "could only have owed its origin to a sense of common danger; in its very nature it must be conservative; it cannot threaten either the security or the liberties of other States."[55] It is no accident that most of the major campaigns of expansion have been waged by one dominant nation (for example, Napoleon's France and Hitler's Germany), and that coalitions among relative equals are usually found defending the status-quo. Most gains from conquest are too uncertain and raise too many questions of future squabbles among the victors to hold an alliance together for long. Although defensive coalitions are by no means easy to maintain—conflicting national objectives and the free-rider problem partly explain why three of them dissolved before Napoleon was defeated—the common interest of seeing that no state dominates provides a strong incentive for solidarity.

Weapons that are particularly effective in reducing fortifications and barriers are of great value to the offense. This is not to deny that a defensive power will want some of those weapons if the other side has them: Brodie is certainly correct to argue that while their tanks allowed the Germans to conquer France, properly used French tanks could have halted the attack. But France would not have needed these weapons if Germany had not acquired them, whereas even if France had no tanks, Germany could not have foregone them since they provided the only chance of breaking through the French lines. Mobile heavy artillery is,

---

53  The French made this argument in the interwar period; see Richard Challener, *The French Theory of the Nation in Arms* (New York: Columbia University Press 1955), 181-82. The Germans disagreed; see Boggs, 44-45.

54  Oman, 57-58.

55  Quoted in Charles Webster, *The Foreign Policy of Castereagh,* II, *1815-1822* (London: G. Bell and Sons 1963), 510.

similarly, especially useful in destroying forti-fications. The defender, while needing artillery to fight off attacking troops or to counterattack, can usually use lighter guns since they do not need to penetrate such massive obstacles. So it is not sur-prising that one of the few things that most nations at the interwar disarmament conferences were able to agree on was that heavy tanks and mobile heavy guns were particularly valuable to a state planning an attack.[56]

Weapons and strategies that depend for their effectiveness on surprise are almost always of-fensive. That fact was recognized by some of the delegates to the interwar disarmament confer-ences and is the principle behind the common national ban on concealed weapons. An earlier representative of this widespread view was the mid-19th-century Philadelphia newspaper that argued: "As a measure of defense, knives, dirks, and sword canes are entirely useless. They are fit only for attack, and all such attacks are of murderous character. Whoever carries such a weapon has prepared himself for homicide."[57]

It is, of course, not always possible to distin-guish between forces that are most effective for holding territory and forces optimally designed for taking it. Such a distinction could not have been made for the strategies and weapons in Europe during most of the period between the Franco-Prussian War and World War I. Neither naval forces nor tactical air forces can be readily classified in these terms. But the point here is that when such a distinction is possible, the cen-tral characteristic of the security dilemma no longer holds, and one of the most troublesome consequences of anarchy is removed.

*Offense-Defense Differentiation and Strategic Nuclear Weapons.* In the interwar period, most statesmen held the reasonable position that weapons that threatened civilians were offensive.[58]

But when neither side can protect its civilians, a counter-city posture is defensive because the state can credibly threaten to retaliate only in re-sponse to an attack on itself or its closest allies. The costs of this strike are so high that the state could not threaten to use it for the less-than-vital interest of compelling the other to abandon an established position.

In the context of deterrence, offensive weapons are those that provide defense. In the now familiar reversal of common sense, the state that could take its population out of hostage, ei-ther by active or passive defense or by destroying the other's strategic weapons on the ground, would be able to alter the status-quo. The desire to prevent such a situation was one of the rationales for the anti-ABM agreements; it explains why some arms controllers opposed building ABM's to protect cities, but favored sites that covered ICBM fields. Similarly, many analysts want to limit warhead accuracy and favor multiple re-entry vehicles (MRV's), but oppose multiple independently targetable re-entry vehicles (MIRV's). The former are more useful than single warheads for penetrating city defenses, and en-sure that the state has a second-strike capability. MIRV's enhance counterforce capabilities. Some arms controllers argue that this is also true of cruise missiles, and therefore do not want them to be deployed either. There is some evidence that the Russians are not satisfied with deterrence and are seeking to regain the capability for defense. Such an effort, even if not inspired by aggressive designs, would create a severe security dilemma.

What is most important for the argument here is that land-based ICBM's are both offensive and defensive, but when both sides rely on Polaris-type systems (SLBM's), offense and defense use different weapons. ICBM's can be used either to destroy the other's cities in retaliation or to initiate

56 Boggs, 14-15, 47-48, 60.
57 Quoted in Philip Jordan, *Frontier Law and Order* (Lincoln: University of Nebraska Press 1970), 7; also see 16-17.
58 Boggs, 20, 28.

hostilities by attacking the other's strategic missiles. Some measures—for hardening of missile sites and warning systems—are purely defensive, since they do not make a first strike easier. Others are predominantly offensive—for instance passive or active city defenses, and highly accurate warheads. But ICBM's themselves are useful for both purposes. And because states seek a high level of insurance, the desire for protection as well as the contemplation of a counterforce strike can explain the acquisition of extremely large numbers of missiles. So it is very difficult to infer the other's intentions from its military posture. Each side's efforts to increase its own security by procuring more missiles decreases, to an extent determined by the relative efficacy of the offense and the defense, the other side's security. That is not the case when both sides use SLBM's. The point is not that sea-based systems are less vulnerable than land-based ones (this bears on the offense-defense ratio) but that SLBM's are defensive, retaliatory weapons. First, they are probably not accurate enough to destroy many military targets.[59] Second, and more important, SLBM's are not the main instrument of attack against other SLBM's. The hardest problem confronting a state that wants to take its cities out of hostage is to locate the other's SLBM's, a job that requires not SLBM's but anti-submarine weapons. A state might use SLBM's to attack the other's submarines (although other weapons would probably be more efficient), but without anti-submarine warfare (ASW) capability the task cannot be performed. A status-quo state that wanted to forego offensive capability could simply forego ASW research and procurement.

There are two difficulties with this argument, however. First, since the state's SLBM's are potentially threatened by the other's ASW capabilities, the state may want to pursue ASW research in order to know what the other might be able to do and to design defenses. Unless it does this, it cannot be confident that its submarines are safe. Second, because some submarines are designed to attack surface ships, not launch missiles, ASW forces have missions other than taking cities out of hostage. Some U.S. officials plan for a long war in Europe which would require keeping the sea lanes open against Russian submarines. Designing an ASW force and strategy that would meet this threat without endangering Soviet SLBM's would be difficult but not impossible, since the two missions are somewhat different.[60] Furthermore, the Russians do not need ASW forces to combat submarines carrying out conventional missions; it might be in America's interest to sacrifice the ability to meet a threat that is not likely to materialize in order to reassure the Russians that we are not menacing their retaliatory capability.

When both sides rely on ICBM's, one side's missiles can attack the other's, and so the state cannot be indifferent to the other's building program. But because one side's SLBM's do not menace the other's, each side can build as many as it wants and the other need not respond. Each side's decision on the size of its force depends on technical questions, its judgment about how much destruction is enough to deter, and the amount of insurance it is willing to pay for—and these considerations are independent of the size of the other's strategic force. Thus the crucial nexus in the arms race is severed.

Here two objections not only can be raised but have been, by those who feel that even if American second-strike capability is in no danger, the United States must respond to a Soviet buildup. First, the relative numbers of missiles and warheads may be used as an index of each side's power and will. Even if there is no military need to increase American arms as the Russians

59 See, however, Desmond Ball, "The Counterforce Potential of American SLBM Systems," *Journal of Peace Research,* XIV (No. 1, 1977), 23-40.

60 Richard Garwin, "Anti-Submarine Warfare and the National Security," *Scientific American,* Vol. 227 (July 1972), 14-25.

increase theirs, a failure to respond may lead third parties to think that the U.S. has abandoned the competition with the U.S.S.R. and is no longer willing to pay the price of world leadership. Furthermore, if either side believes that nuclear "superiority" matters, then, through the bargaining logic, it will matter. The side with "superiority" will be more likely to stand firm in a confrontation if it thinks its "stronger" military position helps it or if it thinks that the other thinks its own "weaker" military position is a handicap. To allow the other side to have more SLBM's—even if one's own second-strike capability is unimpaired—will give the other an advantage that can be translated into political gains.

The second objection is that superiority *does* matter, and not only because of mistaken beliefs. If nuclear weapons are used in an all-or-none fashion, then all that is needed is second-strike capability. But limited, gradual, and controlled strikes are possible. If the other side has superiority, it can reduce the state's forces by a slow-motion war of attrition. For the state to strike at the other's cities would invite retaliation; for it to reply with a limited counterforce attack would further deplete its supply of missiles. Alternatively, the other could employ demonstration attacks—such as taking out an isolated military base or exploding a warhead high over a city—in order to demonstrate its resolve. In either of these scenarios, the state will suffer unless it matches the other's arms posture.[61]

These two objections, if valid, mean that even with SLBM's one cannot distinguish offensive from defensive strategic nuclear weapons. Compellence may be more difficult than deterrence,[62] but if decision makers believe that numbers of missiles or of warheads influence outcomes, or if these weapons can be used in limited manner,

then the posture and policy that would be needed for self-protection is similar to that useful for aggression. If the second objection has merit, security would require the ability to hit selected targets on the other side, enough ammunition to wage a controlled counterforce war, and the willingness to absorb limited countervalue strikes. Secretary Schlesinger was correct in arguing that this capability would not constitute a first-strike capability. But because the "Schlesinger Doctrine" could be used not only to cope with a parallel Russian policy, but also to support an American attempt to change the status-quo, the new American stance would decrease Russian security. Even if the U.S.S.R. were reassured that the present U.S. Government lacked the desire or courage to do this, there could be no guarantee that future governments would not use the new instruments for expansion. Once we move away from the simple idea that nuclear weapons can only be used for all-out strikes, half the advantage of having both sides rely on a sea-based force would disappear because of the lack of an offensive-defensive differentiation. To the extent that military policy affects political relations, it would be harder for the United States and the Soviet Union to cooperate even if both supported the status quo.

Although a full exploration of these questions is beyond the scope of this paper, it should be noted that the objections rest on decision makers' beliefs—beliefs, furthermore, that can be strongly influenced by American policy and American statements. The perceptions of third nations of whether the details of the nuclear balance affect political conflicts—and, to a lesser extent, Russian beliefs about whether superiority is meaningful—are largely derived from the American strategic debate. If most American

---

61 The latter scenario, however, does not require that the state closely match the number of missiles the other deploys.

62 Thomas Schelling, *Arms and Influence* (New Haven: Yale University Press 1966), 60-78. Schelling's arguments are not entirely convincing, however. For further discussion, see Jervis, "Deterrence Theory Re-Visited," Working Paper No. 14, UCLA Program in Arms Control and International Security.

spokesmen were to take the position that a secure second-strike capability was sufficient and that increments over that (short of a first-strike capability) would only be a waste of money, it is doubtful whether America's allies or the neutrals would judge the superpowers' useful military might or political will by the size of their stockpiles. Although the Russians stress war-fighting ability, they have not contended that marginal increases in strategic forces bring political gains; any attempt to do so could be rendered less effective by an American assertion that this is nonsense. The bargaining advantages of possessing nuclear "superiority" work best when both sides acknowledge them. If the "weaker" side convinces the other that it does not believe there is any meaningful difference in strength, then the "stronger" side cannot safely stand firm because there is no increased chance that the other will back down.

This kind of argument applies at least as strongly to the second objection. Neither side can employ limited nuclear options unless it is quite confident that the other accepts the rules of the game. For if the other believes that nuclear war cannot be controlled, it will either refrain from responding—which would be fine—or launch all-out retaliation. Although a state might be ready to engage in limited nuclear war without acknowledging this possibility—and indeed, that would be a reasonable policy for the United States—it is not likely that the other would have sufficient faith in that prospect to initiate limited strikes unless the

state had openly avowed its willingness to fight this kind of war. So the United States, by patiently and consistently explaining that it considers such ideas to be mad and that any nuclear wars will inevitably get out of control, could gain a large measure of protection against the danger that the Soviet Union might seek to employ a "Schlesinger Doctrine" against an America that lacked the military ability or political will to respond in kind. Such a position is made more convincing by the inherent implausibility of the arguments for the possibility of a limited nuclear war.

In summary, as long as states believe that all that is needed is second-strike capability, then the differentiation between offensive and defensive forces that is provided by reliance on SLBM's allows each side to increase its security without menacing the other, permits some inferences about intentions to be drawn from military posture, and removes the main incentive for statusquo powers to engage in arms races.

## IV. Four Worlds

The two variables we have been discussing—whether the offense or the defense has the advantage, and whether offensive postures can be distinguished from defensive ones—can be combined to yield four possible worlds.

The first world is the worst for status-quo states. There is no way to get security without menacing others, and security through defense is

|  | Offense Has the Advantage | Defense Has the Advantage |
|---|---|---|
| Offensive Posture not Distinguishable From Defensive One | 1<br>Doubly dangerous | 2<br>Security dilemma, but security requirements may be compatible. |
| Offensive Posture Distinguishable From Defensive One | 3<br>No security dilemma, but aggression possible. Status-quo states can follow different policy than aggressors. Warning given | 4<br>Doubly stable |

terribly difficult to obtain. Because offensive and defensive postures are the same, status-quo states acquire the same kind of arms that are sought by aggressors. And because the offense has the advantage over the defense, attacking is the best route to protecting what you have; status-quo states will therefore behave like aggressors. The situation will be unstable. Arms races are likely. Incentives to strike first will turn crises into wars. Decisive victories and conquests will be common. States will grow and shrink rapidly, and it will be hard for any state to maintain its size and influence without trying to increase them. Cooperation among status-quo powers will be extremely hard to achieve.

There are no cases that totally fit this picture, but it bears more than a passing resemblance to Europe before World War I. Britain and Germany, although in many respects natural allies, ended up as enemies. Of course much of the explanation lies in Germany's ill-chosen policy. And from the perspective of our theory, the powers' ability to avoid war in a series of earlier crises cannot be easily explained. Nevertheless, much of the behavior in this period was the product of technology and beliefs that magnified the security dilemma. Decision makers thought that the offense had a big advantage and saw little difference between offensive and defensive military postures. The era was characterized by arms races. And once war seemed likely, mobilization races created powerful incentives to strike first.

In the nuclear era, the first world would be one in which each side relied on vulnerable weapons that were aimed at similar forces and each side understood the situation. In this case, the incentives to strike first would be very high—so high that status-quo powers as well as aggressors would be sorely tempted to preempt. And since the forces could be used to change the status-quo as well as to preserve it, there would be no way for both sides to increase their security simultaneously. Now the familiar logic of deterrence leads both sides to see the dangers in this world. Indeed, the new understanding of this situation was one reason why vulnerable bombers and missiles were replaced. Ironically, the 1950's would have been more hazardous if the decision makers had been aware of the dangers of their posture and had therefore felt greater pressure to strike first. This situation could be recreated if both sides were to rely on MIRVed ICBM'S.

In the second world, the security dilemma operates because offensive and defensive postures cannot be distinguished; but it does not operate as strongly as in the first world because the defense has the advantage, and so an increment in one side's strength increases its security more than it decreases the other's. So, if both sides have reasonable subjective security requirements, are of roughly equal power, and the variables discussed earlier are favorable, it is quite likely that status-quo states can adopt compatible security policies. Although a state will not be able to judge the other's intentions from the kinds of weapons it procures, the level of arms spending will give important evidence. Of course a state that seeks a high level of arms might be not an aggressor but merely an insecure state, which if conciliated will reduce its arms, and if confronted will reply in kind. To assume that the apparently excessive level of arms indicates aggressiveness could therefore lead to a response that would deepen the dilemma and create needless conflict. But empathy and skillful statesmanship can reduce this danger. Furthermore, the advantageous position of the defense means that a status-quo state can often maintain a high degree of security with a level of arms lower than that of its expected adversary. Such a state demonstrates that it lacks the ability or desire to alter the status-quo, at least at the present time. The strength of the defense also allows states to react slowly and with restraint when they fear that others are menacing them. So, although status-quo powers will to some extent be threatening to others, that extent will be limited.

This world is the one that comes closest to matching most periods in history. Attacking is usually harder than defending because of the strength of fortifications and obstacles. But purely defensive postures are rarely possible because fortifications are usually supplemented by armies and mobile guns which can support an attack. In the nuclear era, this world would be one in which both sides relied on relatively invulnerable ICBM's and believed that limited nuclear war was impossible. Assuming no MIRV's, it would take more than one attacking missile to destroy one of the adversary's. Pre-emption is therefore unattractive. If both sides have large inventories, they can ignore all but drastic increases on the other side. A world of either ICBM's or SLBM's in which both sides adopted the "Schlesinger Doctrine" would probably fit in this category too. The means of preserving the status-quo would also be the means of changing it, as we discussed earlier. And the defense usually would have the advantage, because compellence is more difficult than deterrence. Although a state might succeed in changing the status-quo on issues that matter much more to it than to others, status-quo powers could deter major provocations under most circumstances.

In the third world there may be no security dilemma, but there are security problems. Because states can procure defensive systems that do not threaten others, the dilemma need not operate. But because the offense has the advantage, aggression is possible, and perhaps easy. If the offense has enough of an advantage, even a status-quo state may take the initiative rather than risk being attacked and defeated. If the offense has less of an advantage, stability and cooperation are likely because the status-quo states will procure defensive forces. They need not react to others who are similarly armed, but can wait for the warning they would receive if others started to deploy offensive weapons. But each state will have to watch the others carefully, and there is room for false suspicions. The costliness of the defense and the allure of the offense can lead to unnecessary mistrust, hostility, and war, unless some of the variables discussed earlier are operating to restrain defection.

A hypothetical nuclear world that would fit this description would be one in which both sides relied on SLBM's, but in which ASW techniques were very effective. Offense and defense would be different, but the former would have the advantage. This situation is not likely to occur; but if it did, a status-quo state could show its lack of desire to exploit the other by refraining from threatening its submarines. The desire to have more protecting you than merely the other side's fear of retaliation is a strong one, however, and a state that knows that it would not expand even if its cities were safe is likely to believe that the other would not feel threatened by its ASW program. It is easy to see how such a world could become unstable, and how spirals of tensions and conflict could develop.

The fourth world is doubly safe. The differentiation between offensive and defensive systems permits a way out of the security dilemma; the advantage of the defense disposes of the problems discussed in the previous paragraphs. There is no reason for a status-quo power to be tempted to procure offensive forces, and aggressors give notice of their intentions by the posture they adopt. Indeed, if the advantage of the defense is great enough, there are no security problems. The loss of the ultimate form of the power to alter the status-quo would allow greater scope for the exercise of nonmilitary means and probably would tend to freeze the distribution of values.

This world would have existed in the first decade of the 20th century if the decision makers had understood the available technology. In that case, the European powers would have followed different policies both in the long run and in the summer of 1914. Even Germany, facing powerful enemies on both sides, could have made herself secure by developing strong defenses. France could also have made her frontier almost impregnable. Furthermore, when crises arose, no one would have had incentives to strike first. There would have been no competitive mobilization races reducing the time available for negotiations.

In the nuclear era, this world would be one in which the superpowers relied on SLBM's, ASW technology was not up to its task, and limited nuclear options were not taken seriously. We have discussed this situation earlier; here we need only add that, even if our analysis is correct and even if the policies and postures of both sides were to move in this direction, the problem of violence below the nuclear threshold would remain. On issues other than defense of the homeland, there would still be security dilemmas and security problems. But the world would nevertheless be safer than it has usually been.

# 17: The Balance of Power

*Edward Vose Gulick*

## Preserve Independence and Secure Survival

The basic aim of the balance of power was to insure the survival of independent states. This may be taken as fundamental to the classical balance-of-power system and should be distinguished from those goals, such as "peace" and (to a lesser degree) the "status quo," which were incidental to it.

Writers on the balance of power expressed their recognition of this basic aim in various ways. Brougham, for example, held that "the whole object of the [balance of power] system is to maintain unimpaired the independence of nations."[1] Heeren spoke of the balance of power as the "mutual preservation of freedom and independence, by guarding against the preponderance and usurpation of an individual."[2] Vattel, in elucidating the "general Principles of the Duties of a Nation to Itself," summarized them with the dictum: "To preserve and perfect one's existence is the sum of all duties to self."[3] We find in all three a repeated emphasis on the primacy of the survival of independent states. Similarly, where the old British Mutiny Act provided for the levy of troops, it was associating an instrument of war (the levy) with the two ideas of "the Safety of the United Kingdom . . . and the Preservation of the Balance of Power in Europe," and was by implication asserting that survival took precedence over peace as an aim of the balance of power.[4]

## Preserve the State System

Taking the survival of the independent state as his base, the equilibrist erected his aims by piling two more blocks on top of the first. The second block consisted of the argument that the best way to preserve the individual state was to preserve the system of which it was a part. Self-interest, according to this line of reasoning, could best be pursued by attention to group interest. By preserving the state system you would preserve the parts thereof. . . .

## No One State Shall Preponderate

Once the second block was in place, there was no choice about the third. If one granted that the survival of independent states was the primary aim and added that the best chance of achieving it resided in preserving the state system, a relentless logic led to the obvious axiom of preventing the proponderance of any one member of the state system. "Nations [should] unite, or . . . prepare for their defense, as soon as they perceive anyone becoming dangerously powerful."[5]

---

1  Brougham, *Works*, VIII, 80.
2  A. H. L. Heeren, *History of the Political System of Europe and Its Colonies* (Northampton, Mass., 1829), I, 12-13.
3  Vatte I, *Law of Nations*, III, 13, no. 14.
4  Cited by T. J. Lawrence, *Principles of International Law* (Boston, 1910), 130. Text may be found in George K. Rickards (ed.), *The Statutes of the United Kingdom of Great Britain and Ireland* (London, 1804-69), XXVIII, pt. I, 34.
5  Brougham, *Works*, VIII, 73.

Reprinted from Edward Vose Gulick: *Europe's Classical Balance of Power: A Case History of the Theory and Practice of One of the Great Concepts of European Statecraft*, pp. 30-31, 33-37, 52-55, 58-79, 89-91. © 1955 by the American Historical Association. Used by permission of the publisher, Cornell University Press.

Failure to do so was "an inexcusable breach of duty."[6] Similar formulations have often been made by writers, typical of whom again was Friedrich Gentz in his assertion. "That if the states system of Europe is to exist and be maintained by common exertions, no one of its members must ever become so powerful as to be able to coerce all the rest put together."[7] . . .

## Comments

### Peace

We may say that survival, a degree of cooperation, and the prevention of a hostile predominance were all germane to the balance-of-power theory, as indicated. We may also say that peace was not germane. However desirable it may have been, however passionately the theorist may have longed for it, however devotedly he may have consecrated his life to its realization, peace was no more essential to equilibrist theory than the barnacle to the boat.

An appreciable amount of confusion has arisen on this point as the result of mistaken analysis of balance-of-power theory. Indeed, peace has occasionally been urged as the preeminent aim of balance-of-power policies: "A balance of power aims primarily to preserve peace and the *status quo*."[8] The same idea is often found in treaties when the balance of power is mentioned; witness one of the treaties of Utrecht, that between Great Britain and Spain (July 2/13, 1713), which contains the following phrase: "in order to secure and stabilize the peace and tranquility of the Christian world by a just equilibrium of power (which is the best and most solid basis of mutual friendship and durable harmony)."[9] Although many who have written on the balance of power have adopted this point

of view, there are reasons why their position is untenable.

Consider, for example, the striking content of the diplomatic history of the last five hundred years in Europe, from the Italian Renaissance to the present, which has literally brimmed with parallel evidence of both balance of power and war, during the very period when the balance of power was at its height. Accepting such a finding, it is possible to deal with this coincidence in two ways: one may say that the balance of power aimed at peace but perennially failed, or that balance-of-power theory aimed at the survival of the state system and regarded war as a means of preventing the breakdown of that system. With regard to the first of these propositions, we cannot help asking if the balance-of-power system was, in the period of its most consistent practice, as ineffectual as the proposition suggests. It is tempting to say yes and drive another nail into the balance-of-power coffin, but the answer surely lies in the direction of the second proposition, and for several reasons.

It is noticeable that wars were fought in the name of balance of power against Charles V, Louis XIV, and Napoleon, to mention only the most outstanding and to ignore myriad examples of lesser importance. One also notices that the clearest-headed theorists of equilibrium have not only *not* claimed peace as the principal aim, but have actually envisaged war as an instrument for balancing power: Vattel, Gentz, Brougham, Christian Wolff, in company with such practical statesmen as Talleyrand, Metternich, and Castlereagh, all thought of war as an instrument to preserve or restore a balance of power. One observes also the almost placid acceptance by Rousseau and Kant of the hideous nature of competition within the state system and their

---

6  *Ibid.*, 72.
7  Gentz, *Fragments*, 61-62.
8  Sidney B. Fay, "Balance of Power," *Encyclopaedia of the Social Sciences* (New York, 1937), I, 397.
9  J. Dumont, *Corps universel diplomatique du droit des gens* (Amsterdam, 1731), VIII, 391, col. 7.

obvious belief in a successful balancing system in spite of it. The argument of these advocates conforms to theory and fact by showing that the incidence of war was not evidence of the ineffectiveness or absence of balance-of-power policies but that such incidence indicated widespread practice (often malpractice, to be sure) of the balance of power, of which war was an instrument. Their contention explains where the first proposition obscures, and, by explaining, effectively cuts the ground from under the "peace" point of view.

We would be correct in listing peace as one of the incidental by-products of equilibrist policy, or as one of its secondary aims. There is no doubt that peace has often been temporarily preserved as a result of balance strategy; but we may also be sure that a system of independent, armed, and often mutually hostile states is inherently incapable of remaining at peace over a considerable period of time merely by the manipulation of balance techniques. . . .

We can now discern the basic assumptions and aims of the balance-of-power, and we have scraped off some of the obscurities which encrusted it. Given the assumptions and aims, it is possible to enumerate the means and show their proper relationship to the foregoing, much as a Euclidian geometrist, having made assumptions with regard to points, lines, planes and numbers can build with corollaries an entire theoretical system, self-consistent and demonstrable. . . .

### Vigilance

Lord Brougham put his finger on the first corollary of the balance of power when he spoke of "the prevalence of that national jealousy, and anxious attention to the affairs of other states, which is the master principle of the modern balance of power system."[10] That system, consecrated to the independence of the members of the state system, must necessarily employ vigilance as one of its primary means. An equilibrist statesman could never direct policy toward a desired end without having some real understanding of the problems at hand. And since his problems often relate to the expansion of neighboring powers, he must at all times "be instructed in all that passes outside of his kingdom which has relation to him, to his allies, [and] to his enemies."[11] The foreign ministry and its officers have to be watchful of foreign developments, of army and navy increases, of important economic gains and losses, and many other aspects of foreign life.

Watchfulness is not, of course, peculiar to the balance-of-power system. It is just as essential to the preservation of any system. Democracy is by no means self-perpetuating, and its continued existence clearly depends upon the constant vigilance of those citizens who cherish it. The same is true of the members of a state system where watchfulness has been of such singular importance to the balance of power that theorists have taken pains to emphasize it. Lord Bacon, writing in the seventeenth century on this problem, used a fine catch phrase when he wrote of a "general rule . . . which ever holdeth; which is that princes do keep due sentinel, that none of their neighbours do overgrow."[12] Brougham also spoke of the necessity of "constantly watching over the state of public affairs, even in profound peace."[13] By this he meant an intimate scrutiny of all relevant domestic problems

---

10 Brougham, *Works*, VIII, 8. See also the comment of Sir James Mackintosh on "that mutual jealousy which made every great Power the opponent of the dangerous ambition of every other" (House of Commons, April 27, 1815; text in C. K. Webster [ed.], *British Diplomacy, 1813-15* [London, 1921], 409). This work will be cited hereafter as Webster, *Brit. Dipl.*

11 Réal, *Science du gouvernement*, VI, 341-342 (translation mine).

12 Francis Bacon, "Essay on Empire"; quoted by Cobden, *Political Writings*, I, 266-267.

13 Brougham, *Works*, VIII, 17.

in the member states of the system. He argued that "no one power should view with indifference the domestic affairs of the rest, more particularly those affairs which have a reference to the increase or consolidation of national resources."[14] Vattel, Gentz, Fénelon, de Réal, and others all urged the necessity of constant watchfulness. There can be no question of either the logical validity of their point or of the vast extent to which it has been practiced in the conduct of balance-of-power policies. . . .

## The Alliance

At an earlier point it was shown that balance of power aims to prevent or check preponderance, because "the greatness of one Prince is . . . the ruin or the diminution of the greatness of his neighbor."[15] In a discussion of the means by which this preponderance might be avoided or checked, one recognizes that theoretically it might be accomplished, as has often been asserted, by giving states equal shares of territory. In a witty and anonymous eighteenth-century lampoon of the balance of power, quoted earlier, a catechist drills "Europa" in this doctrine of equal shares:

Catechist: Hold, my pretty Child—one Word more.—You have been ask'd concerning the Ballance of Power.—Tell me what it is?

Europa: It is such an equal Distribution of Power among the Princes of Europe, as makes it impracticable for the one to disturb the Repose of the other.[16]

In another eighteenth-century work, the Abbé de Mably ascribed to Queen Elizabeth of England the assertion that "it is a matter of dividing Europe into states almost equal in order that, their forces being in balance, they will fear to offend one another, and hesitate to plan too great designs."[17] It is of little importance whether or not Queen Elizabeth ever spoke those words; on the other hand, it is important to realize that such a conception of equal power was an intellectual cliche that was brandished repeatedly by commentators on the balance of power. It had its defenders and its powerful critics. In using the supposed words of Queen Elizabeth, the Abbé de Mably was eager to attack her plan as *"impossible de réaliser."* His attitude was similar to the line adopted later by Gentz, Talleyrand, and others, who pointedly denied the feasibility of such an equality. Gentz spoke of it as an "imaginary principle."[18] Talleyrand held that "an absolute equality of forces among all the States, aside from the fact that it can never exist, is not necessary to the political equilibrium, and would perhaps in some respects be harmful to it."[19] Vattel rejected equal shares as hopeless: "Once this equality were established, how could it be regularly maintained by lawful means? Commerce, industry, the military virtues, would soon put an end to it."[20] Since the idea of a necessary equality has had a perennial virility in balance theory, it is necessary to point out here the justice of the claims of these critics. Their view is sustained by two very important and obvious facts. The first is that, since the fifteenth century and

---

14 *Ibid.*, 33-34.
15 Réal, *Science du gouvernement*, VI, 442; quoted above p. 34.
16 *Europe's Catechism* (London, 1741), 11-12.
17 Abbé de Mably, *Collection complète des oeuvres* (Paris, 1794-95), V, 65 (translation mine).
18 Gentz, *Fragments*, 56.
19 *Mémoires du prince de Talleyrand, publiés par le duc de Broglie* (Paris, 1891-92), II, 237-238 (translation mine). Hereafter cited as Talleyrand, *Mémoires.*
20 Vattel, *Law of Nations*, III, 251, no. 48.

for a variety of reasons, it has never been feasible to redistribute territory among the rulers of Europe in such a way that all would have equal power. Secondly, the ever-present, persistent, and fundamental fact of continuous change in history precludes any equal distribution which could remain equal for any substantial length of time. Even assuming territory to remain the same, internal changes would so alter the power of states as to nullify any original territorial equality.

These two reasons suffice to dispose of the fallacy of necessary equality. For a balance-of-power theorist to insist on equality is for him to admit at the start that balance of power is impossible. Some intelligent theorists who clearly recognize the problem, however, felt that a successful balance of power required that a number, or even a majority, of the *major* states in the equilibrium possess an approximate equality of power. Such a condition is desirable for a balance-of-power system, although not an easy condition to create and sustain. Policy was directed in a limited sense toward an equality of key states in the settlement at Vienna in 1814-1815, when the attempt was made by Talleyrand, Castlereagh, and Metternich to thwart Russian retention of large Polish territories, and again when Prussian power was increased to create an adequate mass to check France on the one hand and Russia on the other. There was, however, never any real question of general equality, for both Russian and Austrian holdings were vastly greater than Prussian, while England's empire gave her a great overseas ascendancy. Moreover, there were still numerous states of insignificant power in Germany and Italy, not to mention the second-rate powers of Sweden, Denmark, Holland, Spain, and Portugal. We may, then, relegate the theory of general equality in power to a position of relative unimportance in a discussion of the means by which the aims of balance of power may be realized.

In our retreat from the idea of "an equal Distribution of Power among the Princes," we dig in at a second line of defense, which prescribes the dexterous use of artificial bonds to create the equality (or more often the defensive preponderance) which is necessary to a balance-of-power system. Vattel indicated the necessary logical step with simplicity and clarity when he wrote the following:

> The surest means of preserving this balance of power would be to bring it about that no State should be much superior to the others, that all the States or at least the larger part, should be about equal in strength. This idea has been attributed to Henry IV, but it is one that could not be realized without injustice and violence. . . . It is simpler, easier and more just to have recourse to the method . . . of forming alliances in order to make a stand against a very powerful sovereign and prevent him from dominating.[21]

In other words, Vattel was arguing for a kind of equality of power, but an equality which was based on blocs of allied power and not on a hoped-for redistribution of land along the lines of equal shares. He willingly accepted the fact that states were unequal in power and could never be made equal like so many red bricks in a wall. He did not, however, give up hope for achieving a balance of power, but argued that the territorial inequality of states might be corrected by alliances. States A and B might each be smaller and weaker than C, but allied they might well be equal to, or greater than, C.

The alliance, then, becomes one of the prominent means of putting balance theory to work. It is at once one of the commonest, as well as one of the most complicated, means of checking

---

21 *Ibid.*

preponderance and preserving the state system. Sir Robert Walpole put the relationship most winningly, after the oratorical manner of his period:

> The use of alliances, Sir, has in the last age been too much experienced to be contested. It is by leagues, well concerted and strictly observed, that the weak are defended against the strong, that bounds are set to the turbulence of ambition, that the torrent of power is restrained, and empires preserved from those inundations of war that, in former times, laid the world in ruins. By alliances, Sir, the equipoise of power is maintained, and those alarms and apprehensions avoided, which must arise from vicissitudes of empire and the fluctuations of perpetual contest.[22]

For historical occurrences of alliances as balance-of-power devices in the eighteenth century, one may examine the alliances of the Seven Years' War, where Britain and Prussia joined against France and Austria, or the broader system of French alliances which included Sweden, the Ottoman Empire, Spain, and some of the smaller German states—the pattern being carefully devised to supply a whole series of stabilizing checks against aggressive power.

## Intervention

Both watchfulness and a concern with checks against preponderance imply a further necessity—intervention. The problem of intervention in the name of the balance of power has been a persistent difficulty for supporters of equilibrist policy. They ride the horns of a dilemma, and the problem is, in fact, a difficult one for the balance-of-power theorist, more especially for an idealist like Lord Brougham. To him the cornerstone of the whole system of equilibrium was independence, and he recognized the ugly illogic of interfering with the independence which was being disregarded.[23] Intervention not only put the cart before the horse but fouled up the harness and elicited unnerving remarks from the bystanders. Brougham attempted to unravel the paradox by emphasizing the expediency and rightness of inviolable independence, then made suggestions for avoiding the necessity of intervention, and finally admitted that necessity in the event of "a great and manifest, and also an immediate danger."[24]

He held that to avoid intervention a state should build up its own strength sufficiently to correct the threatened preponderance of a neighbor. He called this "the right of proportional improvement,"[25] and he felt that it could be useful

---

22 Hansard, *Parl. Hist.*, XII, 168-169; quoted by Kovacs, "Development of the Principle of the Balance of Power," App. X, F. There is abundant evidence on the alliance as an instrument of the balance of power among the theoretical writers. Brougham asserted, "When any one state menaces the independence of any other, . . . that other ought to call in the aid of its allies, or to contract alliances for its protection, if none have already been formed" (*Works*, VIII, 69-70). He even tried to develop a thesis of "natural enmity" and "natural alliances," to enable a statesman to determine the best direction for policy: "The circumstances which are found to constitute a natural enmity between nations are threefold: *proximity* of situation, *similarity* of pursuits, and near *equality* of power. From the opposite causes arise the natural indifference or relative neutrality of states; a reasonable *distance, diversity* of objects and considerable inequality of resources; while natural alliance results from the common enmity produced by a concurrence of the three causes first mentioned, in the relations of two or more powers towards the same third power" (*ibid.*, 39-40). Metternich indicated his equilibrist outlook on alliances by asserting, "Any alliance of Austrian forces with those of any other Power, whose exclusive design is the destruction of the present order of affairs, and whose plans are aimed at dominion, would be a war against holy immutable principles, and against Austria's direct interests" (*Memoirs*, II, 485). See also Vattel's statement that "force of arms is not the only means of guarding against a formidable State. There are gentler means, which are always lawful. The most efficacious of these is an alliance of other less powerful sovereigns, who, by uniting their forces, are enabled to counterbalance the sovereign who excites their alarm" (*Law of Nations*, III, 250, no. 46).

23 See Brougham, *Works*, VIII, 81.

24 *Ibid.*, 82.

25 *Ibid.*, 35.

in perpetuating the equilibrium. An alliance structure could perhaps solve the problem, which the above policy could not, by the added support of an ally against the unsettling increase of power in an unruly neighbor.

In extreme cases, however, he did reluctantly admit the correctness of intervention:

> Whenever a sudden and great change takes place in the internal structure of a State, dangerous in a high degree to all neighbours, they have a right to attempt, by hostile interference, the restoration of an order of things safe to themselves; or, at least, to counterbalance, by active aggression, the new force suddenly acquired.

> The right can only be deemed competent in cases of sudden and great aggrandizement, such as that of France in 1790; endangering the safety of the neighbouring powers, so plainly as to make the consideration immaterial of the circumstances from whence the danger has originated.[26]

Brougham was clearly aware of the dilemma in which he found himself. There is no lack of intelligence in his essays on the balance of power, although his opinions on intervention underwent some change. In the essay dated 1803, he was somewhat more willing to permit interference than in the one dated 1843. Doubtless the immediacy of the early nineteenth-century crisis in balance of power influenced his attitude. His awareness of the complexity of the problem and of the wide ramifications of the concept of interference led him to characterize, quite without irony, the whole system of balance of power as "the refined system of interference, which has regulated . . . Europe in foreign affairs."[27]

Other writers have reflected much the same chary attitude toward intervention. Vattel lay similar emphasis upon internal "self-determination," stating it very strictly:

> A Nation has full right to draw up for itself its constitution, to uphold it, to perfect it, and to regulate at will all that relates to the government, without interference on the part of anyone.

> . . . All such matters [constitutional changes] are of purely national concern, and no foreign power has any right to interfere otherwise than by its good offices, unless it be requested to do so or be led to do so by special reasons.[28]

He did not, of course, ignore the necessity of occasional intervention under some guise, but he was eager to confine it to legal channels. His particular solution was to bring the matter into the open:

> Power alone does not constitute a threat of injury; the will to injure must accompany the power. . . . As soon as a State has given evidence of injustice, greed, pride, ambition, or a desire of domineering over its neighbours, it becomes an object of suspicion which they must guard against. They may . . . demand securities of it; and if it hesitates to give these, they may prevent its designs by force of arms.[29]

Friedrich Gentz recognized the problem and admitted the need for intervention, in such matters, under rare and revolutionary conditions: "when by a mortal distemper in the vital parts of this kingdom, by a violent overthrow of its government, by a dissolution of all social ties, a cessation (though perhaps only a momentary one) of political existence ensues."[30] A statesman did

---

26 *Ibid.*, 37, 38.
27 *Ibid.*, 14.
28 Vattel, *Law of Nations*, III 18, no. 31; 19, no. 37.
29 *Ibid.*, 249, no. 44.
30 Gentz, *Fragments*, 112.

not have to read balance-of-power theory, such as the above, to feel the necessity of intervention in order to preserve the balance of power. The wars of the French Revolution began with just such a measure on the part of Austrian and Prussian leaders in 1791-1792. Burke, writer on, and respecter of, balance-of-power traditions, categorically urged on the government of Great Britain a policy of intervention in French affairs in 1791, arguing that it was in the best interest of France as well as of Europe and that a merely defensive posture was not enough.[31]

### Holding the Balances

An anonymous eighteenth-century commentator on the European balance of power spoke of a fourth corollary in the following way: "Experience as well as Reason will enable us to perceive that some one Power or other generally hinders the rest from going wrong, and this Power is said, I think not without cause, to hold the Balance. A most honourable, a most laudable Office surely!"[32] "Holding the balance" is probably the most familiar of all terms in the theory and practice of balance of power. The phrase is used to describe the role of a third party interested in preserving a simple balance between two other powers or two other blocs of powers. When one side threatens the security and survival of the other, the third party steps in on the side of the weaker and sees that a balance between independent powers is restored. Cartoons on the balance of power have often shown a human figure, symbolic of the "balancer" country, with scales in hand, weighing two other countries in order to determine which side was the lighter and therefore more needful of help to "redress the balance." England is the textbook example of the

balancer, and historians are fond of quoting the words attributed to Henry VIII: *"Cui adhaereo, prae-est."* Britain's location as an island, separate from the continent and yet close to it, gave her security, aloofness, and flexibility which were only partly compromised by the Hanoverian possessions of her monarchs. Great Britain herself, sharing territorial frontiers with no modern European power and avoiding that type of vulnerability, was yet a kind of immediate neighbor of all, because of her generous development of water communications. These factors all contributed to a strong balance-of-power tradition in British foreign policy and gave particular emphasis to the balancer conception of policy, which has been so important in English history.

This information is widely recognized. Less commonly realized is the fact that the idea of "holding the balance" is a familiar aspect of equilibrist history not at all peculiar to modern England alone. England's geographical position, to be sure, was ideal for such a role, but European states less fortunate in that respect often consciously adopted a policy of "holding the balance." De Réal quite rightly wrote of this policy as a general phenomenon and not as something confined to the British.[33]

As a continental example of "holding the balance" on a small although almost ludicrously ambitious scale, Favier cited the policy of the court of Turin in northwestern Italy, where one of the lesser sovereignties of Europe controlled an important pass through the Alps and tried to utilize "this local advantage to hold the balance between the two Houses of Bourbon and Austria."[34] With regard to a more important matter, the same author spoke of France's holding the balance between England and Holland during part of the reign of Louis XIV: "In the great days of Louis XIV, France profited

---

31 Hoffman and Levack, *Burke's Politics*, 431-434.
32 *Appendix to the Memoirs of the Duke de Ripperda*, 359.
33 Réal, *Science du gouvernement*, VI, 443.
34 Favier, *Politique de tous les cabinets*, III 48-49. (Translations from this work are mine.)

from the national animosity, and from the commercial jealousy between the English and Dutch to hold the balance between the two maritime powers."[35] As to relations within the Empire, he held that France could exploit the simple balance between Prussia and Russia.[36] Vergennes, in a memoir to Louis XVI, stated the same argument: France, in need, could count on Prussia and Austria to offset each other's power, thus enabling France to hold the balance between them.[37]

## Mobility of Action

More broadly, "holding the balance" implies the need for a ready mobility in the direction of policy. Statesmen must be able to act quickly and expertly in cutting encumbering ties or making new ones as balance necessities dictate. In the writing of Ségur, already referred to, one gets a very clear sense of the mobility of French policy, as he conceived it, in its dealings with the Holy Roman Empire. Austria and Prussia were to be kept in balance and France's weight to be thrown on the side of the weaker. The same mobility was necessary to any foreign office which sought to act as a "balancer." The Abbé de Mably assigned this role generally to all powers except the two most powerful. The latter were to be held in a simple balance by the fluctuations of the former, all of whom were balancers on the middle of the seesaw. The very smallest states were treated as exceptions and were advised, because of their impotence, to remain scrupulously neutral.[38] The necessity of mobility is seen in the work of the Abbé de Pradt when he points out that in crises of the balance system "enemies come together for common defense, and allies momentarily separate for the same reason."[39]

The eighteenth century, so abundant in its materials on the balance of power, is typically open-handed in its supply of actual examples of flexibility in foreign policy. Great Britain serves as a ready illustration in her policies toward the continental states in the decade immediately after 1713. At the beginning of this era, Great Britain and Europe were emerging from the long War of the Spanish Succession. British statesmen forestalled a withdrawal into isolation and kept Britain active in the continental alliance systems, starting with participation in the Barrier Treaty (1715) with Austria and Holland against France and an alliance with Austria (1716). This system was then paralleled by a triple alliance (1717) of Britain, Holland, and France, which in turn was elaborated by the inclusion of Austria in a well-known quadruple alliance (1718) created to check Spanish aggression. By 1721, however, we find Britain and France, having dropped their earlier alliance structure against Spain, now going into an alliance *with* Spain. By 1725 Britain, France, and Prussia were allies against Austria; in 1725 Britain renewed the earlier triplice with Spain and France; and in the 1730's Britain was back in an Austrian alliance (1731) and later at war (1739ff) with her erstwhile Spanish ally. These details are anything but fascinating when stripped of their historical context, but they do show the rapid fluctuations which were characteristic of balance-of-power policy.

Elaborate documentation is unnecessary to show that mobility is of real importance to balance policies, but there are two important ramifications of this assertion which need comment. One is that the balance of power is best adapted to absolutism and the other that balance of power is basically amoral. The first of these

---

35 *Ibid.*, 92.

36 In his article on England (*ibid.*, II. 165).

37 *Ibid.*, 111, 161.

38 Abbé de Mably, *Collection complète*, V, 49, 84, 86-91.

39 Pradt, *La Prusse et sa neutralité*, 85-86.

two implications may claim both a theoretical and historical basis. The former lies in the compatibility between absolutism and quick, decisive action; the latter, in the disability with which balance of power has been saddled under democratic procedures. Policy must be continually readjusted to meet changing circumstances if an equilibrium is to he preserved. A state which, by virtue of its institutional make-up is unable to readjust quickly to altered conditions will find itself at a distinct disadvantage in following a balance-of-power policy, especially when other states do not labor under the same difficulties. Historically, this fact has meant that democracy, with its slow-moving processes, has been less well adapted to the pursuit of balanced power than absolutism, which has benefited, in this sense, from more swiftly moving machinery in foreign policy. It was not a coincidence that balance of power should have reached the zenith of its popularity in the eighteenth century, when absolutism was still one of the basic conditions in the conduct of diplomacy; nor was it a coincidence that equilibrist diplomacy should have been both unpopular and unsuccessful in the third and fourth decades of the twentieth century. There were other contributing causes, but it seems highly probable that democratic procedure was in itself an important cause for failure.

Mobility of action implies that a foreign minister must be ready to make and remake policy as the international planets wheel in their orbits. According to balance theory, a freshly inked treaty, contracted with all apparent good faith and replete with invocations to Deity, may quickly and justifiably be scrapped, if events prove that treaty incompatible with the necessities of preserving the balance of power. Indeed, under the circumstances, no time should be wasted in scrapping it. Bolingbroke put it cleverly:

"Pique must have no more a place than affection, in deliberations of this kind."[40]

Balance-of-power writers naturally did not dwell as a rule on the iniquities of the system which they championed, any more than enthusiasts and partisans usually do. They invented certain euphemisms to cover policies which might well have been described in sharper language. Lord Brougham, instead of exhorting equilibrists to break their pledges, scrap treaties, violate their given words, be insincere, and adopt unchristian conduct, urged a certain "impartiality" on statesmen as they sought to hold an equilibrium— an impartiality which could serve the higher interest of the state system and ignore special cultural affinities and friendships between nations:

> All particular interests, prejudices, or partialities must be sacrificed to the higher interest . . . of uniting against oppression or against the measures which appear to place the security of all in jeopardy. No previous quarrel with any given State, no existing condition even of actual hostility, must be suffered to interfere with the imperative claims of the general security.[41]

What his pronouncement did not make clear was that ordinary morality had little or no place in the balance system, when the "higher interest" was at stake. The history of the balance of power is littered with the carcasses of violated pledges, broken treaties, and abortive friendships among nations. Where this has been the result of equilibrist policy, clearly conceived and rigorously executed, the balance theorist must defend it. In short, the balancing system emphasized the urgency of preserving the state system and stressed the conformity of means to that end rather than the conformity of means to a moral standard. Thus,

---

40 Lord Bolingbroke, *Works*, II, 293; cited by Kovacs, *op. cit.*, App. XI, 3.
41 Brougham, *Works*, VIII, 72.

the alienation of liberal opinion from the balance of power in the nineteenth century was no casual estrangement, but a deep-seated antagonism, where one stood for the "higher interest" of the state system and the other could not condone an abandonment of the morality of liberalism.[42]

## Reciprocal Compensation

The balance-of-power statesman could not always direct his policy in such a way as to prevent aggrandizement by another power. On occasions he had more to lose than to gain by opposition, when opposition might not affect the state system as a whole. Under such circumstances, the equilibrist might fall back on the idea of "reciprocal compensation" or "proportional aggrandizement."[43] This concept stated that aggrandizement by one power entitled other powers to an equal compensation[44] or, negatively, that the relinquishing of a claim by one power must be followed by a comparable abandonment of a claim by another.

It was not possible to justify this principle in terms of "idealistic" balance of power. What justification it could muster was based on the contention that the balance system was not only run by the big powers but was also run for them. It was clearly impossible for reciprocal compensation to operate on behalf of many members in the state system, unless there was an abnormal situation as in the latter half of the nineteenth century, when many of the European powers could help themselves to overseas territory in Africa, Asia, or the Pacific. If the compensation had to

originate within the confines of the state system itself, however, proportional aggrandizement became manifestly impossible for many states, because the European loaf would soon be consumed by slicing.

From the standpoint of balance theory (with emphasis on the word *theory*), such compensation must be regarded as a corrupt practice of the powerful states at the expense of the less powerful, a policy to be justified only as a "realistic" retrenchment when the usual balance techniques fail to solve the problem of aggrandizement. The fact that international law, in its narrow sense, could not and did not provide for the idea of proportional aggrandizement, even when its codifiers were well aware of the intimacy between international law and balance of power, was an indication of the "corruptness" of the practice. On the other hand, the appearance of the principle of proportional aggrandizement in the history of balance of power was no doubt inevitable. Virtually all western diplomacy and international relations have been based fundamentally on the idea of *quid pro quo*. The theory and practice of balance strategy could not long dissociate itself from an idea to which it bore such obvious affinity, nor did it. The linkage has been strong throughout modern history. Historical examples of reciprocal compensation may be unearthed in the Westphalia settlement in 1648, when many of the small German principalities were parcelled out among the Empire, Sweden, Bavaria, and Brandenburg. The partitions of Poland in 1772, 1793, and 1795 are other and more spectacular illustrations, and the

---

42  Attention is called to the paradox of a system, basically amoral, which nevertheless had no lack of enthusiastic and idealistic admirers. See above, pp. 47-51.

43  Writers' tastes have run to different phraseology in identifying this corollary: "reciprocal compensation" (Geoffrey Bruun, *Europe and the French Imperium, 1799-1814* [New York and London, 1938], 36, 38); "proportional aggrandizement" (Brougham, *Works*, VIII, 8); "proportional mutual aggrandizement" and "reciprocal reduction" (Burke in Hoffman and Levack, *Burke's Politics*, 407, 408); "accroissemens proportionnels" (Pradt, *La Prusse el sa neutralité* 67).

44  See, for example, Hardenberg's assertion of the principle of reciprocal compensation in his demand for Prussia of "a strengthening analogous to that which all the allies and so many other States are obtaining" (Hardenberg to Alexander, Dec. 16, 1814, in d'Angeberg, *Congrès de Vienne*, I, 533).

nineteenth century furnishes an even larger canvas whereon the color patterns of various continental flags were painted, as European imperialists moved throughout the world, to a measurable extent governed by this same idea. In the dictum of Ségur on French policy toward the Ottoman Empire: "France has only two parts to take: that of preventing the dismemberment of the Ottoman Empire, or of cooperating in it."[45] In 1808, Metternich, at that time the Austrian ambassador in Paris, urged a similar attitude toward the partition of the Porte then being considered. He counseled his foreign minister: "If we cannot arrive at an agreement with Russia by persuasion, to stop the destructive plans of Napoleon against the Porte, it would be necessary to take an active part in them."[46] He was willing to see Austria "join in the partition only when it is impossible to arrest it."[47] In short, "If the cake could not be saved, it must be fairly divided."[48]

### Preservation of Components: Moderation

An equilibrium cannot perpetuate itself unless the major components of that equilibrium are preserved. Destroy important makeweights and you destroy the balance; or, in the words of Fénelon to the grandson of Louis XIV early in the eighteenth century: "never . . . destroy a power under pretext of restraining it."[49]

This necessity of preserving the components of the system may be taken as a corollary of the

balance of power, and a most important one. Machiavelli once wrote that "men ought either to be well treated or crushed, because they can avenge themselves of lighter injuries, of more serious ones they cannot; therefore the injury that is to be done to a man ought to be of such a kind that one does not stand in fear of revenge."[50] His injunction is at once so well expressed, cynical, and arresting that one is tempted to snip it out of context and graft it, after trimming, onto the branches of balance of power. By paraphrasing his statement and applying it to international relations, one can make it say that if one is not to crush a defeated state, one must treat it well, because it has work to do and a place to fill in the general balance. Montesquieu came much closer than Machiavelli to putting the sentiment into the context of the balance of power in one of the most interesting of all his assertions: the "law of nations is naturally founded on this principle, that different nations ought in time of peace to do one another all the good they can and in time of war as little injury as possible, without prejudicing their real interest."[51] His remark suggests the immediate relevance of moderation to the balance of power. The evidence on this corollary is easily multiplied. Vergennes wrote to Louis XVI in 1784 that all France's influence "ought to be directed toward the maintenance of the public order, and to prevent the different powers which compose the European equilibrium from being destroyed."[52] Ségur, in a comment on Vergennes' letter, spoke of "the importance of conserving

---

45 Favier, *Politique de tous les cabinets*, III, 156.

46 Metternich to Stadion, Paris, April 27, 1808, in Metternich, *Memoirs*, II, 208.

47 Metternich to Stadion, Paris, February 26, 1808, *ibid.*, 194.

48 Remark of Count Tolstoy, (1769-1844), Russian general, ambassador to Paris during the period of the French alliance (*Ibid.*, 197-198).

49 Fénelon, "Supplément," III, 361. Similarly, "the weakening of a power which serves as a counter-weight can be as dangerous as the positive aggrandisement of such another." Quoted in Alexandre de Stieglitz, *De l'équilibre politique, du légitimisme et du principe des nationalités* (Paris, 1893-97), I, 125.

50 *The Prince*, 19.

51 *The Spirit of the Laws* (London, 1906; trans. by Thomas Nugent from *L'esprit des lois*, Geneva, 1748), I, 6.

52 Favier, *Politique, de tous les cabinets*, II, 201.

Prussian power, without aggrandisement or diminution, in order to maintain the equilibrium in Europe."[53] A similar concern for the preservation of Prussia as a useful component in the European balance was voiced by the Abbé de Pradt, in his analysis of Prussian neutrality:

> The preservation and the integrity of Prussia are important not only to the Empire, to Sweden, Denmark, Turkey, England, and above all to France . . .; but it is further important to the powers which seem to menace it: because each . . . should prefer its actual state to the excessive expansion of the other, and consequently is interested in its preservation.[54]

Ségur, at another point, accused Louis XV of having attempted in the Seven Years' War "to destroy totally the Prussian monarchy; which would have entirely disrupted the balance in Europe."[55] A central Europe, unbuttressed in the north by an independent, effective, and vigorous Prussia, would involve a profound readjustment of French policy toward her eastern neighbors.

Edmund Burke, not an observer given to underestimating the menace of the French Revolution, nevertheless made very clear the basic restraint in his attitude toward France. In 1791 he declared:

> It is always the interest of Great Britain that the power of France should be kept within the bounds of moderation. It is not her interest that that power should be wholly annihilated in the system of Europe. Though at one time through France the independence of Europe was endangered, it is, and ever was, through her alone that the common liberty of Germany can be secured against the single or the combined ambition of any other power.[56]

He felt French power, for the security of the European system, had to be maintained at a high level: "As to the power of France as a state, and in its exterior relations, I confess my fears are on the part of its extreme reduction. . . . the liberties of Europe cannot possibly be preserved but by her remaining a very great . . . power."[57]

In stating this he was emphasizing a policy of moderation which he felt to be a necessary accompaniment to a successful balance of power. Ségur urged the same middle course when, in speaking of peace treaties, he wrote that peace "will be solid and become a glorious and lasting monument only as long as it will be sufficiently advantageous to guarantee our security and that of our allies, and sufficiently moderate to permit no reasonable cause of hatred to exist among our enemies."[58] We might well demand to know what meaning can be applied to "moderation" here. Pursuit of balance-of-power policies has often shown itself most immoderate: coalition wars cannot be called moderate, and the extinction of weak powers under the plea of balance of power surely cannot be termed moderate. The fear, suspicion, and rapid changes of policy which have characterized much of the history of balance of power do not by any stretch of the imagination appear to have been moderate.

There is, however, a limited sense, and a very important sense, in which this term can be applied. Statesmen have often been moderate in their studied attempts to avoid humiliating a defeated power. In a recent period Bismarck offers a classical example of this moderation—in the Prussian war against Austria in 1866, when as principal civilian adviser to the Prussian monarch, he insisted that the war be ended almost as soon as Prussian military victory was

---

53 *Ibid.*, 220.
54 Pradt, *La Prusse et sa neutralité*, 90.
55 Favier, *Politique de tous les cabinets*, I, 297.
56 Hoffman and Levack, *Burke's Politics*, 408.
57 *Ibid.*, 450.
58 Favier, *Politique de tous les cabinets*, III, 369-370.

indicated. In spite of the storm of objections which this policy evoked, his line was adopted; no victory march in Vienna was permitted the victorious Prussian soldiers, a "soft" treaty was given the defeated Austrians, and at Bismarck's insistence, every attempt was made to avoid humiliating Austria.

The student may find ample precedent for Bismarck's action in the record of earlier European history. Successful equilibrist statesmen have almost invariably recognized the imperative necessity of maintaining the essential weights which comprise an equilibrium, a necessity which has manifested itself, for example, in the restoration of complete sovereignty to defeated powers. European wars in the eighteenth century "were ended . . . by treaties which, more often than not, represented a compromise, and in their forms studiously respected the dignity of the defeated party."[59]

The fact that such a policy of moderation was prescribed as well by self-interest does not make it any the less a balance-of-power policy. Statesmen have been as persistent as they have been in pursuit of balance of power because of its relation to a kind of higher self-interest. We can be sure that any use of the word moderation to describe balance of power does not imply an absolute moral standard. Nevertheless, this concept of moderation is useful and meaningful in describing the large policy of statesmen in their search for equilibrium. It is a very roughhewn and inexact usage, to be sure, but it contains a modicum of truth.

If we seek to uncover this kernel of truth, we will find that moderation, when it has been used, has been extended most often to large, and not small, powers, unless the latter have somehow been useful to the former, as in the case of

Belgium to Great Britain from 1837 to 1939. The importance of moderation as far as balance of power is concerned lies in the necessity of preserving the significant counterweights in the system of equilibrium. Moderation is probably necessary to successful equilibrist diplomacy, and its absence may mean failure to establish a workable balance.

The spirit of moderation is often one of the keys to a statesman's balance-of-power policy, because only such an attitude can carry with it a willingness to think of the state system as a whole, and not exclusively of one state. As Talleyrand put it, in connection with the creation of an alliance: "It is necessary to exercise great care . . . , for it [the alliance] must be drawn up in the interest of Europe at large, indeed, of everyone."[60] Moderation has been especially difficult and praiseworthy when shown by statesmen who have been on the victorious side in a bitter war. A case in point is the persistent distinction which allied statesmen, in the period 1813-1815, made between the government and the people of France. Their policy, they were careful to assert, was directed against the government of Napoleon and not against his subjects. And more important than their mere assertion was the stunning willingness of the same men to reduce their policy to practice in the subsequent peace settlement, as though they had taken to heart the wise words of the international jurist:

A treaty of peace can be nothing more than a compromise. . . . Since, however just our cause may be, we must after all look to the restoration of peace and direct our efforts constantly to that salutary object, the only recourse is to compromise the claims and grievances on both sides, and to put an end to all differences by as fair an agreement as can be reached.[61]

---

59 Phillips, *Confederation of Europe*, 7.
60 The wording is from the translation by Raphaël Ledos de Beaufort, *Memoirs of the Prince de Talleyrand* (New York and London, 1891-92), V, 354.
61 Vattel, *Law of Nations*, III, 350, no. 18.

## The Coalition

The alliance has been as common as the pox and has made a very usual, peacetime appearance in a balance-of-power system. The coalition, on the other hand, has typically appeared only in the great war crises of the balance of power, at times when the very existence of the state system seemed shaken and in danger. Among the most obvious examples of coalitions, in addition to those against Louis XIV and Napoleon, are those which were formed against Charles V, the Central Powers in 1914-1918, and the Axis in 1939-1945. It is noteworthy that only five major examples of coalitions are readily cited for a span of four hundred years of modern history, whereas a listing of alliances would sound like someone reading from a telephone book, so bewilderingly abundant are they in the same period.

Care must be taken to distinguish the alliance from the coalition, since they differ in important respects. An alliance, in this context, is taken to mean a bilateral or trilateral agreement for offensive or defensive purposes; and a coalition, to indicate either a similar agreement signed by four or more powers or a conjunction of several alliances directed toward the same end. Thus the critical distinction is one of size, the alliance becoming a coalition when four or more states are included. There are other differences which arise out of the property of size and which will be discussed below.

One of the persistent reasons for the relative rarity of coalitions as opposed to alliances is the difficulty of constructing them and the further problem of holding them together. Coalitions, being larger, are usually harder to create and therefore rarer in occurrence. De Réal, with a Frenchman's preference for images of courtship, remarked that among the members of a coalition the first ardor was soon frozen by mistrust and consequent disunity.[62] Standard examples of suspicion and discord are to be found in the conflicts which took place between the beginning of the wars of the French Revolution in 1792 and the fall of Napoleon in 1815. For twenty long and disheartening years, each of the coalitions against France fell apart. The story is told by numerous "diplomatic revolutions" in the European scene during those two decades. For example, Austria, at war with France off and on between 1792 and 1809, became the ally of Napoleon and assisted his Russian campaign in 1812—against her former Russian ally. Prussia, an enemy of France between 1792 and 1795 and again in 1806, began the same Russian campaign in 1812 as an ally of Napoleon, later to change sides again and fight the French as Austria did. Russia herself, an enemy of France in the second and third coalitions, became a French ally by the Treaty of Tilsit in 1807, later reversing herself again. Vacillation of the small states was just as pronounced, the German states aiding France at one time and later entering the enemy camp against her.

The necessity of forming coalitions is a clear one, according to the rationale of the balance of power: "Confederations would be a sure means of preserving the balance of power and thus maintaining the liberty of Nations, if all sovereigns were constantly aware of their true interests, and if they regarded their policy according to the welfare of the State."[63] Among neighboring states there was a "mutual duty of defense of the common safety against a neighboring state which became too powerful."[64] Or, as expressed in *Europe's Catechism*:[65]

> Catechist: When any Potentate hath arriv'd to an exorbitant Share of Power ought not the Rest to league together in order to reduce him to his due Proportion of it?

---

62 Réal, *Science du gouvernement*, VI, 354.
63 Vattel, *Law of Nations*, III, 25 1, no. 49.
64 Fénelon, "Supplément," III, 362 (translation mine).
65 See above, p. 2.

Europa: Yes, certainly.—Otherwise there is but one Potentate, and the others are only a kind of Vassals to him.

Brougham urged that "leagues or alliances of a defensive kind ought to be formed among States which, from their position, are exposed in common to the hazard of being attacked by any powerful neighbours."[66] . . .

## War

It would be difficult to study the stated assumptions, aims, and means and still be unaware of the connection between balance of power and that most disheartening of all human institutions—warfare. As mentioned, the ablest theorists universally accepted the connection and thought of war as one more corollary of the balance of power. Vattel was typical of these in his assertion that governments, when faced with danger from a powerful neighbor, "may prevent its designs by force of arms." War was an instrument to be used when other devices failed and to be used relatively deftly and sparely. One of the pleasanter things to recall about the seventeenth and eighteenth centuries is the fact that European warfare was appreciably different in that era from its more catastrophic descendant in ours.[67] Armies were smaller and more apt to be personal than national. A colonel losing his regiment was not apt to get another; strategy reflected this fact and tended to create a war of maneuver rather than a war of decisive battles. In a prenational period, generally devoid of fierce loyalties to the state, the ranks were often filled by professional soldiers and mercenaries whose loyalties were fluid and whose disciplining

was harsh in the extreme. The officers, like the Duke of Plaza Toro, marched behind their men to keep a watchful eye on them; and tactical deployment was unwise under the circumstances, because the men might desert. These points help to explain the old prints which embrace in single plates entire battlefields, usually an impossibility for a comparable twentieth-century battle.

The limited war of the eighteenth century meant limited objectives, the reliance on fortresses, and a consequent emphasis on the science of siege warfare. Limited war also made possible a workable distinction between soldier and civilian. The numerous and important advantages of eighteenth-century warfare over its twentieth-century counterpart were unfortunately balanced by the utterly inadequate medical care which resulted in the loss of many more soldiers from disease than from battle. In glancing back at earlier methods of fighting, one of the points that commands attention is the relative appropriateness of the balance-of-power theory to an era of limited warfare and its relative inappropriateness to the more modern era. With the 1790's warfare began to change profoundly. The *levée en masse,* the mass army, the development of a new and fanatical concept of loyalty to the nation-state, the emergence of a new discipline, changes in supply, the greater strategic reliance on wars of decisive battles, the ultimate marriage of warfare to the industrial revolution—all these elements altered the facts of war. In passing, they took a screw driver from the hands of the equilibrist, replacing it with a sledge hammer. In the twentieth century tinkering became impossible, and when the machine was out of repair it was likely to be pounded.

---

66 Brougham, *Works*, VIII, 70.
67 See the Montesquieu quotation above, 73.

# 18: Conflict and Cooperation in the Absence of Hegemony

*Robert O. Keohane*

## Interdependence, Institutions, and Regimes

Interdependence in the world political economy generates conflict. People who are hurt by unexpected changes emanating from abroad, such as increases in the prices that producers charge for oil or that banks charge for the use of money, turn to their governments for aid. So do workers, unemployed because of competition from more efficient or lower-wage foreign production. Governments, in turn, seek to shift the costs of these adjustments onto others, or at least to avoid having them shifted onto themselves. This strategy leads them to pursue incompatible policies and creates discord.

If discord is to be limited, and severe conflict avoided, governments' policies must be adjusted to one another. That is, cooperation is necessary. One way of achieving such mutual policy adjustment is through the activities of a hegemonic power, either through *ad hoc* measures or by establishing and maintaining international regimes that serve its own interests while managing to be sufficiently compatible with the interests of others to be widely accepted. As we saw . . . the United States played this role during the first fifteen or twenty years after World War II; hegemonic cooperation was a reality. . . . The United States is still the most important country in the world political economy and that it remains an essential participant in international regimes. Indeed, U.S. involvement is usually necessary if cooperation is to be fostered successfully.

Nevertheless. . . the ability and willingness of the United States to devote substantial resources to maintaining international economic regimes have both declined since the mid-1960s. As noted earlier, it seems unlikely that the United States will reassume the dominant position that it had during the 1950s, or that any other country will come to occupy such a position, in the absence of a wrenching upheaval such as occurred in the past as a result of major wars. Since war in the nuclear age would have altogether different and more catastrophic effects than the world wars of the past, it is probably safe to assume that hegemony will not be restored during our lifetimes. If we are to have cooperation, therefore, it will be cooperation without hegemony.

Nonhegemonic cooperation is difficult, since it must take place among independent states that are motivated more by their own conceptions of self-interest than by a devotion to the common good. Nothing in this book denies this difficulty, nor do I forecast a marvelous new era of smooth mutual policy adjustment, much less one of harmony. But, despite the persistence of discord, world politics is not a state of war. States do have complementary interests, which make certain forms of cooperation potentially beneficial. As hegemony erodes, the demand for international regimes may even increase, as the lack of a formal intergovernmental oil regime in the 1950s, and the institution of one in 1974, suggest. Furthermore, the legacy of American hegemony persists, in the form of a number of international regimes. These regimes create a more favorable institutional environment for cooperation than would otherwise exist; it is easier to maintain them than it would be to create new ones. Such regimes are important not because they constitute centralized quasi-governments, but because they can facilitate agreements, and decentralized enforcement of agreements, among governments. They enhance the likelihood of cooperation by reducing the costs of making transactions that are consistent with the principles of the regime. They create the conditions for orderly multilateral negotiations, legitimate and delegitimate different types of state action, and facilitate linkages among issues within regimes and between regimes. They increase the symmetry and improve the quality of the information that governments receive. By clustering issues together in the same forums over a long period of time, they help to bring governments into continuing interaction with one another, reducing incentives to cheat and enhancing the value of reputation. By establishing legitimate standards of behavior for states to follow and by providing ways to monitor compliance, they create the basis for decentralized enforcement founded on the principle of reciprocity. The network of international regimes bequeathed to the contemporary international political economy by American hegemony provides a valuable foundation for constructing post-hegemonic patterns of cooperation, which can be used by policymakers interested in achieving their objectives through multilateral action.

The importance of regimes for cooperation supports the Institutionalist claim . . . that international institutions help to realize common interests in world politics. An argument for this view has been made here not by smuggling in cosmopolitan preferences under the rubric of "world welfare" or "global interests," but by relying on Realist assumptions that states are egoistic, rational actors operating on the basis of their own conceptions of self-interest. Institutions

are necessary, even on these restrictive premises, in order to achieve *state* purposes.

Realism provides a good starting-point for the analysis of cooperation and discord, since its taut logical structure and its pessimistic assumptions about individual and state behavior serve as barriers against wishful thinking. Furthermore, it suggests valuable insights that help us interpret the evolution of the world political economy since the end of World War II. Yet it is in need of revision, because it fails to take into account that states' conceptions of their interests, and of how their objectives should be pursued, depend not merely on national interests and the distribution of world power, but on the quantity, quality, and distribution of information. Agreements that are impossible to make under conditions of high uncertainty may become feasible when uncertainty has been reduced. Human beings, and governments, behave differently in information-rich environments than in information-poor ones. Information, as well as power, is a significant systemic variable in world politics. International systems containing institutions that generate a great deal of high-quality information and make it available on a reasonably even basis to the major actors are likely to experience more cooperation than systems that do not contain such institutions, even if fundamental state interests and the distribution of power are the same in each system. Realism should not be discarded, since its insights are fundamental to an understanding of world politics (Keohane, 1983), but it does need to be reformulated to reflect the impact of information-providing institutions on state behavior, even when rational egoism persists.

Thus when we think about cooperation after hegemony, we need to think about institutions. Theories that dismiss international institutions as insignificant fail to help us understand the conditions under which states' attempts at cooperation, *in their own interests,* will be successful. This is especially true in the contemporary world political economy, since it is endowed with a number of important international regimes, created under conditions of American hegemony but facilitating cooperation even after the erosion of U.S. dominance. We seem now to be in a period of potential transition between the hegemonic cooperation of the two decades after World War II and a new state of affairs, either one of prevailing discord or of post-hegemonic cooperation. Whether discord or cooperation prevails will depend in considerable measure on how well governments take advantage of established international regimes to make new agreements and ensure compliance with old ones.

Yet an awareness of the importance of institutions—defined broadly as sets of practices and expectations rather than in terms of formal organizations with imposing headquarters buildings—must not lead us to lapse into old habits of thought. It is not particularly helpful to think about institutions in terms of "peace through law" or world government. Institutions that facilitate cooperation do not mandate what governments must do; rather, they help governments pursue their own interests through cooperation. Regimes provide information and reduce the costs of transactions that are consistent with their injunctions, thus facilitating interstate agreements and their decentralized enforcement. It is misleading, therefore, to evaluate regimes on the basis of whether they effectively centralize authority. Nor do institutions that promote cooperation need to be universal. Indeed, since regimes depend on shared interests, and on conditions that permit problems of collective action to be overcome, they are often most useful when relatively few like-minded countries are responsible for both making the essential rules and maintaining them. Finally, international institutions do not need to be integrated into one coherent network. Cooperation is almost always fragmentary in world politics: not all the pieces of the puzzle will fit together.

Building institutions in world politics is a frustrating and difficult business. Common interests are often hard to discover or to maintain. Furthermore, collective action invites myopic behavior: as in Rousseau's well-known tale, the hunters may chase individually after rabbits rather than cooperate to capture the deer (1755/1950, p. 238). Yet institutions are often worth constructing, because their presence or absence may determine whether governments can cooperate effectively for common ends. It is even more important to seek to maintain the valuable international institutions that continue to exist, since the effort required to maintain them is less than would be needed to construct new ones, and if they did not exist, many of them would have to be invented. Information-rich institutions that reduce uncertainty may make agreement possible in a future crisis. Since they may facilitate cooperation on issues that were not thought about at the time of their creation, international regimes have potential value beyond their concrete purposes. Such institutions cannot, therefore, be evaluated merely on the basis of how well they serve the perceived national interest at a given time; on the contrary, an adequate judgment of their worth depends on an estimate of the contribution they are likely to make, in the future, to the solution of problems that cannot yet be precisely defined. Such estimates should reflect an awareness that, in world politics, unexpected events—whether assassinations, coups, or defaults on debts—are likely, and that we need to insure against them.

The significance of information and institutions is not limited to political-economic relations among the advanced industrialized countries, although that is the substantive focus of this book. The theory presented here is relevant to any situation in world politics in which states have common or complementary interests that can only be realized through mutual agreement. As we have seen, there are almost always conflictual elements in these relationships as well. Like Prisoners' Dilemma, most of these situations will be "mixed-motive games," characterized by a combination of conflicting and complementary interests (Schelling, 1960/1980). Building information-rich institutions is as important in relations among the superpowers, where confidence is a key variable, and in arms control negotiations, in which monitoring and verification are of great importance, as in managing political-economic relations among the advanced industrialized countries. Institution-building may be more difficult where security issues are concerned, but is equally essential if cooperation is to be achieved.

### Foreign Policy and the Costs of Flexibility

It is often assumed that makers of foreign policy should maintain flexibility of action as much as possible. They are urged to "keep their options open." At first glance, this appears to be good advice, since the unpredictability of events in world politics makes it prudent to be able to change policy in response to new information. Yet governments are continually making commitments of one sort or another. For some reason they seem unable to follow the prescriptions of those who emphasize the value of retaining maximum room for maneuver.

The argument of this book helps to account for this discrepancy between the conventional wisdom of foreign policy analysis and the practices of states. Uncertainty pervades world politics. International regimes reduce this uncertainty by providing information, but they can only do this insofar as governments commit themselves to known rules and procedures and maintain these commitments even under pressure to renege. As we have seen, the fact that governments anticipate a future need for agreements with the same countries to which they currently have commitments gives them incentives to fulfill those commitments even when it is painful to do so. Furthermore, theories of bounded rationality make us aware that, even apart from their adherence to international regimes, governments do not have the capability to maintain as high a degree of flexibility as would purely rational actors. They need rules of thumb to guide their actions.

If there were an infinitely large number of equally small actors in world politics, the general desirability of reducing uncertainty through the formation of international regimes would not lead to the creation of such institutions. International conditions would more closely approximate the Hobbesian model in which life is "nasty, brutish, and short." But as we have seen, the fact that the number of key actors in the international political economy of the advanced industrialized countries is typically small gives each state incentives to make and keep commitments so that others may be persuaded to do so.

Committing oneself to an international regime implies a decision to restrict one's own pursuit of advantage on specific issues in the future. Certain alternatives that might otherwise appear desirable—imposing quotas, manipulating exchange rates, hoarding one's own oil in a crisis—become unacceptable by the standards of the regime. Members of a regime that violate these norms and rules will find that their reputations suffer more than if they had never joined at all. A reputation as an unreliable partner may prevent a government from being able to make beneficial agreements in the future.

Reputation is important, but may not provide a sufficient basis for others to estimate the value of one's commitments. . . Diplomats have to deal with "quality uncertainty," much like buyers of used cars. That is, they need information about the real intentions and capabilities of their prospective partners: they may be prepared to enter into agreements only if they can gather convincing evidence that intentions are benign and capabilities sufficient to carry them out, and that the information at their disposal is not significantly worse than that possessed by their partners. Admittedly, governments such as that of the United States—whose bureaucratic struggles take place in public, and whose legislatures often fail to do the bidding of their executives— may earn reputations for unreliability, and their leaders may be viewed abroad as not having the capability to implement their agreements. Yet . . . there is another side to this question. Governments that close off their decisionmaking processes to outsiders, restricting the flow of information about their true preferences or their likely future actions, will have more difficulty providing high-quality evidence about their intentions than their less tightly organized counterparts, and will therefore find it harder to make mutually beneficial agreements.

These arguments suggest that governments should seek to combine reliability of action with the provision of high-quality information to their partners. International regimes facilitate both of these objectives, by providing rules that constitute standards for evaluating state behavior and by facilitating the establishment of contacts among governments that help to provide information not merely about policies but about intentions and values. Both the value of a reputation for reliability and the gains to be made from providing high-quality information to others challenge the traditional *Realpolitik* ideal of the autonomous, hierarchical state that keeps its options open and its decisionmaking processes closed. Maintaining unrestrained flexibility can be costly, if insistence on it makes a government an undesirable partner for others. Admittedly, there are tactical gains to be made from concealing preferences and "keeping others guessing." But such a policy can undermine one's ability to make beneficial agreements in the future. Being

unpredictable not only disconcerts one's partners but reduces one's own ability to make credible promises. Where there are substantial common interests to be realized through agreement, the value of a reputation for faithfully carrying out agreements may outweigh the costs of consistently accepting the constraints of international rules. To pursue self-interest does not require maximizing freedom of action. On the contrary, intelligent and farsighted leaders understand that attainment of their objectives may depend on their commitment to the institutions that make cooperation possible.

### Bibliography

Finifter, Ada W. ed., 1983. *Political Science: The State of the Discipline* (Washington D.C.: American Political Science Association).

Keohane, Robert O., 1983. Theory of world politics: structural Realism and beyond. In Finifter, 1983, pp. 503-40.

Okin, Susan Moller, 1984. Taking the bishops seriously. *World Politics*, vol. 36, no. 4 (July).

Rousseau, Jean-Jacques, 1755/1950. *A Discourse on the Origin of Inequality* (New York: Oxford University Press).

Schelling, Thomas C., 1960/1980. *The Strategy of Conflict* (Cambridge: Harvard University Press).

# 19: Marxist and Liberal Explanations

*Stephen D. Krasner*

## Marxism

Scholars in the Marxist tradition have presented the most extensive analysis of foreign economic policy. Marx himself was primarily concerned with developments within national economies, although he did not entirely ignore international problems. With Lenin's *Imperialism* the international aspects of capitalism assumed a place of first importance for Marxist scholars. The analytic assumptions of this paradigm differ in a number of fundamental ways from the state-centric approach of this study.

Marxist theories can be divided into two basic types: instrumental and structural.[1] Instrumental Marxist theories view government behavior as the product of direct societal pressure. In its most primitive form, this kind of argument emphasizes personal ties between leading capitalists and public officials.[2] In its more sophisticated form, instrumental Marxist arguments analyze the general ties between the capitalist sector and public officials. Ralph Miliband is the leading recent exponent of this kind of argument. He maintains that there is a cohesive capitalist class. This class controls the state because public officials are heavily drawn from the middle and upper classes, are in frequent contact with businessmen, and depend on the cooperation of private firms to carry out public policy. In addition, cultural institutions such as the media and churches reflect the dominant conservative ideology. Harold Laski took a very similar position, arguing that "historically, we always find that any system of government is dominated by those who at the time wield economic power; and what they mean by 'good' is, for the most part, the preservation of their own interests."[3] From an instrumental Marxist perspective, the state is the executive committee of the bourgeoisie.[4]

Structural Marxist arguments take a different tack. They do not attempt to trace the behavior of the state to the influence of particular capitalists

---

1   Gold, Lo, and Wright, "Recent Developments in Marxist Theories of the Capitalist State." This excellent essay also discusses a third approach, Marxist Hegelianism. A similar distinction is made in Wolfe, "New Directions in the Marxist Theory of Politics," pp. 133–36. Nicos Poulantzas, who is generally described as one of the leading proponents of the structuralist position, has argued that the distinction does not make sense. However, Poulantzas defines structuralism as either the view that does "not grant sufficient importance to the role of concrete individuals . . . " or the view that "neglects the importance and weight of the class struggle in history. . . ." See his essay "The Capitalist State," pp. 70 and 71. This is hardly what those who have described Poulantzas as a structuralist have in mind. Poulantzas dismisses his American Marxist critics with the statement that "the academic and ideologico-political conjuncture in the United States" is responsible for their misreading (p. 76).

2   For examples of such reasoning in the area of raw materials see Engler, *Brotherhood of Oil;* Goff and Locker, "The Violence of Domination"; and the much more sophisticated argument of Lipson. "Corporate Preferences and Public Choices."

3   *Foundations of Sovereignty*, p. 289, and *The State in Theory and Practice.*

4   See Kolko, *Roots of American Foreign Policy*, and Miliband, *The State in Capitalist Society*, for applications of instrumental Marxism to the concerns of this study. Recently, Miliband has taken a more structuralist position.

or the capitalist class. Instead, they see the state playing an independent role within the overall structure of a capitalist system. Its task is to maintian the cohesion of the system as a whole. At particular times this may require adopting policies opposed by the bourgeoisie, but generally official action and the preferences of leading elements in the capitalist class will coincide.

For structural Marxism, the behavior of the state involves an effort to deal with economic and political contradictions that are inherent in a capitalist system. Economically, capitalism is not seen as a self sustaining system tending toward equilibrium. Rather, over the long-term profit rates decline because capitalists can only secure profit through the exploitation of labor, but technological innovation reduces the long-term equilibrium ratio of labor to capital. This process also leads to underconsumption: the system produces more goods than its members can consume. It promotes concentration because weaker firms are driven out of the market. Excess capital is accumulated because there is no market for the goods that would be produced by more investment.

Politically, concentration—what Marxists call the increased socialization of the production process—produces tensions. As societies develop, they become more complex and interdependent. However, control is increasingly concentrated in the hands of an ever smaller group of the owners or managers of capital. At the same time, the working class grows and workers come into more intimate and constant contact with each other. The increased socialization of the production process itself and the continued private appropriation of power and profit produce political and social tensions that threaten the stability of the system.

From a structural Marxist perspective, policy analysis can be viewed as a catalogue of state efforts to cope with these tensions. In the area of foreign economic policy the major conclusion is that the state must follow an expansionary, an imperialist, foreign policy. Early Marxist writers elaborated the relationship between colonialism and expanded opportunities for trade and investment. The opening of new areas could help alleviate underconsumption because capitalists could find new markets by eliminating local artisans. Colonies also offered opportunities for surplus capital. This is the major argument presented by Lenin. These contentions have not been sustained by empirical investigations, however. Even in the heyday of empire only a small proportion of goods and capital moved from the mother country to colonial areas.[5] Recent radical analyses have suggested somewhat different motivations for expansion, including protection of the oligopolistic position of large firms, militarism, and the quest for raw materials.

The relationship between advanced capitalist societies, giant firms, and foreign activity has been emphasized by two recent Marxist analysts, Harry Magdoff and James O'Connor. Using arguments from the behavioral theory of the firm, Magdoff suggests that corporations are systems of power. Each firm strives to control its own market. This objective could not be realized during the early stages of capitalism because the level of competition was too high. As concentration increases, however, "the exercise of controlling power becomes not only possible but increasingly essential for the security of the firm and its assets."[6] Businesses seek to maximize control over actual and potential sources of raw materials and over foreign markets. Foreign investment is a particularly effective device for guaranteeing such control, although trading opportunities are not ignored. If control is lost, either to competitors or to socialist regimes, the

---

5  Barrett Brown, "A Critique of Marxist Theories of Imperialism," p. 44; Fieldhouse, "Imperialism"; Cohen, *The Question of Imperialism*, Ch. 2.
6  "Imperialism Without Colonies." p. 157.

oligopoly can be destroyed. Since these corporations are the foundation of the American capitalist system, their political power is great, and their collapse would precipitate a deep economic crisis. There are impelling reasons for the United States, the world's leading capitalist nation, to maintain an international economic system with minimum constraints on the operations of giant multinational firms.[7]

James O'Connor has taken an even more classical Marxist position. He maintains that the monopoly sector in modern capitalist systems is the most important source of profits. However, there is an inherent tendency for the productive capacity of the monopoly sector to expand more quickly than demand or employment. This leads to pressure for an aggressive foreign economic policy. Overseas activity can increase sales and profit, and offer opportunities for new investment. The purpose of foreign assistance and more direct military intervention is to keep foreign client states within the capitalist order.

Magdoff, O'Connor, and other structural Marxist analysts have also postulated an intimate relationship between the economic needs of the capitalist system, military expenditure, and imperialism. Military expenditures are a primary source of revenue for some major firms in the monopoly sector. Such expenditures help maintain the stability of the system because they are not subject to the rational calculations of profit and loss that are an inherent part of the capitalist ideology. Finally, militarism is important in a direct sense because the use of force may be necessary to keep foreign areas open to trade and investment.[8]

An argument directly related to the empirical concerns of this study, which has received new emphasis from Marxists, is that capitalists must have foreign raw materials. This aim was not ignored by classical Marxist writers. Lenin stated that capitalists were driven to control ever increasing amounts of even apparently worthless land because it might contain some unknown material that could lead to economic disaster if it were to fall into the hands of a competitor. Cheap raw materials also contributed to staving off the inevitable tendency toward declining rates of profits: new and rich discoveries could, at least temporarily, provide high profits. Magdoff has maintained that the search for raw materials is part of the general quest of giant corporations for security and oligopolistic profits. Only through vertical integration from mine to final sale can these firms assure themselves of tight market control. Furthermore, the United States and other capitalist states are seen as being vitally dependent on foreign sources for some commodities that are essential for industrial operations and advanced military equipment.[9] One author has argued that all American foreign policy can be explained by the need "to insure that the flow of raw materials from the Third World is never interrupted."[10]

While Marxist writers have dropped some arguments, modified others, and found new ones, there is a central thread that runs through their position. Foreign economic expansion is a necessity. It is not a matter of the preferences of particular enterprises. It is not a policy that has a marginal effect on profits. It is an issue that touches the very core of capitalism's continued viability. Cut off from the rest of the world, the economies of advanced capitalist states would confront problems of great severity. "For Marxism," Tom Kemp avers, "imperialism is not a political or ideological phenomenon but expresses the imperative necessities of advanced capitalism."[11]

---

7  *Age of Imperialism*, pp. 34-35 and Ch. 5.

8  O'Connor, *Fiscal Crisis*, Ch. 6.

9  Lenin, *Imperialism*, pp. 83-84; Magdoff, *Age of Imperialism*, pp. 52, 156; Kolko, *Roots of American Foreign Policy*, pp. 50-54.

10 Dean, "Scarce Resources," p. 149.

11 "The Marxist Theory of Imperialism," p. 17. See also Mack, "Comparing Theories of Economic Imperialism," p. 40.

For structural Marxists, the state can be treated as having autonomy, not from the needs of the system as a whole, but from direct political pressure from the capitalist class. Indeed, such autonomy is necessary because internal divisions preclude effective bourgeois political organization. To maintain cohesion the state must mitigate the social and political pressures arising from the increasing socialization of the production process coupled with the continuing private appropriation of profits and control. Carrying out this task requires it to pose as a representative of all the people. To appear to follow the explicit preferences of powerful capitalists too slavishly would weaken the stability of the whole system. Compromises, such as the recognition of unions and higher social welfare payments, are essential, even if they are opposed by the capitalist class. Such policies protect the existing structure of economic relationships by disarming and disuniting potential opposition from the oppressed.[12]

The analytic assumptions of Marxist theories, whether of the instrumental or structural variety, differ from the statist approach of this study in at least three ways. First, the notion of national interest is rejected by Marxists. The aims pursued by the state mirror the preferences of the capitalist class or some of its elements, or the needs of the system as a whole. State behavior does not reflect either autonomous power drives or the general well-being of the society. Second, the behavior of the state is taken by them to be intimately related to economic goals; other objectives are instrumental, not consummatory. In particular, ideological objectives cannot be independent of economic considerations. Ideology is a mask that hides the reality of exploitation and thus helps mislead and mollify those who have no real power. Third, even though structural Marxists may view the state as relatively autonomous, they do not believe that it can really be understood outside of its societal context. The state has peculiar tasks within the structure of a capitalist system, but they are ultimately associated with the interests of a particular class.

## Liberalism

A statist argument can also be highlighted by contrasting it with another major paradigm—liberalism. Liberal, interest-group, or pluralist theories constitute the most prevalent approach to the study of politics in the United States. They are apparent not only in the analytic framework used by most political scientists but also in the rhetorical expressions of American political leaders.

Analytically, liberalism, like Marxism, begins with the society. Its basic unit of analysis is the group. Politics is viewed as a competition among organized interests. Government policy is understood to be the "resultant of effective access by various interests. . ."[13] In its most simplified and schematic form, interest-group theories view politics as a vector diagram in which a series of pressures are brought to bear on the state, which then moves in the direction it is pushed by the strongest societal forces. Pluralist analysis differs from instrumental Marxism not in the basic structure of its argument (both view formal government institutions as relatively passive recipients of societal pressure), but in its judgment of the kinds of societal formations that have political influence. For Marxists, power is basically in the hands of the capitalist class; for pluralists, it may be exercised

---

12 Poulantzas, *Political Power and Social Classes*; O'Connor, *Fiscal Crisis*, esp. Ch. 1; Poulantzas, "The Capitalist State," p. 73; and Gough, "State Expenditure in Advanced Capitalism," pp. 64–65. It is not my purpose here to critique a structural Marxist position, but it is important to note that granting the state the kind of autonomy imputed to it by this approach weakens any dialectical analysis of capitalism. The state appears to be so independent and prescient that it can save capitalism from its own infirmities.

13 Truman, *The Governmental Process*, p. 507.

by individuals motivated by any interest that is salient enough to affect behavior.

Studies using a pluralist perspective have been most frequently concerned with local government. Since the Second World War most American investigations of foreign policy have been concerned with national security and have been written from a conventional state-centric perspective. However, during the last decade a new approach, the bureaucratic politics paradigm, has been offered as an alternative to conventional views. Bureaucratic politics applies the logic of pluralism to policy-making within government. Societal groups are replaced by government bureaus. Official policy is viewed as the outcome of bargaining among competing administrative units. Each of these units is motivated by its own interests. Though the President may formally make the final determination of policy, his action is explained by pressures and information that have come to him from the bureaucracy. Like governmental institutions in pluralist analyses of urban politics, the Presidency is basically a passive reactor to external forces.[14]

Interest-group theory can be applied to foreign policy questions in a more direct way when economic issues are at stake. Here it is not difficult to establish a relationship between official policy and the preferences of particular groups. Unlike national security, which has a relatively undifferentiated impact on all political groups, economic policy benefits some more than others. Commercial arrangements or foreign investment usually have a very salient impact on particular actors and a diffuse effect on the society as a whole. In such situations interest-group theory suggests that public policy will be very strongly affected by specific interests: it is very likely that governmental activity will reflect the demands of particular social groups. Probably the most well-known application of this line of reasoning is E. E. Schattschneider's *Politics, Pressures and the Tariff*. This study explains the Smoot-Hawley Tariff of 1930 as a product of the desires of a multiplicity of private economic actors. Each wanted protection for itself and was willing to accept protection for others. Government policy was simply a summation of private goals.

Analysts adopting a liberal or pluralist perspective have been very critical of the concept of the national interest. An inescapable implication of their position is that government policy is a reflection of whatever groups have power in the society. The concept of the public interest slips away. David Truman argues that in a complex modern nation "we do not need to account for a totally inclusive interest, because one does not exist."[15] Stephen Bailey writes that there "is perhaps no better example in all language of the utility of myth than the phrase 'the public interest.'"[16] Robert Dahl states that "if one rejects the notion that public interest is some amalgamation of private interests, there is little philosophical mileage to be gained from using the concept at all."[17] In respect to substance, from a liberal perspective, the public or national interest can only mean some summation of private interests.[18]

Liberal conceptions of politics also have little use for the notion of the state as an autonomous actor motivated by drives associated with its own need for power or with the well-being of the society as a whole. Governmental institutions

---

14  For examples see Allison, *Essence of Decision*, and Halperin, *Bureaucratic Politics*. For a study from this perspective dealing with the problems of this book see Einhorn, *Expropriation Politics*. For critiques see Krasner, "Are Bureaucracies Important?" and Art, "Bureaucratic Politics and American Foreign Policy." Art makes a critical distinction between first- and second-wave bureaucratic theorists and their treatment of the President.

15  *Governmental Process,* p. 51.

16  "The Public Interest," p. 97.

17  Quoted in Colm, "The Public Interest," pp. 116–17.

18  This argument is developed in Flathman, *The Public Interest*, pp. 21 ff.

merely process inputs and outputs. The state is seen as a set of formal structures, not an autonomous actor. There is no cohesive center of decision-making. The locus of power may move from one bureau to another, or from one branch of government to another, depending on the interests and power resources associated with particular issues.[19] At best, from a pluralist perspective, governmental institutions become but one interest group among many; at worst, public policy is corrupted by the influence of particular private actors.[20]

If the state has any active role to play, from a liberal perspective, it is to maintain the basic rules of the game: to make sure that all groups have an equal opportunity to compete. Government activity must be characterized by fairness. It must create an order within which individuals can express their own needs and wants and within which, one may hope, they can learn to exercise higher human virtues. Indeed, some liberal thinkers have argued that the public interest can be understood essentially in these procedural terms.[21]

---

19 Truman, p. 508. For a critique see Nettl, p. 569.

20 Truman, at least, is keenly aware of this problem. He argues that the worst is not likely to happen because of cross-cutting cleavages and the existence of what he calls latent groups that reflect widespread adherence to certain basic values such as civil liberties.

21 For a discussion of Smith and Ricardo see Flathman, p. 57; Billet, "The Just Economy"; and O'Leary, "Systems Theory and Regional Integration."

# 20: Domestic Factors

## Jack S. Levy

Although most of the leading theories of the causes of war in the political science literature minimize the importance of domestic political variables, one can find individual hypotheses that link these variables to war. Although these hypotheses are not integrated into a larger theoretical system, it is useful to examine some of them here.

### National Attributes and War

Although international war is a widespread phenomenon, frequencies of war involvement for different states are not equal, which suggests that the attributes of states may constitute important variables contributing to war. It is sometimes asserted that certain political cultures, ideologies, or religions are more warlike than others, but this proposition finds little support from the quantitative empirical literature. Studies by Richardson, Rummel, Haas, and others have found essentially no relationship between national attributes and foreign conflict behavior.[1]

These and other scholars hence look for explanations for war not in the characteristics of individual states but in the *differences* between states. One common view is that national differences in religion, language, and other characteristics contribute to war, whereas similarities along these dimensions facilitate peace. Nef argues that a "common universe of customs and beliefs" is the "true basis for international peace." Some balance of power theorists, who emphasize the role of power distributions in determining behavior and outcomes, have also suggested that a common intellectual and moral framework is a precondition for stability and peace. There have been some attempts to test these hypotheses empirically. Although many of the results are contradictory, the bulk of the evidence points to positive but weak relationships between societal differences and the incidence of war.[2]

---

1   For the variation in war behavior among states, see Quincy Wright, A *Study of War* (Chicago, 1965, 2nd ed.), Tables 31-42; J. David Singer and Melvin Small, *The Wages of War, 1815-1965* (New York, 1972), 257-287. On the disproportionate incidence of great power war behavior, see Levy, *War in the Modern Great Power System, 1495-1975* (Lexington, Kentucky, 1983). Lewis F. Richardson, *Statistics of Deadly Quarrels* (Chicago, 1960), 168-183, 211-246; Rudolph Rummel, "National Attributes and Foreign Collective Behavior," in Singer (ed.), *Quantitative International Politics* (New York, 1968), 187-214; Michael Haas, "Societal Approaches to the Study of War," *Journal of Peace Research*, IV (1965), 307-323; Raymond Tanter, "Dimensions of Conflict Behavior within and between Nations, 1958-1960," *Journal of Conflict Resolution*, X (1966), 41-64; Wright, *War*, 828-829. It is difficult to generalize from these studies, however, because many of them follow Rummel and are limited to the 1955-1960 period.

2   On the importance of a common cultural or moral framework, see John Nef, *War and Human Progress*, (Cambridge, Mass., 1950), 257-258; Hans J. Morganthau, *Politics Among Nations* (New York, 1967; 4th ed.) 208-215; Edward Vose Gulick, *Europe's Classical Balance of Power*, (New York, 1955), 19-24. For quantitative empirical work on this see Wright, *War*, 1240-1260; Haas, "Communication Factors in Decision Making," *Peace Research Society (International) Papers*, XII (1969), 65-86; Richardson, *Deadly Resolution*, 211-246; Rummel, "Dimensions of Dyadic War, 1820-1952," *Journal of Conflict Resolution*, XI (1967), 176-183; Francis A. Beer, *Peace Against War* (San Francisco, 1981), 169. Beer estimates that political, linguistic, and religious differences together account for about 20% of the variance in foreign conflict.

Reprinted from *The Journal of Interdisciplinary History*, XVIII (1988), 657-670, with the permission of the editors of *The Journal of Interdisciplinary History* and the MIT Press, Cambridge, Massachusetts. © 1988 by the Massachusetts Institute of Technology and the editors of *The Journal of Interdisciplinary History*.

The implications of these findings are unclear, however, for the absence of a well-defined theoretical framework guiding these studies precludes a meaningful interpretation of the observed empirical associations. There needs to be greater specification of the types of states and conditions under which these empirical relationships are valid. There also needs to be far more theoretical attention to the causal mechanisms by which these factors are translated into decisions for war. For example, do these differences generate conflicting interests which lead to war by creating expectations of gains from war, or do they generate misleading images of the adversary which contribute to war through misperceptions of adversary intentions or capabilities?

## Democracy and War

Although earlier studies found no consistent relationship between type of regime and war behavior, there has recently been renewed interest in the Kantian proposition that democracies are inherently peaceful and that non-democratic regimes are more warlike. Kant's basic argument is that in a republican regime (characterized by a constitutional, representative government and separation of powers) the citizens rule, and "those who would have to decide to undergo all the deprivations of war will very much hesitate to start such an evil game." Decision-makers in non-democratic states are more likely to engage in war, even "for the most trivial reasons" because they do not themselves directly suffer its human consequences and because they are not constrained by a system of checks and balances or electoral accountability.[3]

Many who accept the basic Kantian argument concede that, once aroused, democracies adopt a crusading spirit and often fight particularly destructive wars. Democratic polities transform conflicts of interests into moral crusades, demand nothing less than total victory and unconditional surrender, and engage in "liberal interventionism" to promote their own vision of the morally proper international order. Thus Churchill asserted in 1901 that "democracy is more vindictive than Cabinets. The wars of peoples will be more terrible than those of kings." Lippmann reflected the paradox of democracy and foreign policy when he argued that public opinion has forced governments "to be too late with too little, or too long with too much, too pacifist in peace and too bellicose in war, too neutralist or appeasing in negotiation or too transient."[4]

There are other characteristics of decision-making in democratic states which may affect their tendency to become involved in wars, although the linkages to war are not always made explicit. Many have argued that the democratic decision-making process is flawed with respect to the conduct of foreign policy. In a well-known remark, de Tocqueville concluded that "foreign politics demand scarcely any of those qualities which are peculiar to a democracy; they require, on the contrary, the perfect use of almost all those in which it is deficient." Morgenthau emphasizes the importance of a democratic government se curing popular approval for its policies, but argues that "the conditions under which popular support can be obtained for a foreign policy are not necessarily identical with the conditions under which a foreign policy can be successfully pursued." Similarly,

---

3   Immanuel Kant, "Eternal Peace," in Carl J. Frederich (ed.), *The Philosophy of Kant* (New York, 1949), 430-476; Kenneth N. Waltz, *Man, the State, and War* (New York, 1954), 80-123; *idem*, "Kant, Liberalism, and War," *American Political Science Review*, LVI (1962), 331-340; Michael W. Doyle, "Kant, Liberal Legacies, and Foreign Affairs: Part I," *Philosophy and Public Affairs*, XII (1983), 205-235.

4   Winston Churchill, speech in the House of Commons (May 13, 1901), in Martin Gilbert (ed.), *Churchill* (Englewood Cliffs, 1967), 21-22; Walter Lippmann, *The Public Philosophy* (Boston, 1955), 20.

Kennan argues that public and congressional involvement are "congenital deficiencies" with respect to the effective conduct of foreign policy. More specifically, the factors that are said to be necessary for the effective conduct of foreign policy in a hostile world but are uncharacteristic of democracies include coherence, long-range planning and continuity, flexibility, dispatch, and secrecy. Waltz, however, disputes the argument that authoritarian states have decisive advantages in international security affairs, and suggests that the impact of internal politics on foreign policy may be even greater in authoritarian states than in democracies.[5]

Even if it were true that liberal democratic regimes are less inclined to *initiate* foreign wars, it would not automatically follow that they are less likely to become *involved* in international wars.[6] A reduced willingness to prepare for war or to resort to the threat or use of force may under some conditions make war more likely by undermining deterrence. Thus Wright and many others have argued that democracies are ill-adapted to the successful use of threats and force as instruments of foreign policy and often fail to preserve peace by balancing power. Many balance of power theorists argue more generally that the stability of the international system, and hence a low likelihood of major war, depends in part on the freedom of decision-makers to pursue realpolitik without internal constraints. Democratic public opinion impedes the formation of alliances with ideologically hostile states and the sudden shifts in alignments that may be necessary for the maintenance of a proper balance of military power in

the system or, more generally, the military commitments that may be necessary for the purposes of deterrence. Public demands for an open foreign policy process also preclude the secrecy that is often necessary, realists argue, for delicate negotiations with an adversary. Many have argued, for example, that a definitive British commitment to France before 1914 would probably have been sufficient to deter Germany from its aggressive policies and hence would have avoided a continental war, but that British public opinion precluded such a commitment. It has also been argued that public opinion in Britain was the primary reason for British diplomatic and military passivity during the enormous shifts in power between 1864 and 1875 which created the disequilibrium that undermined stability.[7]

The debate regarding the relative likelihood of democratic and non-democratic regimes going to war has been conducted at the empirical as well as the theoretical level. Most analyses have confirmed the findings of a 1976 study by Small and Singer that there have been no significant differences between democratic or non-democratic states in terms of the proportional frequency of their war involvement or the severity of their wars. Democratic states maybe slightly less inclined to initiate wars than non-democratic states, but the evidence is not conclusive. The debate has been rekindled by Rummel's study which suggests that libertarian states are more peaceful, but Rummel's conclusions have been challenged on the grounds that they are due almost entirely to biases in his empirical indicators and the excessively narrow

---

5    Alexis de Tocqueville, *Democracy in America* (New York, 1975), I, 234-235; Morgenthau, *Politics*, 241; George Kennan, *The Cloud of Danger* (Boston, 1977), 3-4; Waltz, *Foreign Policy and Democratic Politics* (Boston, 1967), 308-311.

6    I use the concepts of war involvement or participation to refer to behavior in which no distinction is made as to who initiates the war.

7    On domestic politics and the balance of power, see Wright, *War*, 842-848; Inis L. Claude, Jr., *Power and International Relations* (New York, 1962), 40-93; Morgenthau, *Politics*, 141-144. On public opinion and the British non-commitment in 1914 and earlier, see Mayer, "Internal Causes," 298-299; Gordon, "Domestic Conflict," 195-198. On British passivity during the rise of Prussia, see Paul Kennedy, *The Realities behind Diplomacy* (London, 1981), 74-139; R. W. Seton-Watson, *Britain in Europe, 1789-1914* (Cambridge, 1955), 466-504.

and unrepresentative temporal domain of most of his analyses.[8]

The evidence is conclusive that democratic states have been involved, proportionately, in as many wars as non-democratic states. There is one aspect of the military behavior of democratic states, however, that is clearly distinguished from that of non-democratic states: liberal or democratic states do not fight each other. This observation was first emphasized by Babst in 1972 and reconfirmed in most of the subsequent studies surveyed earlier. The number of wars between democracies during the past two centuries ranges from zero to less than a handful depending on precisely how democracy is defined, but these are marginal deviations from a robust finding generated by rigorous and systematic empirical investigations. Moreover, in general wars involving all or nearly all of the great powers, democratic states have never fought on opposite sides. This absence of war between democracies comes as close as anything we have to an empirical law in international relations.[9]

Although a number of plausible explanations for the absence of war between democracies have been proposed, none has been rigorously and systematically tested. One reasonable conclusion, however, is that purely structural explanations, which do not differentiate between states on the basis of their internal characteristics, cannot account for the observed behavioral differences between democratic and non-democratic states. The answer probably lies in variables internal to the states.[10]

## Economic Structure

The most comprehensive of all societal-level approaches to international conflict is Marxist-Leninist theory, which focuses on economic structure as the key independent variable. The basic argument is that the inequitable distribution of wealth in capitalist societies generates overproduction, inadequate domestic investment opportunities, and generally stagnant economies. These effects lead to expansionist and imperialist policies abroad; competition between capitalist enterprises for access to markets, investment opportunities, and raw materials; and ultimately to wars between capitalist states. Capitalist economic systems also generate war economies and high levels of military spending as replacement markets to absorb excess capital, which can lead to war through arms races, international tensions, and a conflict spiral. Capitalist states may also initiate wars against socialist states in a desperate attempt to prevent the further deterioration of their own positions.[11]

---

8  Small and Singer, "The War-Proneness of Democratic Regimes, 1816-1965," *Jerusalem Journal of International Relations*, I (1976), 50-69; Rummel, "The Relationship between National Attributes and Foreign Policy Behavior," in Singer, *International Politics*, 187-214; Rummel, "Libertarianism and International Violence," *Journal of Conflict Resolution*, XXVII (1983), 27-71. On the question of war initiation, Small and Singer, "War-Proneness," 64-66, find no difference between democratic and non-democratic states, whereas Chan finds a small but non-statistically significant tendency for democratic states to initiate proportionately fewer wars. Steve Chan, "Mirror, Mirror on the Wall . . . Are the Freer Countries More Pacific?" *Journal of Conflict Resolution*, XXVIII (1984), 617-648. See Chan for a critique of Rummel.

9  Although there is some variation in the definitions of democratic or liberal political system in this literature, most definitions are comparable to that of Small and Singer in "War-Proneness," 55: "bourgeois democracies" involve 1) regular elections and the free participation of opposition parties, 2) at least 10% of the adult population being able to vote for 3) a parliament that either controlled or shared parity with the executive branch. In this article I do not distinguish between liberal and democratic regimes. Dean Babst, "A Force for Peace," *Industrial Research* (April 1972), 55-58. For possible exceptions, see Small and Singer, "War Proneness," 19; Rummel, "Libertarianism," 42; Doyle, "Liberal Legacies, I," 209-217.

10 For alternative explanations of this phenomenon see Small and Singer, "War-Proneness," 67; Doyle, "Kant, Liberal Legacies, and Foreign Affairs, Part II," *Philosophy and Public Affairs*, XII (1983), 323-353.

11 Vladimir Ilyich Lenin, *Imperialism* (New York, 1939); John A. Hobson, *Imperialism* (London, 1954).

There are numerous critiques of the theoretical coherence and historical validity of the Marxist-Leninist theory of imperialism; a few points will suffice here: First, even if one were to accept the link between capitalism and imperialism, the theoretical linkages between imperialism and war, particularly interstate war, have never been convincingly demonstrated. It is equally plausible that imperialist expansion, particularly in an era of an open colonial frontier, reduces the likelihood of major war by diverting great power competition from the core of the system into the periphery, where their vital interests are much less likely to conflict and where compromise solutions are more feasible. Kautsky suggested that imperialist competition would lead to "ultraimperialism," the cooperation among capitalist states for the joint exploitation of the periphery. Second, on the empirical level, if we assume a strong association between liberal democratic political systems and capitalist economic systems, Marxist-Leninist theory makes two predictions that are directly contradicted by the observed empirical relationships between liberal democracy and war. The predicted wars between liberal capitalist states have not been commonplace, and capitalist states have not been disproportionately war prone or more likely to initiate wars than other states in the international system.[12]

Liberal theory also explains international war largely in terms of the structure of economic relationships, but reaches the opposite conclusions from Marxist-Leninists. The Manchester liberals argued strongly that free trade promotes economic efficiency and prosperity, which in turn promotes peace. Any interference with the operation of the market mechanism, such as constraints on trade, reduces profits and increases conflict. Veblen, Schumpeter, and others emphasized the radical opposition of the industrial spirit and the military spirit. They argued that imperialism and war only squander the riches generated by industrial capitalism and are contrary to the interests of the masses as well as the bourgeoisie. Liberal states have material incentives to avoid hostile policies that might lead others to break their established economic ties. Moreover, in relationships between liberal states, difficult questions of production, distribution, price, and other aspects of trade and finance are resolved through impersonal market forces, and interstate conflicts over these issues are minimized. Economic relations between centralized economies, however, tend to be determined by considerations of power rather than by the market, and this politicization of economic conflicts introduces additional tensions into interstate relations.[13]

## Nationalism and Public Opinion

For Kant, Bentham, and most liberals, public opinion is inherently peaceful, and it is widely believed that when wars occur it is because

---

12  These particular arguments regarding the empirical inaccuracy of Marxist-Leninist theory depend on the assertion that liberal democratic political systems have historically tended to coincide with capitalist economic systems. For critiques of the Marxist-Leninist theory, see Lionel Robbins. *The Economic Causes of War* (London, 1939), 19-59; Waltz, *Theory of International Politics* (Reading, Mass., 1979), 18-37. On the safety valve hypothesis, see Morgenthau, *Politics*, 340-343; T. Clifton Morgan and Levy, "The Structure of the International System and the Relationship between the Frequency and Seriousness of War," in Margaret P. Karns (ed.), *Persistent Patterns and Emergent Structures in a Waning Century* (New York, 1986), 75-98. Karl Kautsky, "Ultra-imperialism," *New Left Review*, LIX (1970), 41-46.

13  For surveys of liberal theories of war, see A. Geoffrey Blainey, *The Causes of War* (New York, 1973), 18-32; Edmund Silberner (trans. Alexander H. Krappe) *The Problem of War in Nineteenth Century Economic Thought* (Princeton, 1946); Barry Buzan, "Economic Structure and International Security: The Limits of the Liberal Case," *International Organization*, XXXVIII (1984), 597-624. On the relationship between industrialism, capitalism, democracy, and peace, see Thorstein Veblen, *Imperial Germany and the Industrial Revolution* (Ann Arbor, 1966); Schumpeter, *Imperialism*; Raymond Aron, *War and Industrial Society* (London, 1958). On the politicization of international economic relations between states with centralized economies, see *idem, War*; Benjamin J. Cohen, *The Question of Imperialism* (New York, 1973).

political leaders force war on an unwilling public. There appear to be numerous examples, however, of precisely the opposite: of a hawkish public pressuring political elites into war, or into adopting more hardline policies than they would otherwise prefer. Some examples include the United States in the War of 1812, both the United States and Spain in the Spanish-American War, and Britain and possibly France in the Crimean War. With respect to the Spanish-American War, for example, May writes that, because of domestic politics, President William McKinley "led his country unhesitatingly toward a war which he did not want for a cause in which he did not believe."[14]

Peoples in both democratic and non-democratic states are often highly enthusiastic at the beginning of wars, although this support may decline rapidly if the war becomes prolonged and costly. In American politics popular support for a president invariably increases immediately after the use of force, regardless of the wisdom or success of that military action. This pattern has been explained by the tendency of the public to rally around the flag, the president, and the party, and ultimately by the phenomenon of modern nationalism.[15]

Nationalism has created the sense of a common interest in the nation, a concept of the national interest as the highest value, and an intense commitment to the well-being of the state. This commitment is strengthened by national myths regarding the omniscience and omnipotence of the nation and the congruence of one's national morality with a supranational ethic. Such myths and doctrines can be used by elites to advance their own view of the national interest or their own political interests, but, once created, these myths and doctrines take on a life of their own. Assertive national policies and even war can be psychologically functional for individuals by increasing their sense of power and control over an oppressive environment and by reinforcing the tendency of some individuals to seek their identity and fulfillment through the state. Thus Proudhon wrote that war had acquired the status of religion: "For the masses, the real Christ is Alexander, Caesar, Charlemagne, Napoleon." Thus nationalism can generate a hardline public opinion which imposes major constraints on states-men who recognize the limits of power and who would prefer to act with more prudence in their interactions with other states. In Morgenthau's words, "compromise, the virtue of the old diplomacy, becomes the treason of the new." Thus statesmen are sometimes pressured by a jingoistic public to pursue bellicose policies for which the risk of war far outweighs the interests at stake and to forego compromises which are in the best interests of all.[16]

Public opinion is not always hawkish, and there are numerous examples of public opinion constraining decision-makers from taking more hardline policies. Although it would be useful to know whether public opinion is usually more hawkish or more dovish, there are other questions that are probably more important. One

14 Jeremy Bentham (ed. John Bowring), *The Works of Jeremy Bentham* (Edinburgh, 1843), II-IV. On public opinion, party politics, and the origins of the War of 1812, see Roger Brown, *The Republic in Peril* (New York, 1964). On the Spanish-American War, see Richard Hofstadter, *The Age of Reform* (New York, 1955); Ernest May, *Imperial Democracy* (New York, 1961). On Britain and the Crimean War, see Olive Anderson, *A Liberal State at War* (London, 1967).

15 The support of presidential actions by the American public is analyzed by John E. Mueller, *War, Presidents and Public Opinion* (New York, 1973). For some recent empirical work which qualifies the rally-around-the-flag hypotheses, see Richard Stoll, "The Guns of November," *Journal of Conflict Resolution*, XXVII (1984), 231-246; Charles W. Ostrom, Jr., and Brian L. Job, "The President and the Political Use of Force," *American Political Science Review*, LXXX (1986), 541-566.

16 John Breuilly, *Nationalism and the State* (Chicago, 1985); Erich Fromm, *Escape from Freedom* (New York, 1941); Pierre-Joseph Proudhon, *La Guerre et la paix* (Paris, 1891), quoted in Nef, *War*, 405; Morgenthau, *Politics*, 532-550.

concerns the conditions under which public opinion prefers more belligerent policies and the conditions under which it prefers more conciliatory policies. Another concerns the particular kinds of military actions that the public is likely to support (for example, the quick and massive use of force as opposed to gradual and limited actions). An even more basic question is the extent to which public preferences influence state decisions relating to war and peace. These are complex questions, particularly because of the diversity of political systems and historical circumstances over which we want to generalize. In addition, political elites are not only constrained by public opinion, but they can also actively manipulate public opinion for their own purposes. The nature of this reciprocal relationship between political elites and the mass public is poorly understood. The complexity of the relationship between public opinion and foreign policy decision-making is undoubtedly one of the reasons for the absence of a theory of public opinion and war.

### The Scapegoat Hypothesis

The tendency of peoples in a wide range of circumstances to support assertive national policies which appear to enhance the power and prestige of the state may lead decision-makers, under certain conditions, to embark on aggressive foreign policies and sometimes even war as a means of increasing or maintaining their domestic support. This old idea is often referred to as the scapegoat or diversionary theory of war, for political elites can use a foreign war to divert popular attention from internal social, economic, and political problems.[17]

Theoretically, the scapegoat theory is based on the in-group/out-group hypothesis in sociology. Simmel, in the first systematic treatment of the subject, argued that conflict with an out-group increases the cohesion and political centralization of the in-group, and generalized to international relations: "war with the outside is sometimes the last chance for a state ridden with inner antagonisms to overcome these antagonisms, or else to break up definitely." Coser modified many of Simmel's propositions. He argues that the cohesion of the in-group will be increased only if there already exists some minimal level of internal cohesion and only if it is generally perceived that the external threat menaces the group as a whole and not just some part of it. Otherwise, external conflict will lead to internal conflict and disintegration rather than cohesion. Coser is the most widely cited authority on the in-group/out-group hypothesis, but this important qualification is not always recognized.[18]

There has been a great deal of empirical research on the in-group/out-group hypothesis by psychologists, anthropologists, sociologists, and political scientists. This literature has been thoroughly reviewed elsewhere, and a brief summary of the political science literature will suffice. Numerous quantitative studies, which simply correlate a variety of indicators of the internal and foreign conflict behavior of states, have generally agreed that there exists no relationship between the two. However, some studies which attempt to control for other variables (such as type of

---

17 A different theoretical question, which is not discussed here, concerns the symbiotic relationship between domestic politics and external war in the processes involved in the development of the modern state. See Charles Tilly, "War Making and State Making as Organized Crime," in Peter B. Evans, Dietrich Rueschemeyer, and Theda Skocpol (eds.), *Bringing the State Back In* (Cambridge, 1985), 169-191; Tilly (ed.), *The Formation of National States in Western Europe* (Princeton, 1975).

18 Georg Simmel (trans. Kurt H. Wolff), *Conflict* (Glencoe, Ill., 1955), 93; Lewis Coser, *The Functions of Social Conflict* (Glencoe, Ill., 1956).

regime) have found positive but weak relationships between internal and external conflict.[19]

Some comparative historical studies have found, contrary to the large-N correlational studies, a much stronger relationship between internal instability and external war. Rosecrance concludes that the primary determinant of international stability and peace in the European system from 1740 to 1960 was internal stability and the resulting security of elites, whereas domestic instability and elite insecurity were - associated with war. Rosecrance argues, contrary to some of the quantitative correlational studies, that this relationship holds regardless of the political structure or ideology of the regime. In addition, there have been numerous historical case studies suggesting that a major cause of individual wars was the motivation of political leaders to solve their internal problems through a diplomatic or military victory abroad.[20]

The arguments by Kehr, Mayer, and others that the aggressive policies of Germany and other powers in 1914 were driven by the hope that they would help maintain a precarious domestic status quo against the forces of democracy and socialism have already been mentioned, and there are numerous other cases. Michon adopts a scapegoat interpretation of French policy in 1792: "War was willed solely to act as a diversion from the social problems. . . . [War] would give the government dictatorial

powers and would allow it to eliminate its detested enemies. For these groups the war was a grand maneuver of domestic politics." Many trace the origins of the Russo-Japanese War to the motivation articulated by the Russian minister of the interior: "What this country needs is a short victorious war to stem the tide of revolution." Hitler also used an aggressive foreign policy to consolidate his internal political position (although this was probably not the primary cause of the war), and similar motivations have been widely attributed to the Argentine junta in their 1982 attempt to seize the Falkland (Malvinas) Islands from Britain. Thus the quantitative empirical research bearing on the scapegoat hypothesis contradicts much of the historical literature, and it is not clear which (if either) is correct.[21]

Although the quantitative studies of the relationships between domestic and foreign conflict are beset by numerous methodological problems, the conceptual problems are even more serious.[22] These studies have not been based on or guided by theory, but instead have been driven too much by method and (after Rummel) by data availability. They have focused on the question of whether there exists an empirical association between internal and external conflict without regard for the causal processes which might produce such a result. Their strictly correlational methodology fails to distinguish processes in

---

19 See Rummel, "The Dimensions of Conflict Behavior within and between Nations," *General Systems Yearbook*, VIII (1963), 1-50; Tanter, "Dimensions of Conflict"; Jonathan Wilkenfeld, (ed.), *Conflict Behavior and Linkage Politics* (New York, 1973), 148-190. For more detailed reviews of this literature, see Arthur A. Stein, "Conflict and Cohesion," *Journal of Conflict Resolution*, XX (1976), 143-172; Michael Stohl, "The Nexus of Civil and International Conflict," in Gurr (ed.), *Handbook*; Zinnes, "Why War?" 341-344.

20 Richard Rosecrance, *Action and Reaction in World Politics* (Boston, 1963).

21 Georges Michon is quoted by Blanning, *French Revolutionary Wars*, 71. William L. Langer, "The Origin of the Russo-Japanese War," in *idem, Explorations in Crises* (Cambridge, Mass., 1969), 3-45; Max Hastings and Simon Jenkins, *The Battle for the Falklands* (New York, 1983).

22 One serious flaw in the research design of these quantitative studies is the 1955-1960 period upon which most of them are based. This is not only too narrow a temporal domain but also coincides with a period which is relatively peaceful and entirely unrepresentative of "normal" international political behavior, and thus restrict the generalizability of the findings. For an excellent methodological critique, see Joseph M. Scolnick, Jr., "An Appraisal of Studies of the Linkages between Domestic and International Conflict," *Comparative Political Studies*, VI (1974), 485-509.

which internal conflict generates external conflict from those in which external conflict generates internal conflict.[23]

The first of these processes can be further subdivided. Conflict within state A may tempt A's leaders to resort to the use of force externally for diversionary purposes, as suggested by the scapegoat hypothesis. Alternatively, conflict within state A may tempt state B to intervene, either to exploit a temporary military advantage created by the impact of A's turmoil on its military strength, or to attempt to influence the outcome of the struggle for power in A. It is possible that both of these processes may be operative. Conflict within A may generate weaknesses which provide an opportunity for B to attack, which in turn provides the political leadership of A with a real external threat which can be exploited for its own domestic political purposes. This external threat can be particularly useful for revolutionary regimes, as suggested by the cases of France in 1792, Russia in 1918, and Iran in 1980.[24]

Another weakness of empirical studies of the in-group/out-group hypothesis is their failure to identify the conditions under which the proposition is likely to hold. The resulting correlational analyses over a universe of cases have a minimum of scientific controls and may be masking stronger relationships that hold in more restricted circumstances. Although many of these empirical studies refer to Coser, they generally neglect his qualification that if the level of pre-existing internal conflict is too high, foreign conflict will increase rather than decrease internal conflict. If this is true, the point at which the relationship reverses must be specified before the hypothesis can be tested. External constraints are also important. A diplomatic defeat usually (but not always) intensifies internal political divisions, and therefore a state's relative power position may be an important factor affecting scapegoating. The rate of change in military power may also have an impact. Decision-makers faced with a decline in military strength as well as internal divisions may be particularly willing to gamble on a war that might solve their external and internal problems simultaneously, and thus be driven to war by the interaction of scapegoat and preventive motivations. Fischer and others argue that these were the two primary motivations leading Germany to precipitate a war in 1914. Lebow's work suggests that this phenomenon may be more general. In fact, internal conflict— and the social and economic problems that often generate it—may sometimes be an important cause of national decline.[25]

---

23 External war often results in an increase in the government's extraction of resources from society to fund the war effort, which under certain conditions generates resistance from key elites or masses. War may also weaken the government's repressive capacity and encourage its internal enemies to rebel. See Tilly, "Reflections on the History of European State-making," in *idem, Formation*, 74.

24 Blainey, *Causes of War*, 68-86, argues that external attacks to exploit internal weaknesses have historically been more common than diversionary actions, but this claim is an unresolved empirical question. The possibility of a revolutionary regime responding to an externally initiated attack in a way that helps consolidate its own political power was emphasized to me by Joseph Nye.

25 Fischer, *War*, 398; Lebow, *Between Peace and War*; Levy, "Declining Power and the Preventive Motivation for War," *World Politics*, XL (1987), 82-107.

# 21: Ethnic Nationalism and International Conflict

## V.P. Gagnon, Jr.

Does ethnicity affect the international system? What are the causes of violent conflict along ethnic lines? Since the collapse of the Soviet Union and the outbreak of war in the Balkans, these questions have seized the attention of international relations scholars and policy makers.[1] In the former Yugoslavia, war conducted in the name of ethnic solidarity has destroyed the Yugoslav state, leveled entire cities, and resulted in hundreds of thousands of casualties and millions of refugees.[2] It has also brought NATO's first out-of-area actions, the largest United Nations peacekeeping operation in history, and the very real possibility of war spreading to other parts of the Balkans.

Is the Yugoslav case a look into the future of international relations? Are ethnically-mixed regions in the post–Cold War era inevitably the sites of violent conflict that will spill over into the international arena? If so, the only apparent solution would be the creation of ethnically pure states; yet the greatest threats to peace in this century have tended to come from those regions in which partitions along ethnic or religious lines have taken place.[3] This paradox is a major challenge to international peace and stability, especially given the growing number of violent conflicts described and justified in terms of ethnicity, culture, and religion.

I argue that such violent conflict is caused not by ethnic sentiments, nor by external security concerns, but rather by the dynamics of within-group conflict.[4] The external conflict, although justified and described in terms of relations with other ethnic groups and taking place

---

1   See, for example, John Mearsheimer, "Back to the Future: Instability in Europe After the Cold War," *International Security,* Vol. 15, No. 1 (Summer 1990), pp. 5–56; Stephen Van Evera, "Hypotheses on Nationalism and War," *International Security,* Vol. 18, No. 4 (Spring 1994), pp. 5–39; Jack Snyder, "The New Nationalism," in Richard Rosecrance and Arthur A. Stein, eds., *The Domestic Bases of Grand Strategy* (Ithaca, N.Y.: Cornell University Press, 1993), pp. 179–200; Michael E. Brown, ed., *Ethnic Conflict and International Security* (Princeton, N.J.: Princeton University Press, 1993).

2   The best English-language sources on the Yugoslav wars include Lenard Cohen, *Broken Bonds: The Disintegration of Yugoslavia* (Boulder, Colo.: Westview, 1993); James Gow, *Legitimacy and the Military: The Yugoslav Crisis* (New York: St. Martin's Press, 1992); Rabia Ali and Lawerence Lifshutz, eds., *Why Bosnia? Writings on the Balkan War* (Stony Creek, Conn.: Pamphleteers Press, 1993).

3   Examples include Greece-Turkey (1922), Ireland (1921), the Sudetenland (1938), India-Pakistan (1947), South African apartheid (1948), Palestine (1948), and Cyprus (1974). John Mearsheimer and Robert Pape, "The Answer: A Partition Plan for Bosnia," *The New Republic,* June 14, 1993, pp. 22–28, argue for partition of Bosnia-Hercegovina as the best solution to the current conflict.

4   One work that explores the domestic roots of conflictual nationalist policy is Snyder, "The New Nationalism." For a review of earlier works that look at domestic sources of international conflict, see Jack Levy, "The Diversionary Theory of War: A Critique," in Manus I. Midlarsky, ed., *Handbook of War Studies* (Boston: Unwin Hyman, 1989), pp. 259–288.

within that context, has its main goal within the state, among members of the same ethnicity.[5]

I argue that violent conflict along ethnic cleavages is provoked by elites in order to create a domestic political context where ethnicity is the only politically relevant identity. It thereby constructs the individual interest of the broader population in terms of the threat to the community defined in ethnic terms. Such a strategy is a response by ruling elites to shifts in the structure of domestic political and economic power: by constructing individual interest in terms of the threat to the group, endangered elites can fend off domestic challengers who seek to mobilize the population against the status quo, and can better position themselves to deal with future challenges.

The dominant realist approach in international relations tells us very little about violent conflict along ethnic lines, and cannot explain the Yugoslav case. Focusing on external security concerns, this approach argues that conflictual behavior in the name of ethnic nationalism is a response to external threats to the state (or to the ethnic group).[6] The general literature on ethnic conflict likewise uses the "ethnic group" as actor and looks to factors outside the group to explain intergroup conflict.[7] But in fact, the Serbian leadership from 1987 onward actively created rather than responded to threats to Serbs by purposefully provoking and fostering the outbreak of conflict along ethnic lines, especially in regions of Yugoslavia with histories of good interethnic relations.[8]

A common explanation for violent conflicts along ethnic lines, particularly for the Yugoslav case, is that ancient ethnic hatreds have burst to the surface.[9] But this too is unsupported by the evidence: in fact, Yugoslavia never saw the kind of religious wars seen in Western and Central Europe, and Serbs and Croats never fought before this century;[10] intermarriage rates were

---

5　This type of conflict is one example of the more general phenomenon of violent conflict in the international arena which is described and justified by national leaders in terms of ideas such as religion, class, and culture, as well as ethnicity. Given the extent to which international conflicts have been justified not in purely security terms but rather in such ideational terms, identifying the causal link between such ideas and violent conflicts carried out in their names is clearly of importance.

6　Mearsheimer, "Back to the Future"; Posen, "Nationalism, the Mass Army, and Military Power." For a realist approach that takes ethnic groups rather than states as actors, see Barry Posen, "The Security Dilemma and Ethnic Conflict," *Survival*, Vol. 35, No. 1 (Spring 1993), pp. 27–47.

7　Horowitz, *Ethnic Groups in Conflict;* and "Democracy in Divided Societies," *Journal of Democracy*, Vol. 4, No. 4 (October 1993), pp. 18–38.

8　In both Croatia and Bosnia, forces allied with Belgrade went to great lengths to destroy the long-standing harmony between Serbs and non-Serbs. Although the Croatian regime had resorted to nationalist rhetoric and actions worrisome to local Serbs, both sides were willing to negotiate over key issues until Belgrade began terrorizing moderate Serbs. This strategy was repeated in Bosnia. In Serbian-controlled regions of Croatia and Bosnia, the extremists in power have silenced and even killed dissenting Serbs. See *NIN*, November 8, 1991, p. 15; *Vreme*, November 4, 1991, pp. 12–15; Milorad Pupovac, head of the Zagreb-based moderate Serbian Democratic Forum, in *Vreme*, October 21, 1991, pp. 12–14; Peter Maass, "In Bosnia, 'Disloyal Serbs' Share Plight of Opposition," *Washington Post*, August 24, 1992, p. 1.

9　See, for example, Robert Kaplan, "Ground Zero," *New Republic*, August 2, 1993, pp. 15–16, "A Reader's Guide to the Balkans," *New York Times Book Review*, April 18, 1994; "History's Cauldron," *Atlantic Monthly*, June 1991, pp. 92–104; and Robert Kaplan, *Balkan Ghosts: A Journey Through History* (New York: St. Martin's Press, 1993). See also Elizabeth Drew, "Letter from Washington," *New Yorker*, July 6, 1992, p. 70.

10　On the history of relations between Serbs and Croats in Croatia before this century, see, for example, Wolfgang Kessler, *Politik, Kultur und Gesellschaft in Kroatien und Slawonien in der ersten Hälfte des 19. Jahrhunderts* (Munich: R. Oldenbourg, 1981); Sergei A. Romanenko, "National Autonomy in Russia and Austro-Hungary," in *Nationalism and Empire* (New York: St. Martin's Press, 1992); Ivo Banac, *The National Question in Yugoslavia: Origins, History, Politics* (Ithaca, N.Y.: Cornell University Press, 1984), p. 410. On cooperation in the first Yugoslavia between Serb and Croat parties in Croatia against Belgrade, see Ljubo Boban, *Svetozar Pribićević u opoziciji (1928–1936)* (Zagreb: Institut za

quite high in those ethnically-mixed regions that saw the worst violence;[11] and sociological polling as late as 1989–90 showed high levels of tolerance, especially in these mixed regions.[12] Although some tensions existed between nationalities and republics, and the forcible repression of overt national sentiment added to the perception on all sides that the existing economic and political system was unjust, the evidence indicates that, notwithstanding claims to the contrary by nationalist politicians and historians in Serbia and Croatia, "ethnic hatreds" are not the essential, primary cause of the Yugoslav conflict.

### Domestic Power and International Conflict: A Theoretical Framework

This section lays out a framework and proposes some hypotheses about the link between ethnicity (and other ideas such as religion, culture, class) and international conflict. It is based on the following four premises: first, the domestic arena is of central concern for state decision-makers and ruling elites because it is the location of the bases of their power. Ruling elites will thus focus on preserving these domestic bases of power. Second, persuasion is the most effective and least costly means of influence in domestic politics. One particularly effective means of persuasion is to appeal to the interest of politically relevant actors as members of a group. Third, within the domestic arena, appeals for support

must be directed to material and nonmaterial values of the relevant target audiences—those actors whose support is necessary to gain and maintain power. Ideas such as ethnicity, religion, culture, and class therefore play a key role as instruments of power and influence, in particular because of their centrality to legitimacy and authority.

Finally, conflict over ideas and how they are framed is an essential characteristic of domestic politics, since the result determines the way political arguments can be made, how interests are defined, and the values by which political action must be justified. The challenge for elites is therefore to define the interest of the collective in a way that coincides with their own power interests. In other words, they must express their interests in the "language" of the collective interest.

These premises lead to the following hypotheses about the conditions under which national leaders will resort to conflictual policies described and justified in terms of threats to the ethnic nation.

First, if ruling elites face challenger elites who seek to mobilize the majority of the politically relevant population in a way that threatens the rulers' power or the political or economic structure on which their power is based, the ruling elites will be willing to respond by undertaking policies that are costly to society as a whole, even if the costs are imposed from outside. Behavior *vis-à-vis* the outside may thus have its

---

hrvatsku povijest, 1973); Drago Roksandić, *Srbi u Hrvatskoj od 15. stoljeća do naših dana* (Zagreb: Vjesnik, 1991). During World War II, the ruling Ustaša forces in the puppet Independent State of Croatia perpetrated massive atrocities against Serbs and others; they were a marginal party imposed by the Germans and Italians after the highly popular Croatian Peasant Party refused to collaborate. The Ustaša policy of genocide against Serbs, and its use of Muslims to carry out this policy in Bosnia, combined with its authoritarian repression of Croat and Muslim dissent, rapidly alienated most of the state's population. Fikreta Jelić-Butić, *Ustaše i Nezavisna Država Hrvatska* (Zagreb: Sveučilišna Naklada Liber, 1978). And while the Serbian nationalist Četnik forces perpetrated atrocities against Muslims in Bosnia, most Serbs in Croatia and Bosnia joined the multi-ethnic communist partisan forces rather than the purely nationalistic Četniks. Thus the image of "ethnic groups" in conflict even during World War II must be seen as part of an ideological construct in which "ethnic groups" are portrayed as actors by nationalist politicians and historians.

11 For example, throughout the 1980s, 29 percent of Serbs living in Croatia married Croat spouses. *Demografska statistika* (Belgrade: Savezni zavod za statistiku), 1979–1989 (annual), Table 5–3.

12 Randy Hodson, Garth Massey and Dusko Sekulic, "National Tolerance in the Former Yugoslavia," *Global Forum Series Occasional Papers*, No. 93-01.5 (Durham, N.C.: Center for International Studies, Duke University, December 1993).

main goal in the domestic arena. If the most effective way to achieve domestic goals involves provoking conflict with the outside, then, as long as the net benefit to the threatened elites is positive, they will be willing to undertake such a strategy.

Second, threatened elites will respond to domestic threats in a way that minimizes the danger to the bases of their domestic power. They must gain the support, or neutralize the opposition, of the majority. But if domestic legitimacy precludes the massive use of force against political opponents and depends on respecting certain political forms and "rules of the game," elites are circumscribed in how they can respond to domestic threats. One effective strategy in this context is to shift the focus of political debate away from issues where ruling elites are most threatened—for example, proposed changes in the structure of domestic economic or political power—toward other issues, defined in cultural or ethnic terms, that appeal to the interest of the majority in noneconomic terms.[13] But ethnicity or culture in and of itself does not determine policies; the interest of the collective defined in ethnic terms can be defined in any number of ways.

Competing elites will thus focus on defining the collective interest by drawing selectively on traditions and mythologies and in effect constructing particular versions of that interest. The elite faction that succeeds in identifying itself with the interest of the collective, and in defining the collective interest in a way that maximizes its own ability to achieve its goals, wins an important victory. It has framed the terms of political discourse and debate, and thus the limits of legitimate policy, in a way that may delegitimize or make politically irrelevant the interests of challenger elites and prevent them from mobilizing the population on specific issues or along certain lines.

Third, in this competition over defining the group interest, images of and alleged threats from the outside world can play a key role in this domestic political strategy. A strategy relying on such threatening images can range from citing an alleged threat to provoking conflict in order to create the image of threat; conflict can range from political to military. Since political mobilization occurs most readily around grievances, in order to shift the political agenda, elites must find issues of grievance unrelated to those issues on which they are most threatened, and construct a political context in which those issues become the center of political debate. It is at this point that focus on the interest of the group *vis-à-vis* the outside world proves to be useful. If the grievance or threat is to the collective rather than to individuals, it creates an image of potentially very high costs imposed on the group regardless of the direct impact on individuals. It therefore defines the individual's interest in terms of a particular threat to the group. Moreover, if the threat or grievance is outside the direct experience of the majority of politically relevant actors, there is no way to verify whether the grievance is real, or indeed whether it is being addressed or not. Such a strategy also becomes in effect a self-fulfilling prophecy, as the reactions provoked by the conflictual policies are pointed to as proof of the original contention. Thus is created a grievance that, if violence is involved, is sure to continue for years.

The effect of creating an image of threat to the group is to place the interest of the group above the interest of individuals. This political strategy is crucial because, in the case of aggressive nationalism and images of threats to the ethnic nation, it creates a context where ethnicity is all that counts, and where other interests are no longer relevant. In addition, such an image of overwhelming threat to the group delegitimizes the dissent of those challengers who attempt to

---

13 On agenda setting as a power strategy, see P. Bachrach and M.S. Baratz, "The Two Faces of Power," *American Political Science Review,* Vol. 56, No. 4 (1962), pp. 947–952.

appeal to members of the relevant group as individuals or who appeal to identities other than the "legitimate" identity in a "legitimate" way, especially if dissenters can be portrayed as selfish and uninterested in the well-being of the group, and can therefore be branded as traitors.[14]

The larger and more immediate the threat to the ruling elite, the more willing it is to take measures which, while preserving its position in the short term, may bring high costs in the longer term; in effect it discounts future costs. The intensity and thus costliness of a conflictual strategy depends on the degree of the threat to the old elites. These factors include, first, the time frame of the threat to power. While the conflictual policies may over the long run result in an untenable position and ultimately undermine their bases of political influence, elites' political behavior in a situation of immediate threat is motivated by that threat and by the concern for keeping the power in the short run, which at least leaves open the possibility of their survival in the long run. This also gives them time to fashion alternative strategies for dealing with change, including shifting the bases of their power.

Also, the strength of the challenger elites also affects the immediacy of the threat. If the challenger elites are successfully mobilizing the majority of the politically relevant population against the status quo, ruling elites will feel quite threatened and be willing to incur high costs to preserve their position. Threatened elites will also attempt to recruit other elites, at the local and regional as well as national levels, to prevent such a mobilization.

A further factor is the costs to the threatened elites of losing power; that is, the resources and fallback positions they have if change does take place. If they have everything to lose and nothing to gain, they will be much more likely to undertake conflictual policies costly to society as a whole than if they have resources that would allow them to remain involved in power to some degree.

Threatened elites may use marginal neo-fascist parties as part of their conflictual strategy in conditions where the wider population is included in the political system. Every country has small extremist groups whose mainstay is ethnic hatred and violence; their motivations may be political, personal, or psychological. But the very existence of this option is clearly not enough for it to come to dominate state policy. An advantage of giving neo-fascists media coverage and weapons is that by bringing extremists into the political realm, the right becomes the "center"; a statement that ten years earlier may have been unacceptably racist may be perceived after this kind of strategy as relatively moderate.[15] By making issues of ethnic nationalism the center of political discourse, this strategy also turns those who are archconservatives on economic issues into moderate centrists.

Internal costs of a conflictual strategy are closely monitored, since they must be outweighed by benefits. Of particular importance is the need to prevent popular mobilization against costs of the conflictual external strategy. While conflict remains in the realm of political rhetoric, it may have great support among the population, since it is basically costless. But if military conflict is involved, the costs to the general population rapidly start to mount.[16] Conflict will be undertaken with an eye toward minimizing the costs for those parts

---

14 This strategy is thus especially effective in discrediting those who appeal to liberal democratic ideology, which defines the collective interest of the citizenry as best ensured by ensuring the rights and well-being of the individual.

15 See Anna Marie Smith, *New Right Discourse in Race and Sexuality: Britain 1968–1990* (New York: Cambridge University Press, 1994).

16 Despite the assumption that ethnic political mobilization inevitably pushes politics towards extremism (referred to as "ethnic outbidding" by Horowitz, *Ethnic Groups in Conflict,* p. 348), there is in fact little evidence of a natural inevitable progression from ethnic mobilization to violent ethnic conflict. See V.P. Gagnon, Jr., "Ethnic Conflict as a Political Demobilizer," forthcoming.

of the populations which are key for support, and will therefore tend to be provoked outside the borders of the elite's power base, with great efforts taken to prevent war from spilling over to the domestic territory. Thus, in the Soviet case anti-reform conservatives provoked violent ethnic conflict outside of Russia, in Moldova, Georgia, and the Baltics; in the Yugoslav case armed conflict has not taken place within Serbia itself, and the Croatian conservatives' conflictual strategy affected mainly central Bosnia, rather than Croatia. . . .

### Ethnic Conflict as a Political Strategy

Violent conflict described and justified in terms of ethnic solidarity is not an automatic outgrowth of ethnic identity, or even of ethnic mobilization. Violence on a scale large enough to affect international security is the result of purposeful and strategic policies rather than irrational acts of the masses. Indeed, in the case of the former Yugoslavia there is much evidence that the "masses," especially in ethnically-mixed regions, did not want war and that violence was imposed by forces from outside. The current major conflicts taking place along ethnic lines throughout the world have as their main causes not ancient hatreds, but rather the purposeful actions of political actors who actively create violent conflict, selectively drawing on history in order to portray it as historically inevitable.[17]

If such conflict is driven by domestic concerns, outside actors can try to prevent or moderate it by making the external costs of such conflict so high that the conflict itself would endanger the domestic power structure. The most obvious way is the use of military force. But to prevent such conflicts, the threat of force must be made early, and it must be credible. In the Yugoslav case the international community has not fulfilled either condition.

Such conflict might also be prevented or moderated by international attempts to influence the situation from within, striking at the root cause of conflictual behavior. While assuring minorities of their rights may be important, that alone does not address the roots of the conflict in cases such as this one. Rather, the target must be the real causes of conflictual policy: the provocation of violence by threatened elites, and the reasons for their conflictual behavior. Such a preventative policy must come early, but it is much less costly than a military solution. The international community can undertake policies such as ensuring multiple sources of mass information and active and early support for democratic forces. But in cases where domestic structural changes are being fostered by international actors, those actors must also be very attentive to the domestic political context into which they are intervening, and in particular should take into account the concerns of those who are most negatively affected by domestic changes. An example is to ensure those elites most affected by change of fall-back positions.

What are the implications of this approach for understanding the link between nationalism and violent conflict in other parts of the world? If domestic conflict drives external conflict, and

---

17 On Azerbaijan, see Dmitrii Furman, "Vozvrashchenie v tretii mir," *Svobodnaia mysl'*, No. 11 (1993), pp. 16–28; on various cases in the Caucasus and Central Asia, Georgii Derluguian, "'Ethnic' violence in the post-communist periphery," *Studies in Political Economy*, No. 41 (Summer 1993), pp. 45–81; on Africa, Binaifer Nowrojee, *Divide and Rule: State Sponsored Ethnic Violence in Kenya* (New York: Africa Watch, 1993); *Somalia: A Government at War with its Own People* (New York: Africa Watch, 1990); Amnesty International, *Rwanda: Mass Murder by Government Supporters and Troops* (New York: Amnesty International, 1994); Catherine Watson, et al., *Transition in Burundi* (Washington, D.C.: American Council for Nationalities, 1993); on India, Susanne Hoeber Rudolph and Lloyd I. Rudolph, "Modern Hate," *The New Republic*, March 22, 1993, pp. 24–29; on Lebanon, Barry Preisler, "Lebanon: The Rationality of National Suicide," Ph,D. dissertation, University of California, Berkeley, 1988.

if the potential costs in the outside world are a key part of the domestic calculus, then we would expect such types of external conflict to be less likely in a truly threatening international environment. If the risk is too high, threatened elites will have more motivation to seek a compromise solution with challengers at home. On the other hand, in conditions where the external threat to security is minimal, threatened elites may be more tempted to use conflict in the external arena as one part of their domestic political strategy. The end of the Cold War may therefore have its primary effects on the international arena not directly, through its influence on the structure of the international system, but rather indirectly, in domestic spheres around the world.

# 22: Democratic Peace

## Jack S. Levy

Although Immanuel Kant spoke of a "pacific union" among democracies,[1] and although many have argued that democracies behave differently than do nondemocratic states in international relations, it was not until a number of studies in the mid-1980s offered systematic evidence that democracies rarely if ever go to war with each other that the "democratic peace" became a central focus of scholarly research in international relations. What is striking about this finding is that in a realm as complex as international relations, in which the actions and interactions of states are so historically contingent, and in which the regularized laws of physics are only a dream to scholars in search of a science of international relations, the absence of war between democracies "comes as close as anything we have to an empirical law in international relations."[2] Although interest in the democratic

peace began with a strong empirical finding, it was intensified by the fact that the observed pattern contradicted realist theory,[3] constituted the core of an emerging liberal theory of peace and war, reinforced the ideological foundations of U.S. foreign policy, and provided some basis for optimism that the persistent pattern of international war might one day be broken.

To say that democracies rarely if ever fight each other is not necessarily to say that democracies are more peaceful than other kinds of states. Most of the evidence suggests that democracies are as likely as authoritarian states to get involved in wars; they often fight imperial wars; in wars between democracies and autocracies they are more likely to be the initiators than the targets; and they occasionally engage in covert action against each other.[4] But the fact remains that they have been nearly immune from

---

1 Immanuel Kant, "Eternal Peace," in *The Philosophy of Kant,* ed. C. J. Friederich (New York: Modern Library, 1949), 430-476. Thomas Paine made a similar argument a few years before Kant. See Thomas C. Walker, "The Forgotten Prophet: Tom Paine's Cosmopolitanism and International Relations," *International Studies Quarterly* 44, no. 1 (March 2000): 51-72.

2 Jack S. Levy, "Domestic Politics and War," *Journal of Interdisciplinary History* 18, no. 4 (spring 1988): 662.

3 As a systemic theory, realism argues that state behavior is shaped by international pressures, not domestic structures or processes. This implies that, ceteris paribus, democratic dyads will go to war as often (proportionately) as any other pairs of states.

4 There is also substantial evidence that democratic dyads tend to engage in more peaceful processes of conflict resolution when they do get in disputes. Democracies also tend to win a disproportionate number of the wars they fight, suffer fewer casualties, and end their wars more quickly than other states. These patterns are summarized in James Lee Ray, *Democracy and International Conflict: An Evaluation of the Democratic Peace Proposition* (Columbia: University of South Carolina Press, 1995); Bruce Russett and John R. Oneal, *Triangulating Peace*; (New York: W. W. Norton, 2001); and Bruce Bueno de Mesquita, James D. Morrow, Randolph M. Siverson, and Alastair Smith, "An Institutional Explanation of the Democratic Peace," *American Political Science Review* 93, no. 4 (December 1999): 791-808. Debate continues on the relative frequency of war involvement of democratic and nondemocratic states and of democratic war initiation, with some scholars now claiming that democracies really are more peaceful than authoritarian states. The differences are modest, however, in contrast to the extraordinarily strong relationship between democratic dyads and peace. See R. J. Rummel, "Democracies *Are* Less Warlike Than Other Regimes," *European Journal of International Relations* 1, no. 4 (December 1995): 457-479.

In Chester A. Crocker, Fen Osler Hampson, and Pamela Aall, eds., *Turbulent Peace: The Challenges of Managing International Conflict,* Washington, D.C.: United States Institute of Peace Press, 2001.

war against each other and that there are few if any unambiguous cases of actual wars between democracies.[5] Scholars have also demonstrated that the relative absence of war between democracies cannot be explained by the fact that democratic dyads trade a lot with each other and that potential conflicts between democracies in the period since World War II were suppressed by U.S. hegemonic power or by other economic or geopolitical factors correlated with democracy.

The growing consensus that democracies rarely if ever fight each other is not matched by any agreement on how to best explain this strong empirical regularity, and in the absence of a convincing theoretical explanation there are few grounds for predicting whether the democratic peace will continue into the future. Theorizing about the democratic peace is in its early stages, and new theories will undoubtedly be proposed, but at the present time there are three general types of models.

The "democratic culture and norms model" suggests that democratic societies are inherently averse to war, and particularly to the casualties from war, and that the norms of peaceful conflict resolution that have evolved within democratic political cultures are extended to relations between democratic states. Consequently, when democracies become involved in disputes with each other they resolve their differences through norms of bounded competition rather than through force.

The "institutional constraints model" emphasizes the checks and balances and the dispersion of power that preclude democratic leaders from taking unilateral military action and imposing aggressive wars on a citizenry that must bear most of the costs of those wars. This, combined with the role of a free press that ensures an open debate, means that democracies are more deliberate in their decisions with respect to war.

One can question whether the aversion to casualties is an inherent feature of democracies or a historically contingent aspect of U.S. and European political culture beginning in the later twentieth century. . . . One can also question the institutional model's assumption that leaders have more warlike preferences than do their domestic publics, a point to which we return in our subsequent discussion of the diversionary theory of war. The institutional and cultural models also have difficulty explaining the fact, confirmed repeatedly in empirical studies, that democracies often fight and often initiate wars.

Proponents of the institutional and cultural models respond by arguing that because there are fewer internal constraints on the use of force by authoritarian leaders, autocrats often attempt to exploit the conciliatory tendencies of democracies. This undermines democratic political leaders' expectations that their peaceful conflict resolution strategies will be reciprocated, reduces their internal constraints on the use of force, and provides additional incentives for democratic regimes to use force against authoritarian regimes to eliminate their violent tendencies. This is plausible, but the institutional and cultural models have more trouble explaining why democracies have frequently initiated imperial wars against weaker opponents despite the absence of any risk of being exploited by the latter, or why democracies have fought wars against autocracies with an intensity disproportionate to any plausible security threat.

---

5   Criteria for war include a military conflict involving at least one thousand battle deaths, and criteria for democracy include regular fair elections, tolerance of opposition parties, and a parliament that at least shares powers with the executive. Possible exceptions to this "law" include the American Civil War and the Spanish-American War, among other cases. See Bruce Russett, *Grasping the Democratic Peace* (Princeton, N.J.: Princeton University Press, 1993); and Ray, *Democracy and International Conflict*. Note that it is democratic regime type, not similarity of regimes, that makes a difference, because authoritarian regimes often fight each other.

A third explanation of the democratic peace is the "signaling model," which is based on the "transparency" of democratic political systems ensured by a free press and open political competition. Transparency makes it obvious whether democratic political leaders involved in international crises have the support of the political opposition and the public. Without domestic support, democratic political leaders cannot implement military threats that might escalate to war. The adversary understands this and will adopt a harder line in crisis bargaining. Democratic leaders anticipate the adversary's resolve and avoid getting into crises in the first place unless they anticipate domestic support. This means that if democracies do get into crises, the adversary will then assume that the leader has domestic support and consequently that the leader will be highly resolved. As a result, the adversary behaves more cautiously. Thus crises bargaining involving democratic states is less likely to be characterized by misperceptions regarding the adversary's resolve and thus is less likely to escalate to war because of misperceptions.[6] In this way the signaling model better incorporates the strategic interaction between democratic states and their external adversaries than does either the cultural or institutional model.

The democratic peace also has important policy implications, for it suggests that by promoting the development of democracies around the world the United States can contribute to the elimination of war as well as to the establishment of liberal institutions and political freedom. Some researchers question this prescription, however, and argue that although well-established democratic dyads are peaceful, the *process* of transition to democracy can be a particularly destabilizing period, and that democratizing states occasionally go to war against other states and even against each other. Edward Mansfield and Jack Snyder argue . . . that the democratization process brings new social groups with widely divergent interests into the political process at a time when the state lacks the institutional capacity to accommodate conflicting interests and respond to popular demands. This can create enormous social conflict, which is often exacerbated if democratization is coupled with the introduction of market forces into nonmarket economies, which leads to popular pressures for state protection against the pain of economic adjustment.

Democratization can be particularly destabilizing in multiethnic societies where ethnic groups are uncertain about how fully their rights will be protected, especially if the state in transition is too weak to maintain a monopoly of violence to protect those rights, as Mohammed Ayoob . . . and Gurr . . . each argue. Elites competing for mass political support are tempted to make nationalist appeals and engage in external scapegoating in order to bolster their internal support. This scapegoating is particularly appealing to those elites whose interests are threatened by the democratization process and who believe that an external enemy might help reverse that process and strengthen centralized political power at home.[7]

While these theoretical linkages are plausible, most of the evidence suggests that states in the process of democratization are *not,* on average, more war prone than are other states. Violence is most likely to occur in the very early stages in the transition away from authoritarianism, not as states move closer to democracy.[8] Still, there are

---

6   Kenneth A. Schultz, "Domestic Opposition and Signaling in International Crises," *American Political Science Review* 92, no. 4 (December 1998): 829-844.

7   See the chapter by Edward D. Mansfield and Jack Snyder (chapter 8) in this volume. Also Jack Snyder, *From Voting to Violence: Democratization and Nationalist Conflict* (New York: W. W. Norton, 2000).

8   Andrew J. Enterline, "Driving while Democratizing," *International Security* 20, no. 4 (spring 1996): 183-196; Michael D. Ward and Kristian S. Gleditsch, "Democratizing for Peace," *American Political Science Review* 92, no. 1 (March 1998): 51-61; Russett and Oneal, *Triangulating Peace*; and Edward D. Mansfield and Jack Snyder, "Democratic Transitions, Institutional Strength, and War" (unpublished paper, 2001).

enough historical cases of democratizing states becoming involved in wars, through processes similar to those hypothesized above, to justify more research on the conditions under which this is likely to happen.

One example is the French Revolution, and another is Serbia under Slobodan Milosevic.[9] A key causal mechanism in these cases involves a political leader conducting an aggressive foreign policy, perhaps including the use of force, to increase his or her domestic political support. This pattern is not restricted to democratizing states, of course, but is a strategy that political leaders in a variety of states have adopted through the ages, ranging from the Athenian "Sicilian expedition" during the Peloponnesian War to the Argentinian invasion of the Falkland Islands in 1982.[10]

While scholars have often alluded to external scapegoating, it was not until the 1980s that they began to systematically investigate this phenomenon. The "diversionary theory of war" is theoretically grounded in social identity theory and the in-group/out-group hypothesis . . . which posits that conflict with an out-group increases the cohesion of a well-defined in-group.[11] Political leaders facing substantial domestic unrest or political opposition

at home anticipate this response and sometimes take belligerent action, including the use of force, in order to rally domestic support. They often set the stage for their scapegoating by promoting historical myths that glorify their people's own history and to demonize the adversary.[12]

Internal political insecurity does not always lead to external scapegoating, however, and this raises the question of the conditions under which leaders are most likely to adopt this strategy. Among the conditions that scholars have identified are low to moderate levels of domestic political support and legitimacy, poor economic performance, and the perception that a diplomatic or military victory is feasible with minimal costs. Another possible variable is regime type, and some have suggested that democratic leaders, because of their electoral accountability, may have greater incentives for scapegoating than do authoritarian leaders, but empirical support for this hypothesis is mixed.[13]

Political leaders must balance incentives for scapegoating against its potential costs, however, and recent evidence suggests that democratic leaders who initiate wars, particularly losing wars, are more likely to be removed from office than are nondemocratic

9   Snyder, *From Voting to Violence*; V. P. Gagnon Jr., "Ethnic Nationalism and International Conflict: The Case of Serbia," *International Security* 19, no. 3 (winter 1994-95): 331-367.

10  Donald Kagan, *The Peace of Nicias and the Sicilian Expedition* (Ithaca, N. Y.: Cornell University Press, 1981); Jack S. Levy and Lily I. Vakili, "External Scapegoating in Authoritarian Regimes: Argentina in the Falklands/Malvinas Case," in *The Internationalization of Communal Strife,* ed. Manus J. Midlarsky (London: Routledge, 1992), 118-146.

11  Four centuries ago, for example, Jean Bodin argued that "the best way of preserving a state, and guaranteeing it against sedition, rebellion, and civil war is to . . . find an enemy against whom [the subjects] can make common cause." Cited in Jack S. Levy, "The Diversionary Theory of War," in *Handbook of War Studies*, ed. Manus I. Midlarsky (Boston: Unwin Hyman, 1989), 259.

12  Jack Snyder, *Myths of Empire: Domestic Politics and International Ambition* (Ithaca, N. Y.: Cornell University Press, 1991).

13  Christopher Gelpi, "Democratic Diversions: Governmental Structure and the Externalization of Domestic Conflict," *Journal of Conflict Resolution* 41, no. 2 (April 1997): 255-282; and Ross Miller, "Regime Type, Strategic Interaction, and the Diversionary Use of Force," *Journal of Conflict Resolution* 43, no. 3 (June 1999): 388-402.

leaders.[14] This provides one possible basis for explaining the finding that democratic states tend to win a disproportionate number (75–80 percent) of the wars that they fight: because of the anticipated political costs of military defeat, democratic leaders are more cautious in their decisions for war (whether driven by scapegoating or other motivations) than are authoritarian leaders and tend to start only those wars they are likely to win.[15]

---

14 Bruce Bueno de Mesquita and Randolph M. Siverson, "War and the Survival of Political Leaders: A Comparative Study of Regime Types and Political Accountability," *American Political Science Review* 89, no. 4 (December 1995): 841–855. Although democratic political leaders are more likely than their authoritarian counterparts to be removed from office after a military defeat, the personal costs of removal are undoubtedly greater for many deposed authoritarian leaders, who have fewer legal protections.

15 A related hypothesis is that once involved in war, democracies extract more resources from society for the prosecution of the war effort than autocracies do. See Bueno de Mesquita et al., "An Institutional Explanation of the Democratic Peace." For some evidence that contradicts this, see Dan Reiter and Alan Stam III, *Democracies at War* (Princeton, N.J.: Princeton University Press, forthcoming 2002).

# 23: An Evolutionary Explanation of Human Aggression

## Azar Gat

Arguing that the human motivational system as whole should be approached from the evolutionary perspective, the article begins with an examination of what can be meaningfully referred to as the 'human state of nature,' the 99.5% of the genus *Homo*'s evolutionary history in which humans lived as hunter-gatherers. In this 'state of nature' people's behavior patterns are generally to be considered as having been evolutionarily adaptive. The interaction of biological propensities and cultural development in shaping the causes of war in historical state societies is examined in the second part of the article . . .

## The Human State of Nature

### Subsistence Resources

In contrast to long-held Rousseauian beliefs that reached their zenith in the 1960s, widespread deadly violence within species—including humans—has been found to be the norm in nature (Gat, 2006; Keeley, 1996; LeBlanc with Register, 2003). Competition over resources is a prime cause of aggression and deadly violence. The reason for this is that food, water, and, to a lesser degree, shelter against the elements are tremendous selection forces. As Darwin, following Malthus, explained, living organisms, including humans, tend to propagate rapidly. Their numbers are constrained and checked only by the limited resources of their particular ecological habitats and by all sorts of competitors. Contrary to the Rousseauian imagination, humans, and animals, did not live in a state of primordial plenty. Even in lush environments plenty is a misleading notion, for it is relative, first, to the number of mouths that have to be fed. The more resource-rich a region is, the more people it attracts from outside, and the greater the internal population growth that takes place. As Malthus pointed out, a new equilibrium between resource volume and population size would eventually be reached, recreating the same tenuous ratio of subsistence that was the fate of pre-industrial societies throughout history. Hence the inherent state of competition and conflict found among Stone Age people.

Let us understand more closely the evolutionary calculus that can make the highly dangerous activity of fighting over resources worthwhile. In our affluent societies, it might be difficult to comprehend how precarious people's subsistence in pre-modern societies was (and still is). The specter of hunger and starvation was ever-present. Affecting both mortality and reproduction, they constantly trimmed down population numbers. Thus struggle over resources was very often evolutionarily cost-effective. The benefits of fighting also had to be matched against possible alternatives (other than starvation). One of them was to move elsewhere. This, of course, often happened, especially if one's enemy was much stronger, but this strategy had clear limitations. By and large, there were no 'empty spaces' for people move to. In the first place, space is not even, and the best, most productive, habitats were normally already taken. Furthermore, a move meant leaving a habitat with whose resources and dangers the group's members were intimately familiar. Such a change could involve heavy penalties. Moreover, giving in to pressure from outside might establish a pattern of victimization. Encouraged by its success, the alien group might repeat and even increase its pressure. Standing for one's own might mean lessening the occurrence of conflict in the future. No less, and perhaps more, than actual fighting, conflict is about deterrence.

### Reproduction

The struggle for reproduction is about access to sexual partners of reproductive potential. There is a fundamental asymmetry between males and females in this respect, which runs throughout nature. At any point in time, a female can be fertilized only once. Consequently, evolutionarily speaking, she must take care to make the best of it. It is quality rather than quantity that she seeks. She must select the male who looks the best equipped for survival and reproduction, so that he will impart his genes, and his qualities, to the offspring. In those species, like the human, where the male also contributes to the raising of the offspring, his skills as a provider and his loyalty are other crucial considerations. In contrast to the female, there is theoretically almost no limit to the number of offspring a male can produce. He can fertilize an indefinite number of females, thus multiplying his own genes in the next generations. The main brake on male sexual success is competition from other males . . .

How does all this affect human violent conflict and fighting? The evidence across the range of hunter-gatherer peoples tells the same story. Within the tribal groupings, women-related quarrels, violence, so-called blood feuds, and homicide were rife, often constituting the principal category of violence. Between groups, the picture was not different, and was equally uniform. Warfare regularly involved the stealing of women, who were then subjected to multiple rape, or taken for marriage, or both.

So hunter-gatherer fighting commonly involved the stealing and raping of women, but was this the cause or a side effect of hunter-gatherer fighting? This is a pointless question that has repeatedly led scholars to a dead end. It artificially takes out and isolates one element from the wholeness of the human motivational complex that may lead to warfare, losing sight of the overall rationale that underpins these elements. Both somatic and reproductive elements are present in humans; moreover, both these elements are intimately interconnected, for people must feed, find shelter, and protect themselves in order to reproduce successfully. Conflict over resources was at least partly conflict over the ability to acquire and support women and children, and to demonstrate that ability in advance, in order to rank worthy of the extra wives. Resources, reproduction, and, as we shall see, status are interconnected and interchangeable. Motives are mixed, interacting, and widely refracted, yet this seemingly immense complexity and inexhaustible diversity can be traced back to a central core, shaped by the evolutionary rationale . . .

Polygyny (and female infanticide) created women scarcity and increased men's competition for, and conflict over, them (Divale and Harris, 1976). Among Aboriginal Australian tribes, about 30% of the Murngin adult males are estimated to have died violently, and similar findings have been recorded for the Tiwi. The Plains Indians showed a deficit of 50% for the adult males in the Blackfoot tribe in 1805 and a 33% deficit in 1858, while during the reservation period the sex ratio rapidly approached 50–50 . . .

### Dominance: Rank, Power, Status, Prestige

The interconnected competition over resources and reproduction is the *root* cause of conflict and fighting in humans as in all other animal species. Other causes and expressions of fighting in nature, and the motivational and emotional mechanisms associated with them, are derivative of, and subordinate to, these primary causes, and *originally* evolved this way in humans as well. It is to these 'second-level' causes and motivational mechanisms, directly linked to the first, that we now turn.

Among social animals, possessing higher rank in the group promises one a greater share in the communal resources, such as hunting spoils, and better access to females. For this reason, rank in the group is hotly contested. It is the strong, fierce, and—among our sophisticated cousins, the chimpanzees—also the 'politically' astute that win status by the actual and implied use of force. Rivalry for rank and domination in nature is, then, a proximate means in the competition over resources and reproduction. For this reason people jealously guard their honor. In traditional societies in particular, people were predisposed to go to great lengths in defense of their honor. The slightest offense could provoke violence. Where no strong centralized authority existed, one's honor was a social commodity of vital significance . . .

As with competition over women, competition over rank and esteem could lead to violent conflict indirectly as well as directly. For instance, even in the simplest societies people desired ornamental, ostentatious, and prestige goods. Although these goods are sometimes lumped together with subsistence goods, their social function and significance are entirely different. Body and clothes ornamentation are designed to enhance physically desirable features that function everywhere in nature as cues for health, vigor, youth, and fertility (Darwin, 1871: 467–8; Diamond, 1992: ch. 9; Low, 1979). It is precisely on these products of the 'illusions industry'—cosmetics, fashion, and jewelry—that people everywhere spend so much money. Furthermore, where some ornaments are scarce and therefore precious, the very fact that one is able to afford them indicates wealth and success. Hence the source of what economist Thorstein Veblen, referring to early 20th-century American Society, called 'conspicuous consumption.' In Stone Age societies as well, luxury goods, as well as the ostentatious consumption of ordinary ones, became in themselves objects of desire as symbols of social status. For this reason, people may fight for them.

Indeed, plenty and scarcity are relative not only to the number of mouths to be fed but also to the potentially ever-expanding and insatiable range of human needs and desires. Human competition increases with abundance—as well as with deficiency—taking more complex forms and expressions, widening social gaps, and enhancing stratification. While the consumption capacity of simple, subsistence, products is inherently limited, that of more refined, lucrative ones is practically open-ended. One can simply move up the market.

### Revenge: Retaliation to Eliminate and Deter

Revenge is one of the major causes of fighting cited in anthropological accounts of pre-state societies. Violence was activated to avenge injuries to honor, property, women, and kin. If life was taken, revenge reached its peak, often leading to a vicious circle of death and counter-death.

How is this most prevalent, risky, and often bloody behavior pattern to be explained? From the evolutionary perspective, revenge is retaliation that is intended either to destroy an enemy or to foster deterrence against him, as well as against other potential rivals. This applies to non-physical and non-violent, as well as to physical and violent; action If one does not pay back an injury, one may signal weakness and expose oneself to further injuries. A process of victimization might be created. This rationale applies wherever there is no higher authority that can be relied upon for protection, that is, in so-called anarchic systems. In modern societies it thus applies to the wide spheres of social relations in which the state or other authoritative bodies do not intervene. In pre-state societies, however, it applied far more widely to the basic protection of life and property.

Thus the instinctive desire to strike back is a basic emotional response which evolved precisely because those who struck back were generally more successful in protecting their own. This is remarkably supported by the famous computerized game that found tit-for-tat the most effective strategy a player can adopt (Hamilton and Axelrod, 1984). But tit-for-tat poses a problem.

The offender cannot always be eliminated. Furthermore, the offender has kin who will avenge him, and it is even more difficult to eliminate them as well. In many cases tit-for-tat becomes a negative loop of retaliation and counter-retaliation from which it is very hard to exit. One original offence may produce a pattern of prolonged hostility. Retaliation might produce escalation rather than annihilation or deterrence. In such cases, fighting seems to feed on, and perpetuate, itself, bearing a wholly disproportional relation to its 'original' cause. People become locked into conflict against their wishes and best interests. It is this factor that has always given warfare an irrational appearance that seems to defy a purely utilitarian explanation.

How can this puzzle be explained? In the first place, it must again be stressed that both the original offence and the act of retaliation arise from a fundamental state of inter-human competition that carries the potential of conflict, and is consequently fraught with suspicion and insecurity. Without this basic state of somatic and reproductive competition and potential conflict, retaliation as a behavior pattern would not have evolved. However, while explaining the root cause of retaliation, this does not in itself account for retaliation's escalation into what often seems to be a self-defeating cycle. A prisoner's dilemma situation is responsible for the emergence of such cycles. In the absence of an authority that can enforce mutually beneficial cooperation on people, or at least minimize their damages, the cycle of retaliation is often their only rational option, though, exposing them to very heavy costs, is not their best option . . .

### Power and the Security Dilemma

Revenge or retaliation is an active reaction to an injury, emanating from a competitive and, hence, potentially conflictual basic state of relations. However, as Hobbes saw (*Leviathan*: ch. 13), the basic condition of competition and potential conflict, which gives rise to endemic suspicion and insecurity, invites not only reactive but also pre-emptive responses, which further magnify mutual suspicion and insecurity. It must be stressed that the source of the potential conflict here is again of a 'second level.' It does not necessarily arise directly from an actual conflict over the somatic and reproductive resources themselves, but from the fear, suspicion, and insecurity that the potential of those 'first-level' causes for conflict creates. Potential conflict can thus breed conflict. When the 'other' must be regarded as a potential enemy, his very existence poses a threat, for he might suddenly attack one day. For this reason, one must take precautions and increase one's strength as much as possible. The other side faces a similar security problem and takes similar precautions. Things do not stop with precautionary and defensive measures, because such measures often inherently possess some offensive potential. Thus measures that one takes to increase one's security in an insecure world often decrease the other's security and vice versa . . .

### World-view and the Supernatural

But what about the world of culture that after all is our most distinctive mark as humans? Do not people kill and get killed for ideas and ideals? From the Stone Age on, the spiritual life of human communities was imbued with supernatural beliefs, sacred cults and rituals, and the practice of magic.

The evolutionary status of religion is beyond our scope here. Like warfare, religion is a complex phenomenon that is probably the result of several different interacting factors. For example, from Emile Durkheim (1965) on, functionalist theorists have argued that religion's main role was in fostering social cohesion, *inter alia* in war.[1] This means that in those groups in

---

1  Durkheim was followed in the functionalist tradition by Bronislav Malinovski and A.R. Radeliffe-Brown. More recently see Heiden (2003); and for an evolutionary perspective: Ridley (1996: 189-93); Wilson (2002).

which common ritual and cult ceremonies were more intensive, social cooperation became more habitual and more strongly legitimized, which probably translated into an advantage in warfare.

But how did hunter-gatherers' supernatural beliefs and practices affect the reasons for conflict and fighting? I argue that on the whole they added to, sometimes accentuating, the reasons we have already discussed. The all-familiar glory of the gods, let alone missionary quests, never appear as reasons for hunter-gatherers' warfare. These will appear later in human cultural evolution. The most regular supernatural reason cited by anthropologists for fighting among hunter-gatherers is fear and accusations of sorcery. It should be noted, however, that these did not appear randomly, but were directed against people whom the victim of the alleged sorcery felt had reasons to want to harm him. This, of course, does not necessarily mean that they really did. What it does mean is that competition, potential conflict, animosity, and suspicion were conducive to fears and accusations of sorcery. To a greater degree than with the security dilemma, the paranoia here reflects the running amok of real, or potentially real, fears and insecurity, thus further exacerbating and escalating the war complex.

### Conclusion: Fighting in the Evolutionary State of Nature

Conflict and fighting in the human state of nature, as in the state of nature in general, was fundamentally caused by competition. While violence is evoked, and suppressed, by powerful emotional stimuli, it is not a primary, 'irresistible' drive; it is a highly tuned, both innate and optional, evolution-shaped tactic, turned on and off in response to changes in the calculus of survival and reproduction. It can be activated by competition over scarce resources, as scarcity and competition are the norm in nature because of organisms' tendency to propagate rapidly

when resources are abundant. Deadly violence is also regularly activated in competition over women, directly as well as indirectly, when men compete over resources in order to be able to afford more women and children.

From these primary somatic and reproductive aims, other, proximate and derivative, 'second-level,' aims arise. The social arbiters within the group can use their position to reap somatic and reproductive advantages. Hence the competition for—and conflict over—esteem, prestige, power, and leadership, as proximate goods. An offense or injury will often prompt retaliation, lest it persists and turns into a pattern of victimization. Tit-for-tat may end in victory or a compromise, but it may also escalate, developing into a self-perpetuating cycle of strikes and counter-strikes, with the antagonists locked in conflict in a sort of prisoner's dilemma situation . . .

Once humans developed agriculture some ten thousand years ago, which led to the growth of the first states about five thousand years ago, they set in motion a continuous chain of developments that have taken them far away from their evolutionary natural way of life. Original, evolution-shaped, innate human wants, desires, and proximate behavioral and emotional mechanisms now expressed themselves in radically altered, 'artificial' conditions. In the process, they were greatly modified, assuming novel and diverse appearances. All the same, cultural evolution did not operate on a 'clean slate,' nor was it capable of producing simply 'anything.' Its multifarious and diverse forms have been built on a clearly recognizable deep core of innate human propensities. Cultural take-off took place much too recently to affect human biology in any significant way. Biologically, we are virtually the same people as our Stone Age forefathers and are endowed with the same predispositions. With cultural evolution all bets are not off—they are merely hedged. We now turn to examine these gene–culture interactions to see how they shaped the motives for human fighting throughout history.

## Historical State-Societies

As we have seen, the motivations that lead to fighting are fundamentally derived from the human motivational system in general. Fighting, to extend Clausewitz's ideas, is a continuation of human aims, and the behavior designed to achieve them, by violent means, and, now, on a progressively larger scale and with increasing organization, mainly associated with the state. How did cultivation, accumulated resources, stratification, coercive structuring, and a growing scale affect the motivational system that led to fighting?

### *Resources*

Territories for cultivation (and for pasture) replaced hunting and foraging territories as an object for competition. However, where both of the above involved competition over the right of access to nature, the real novelty brought about by cultivation was the exploitation of human labor. With cultivation it became possible to live off other people's work. Accumulated foodstuffs and livestock could be appropriated by looting. Other somatic-utility objects, such as fabrics, tools, and metal, were also desirable targets. In addition to their utility value, objects possessed decorative status, and prestige value. Precious objects that acquired the role of money, most notably precious metals, became the most highly prized booty. Control over both natural sources of raw materials and trade intensified as a source of competition. Furthermore, not only products but also the producers themselves could be captured and carried back home as slaves, to labor under direct control. Finally, looting could be further upgraded into tribute extraction, a more systematic and efficient appropriation of labor and resources through political subjugation,

which did not involve great destruction, waste, and disruption of productive activity.

The balance of costs and gains is the most intricate and intriguing issue here. Cultivation greatly increased the material costs of fighting. Hunter-gatherers' fighting harmed mainly the antagonists and their productive activity, but (with minor exceptions) barely the resources themselves. Cultivation, however, added to the above the ability to inflict direct damage on the resources and on other somatic and labor-intensive hardware. Antagonists regularly ravaged crops, livestock, production implements, and settlements in order to weaken and/or increase the cost of war incurred by the opponent. Furthermore, growing political units and technological advancement meant that fighting no longer took place close to home, during lulls in productive activity, and with simple arms and improvised logistics. Metal weapons, fortifications, horses, ships, pay for long-term soldiers, and provisions consumed huge resources. Exact data are sparse, but it is clear that military expenditure regularly constituted by far the largest item of states' expenditure, in most cases the great majority of it. States' tax revenues may have reached as much as 10% of the national product and rose to even higher levels during military emergencies.[2] In pre-modern subsistence economies, where malnutrition was the norm and starvation an ever-looming prospect, such a burden literally took bread out of people's mouths.

Resources ravaged by and invested in war thus constituted a new, massive addition to the cost side of fighting. Whereas among hunter-gatherers the struggle for resources approximated a zero-sum game, wherein resource quantity remained generally unaffected, fighting now invariably *decreased* the *sum total* of resources, at least so long as the fighting went on. Only the relative *distribution* of these decreased resources and, moreover, the

---

2  Rome is the best documented case: Frank (1959, i: 146, 228, and *passim;* v: 4-7, and *passim*); Hopkins (1980); more broadly see Goldsmith (1987: 18, 31-2) [Athens]; 48 [Rome]; 107, 121 [Moghal India]; 142 [Tokugawa Japan]).

re-channeling of their *future yield* might result in net gains for one at the expense of the other.

Who was that 'one'? Neither humanity nor even individual societies counted as real agents or units of calculation in the competition. Unequal distribution was the rule not only between but also within rival sides. Chiefs and their war hosts might accumulate wealth through raiding, while the rest of the tribal people suffered the consequences, in the form of enemy reprisals, counter-raiding, and ravaging. Indeed, the state itself was largely the outgrowth of such processes: power gave wealth, which, in a self-reinforcing spiral, accentuated intra-social power relations in a way that obliged people down a progressively more hierarchic social pyramid to follow their superiors while receiving a lesser and lesser share of the benefits.

Thus cultivation, resource accumulation, and the state for the first time made possible predatory, 'parasitical' existence on the fruits of other people's labor. Whereas productivity-related competition generally increases productive efficiency, predatory-parasitical competition increases predatory-parasitic efficiency while decreasing productive efficiency. All the same, by being efficient in the predatory competition, one was able to secure the benefits of production.

There were also 'spin-off' and long-term net productive gains resulting from the power race. How much of a substantial independent 'spin-off' effect military innovation in metallurgy, engineering, horse breeding, naval architecture, and supply had on society is difficult to establish. But the most significant spin-off effects seem to have come from the state itself. It was through violence that one power established authority over a territory or society, thereby securing increased internal peace and imposing coordinated collective efforts, some of which, at least, were for the common good, decreasing 'free riding.' Large states introduced economies of scale, and, as long as they did not become monopolistically big and overburdened by overheads, they generated and accelerated innovation (see Mann, 1988: 64–5). War was a 'two-level game,' in which both external and internal power relations and external and internal benefit extraction were linked.

### Sex and Harems

The same logic applies to that other principal source of human competition—the sexual—considered from the perspective of male fighting. Students of war scarcely think of sexuality as a motive for fighting. The underlying links that connect the various elements of the human motivational system have largely been lost sight of.[3]

Silence is one reason for this blind spot. While some aspects of sexuality are among the most celebrated in human discourse, others are among the least advertised and most concealed by all sides involved. Nonetheless, the evidence is overwhelming and has recently returned to the headlines, shocking the Western public with mass documentation from the wars in Bosnia, Rwanda, and the Sudan. Throughout history, widespread rape by soldiers went hand in hand with looting as an inseparable part of military operations. Indeed, like looting, the prospect of sexual adventure was one of the main attractions of warlike operations which motivated people to join in. Young and beautiful captured women were a valued prize, in the choice of which—as with all other booty—the leaders enjoyed a right of priority. While in heroic sagas of semi-barbaric societies, such as the *Iliad*, the sexual value of that prize was barely veiled, the practice was no less in force—openly or more discretely—in the armed forces of more civilized societies.[4]

---

3   Even Thayer generally shies away from sexuality in his evolutionary account of war. There have been, of course, attempts to connect sexuality with politics, most famously, in Freud's footsteps, those by Wilhelm Reich and Michel Foucault.

4   Thornhill and Palmer (2000) is an evolution-informed study. See also Buss and Malamuth (1996); Goldstein (2001: 362-9); van Creveld (2001: 33).

The other major reason—apart from the silence of both victors and victims—for the oversight of sexuality as one of the potential benefits of fighting was the exponential rise in large-scale civilized societies of accumulated wealth, which functioned as a universal currency that could be exchanged for most of the other good things in life. Even more than before, fighting advanced reproductive success not only directly, as women were raped and kidnapped, but also indirectly, as the resources and status won by fighting advanced one in the intra-social competition for the acquisition and upkeep of women domestically. By and large, power, wealth, and sexual opportunity comprised overlapping and interlinked hierarchic pyramids.

Where polygyny was permitted, the rich and powerful acquired a greater number of wives and enjoyed a marked advantage in choosing young, beautiful and otherwise worthy ones. In addition to wives, many societies sanctioned official concubines, and there were, of course, unofficial concubines or mistresses. Yet another avenue of sexual opportunity was females in the household, some of whom were slave girls captured in war and raiding. Finally, there was the sex trade per se, where again the most consummate and graceful exponents of the trade could be very expensive.

The manner in which power, wealth, and sexual opportunity were linked is most strikingly demonstrated at the apex of the hierarchic pyramids, most notably in the figure of the so-called Oriental despot, who had his counterpart in the empires of pre-Columbian America. Rulers possessed large harems. According to the Greek authors (Cook, 1985, ii: 226-7), Alexander the Great captured 329 of King Darius III's concubines after the Battle of Issus (333 BC). Only slightly later, Kautilya's *Arthasastra* (i.20 and i.27) provides a detailed description of the construction and procedures of the harem, as well as an account of the bureaucratic apparatus that supervised the march of prostitutes who were invited to the court.

Bureaucratic records, where they survive, constitute the most solid source from which verified *numbers* can be derived. The most bureaucratic and most magnificent of empires was China. According to the state's records (Bielenstein, 1980: 73–4), the imperial harem of the Early Han (second and first centuries BC) comprised some 2000–3000 women, whereas that of the Later Han (first and second centuries AD) reached 5000–6000. Imperial China represented the ultimate in terms of harem size. The records of the Ottoman Privy Purse indicate (Peirce, 1993: 122–4) that at its zenith, during the first half of the 17th century, the sultan's harem comprised some 400 women, with another 400 kept on a 'retired list.'

### Gardens of Pleasure and Cherubs with a Flaming Sword at their Gates

All this should not be regarded as a piece of exotic piquancy, something peripheral to the real business of government. On the contrary, as with the other elements in the human motivational system, it was for the supreme commanding position over the garden of pleasures that people reached or fought in defense of, killed and were killed. As Ibn Khaldun (1958: ch. 3.1) wrote: 'royal authority is a noble and enjoyable position. It comprises all the good things of the world, the pleasures of the body, and the joys of the soul. Therefore, there is, as a rule, great competition for it. It rarely is handed over (voluntarily), but may be taken away. Thus discord ensues. It leads to war and fighting.' The same reality was vividly captured by the ancient Greek tale of wisdom regarding the sword of Damocles. The ruler, according to this tale, was seated at a table packed full with all the world's delights and objects of desire, while a sword hung on a horse-hair above his head, liable to fall down and kill him at any moment. Ruling was a high-stake–high-risk–high-gain affair, with force as its mainstay.

A rigorous study of royal violent mortality rates has yet to be undertaken. All the same, some data may illustrate the point. According to the Biblical record, only nine out the 19 kings of the northern kingdom of Israel died naturally. Of the others, seven were killed by rebels, one committed suicide to escape the same fate, one fell in battle, and one was exiled by the Assyrians. Four or five out of Achaemenid Persia's 13 kings were assassinated and one was apparently killed in war (Cook, 1985: 227, 331). During the last century of the reign of the Hellenistic Seleucids, practically all of the 19 reigning monarchs became victims (after having been perpetrators) of usurpation and violent death. During the 500 years of the Roman Empire, roughly 70% of its rulers died violently, not to mention the countless contenders who were killed without ever making it to the imperial crown (Southern and Dixon, 1996: x-xii, for the data on the late Empire). During the lifespan of the Eastern Roman Empire or Byzantium (395-1453 AD), 64 out of its 107 emperors, more than 60%, were deposed and/or killed (Finer, 1997: 702). Six out of eight kings of Northumbria in the 7th century AD died in war (Abels, 1988: 12). It is estimated that during the later Viking period more than a third of the Norwegian kings died in battle, and another third were banished (Griffith, 1995: 26).

All these are merely examples taken from countless similar tales of insecurity, violent struggle, and bloodbaths at the apex of political power. Violent usurpations spelled doom not only for the ruler or contender, but also for their families and followers, and, if the struggle turned into a full-fledged civil war, for masses of soldiers and civilians. All the same, there was no shortage of candidates to take up this high-risk–high-gain game.

Was it 'worth it' and in what sense? Did people who engaged in the high-gain-high-cost, intra- and inter-social, 'two-level' game of power politics improve their ultimate reproductive success? The answer to this question seems very difficult to compute. On the one hand, rulers enjoyed much greater reproductive opportunities, most strikingly represented in the autocratic harem. On the other

hand, contenders to the throne, and even incumbent rulers, played a highly risky game for both themselves and their families. Some light is shed on the question by a remarkable study recently conducted on the Y (male) chromosome in Central and Eastern Asia, which demonstrates how great rulers' reproductive advantage could be (Zerjal et al., 2003). It reveals that some 8% of the population in the region (0.5% of the world's population) carry the same Y chromosome, which can only mean that they are the descendants of a single man. Furthermore, the biochemical patterns indicate that this man lived in Mongolia about a thousand years ago. It was not difficult to identify the only likely candidate, Chinggis Khan, an identification confirmed by an examination of the Y gene of his known surviving descendants. This, of course, does not mean that Chinggis Khan alone sired so many children from a huge number of women, an obvious impossibility even if he had ceased his military conquests altogether. The tremendous spread of his Y chromosome is due to the fact that his sons succeeded him at the head of ruling houses throughout Central and East Asia for centuries, all enjoying staggering sexual opportunities.

To be sure, Chinggis Khan was among the greatest warlords ever, and his dynasty probably the most successful. Countless unsuccessful bidders for power, whose lines ceased because of their failures, have to be figured into the other side of the equation. All the same, the apex of the social pyramid held such a powerful attraction for people because it was there that evolution-shaped human desires could be set loose and indulged on a gigantic scale. On a more modest scale, the same considerations held true farther down the social hierarchy.

### The Quest for Power and Glory

Status, leadership, and power were sought out in the evolutionary state of nature because of the advantages that they granted in access to somatic and reproductive resources. With resource accumulation and hierarchic organization, the scope and significance of coercive social power rocketed. Furthermore, since both resources and power could now be accumulated and expanded on a hitherto unimaginable scale, while being closely intertwined and interchangeable, power, like money, grew into a universal currency by which most objects of desire could be secured. Power became the medium through which all else was channeled, and the quest for power thus represented all else. For this reason, the quest for power seemingly acquired a life of its own and was also pursued for its own sake. To be sure, power was desired not only for positive reasons; the security dilemma itself drove people and political communities to expand their power as a defensive measure, for in a competitive race one would rather swallow than be swallowed.

Like status and power and closely linked to them, the quest for honor and prestige was originally 'designed' to facilitate access to somatic and reproductive resources. As such, it too is stimulated by powerful emotional gratifications, which give it a seemingly independent life of its own. Again, the potential for the fulfillment of this quest increased exponentially in large-scale societies. The stellas on which autocrats celebrated their achievements in super-human images are interpreted by scholars as instruments of royal propaganda; but, equally, they express the quest for the ultimate fulfillment of the craving for boundless glory and absolute domination, which could now be extended to the 'four corners of the world' and 'everything under the sun,' as the mightiest of imperial rulers boasted.

All the above also applied to individuals in general and to political communities at large. Community members bathed in their collective glory and were willing to pay for its advancement and protection. This again was derived from the conversion value of honor and glory in terms of power, deterrence, and inter-state bargaining. Individuals and political communities jealously guarded their honor and responded forcefully even to slight infringements not because of the trifling matters involved, but because of the much more serious ones that might follow if they demonstrated weakness.[5] To paraphrase Winston Churchill: choosing shame rather than war might very likely beget shame and then war.

### Kinship, Culture, Ideas, Ideals

Are people only interested in these crude materialistic objectives, which even after humankind's dramatic cultural take-off can ultimately be shown to derive from evolution-shaped sources? Lofty aims exist, but, as already claimed, as a continuation rather than a negation of the above. A highly intricate interface links the natural with the cultural.

Let us begin with the factor of identity. People exhibit a marked, evolution-shaped innate predisposition to favor closer kin over more remote ones, or 'strangers'—that is, to favor those with whom they share more genes. Roughly this means that people in any kin circle struggle among themselves for the interests of their yet closer kin, while at the same time tending to cooperate against more distant circles. In this incessant multi-level game, internal cooperation tends to stiffen when the community is faced with an external threat, while inner rivalries variably diminish, though never disappear. It should, of course, be added that non-kin cooperation and alliances for mutual gain are commonplace, becoming only more so with the growth of large-scale organized society.

While the above limitations on kin cooperation must always be kept in mind, the range of kin affinities and kin bonds expanded dramatically in large-scale state-societies. Wherever they took

5  Two works on the subject are: Mercer (1996), which unpersuasively rejects the significance of that factor in crisis; O'Neill (1999).

place, agricultural expansions in particular created *ethnies* which often encompassed hundreds of thousands, but were divided into separate, competing, and often hostile tribes, tribal confederations, and, later, petty-states. It is not sufficiently recognized that above all it is within such ethnic spaces that larger states tended to emerge and expand, for people of a similar ethnicity could be more easily united and kept united, relying on shared ethnocentric traits and bonds. Indeed, it was primarily on their loyal native ethnic core that states and empires relied when they expanded beyond that core to rule over other ethnicities. Thus, contrary to a widely held view, ethnicity mattered a great deal in determining political boundaries and affinities from the very start, rather than only achieving that effect with modernity.[6]

To be sure, it is overwhelmingly cultural traits rather than genetic gradations that separate ethnicities from one another. The point is entirely different. Since in small hunter-gatherer groups kinship and culture overlapped, not only phenotypic resemblance (similarity in physical appearance) but also shared cultural traits functioned as cues for kinship, as well as proving vital for effective cooperation. Thus, whether or not national communities are genetically related (and most of them are), they feel and function *as if* they were, on account of their shared cultural traits. Independence from foreign domination has been perceived as crucial to a people's prosperity as a community of kinship and culture, often evoking most desperate expressions of communal devotion in its defense. To be blind to the sources and workings of these intricate mental mechanisms of collective identity formation inevitably means to misconceive some of the most powerful bonds that shape human history.

The power of ideas is even more far-reaching. People everywhere kill and get killed over ideas, irrespective of kinship and across nations. How is this lofty sphere—the often most abstract of metaphysical ideas, indeed, all too often seemingly absurd notions—connected to the practicalities of life? The key for understanding this question is our species' strong propensity for interpreting its surroundings as deep and as far as the mind can probe, so as to decipher their secrets and form a mental map that would best help to cope with their hazards and opportunities. *Homo sapiens sapiens* possesses an innate, omnipresent evolution-shaped predisposition for ordering its world, which *inter alia* extends to form the foundation of mythology, metaphysics, and science. We are compulsive meaning-seekers. It is this propensity that is responsible for our species' remarkable career.

Thus the array of ideas regarding the fundamental structure and working of the cosmos and the means and practices required for securing its benevolent functioning have been largely perceived as *practical* questions of the utmost significance, evoking as powerful emotions and motivation for action—including violence—as any other major practical question might (see Boyer, 2001: 135–42). They hold the key to individual, communal, and cosmic salvation in this and/or other worlds, worthy of the greatest dedication and even to die for.

Although religious, and later secular, salvation-and-justice ideologies regularly emerged and sometimes remained grounded within a particular people, they often carried a universal message that transcended national boundaries. Furthermore, the relationship of the new universal religious and secular ideologies with war was complex. The obligation of a 'just war' was already evident in many of the older religions. With the new universal ideologies, this obligation was reinforced, as was the ban on belligerency among the faithful. At the same time, some of the salvation ideologies incorporated a strong missionary zeal that could be translated into holy belligerency against

---

6  Cavalli-Sforza et al. (1994). This is not the place to go into the vast literature on nationalism.

non-believers. Furthermore, militant salvation ideologies generated a terrific galvanizing effect on the holy warrior host . . .[7]

## Conclusion

Wars have been fought for the attainment of the same objects of human desire that underlie the human motivational system in general—*only by violent means,* through the use of force. Politics—internal and external—of which war is, famously, a continuation, is the activity intended to achieve at the intra- and inter-state 'levels' the very same evolution-shaped human aims we have already seen . . .

The desire and struggle for scarce resources—wealth of all sorts—have always been regarded as a prime aim of 'politics' and an obvious motive for war. They seem to require little further elaboration. By contrast, reproduction does not appear to figure as a direct motive for war in large-scale societies. However, as we saw, appearance is often deceptive, for somatic and reproductive motives are the two inseparable sides of the same coin. In modern societies, too, sexual adventure remained central to *individual* motivation in going to war, even if it usually failed to be registered at the level of 'state politics.' This may be demonstrated by the effects of the sexual revolution since the 1960s, which, by lessening the attraction of foreign adventure for recruits and far increasing the attraction of staying at home, may have contributed to advanced societies' growing aversion to war. Honor, status, glory, and dominance—both individual and collective—enhanced access to somatic and reproductive success and were thus hotly pursued and defended, even by force. The security dilemma sprang from this state of actual and potential competition, in turn pouring more oil onto its fire. Power has been the universal currency through which all of the above could be obtained and/or defended, and has been sought after as such, in an often escalating spiral.

Kinship—expanding from family and tribe to peoples—has always exerted overwhelming influence in determining one's loyalty and willingness to sacrifice in the defense and promotion of a common good. Shared culture is a major attribute of ethnic communities, in the defense of which people can be invested as heavily as in the community's political independence and overall prosperity. Finally, religious and secular ideologies have been capable of stirring enormous zeal and violence; for grand questions of cosmic and socio-political order have been perceived as possessing paramount *practical* significance for securing and promoting life on earth and/or in the afterlife. In the human problem-solving menus, ideologies function as the most general blueprints. Rather than comprising a 'laundry list' of causes for war, all of the above partake in the interconnected human motivational system, *originally* shaped by the calculus of survival and reproduction.

This calculus continues to guide human behavior, mostly through its legacy of innate proximate mechanisms—human desires—even where the original link between these proximate mechanisms and the original somatic and reproductive aims may have been loosened or even severed under altered conditions, especially during modernity: more wealth is desired even though above a certain level it has ceased to translate into greater reproduction; with effective contraception much the same applies to sexual success; power, status, honor, and fame—connected to the above—are still hotly pursued even though their reproductive significance has become ambivalent.

To the extent that the industrial-technological revolution, most notably its liberal path, has sharply reduced the prevalence of war, the

---

7   For a similar argument see: Stark (1996: ch. 8: 'The Martyrs: Sacrifice as Rational Choice'); Wilson (2002). Both works overlook the military aspect.

reason for this change is that the violent option for fulfilling human desires has become much less promising than the peaceful option of competitive cooperation. Furthermore, the more affluent and satiated the society and the more lavishly are people's most pressing needs met, the less their incentives to take risks that might involve the loss of life and limb. This does not mean a millenarian era of selfless altruism. People continue to compete vigorously over scarce objects of desire, partly because much of the competition among them concerns relative rather than absolute allocation of gains. On this realists are on firmer ground than radical liberals. However, liberals have been right in stressing that human reality is not static and, indeed, has been changing dramatically over the past generations, with the growth of affluent-liberal society going hand in hand with deepening global economic interdependence and mutual prosperity.[8] As conditions have changed—indeed, *only* for those for whom they have changed, most notably within the world's affluent and democratic 'zone of peace'—the violent option, the 'hammer,' in the human behavioral tool kit seems to have declined in utility for attaining desired aims.

### References

Abels, Richard (1988) *Lordship and Military Obligation in Anglo-Saxon England.* Berkeley, CA: University of California Press.

Bielenstein, Hans (1980) *The Bureaucracy of the Han Times.* Cambridge: Cambridge University Press.

Boyer, Pascal (2001) *Religion Explained: The Evolutionary Origins of Religious Thought.* New York: Basic Books.

Buss, D. and N. Malamuth (eds) (1996) *Sex, Power, Conflict: Evolutionary and Feminist Perspectives.* New York: Oxford University Press.

Cavalli-Sforza, L.L., Paolo Menozzi and Alberto Piazza (1994) *The History and Geography of Human Genes.* Princeton, NJ: Princeton University Press.

Cook, J. (1985) 'The Rise of the Achaemenids and Establishment of their Empire', in I. Gershevitch (ed.) *The Cambridge History of Iran,* vol. ii. pp. 200-91. Cambridge: Cambridge University Press.

Darwin, Charles (n.d. [1871]) *The Origin of the Species and the Descent of Man.* New York: The Modern Library.

Diamond, Jared (1992) *The Rise and Fall of the Third Chimpanzee.* London: Vintage.

Divale, William and Marvin Harris (1976) 'Population, Warfare and the Male Supremacist Complex', *American Anthropologist* 78: 521-38.

Durkheim, Emile (1965) *The Elementary Forms of Religious Life.* New York: Free Press.

Finer, S.E. (1997) *The History of Government from the Earliest Times.* Oxford: Oxford University Press.

Frank, Tenney (1959) *An Economic Survey of Ancient Rome.* Paterson, NJ: Pageant Books.

Gat, Azar (2005) 'The Democratic Peace Theory Reframed: The Impact of Modernity', *World Politics* 58: 73-100.

Gat, Azar (2006) *War in Human Civilization.* Oxford: Oxford University Press.

Goldsmith, Raymond (1987) *Premodern Financial Systems: A Historical Comparative Study.* Cambridge: Cambridge University Press.

Goldstein, Joshua (2001) *War and Gender: How Gender Shapes the War System and Vice Versa.* New York: Cambridge University Press.

Griffith, Paddy (1995) *The Viking Art of War.* London: Greenhill.

Hamilton, W.D. and Robert Axelrod (1984) *The Evolution of Cooperation.* New York: Basic Books.

Heiden, Brain (2003) *A Prehistory of Religion: Shamanism, Sorcerers and Saints.* Washington, DC: Smithsonian.

8 See Modelski (2001: 22); Sterling-Folker (2001); Gat (2005).

Hopkins, Keith (1980) 'Taxes and Trade in the Roman Empire (200 BC–Ad 400)', *Journal of Roman Studies* 70: 101-25.

Ibn Khaldun (1985) *The Muqaddimah: An Introduction to History.* New York: Pantheon.

Keeley, Lawrence (1996) *War before Civilization.* New York: Oxford University Press.

LeBlanc, Steven with Katherine Register (2003) *Constant Battles: The Myth of the Peaceful Noble Savage.* New York: St Martin's Press.

Low, Dobbi (1979) 'Sexual Selection and Human Ornamentation', in N. Chagnon and W. Irons (eds) *Evolutionary Biology and Human Social Behavior,* pp. 462-87. North Scituate, MA: Duxbury.

Mann, Michael (1988) 'States, Ancient and Modern', in M. Mann, *States, War and Capitalism,* pp. 33-72. Oxford: Blackwell

Mercer, Jonathan (1996) *Reputation and International Politics.* Ithaca, NY: Cornell University Press.

Modelski, George (2001) 'Evolutionary World Politics', in W. Thompson (ed.) *Evolutionary Interpretations of World Politics,* pp. 16-29. New York: Routledge.

O'Neill, Barry (1999) *Honor, Symbols and War.* Ann Arbor, MI: University of Michigan Press.

Peirce, Leslie (1993) *The Imperial Harem: Women and Sovereignty in the Ottoman Empire.* New York: Oxford University Press.

Ridley, Matt (1996) *The Origins of Virtue: Human Instincts and the Evolution of Cooperation.* New York: Viking.

Southern, Pat and Karen Dixon (1996) *The Late Roman Army.* London: Batsford.

Stark, Rodney (1996) *The Rise of Christianity.* Princeton, NJ: Princeton University Press.

Sterling-Folker, Jennifer (2001) 'Evolutionary Tendencies in Realist and Liberal IR Theory', in W. Thompson (ed.) *Evolutionary Interpretations of World Politics,* ch. 4. New York: Routledge.

Thayer, Bradley (2004) *Darwin and International Relations: On the Evolutionary Origins of War and Ethnic Conflict.* Lexington, KY: University of Kentucky Press.

Thornhill, Randy and Craig Palmer (2000) *A Natural History of Rape: Biological Bases of Sexual Coercion.* Cambridge, MA: MIT Press.

van Creveld, Martin (2001) *Men, Women and War.* London: Cassell.

Wilson, David S. (2002) *Darwin's Cathedral: Evolution, Religion, and the Nature of Society.* Chicago, IL: University of Chicago Press.

Zerjal, Tatiana, Yali Xue, Giorgio Bertorelle, R. Spencer Wells, Weidong Bao, Suling Zhu et al. (2003) 'The Genetic Legacy of The Mongols', *The American Journal of Human Genetics* 72: 717-21.

# 24: Cognition and Stress

## Richard Ned Lebow

Traditional social science theory depicted decision-making as an essentially rational process. This paradigm assumed that policy-makers processed information in a relatively straightforward and honest manner in order to discover the best policy alternative. To do this, they identified the alternatives, estimated the probability of success of each, and assessed their impact upon the values they sought to maximize. Policy-makers were thought of as receptive to new information. As they learned more about a particular problem they were expected to make more complex and sophisticated judgments about the implications of the various policy alternatives they considered. The rational actor paradigm also assumed that policy-makers confronted tradeoffs squarely, that they accepted the need to make choices between the benefits and costs of competing alternatives in order to select the best policy.

Considerable research points to the conclusion that decision-making in practice differs considerably from the rational process we have just described.[1] This finding has prompted efforts to develop alternative paradigms of decision-making, several of which have already been formulated in considerable detail. Each of these several paradigms claims to represent a more accurate description of the decision-making process than that of the rational actor model.

The variety of models and approaches to decision-making that have been developed in recent years has added immeasurably to our understanding of the decision-making process. The models have made us aware of the complexity of this process and the multiplicity of personal, political, institutional, and cultural considerations that can shape decisions. For this very reason no one perspective provides a satisfactory explanation of decision-making. Each offers its own particular insights and is more or less useful depending upon the analytical concerns of the investigator and the nature of the decision involved.

For our purposes the psychological perspective on decision-making appears to be the most relevant by virtue of the insights it offers into the causes and effects of misperception. Use of the psychological approach is complicated by the fact that there is as yet no integrated statement of psychological principles and processes that could be considered to represent a paradigm of decision-making.[2] There are instead several

---

1   For example, Herbert A. Simon, *Administrative Behavior* (New York: Free Press, 1946); Charles E. Lindblom, "The Science of 'Muddling Through,'" *Public Administration* 19 (Spring 1959): 74-88; Richard Cyert and James March, *A Behavioral Theory of the Firm* (Englewood Cliffs, N.J.: Prentice-Hall, 1963); Graham T. Allison, *Essence of Decision: Explaining the Cuban Missile Crisis* (Boston: Little, Brown, 1971); John D. Steinbruner, *The Cybernetic Theory of Decision* (Princeton: Princeton University Press, 1974).

2   Donald R. Kinder and Janet A. Weiss, "In Lieu of Rationality: Psychological Perspectives on Foreign Policy Decision Making," *Journal of Conflict Resolution* 22 (December 1978): 707-35, offer a thoughtful analysis of the prospects for a psychological paradigm of decision-making. Following a review of the relevant literature the authors identify four common themes they believe will be central to any paradigm. These are (1) the striving for cognitive consistency and its conservative impact upon perception and information processing, (2) systematic biases in causal analysis, (3) distorting effects of emotional stress, and (4) the cognitive construction of order and predictability within a disorderly and uncertain environment.

Richard Ned Lebow, *Between Peace and War* (Baltimore: Johns Hopkins University Press, 1981), pp. 101-19.

different schools of thought, each of which attempts to explain nonrational processes in terms of different causation. The state of psychological theory therefore mirrors that of decision-making theory as a whole. As it is often necessary to employ more than one decision-making perspective to understand the genesis of a policy so one must exploit more than one psychological theory or approach in order to explain the nonrational processes that are involved. In the pages that follow we will accordingly describe two psychological approaches, one cognitive the other motivational, that will be used in analyzing our case material.

## Cognitive Consistency and Misperception

The cognitive approach emphasizes the ways in which human cognitive limitations distort decision-making by gross simplifications in problem representation and information processing. Some psychologists have suggested that human beings may be incapable of carrying out the procedures associated with rational decision-making.[3] Whether or not this is actually the case, there is growing evidence that people process and interpret information according to a set of mental rules that bear little relationship to those of formal logic. Robert Abelson refers to these as yet poorly understood procedures as "psycho-logic."[4]

One principle of psycho-logic that has received considerable empirical verification is the principle of "cognitive consistency." Numerous experiments point to the conclusion that people try to keep their beliefs, feelings, actions, and cognitions mutually consistent. Thus, we tend to believe that people we like act in ways we approve of, have values similar to ours, and oppose people and institutions we dislike. People we dislike, we expect to act in ways repugnant to us, have values totally dissimilar from ours, and to support people and institutions we disapprove of.[5] Psychologists have theorized that cognitive consistency is an economic way or organizing cognition because it facilitates the interpretation,

---

3   Some of the experimental literature on this subject is described in chapter 1, footnote 35. In addition, see G. A. Miller, "The Magical Number Seven Plus or Minus Two: Some Limits on Our Capability for Processing Information," *Psychological Review* 63 (March 1956): 81-94; K. R. Hammond, C. J. Hursch, and F. J. Todd, "Analyzing the Components of Clinical Judgements," *Psychological Review* 71 (November 1964): 438-56; L. R. Goldberg, "Simple Models or Simple Processes? Some Research on Clinical Judgements." *American Psychologist* 23 (July 1968): 83-96; N. Wiggins and E. S. Kohen, "Man vs. Model of Man Revisited: The Forecasting of Graduate School Success," *Journal of Personality and Social Psychology* 19 (July 1971): 100-6. The experimental literature is reviewed by Robert P. Abelson, "Social Psychology's Rational Man," in S. I. Benn and G. W. Mortimore, eds., *Rationality and the Social Sciences: Contributions to the Philosophy and Methodology of the Social Sciences* (Boston: Routledge & Kegan Paul, 1976), pp. 59-89; Melvin Manis, "Cognitive Social Psychology and Attitude Change," *American Behavioral Scientist* 21 (May-June 1978): 675-90.

4   Robert P. Abelson and Milton Rosenberg, "Symbolic Psycho-Logic," *Behavioral Science* 3 (January 1958): 1-13; Robert P. Abelson, "Psychological Implication," in Robert P. Abelson et al., *Theories of Cognitive Consistency: A Sourcebook* (Chicago: Rand McNally, 1968), pp. 112-39, and "Social Psychology's Rational Man," pp. 59-89.

5   Abelson and Rosenberg, in "Symbolic Psycho-Logic," p. 5, define a consistent structure as one in which "All relations among 'good elements' [i.e., those that are positively valued] are positive (or null), all relations among 'bad elements' [i.e., those that are negatively valued] are positive (or null), and all relations among good and bad elements are negative (or null)." The literature on cognitive consistency is considerable. For discussion of this literature, see, Robert Zajonc, "Cognitive Theories in Social Psychology," in Gardner Lindzey and Elliot Aaronson, eds., *The Handbook of Social Psychology*, 2nd ed. (Reading, Mass.: Addison-Wesley, 1968), vol. 1, pp. 345-53; Abelson et al., *Theories of Cognitive Consistency: A Sourcebook*; Stevan Sherman and Robert Wolosin, "Cognitive Biases in a Recognition Task," *Journal of Personality* 41 (September 1973): 395-411; Jesse Delia and Walter Crockett, "Social Schemas, Cognitive Complexity, and the Learning of Social Structures." *Journal of Personality* 41 (September 1973): 412-29.

retention, and recall of information.[6] While this may or may not be true, our apparent need for cognitive order also has some adverse implications for decision-making because it suggests the existence of systematic bias in favor of information consistent with information that we have already assimilated.

At the present time considerable work is being done to analyze the various ramifications of cognitive consistency for decision-making. To date, the most comprehensive effort is that of Robert Jervis whose work is especially relevant for our purposes, because he has made the foreign policy process the specific focus of his study.[7]

Jervis contends that it is impossible to explain crucial foreign policy decisions without reference to policy-makers' beliefs about the world and the motives of other actors in it. These beliefs, organized as "images," shape the way in which policy-makers respond to external stimuli. He suggests that the primary source of images is stereotyped interpretations of dramatic historical events, especially wars and revolutions. These upheavals have a particularly strong impact upon the thinking of younger people whose opinions about the world are still highly impressionable. Images formed by adolescents and young adults can still shape their approach to international problems years later when they may occupy important positions of authority. Jervis believes that this may explain why "generals are prepared to fight the last war and diplomats prepared to avoid it."[8]

Lessons learned from history are reinforced or modified by what policy-makers learn from first-hand experience. Jervis finds that events that are personally experienced can be a "powerful determinant" of images. This too may be a source of perceptual distortion because personal experiences may be unrepresentative or misleading. As with historical lessons, events experienced early in adult life have a disproportional impact upon perceptual predispositions.[9]

The major part of Jervis' study is devoted to analyzing the ways in which images, once formed, affect foreign policy behavior. From the outset he makes an important distinction between what he calls "rational" and "irrational" consistency. The principle of consistency, he argues, helps us to make sense of new information as it draws upon our accumulated experience, formulated as a set of expectations and beliefs. It also provides continuity to our behavior. But the pursuit of consistency becomes irrational when it closes our minds to new information or different points of view. Even irrational consistency can be useful in the short run because it helps to make a decision when the time comes to act. However, persistent denial of new information diminishes our ability to learn from the environment. Policy-makers must strike a balance between persistence and continuity on the one hand and openness and

---

6   The various explanations for cognitive consistency are discussed by Norman Feather, "A Structural Balance Approach to the Analysis of Communication Effects," in Leonard Berkowitz, ed., *Advances in Experimental Social Psychology* (New York: Academic Press, 1967), vol. 3, pp. 99-165.

7   Robert Jervis, "Hypotheses on Misperception," *World Politics* 20 (April 1968): 454-79, and *Perception and Misperception in International Politics* (Princeton: Princeton University Press, 1976). For other analyses by political scientists of the implications of cognitive processes for decision-making, see Robert Axelrod, *Framework for a General Theory of Cognition and Choice* (Berkeley: Institute of International Studies, 1972), and Robert Axelrod, ed., *Structure of Decision: The Cognitive Maps of Political Elites* (Princeton: Princeton University Press, 1976); Steinbruner, *The Cybernetic Theory of Decision.*

8   Jervis, *Perception and Misperception in International Politics*, pp. 117-24, 187, 262-70. Jervis' argument is reminiscent of V. O. Key's thesis that dramatic historical events like the civil war and the great depression significantly influenced the formation of party identification which then endured long after the event and the party's response to it. "A Theory of Critical Elections," *Journal of Politics* 17 (February 1955): 3-18.

9   Ibid., pp. 239-48.

flexibility on the other. Jervis marshals considerable evidence to indicate that they more often err in the direction of being too wedded to established beliefs and defend images long after they have lost their utility.[10]

Irrational consistency can leave its mark on every stage of the decision-making process. Most importantly, it affects the policy-maker's receptivity to information relevant to a decision. Once an expectation or belief has taken hold, new in-formation is assimilated to it. This means that policy-makers are more responsive to information that supports their existing beliefs than they are to information that challenges them. When confronted with critical information, they tend to misunderstand it, twist its meaning to make it consistent, explain it away, deny it, or simply ignore it.

To the extent that a policy-maker is confident in his expectations, he is also likely to make a decision before sufficient information has been collected or evaluated. Jervis refers to this phenomenon as "premature cognitive closure" and sees it as a major cause of institutional inertia. As all but the most unambiguous evidence will be interpreted to confirm the wisdom of established policy and the images of reality upon which it is based, policy-makers will proceed a long way down a blind alley before realizing that something is wrong.[11]

When policy-makers finally recognize the need to reformulate an image, they are likely to adopt the first one that provides a decent fit. This "perceptual satisficing" means that images change incrementally, that a large number of exceptions, special cases, and other superficial alterations will be made in preference to rethinking the validity of the assumptions on which the image is based. It also means that tentative beliefs or

expectations, often made on the basis of very incomplete information, come to exercise a profound influence on policy because once they are even provisionally established incoming information is assimilated to them. This in turn lends credence to their perceived validity.[12]

The tautological nature of information processing is further facilitated by the "masking effect" of preexisting beliefs. As information compatible with an established belief will be interpreted in terms of it, the development of alternative beliefs that the information might also support is inhibited. Thus, the belief that the other side is bluffing, as Jervis points out, is likely to mask the perception that it means what it says because the behaviors that follow from these two intentions resemble each other so closely.[13]

The second way in which irrational consistency influences decision-making is by desensitizing policy-makers to the need to make value "trade-offs." Instead of recognizing that a favored option may advance one or even several valued objectives, but does so at the expense of some other valued objective, policy-makers are more likely to perceive the option as simultaneously supporting all of their objectives. As they come to favor an option, policymakers may even alter some of their earlier expectations or establish new ones all in the direction of strengthening the case for the favored policy.

The failure to recognize trade-offs leads to "belief system overkill." Advocates of a policy advance multiple, independent, and mutually reinforcing arguments in its favor. They become convinced that it is not just better than other alternatives but superior in every way. Opponents on the other hand tend to attack it as ill considered in all its ramifications. In this regard, Jervis cites Dean Acheson's description of Arthur

---

10  Ibid., pp. 17-42, et passim.
11  Ibid., pp. 187-91.
12  Ibid., pp. 191-95.
13  Ibid., pp. 193-95.

Vandenberg's characteristic stand: "He declared the end unattainable, the means harebrained, and the cost staggering." Cognitions ordered in this way facilitate choice as they make it appear that all considerations point toward the same conclusion. Nothing therefore has to be sacrificed. But, as Jervis points out, "the real world is not as benign as these perceptions, values are indeed sacrificed and important choices are made, only they are made inadvertently."[14]

The final way irrational consistency is manifested is in the form of postdecisional rationalization, a phenomenon described by Leon Festinger in his theory of cognitive dissonance.[15] Festinger argues that people seek strong justification for their behavior and rearrange their beliefs in order to lend support to their actions. Following a decision they spread apart the alternatives, upgrading the attractiveness of the one they have chosen and downgrading that of the alternative they have rejected. By doing so they convince themselves that there were overwhelming reasons for deciding or acting as they did. Festinger insists that people only spread apart the alternatives after they have made a decision. The decision must also result in some kind of commitment and the person making it must feel that it was a free decision, i.e., that he had the choice to decide otherwise.[16]

Subsequent research indicates that decisional conflict is positively correlated with the appeal of the rejected alternatives, their dissimilarity from the chosen alternatives and the perceived importance of the choice. In other words, the more difficult the decision the greater the need to engage in postdecisional rationalization. According to Jervis, foreign policy decisions are often characterized by these criteria, and statesmen respond by upgrading their expectations about their chosen policy. By making their decision appear even more correct in retrospect they increase the amount of negative feedback required to reverse it. Postdecisional rationalization therefore makes policymakers less responsive to the import of critical information.[17]

### Decisional Conflicts and Defensive Avoidance

Whereas Jervis stresses the ways in which cognitive processes distort decision-making, another school of psychology emphasizes the importance of motivation as a source of perceptual distortion. They see human beings as having a strong need to maintain images of the self or the environment conducive to their emotional well-being. This need interferes with their ability to act rationally. Harold Lieff observes:

> An important aspect of emotional thinking, including anxious and fearful thinking, is its selectivity. Under the influence of anxiety, a

---

14 Ibid., pp. 128-43.

15 Leon Festinger, *A Theory of Cognitive Dissonance* (Stanford: Stanford University Press, 1957), and Leon Festinger, ed., *Conflict, Decision, and Dissonance* (Stanford: Stanford University Press, 1964); also Jack W. Brehm and Arthur Cohen, *Explorations in Cognitive Dissonance* (New York: Wiley, 1962); Alliot Aronson, "The Theory of Cognitive Dissonance," in Berkowitz, *Advances in Experimental Social Psychology*, vol. 4, pp. 15-17; Robert A. Wicklund and Jack W. Brehm, *Perspectives on Cognitive Dissonance* (Hillsdale, N.J.: Erlbaum, 1976). For a discussion of the literature, see, Jervis, *Perception and Misperception in International Politics*, pp. 382-406; Irving L. Janis and Leon Mann, *Decision Making: A Psychological Analysis of Conflict, Choice, and Commitment* (New York: Free Press, 1977), pp. 309-38, 437-40.

16 Janis and Mann, in *Decision Making*, pp. 81-105, disagree with Festinger on this point. They describe the spreading of alternatives as a form of bolstering, which they see motivated by the need to ward off the stress of decisional conflict and only secondarily by a need to maintain cognitive consistency. Accordingly, they argue for the existence of predecisional bolstering, especially in instances where the conflicted policymaker believes that he already possesses all the relevant information that he will receive.

17 Jervis, *Perception and Misperception in International Politics*, pp. 382-406.

person is apt to select certain items in his environment and ignore others, all in the direction of either falsely proving that he was justified in considering the situation frightening and in responding accordingly, or conversely, of seeking reasons for false reassurances that his anxiety is misplaced and unnecessary. If he falsely justifies his fear, his anxieties will be augmented by the selective response, setting up a vicious circle of anxiety-distorted perception—increased anxiety. If, on the other hand, he falsely reassures himself by selective thinking, appropriate anxieties may be reduced, and he may then fail to take the necessary precautions.[18]

The work of Irving Janis and Leon Mann represents one of the most thought-provoking attempts to construct a motivational model of decision-making. They start from the assumption that decision-makers are emotional beings, not rational calculators, that they are beset by doubts and uncertainties, struggle with incongruous longings, antipathies, and loyalties, and are reluctant to make irrevocable choices. Important decisions therefore generate conflict, defined as simultaneous opposing tendencies to accept and reject a given course of action. This conflict and the psychological stress it generates become acute when a decision-maker realizes that there is risk of serious loss associated with any course of action open to him.[19] More often than not, he will respond to such situations by procrastinating, rationalizing, or denying his responsibility for the decision. These affective responses to stress detract from the quality of decision-making.[20]

Janis and Mann present their "conflict model" of decision-making in terms of the

sequence of questions policy-makers must ask when confronted with new information about policies to which they are committed. Their answers to these questions determine which of five possible patterns of coping they will adopt. . . .

The first of the questions pertains to the risks to the policy-maker of not changing his policy or taking some kind of protective action. If he assesses the risks as low, there is no stress and he can ignore the information. Janis and Mann refer to this state as "unconflicted inertia." Sometimes this is a sensible appraisal as when policy-makers ignore warnings of doom from critics motivated by paranoia or partisan advantage. It is dysfunctional when it is a means of avoiding the stress associated with confronting a difficult decision head on.[21]

If the perceived risks are thought to be serious, the policy-maker must attempt to identify other courses of action open to him. If his search reveals a feasible alternative, Janis and Mann expect that it will be adopted without conflict. "Unconflicted change," as this pattern of coping is called, may once again reflect a realistic response to threatening information although it can also be a means of avoiding stress. Unconflicted change is dysfunctional when it mediates a pattern of "incrementalism." This happens when the original policy is only marginally changed in response to threatening information and then changed slightly again when more trouble is encountered. Such a crude satisficing strategy tends to ignore the range of alternative policies, some of which may be more appropriate to the situation. Janis and Mann suggest that this is most likely to occur when a policy-maker is deeply

---

18  Harold Lieff, "Anxiety Reactions," in Alfred Freedman and Harold Kaplan, eds., *Comprehensive Textbook of Psychiatry* (Baltimore: Williams & Wilkins, 1967), pp. 859-60.

19  Psychological stress is used by Janis and Mann to designate "unpleasant emotional states evoked by threatening environmental events or stimuli." Common unpleasant emotional states include anxiety, guilt and shame.

20  Janis and Mann, *Decision Making*, p. 15.

21  Ibid., pp. 55-56.

committed to his prior course of action and fears that significant deviation from it will subject him to disapproval or other penalties.[22]

If the policy-maker perceives that serious risks are inherent in his current policy, but upon first assessment is unable to identify an acceptable alternative, he experiences psychological stress. He becomes emotionally aroused and preoccupied with finding a less risky but nevertheless feasible policy alternative. If, after further investigation, he concludes that it is unrealistic to hope for a better strategy, he will terminate his search for one despite his continuing dissatisfaction with the available options. This results in a pattern of "defensive avoidance," characterized by efforts to avoid fear-arousing warnings.[23]

Janis and Mann identify three forms of defensive avoidance: procrastination, shifting responsibility for the decision, and bolstering. The first two are self-explanatory. Bolstering is an umbrella term that describes a number of psychological tactics designed to allow policy-makers to entertain expectations of a successful outcome. Bolstering occurs when the policy-maker has lost hope of finding an altogether satisfactory policy option and is unable to postpone a decision or foist the responsibility for it onto someone else. Instead, he commits himself to the least objectionable alternative and proceeds to exaggerate its positive consequences or minimize its negative ones. He may also deny the existence of his aversive feelings, emphasize the remoteness of the consequence or attempt to minimize his personal responsibility for the decision once it is made. The policy-maker continues to think about the problem but wards off anxiety by practicing selective attention and other forms of distorted information processing.[24]

Bolstering can serve a useful purpose. It helps a policy-maker forced to settle for a less than satisfactory course of action to overcome residual conflict and move more confidently toward commitment. But bolstering has detrimental consequences when it occurs before the policy-maker has made a careful search of the alternatives. It lulls him into believing that he has made a good decision when in fact he has avoided making a vigilant appraisal of the possible alternatives in order to escape from the conflict this would engender.[25]

If the policy-maker finds an alternative that holds out the prospect of avoiding serious loss he must then inquire if he has sufficient time to implement it. If his answer to this question is no, his response will be one of "hypervigilance." This pattern of coping is also likely to be adopted if the time pressures are such that the policy-maker does not even believe it possible to initiate a search for an acceptable alternative. Hypervigilance is characterized by indiscriminate openness to all information and a corresponding failure to determine whether or not that information is relevant, reliable, or supportive. Decisions made by persons in a hypervigilant state are likely to be unduly influenced by the will and opinions of others. In its most extreme form, panic, decisions are formulated in terms of the most simpleminded rules, e.g., "Do what others around you are doing. This is why a fire in a theater may prompt the audience to rush irrationally toward only one of several accessible exits."[26]

The patterns described above—unconflicted inertia, unconflicted change, defensive avoidance, and hypervigilance—are all means of coping with psychological stress. But they are hardly likely to lead to good decisions as each

---

22  Ibid., pp. 56-57, 73.
23  Ibid., pp. 57-58, 74, 107-33.
24  Ibid., pp. 74-95.
25  Ibid., pp. 76-79.
26  Ibid., pp. 59-60, 205.

pattern is characterized by some kind of cognitive distortion. "High quality" decision-making occurs when a policy-maker is able to answer "yes," or at least "maybe," to all four questions. "Vigilance," the pattern of coping that leads to good decisions, is therefore associated with the following conditions: the policy-maker realizes that his current policy will encounter serious difficulties; he sees no obvious satisfactory alternative but believes that a good alternative can probably be found and implemented in the time available to him.[27]

The preceding argument makes it apparent that Janis and Mann believe that stress can facilitate good decision-making but only under circumstances so specific that they are not likely to recur very often. In less than ideal circumstances stress can be so acute as to compel the policy-maker to adopt a decision-making strategy to protect him from it. Any of these patterns of coping will impair the quality of the decision.

## Cognitive Processes and Decision-Making Pathologies

The studies we have just described represent two of the most provocative and comprehensive attempts to apply psychological insights to the study of political behavior. Unfortunately for those concerned with developing a psychological paradigm, the principal arguments of these two works are derived from sufficiently different premises to preclude their reformulation into an integrated model of decision-making. For Jervis, the starting point is the human need to develop simple rules for processing information in order to make sense of an extraordinarily complex and uncertain environment. Janis and Mann take as their fundamental assumption the human desire to avoid fear, shame, and guilt. Jervis describes cognitive consistency as the most important organizing principle of cognition. Janis and Mann contend that aversion of psychological stress is the most important drive affecting cognition. Whereas Jervis concludes that expectations condition our interpretation of events and our receptivity to information. Janis and Mann argue for the importance of preferences. For Jervis, we see what we *expect* to see, for Janis and Mann, what we *want* to see.[28]

Despite the differences between these scholars they are in fundamental agreement about the important implications of cognitive distortion for decision-making. Each in his own way emphasizes the tendency of policymakers to fail to see trade-off relationships, engage in postdecisional rationalization and remain insensitive to information that challenges the viability of their commitments. In essence, they are advancing competing explanations for some of the same observable behavior, behavior they both describe as detrimental to good decision-making.

The several kinds of cognitive distortions Jervis and Janis and Mann refer to result in specific kinds of deviations from rational decision-making. These deviations might usefully be described as decision-making "pathologies." To the extent that they are present they diminish the probability that effective policy will be formulated or implemented. For the purpose of

---

27  Ibid., pp. 62-63.

28  Not only do the authors advance different explanations for cognitive failures, they also minimize the importance of the psychological principles upon which the opposing explanation is based. Jervis, pp. 356-81, devotes a chapter to analyzing the influence of desires and fears upon perceptions and concludes that "the conventional wisdom that wishful thinking pervades political decision-making is not supported by the evidence from either experimental or natural settings." For their part, Janis and Mann, p. 85, insist that cognitive consistency may be "a weak need" in many individuals. The effort by these analysts to discredit the principles underlying a different approach is certainly consistent with the principle of cognitive consistency.

analyzing crisis performance the most important of these pathologies appear to be: (1) the overvaluation of past performance as against present reality, (2) overconfidence in policies to which decision-makers are committed, and (3) insensitivity to information critical of these policies. These pathologies warrant some elaboration.

**Overvaluation of Past Success** Policymakers, according to Jervis, learn from history and their own personal experience. Their understanding of why events turned out the way they did constitutes the framework in terms of which they analyze current problems. It facilitates their ability to cope with these problems and provides continuity to their behavior.

Lessons from the past can discourage productive thinking to the extent that they represent superficial learning and are applied too reflexively. Jervis makes the case that this is a common occurrence because people rarely seek out or grasp the underlying causes of an outcome but instead assume that it was a result of the most salient aspects of the situation. This phenomenon gives rise to the tendency to apply a solution that worked in the past to a present problem because the two situations bear a superficial resemblance. Jervis observes: "People pay more attention to *what* has happened than to *why* it has happened. Thus learning is superficial, overgeneralized, and based on *post hoc ergo propter hoc* reasoning. As a result, the lessons learned will be applied to a wide variety of situations without a careful effort to determine whether the cases are similar on crucial dimensions."[29]

Examples of this kind of learning abound in the political and historical literature. A good case in point is the lesson drawn by the British military establishment and most military writers from the allied disaster at Gallipoli in World War I. Because Gallipoli failed, they became obdurate in their opinion that an amphibious assault against a defended shore was impractical and even suicidal. It took the Unites States Marine Corps, which undertook a detailed study of *why* Gallipoli failed (e.g., faulty doctrine, ineffective techniques, poor leadership, and utter lack of coordination) to demonstrate the efficacy of amphibious warfare.[30]

Success may discourage productive learning even more than failure as there is much less incentive or political need to carry out any kind of postmortem following a resounding success. If this is true, the greatest danger of superficial learning is that a policy, successful in one context, will be used again in a different and inappropriate context. The chance of this happening is enhanced by the strong organizational bias in favor of executing programs already in the repertory.[31] The Bay of Pigs invasion is a case in point. The CIA, ordered to overthrow Castro with no overt American participation, resurrected the plan they had used successfully in 1954 to topple the Arbenz government in Guatemala. Although the two situations had only

---

29  Jervis, *Perception and Misperception in International Politics*, pp. 227-28.

30  Sir Roger Keyes, *Amphibious Warfare and Combined Operations* (New York: Macmillan, 1943), p. 53; William D. Puleston, *The Dardanelles Expedition* (Annapolis, Md.: United States Naval Institute, 1927), pp. 1-56. No less of a figure than R. H. Liddell Hart, in *The Defence of Britain* (London: Faber & Faber, 1939), p. 130, concluded that Gallipoli had demonstrated the near impossibility of modern amphibious warfare. He thought that such operations were even more difficult since the advent of airpower. The same argument was made by Alexander Kiralfy, "Sea Power in the Eastern War," *Brassey's Naval Annual, 1942* (London: Brassey's, 1942), pp. 150-60; For a discussion of the development of amphibious warfare in the United States, see, Jeter A. Isely and Philip A. Crowl, *The United States Marines and Amphibious War: Its Theory and Its Practice in the Pacific* (Princeton: Princeton University Press, 1951), pp. 3-44.

31  See Allison, *Essence of Decision*, pp. 67-100, for a discussion of organizational theory. This particular aspect of the theory is discussed in greater detail by Harold Wilensky, *Organizational Intelligence: Knowledge and Policy in Government and Industry* (New York: Basic Books, 1967), pp. 75-94.

a superficial similarity, this plan was implemented with only minor modifications, with results that are well known.[32] Some critics of American foreign policy have suggested that a similar process occurred with the containment policy. Due to its apparent success in Europe it was applied to Asia with consequences that now appear disastrous.[33]

**Overconfidence** Jervis theorizes that irrational consistency encourages overconfidence at every stage of the decision-making process. Before a decision is made policy-makers attempt to avoid value trade-offs by spreading the alternatives. In doing so they tend not only to make the favored alternative more attractive but also to judge it more likely to succeed. As policy decisions often hinge on estimates of their probability of success it is not surprising that Jervis finds that people who differ about the value of an objective are likely to disagree about the possibility of attaining it and the costs that this will entail. Those who favor the policy will almost invariably estimate the chances of success as high and the associated costs as lower than do their opponents.[34]

After a decision is made, postdecisional rationalization enters the picture. It too is a means of minimizing internal conflict by providing increased support for a person's actions. For by revising upwards the expected favorable consequences of a policy and its probability of success, policy-makers further enhance their confidence in the policy. By this point their confidence may far exceed whatever promise of success would be indicated by a more objective analysis of the situation.[35]

Janis and Mann also describe overconfidence as a common decision-making pathology but attribute it to different causes and specify a different set of conditions for its appearance. For them it is a form of bolstering, the variety of psychological tactics that policy-makers employ to maintain their expectations of an outcome with high gains and minimal losses. Policy-makers will display overconfidence and other forms of defensive avoidance to the degree that they (1) confront high decisional conflict resulting from two clashing kinds of threat and, (2) believe that they will not find a better alternative for coping with this threat than their present defective policy. Janis and Mann write: "Whenever we have no hope of finding a better solution than the least objectionable one, we can always take advantage of the difficulties of predicting what might happen. We can bolster our decision by tampering with the probabilities in order to restore our emotional equanimity. If we use our imagination we can always picture a beautiful outcome by toning down the losses and highlighting the gains."[36]

32 Arthur M. Schlesinger, Jr., *A Thousand Days* (Boston: Houghton, Mifflin, 1965), pp. 255-58, 289, 293, 297; Theodore C. Sorensen, *Kennedy* (New York: Harper & Row, 1965), pp. 294-309; Peter C. Wyden, *The Bay of Pigs: The Untold Story* (New York: Simon & Shuster, 1979), pp. 323-24.

33 See, Hans J. Morgenthau, "The Unfinished Business of United States Foreign Policy," (*Wisconsin Idea*, Fall 1953) and, "Vietnam: Another Korea?"(*Commentary*, May 1962), in Hans J. Morgenthau, *Politics in the Twentieth Century*, vol. 2: *The Impasse of American Foreign Policy*, (Chicago: University of Chicago Press, 1962), pp. 8-16, 365-75; John Lukacs, *A New History of the Cold War*, 3d rev. ed. (Garden City, N.Y.: Doubleday, 1966), pp. 69-71, 161, 167; Robert E. Osgood, *Alliances and American Foreign Policy* (Baltimore: Johns Hopkins University Press, 1968), pp. 75-77; Stanley Hoffman, *Gulliver's Troubles, or the Setting of American Foreign Policy* (New York: McGraw-Hill, 1968), pp. 140, 153-54; James A. Nathan and James K. Oliver, *United States Foreign Policy and World Order* (Boston: Little, Brown, 1976); John Lewis Gaddis, *Russia, the Soviet Union, and the United States: An Interpretive History* (New York: Wiley, 1978), pp. 187-89, 193-200, 207-13; Leslie H. Gelb with Richard K. Betts, *The Irony of Vietnam: The System Worked* (Washington, D.C.: Brookings Institution, 1979), pp. 78-79, 181-82.

34 Jervis, *Perception and Misperception in International Politics*, pp. 128-30.

35 Ibid., pp. 382-93.

36 Janis and Mann, *Decision Making*, pp. 79-80, 91-95.

**Insensitivity to Warnings** An important corollary of cognitive consistency theory is that people resist cues that challenge their expectations. They may misinterpret them to make them supportive, rationalize them away, or ignore them. Jervis finds that resistance to critical information increases in proportion to a policy-maker's confidence in his course of action, the extent of his commitment to it, and the ambiguity of information he receives about it. Under these conditions even the most negative feedback may have little impact upon the policy-maker.[37]

For Janis and Mann, insensitivity to warnings is a hallmark of defensive avoidance. When this becomes the dominant pattern of coping "the person tries to keep himself from being exposed to communications that might reveal the shortcomings of the course of action he has chosen." When actually confronted with disturbing information he will alter its implications through a process of wishful thinking. This often takes the form of rationalizations which argue against the prospect of serious loss if the current policy is unchanged. Janis and Mann find that extraordinary circumstances with irrefutable negative feedback may be required to overcome such defenses.[38]

Selective attention, denial, or almost any other psychological tactic used by policy-makers to cope with critical information can be institutionalized. Merely by making their expectations or preferences known, policy-makers encourage their subordinates to report or emphasize information supportive of those expectations and preferences. Policy-makers can also purposely rig their intelligence networks and bureaucracies to achieve the same effect. Points of view thus confirmed can over time exercise an even stronger hold over those who are committed to them.[39] Some effort has been made to explain both the origins and duration of the Cold War in terms of such a process.[40] The danger here is that perceptual rigidity will impair personal and organizational performance. It encourages a dangerous degree of overconfidence which reduces the probability that policy-makers will respond to information critical of their policies. Karl Deutsch warns: "If there are strong tendencies toward eventual failure inherent in all organizations, and particularly governments—as many pessimistic theories of politics allege—then such difficulties can perhaps be traced to their propensities to prefer self-referent symbols to new information from the outside world."[41]

---

37 Jervis, *Perception and Misperception in International Politics*, pp. 187-202.

38 Janis and Mann, *Decision Making*, pp. 74-79.

39 Richard W. Cottam, in *Foreign Policy Motivation: A General Theory and a Case Study* (Pittsburgh: University of Pittsburgh Press, 1977), pp. 10-11, argues that the role structure of foreign policy bureaucracy is likely to mirror the needs of policy as they were perceived when those roles were structured. But once the structure is created a bureaucratic interest develops in perpetuating the world view upon which that structure is based. "Even extraordinarily competent bureaucrats . . . will tend to bring congruence to role and perceptions. Indeed, a central ingredient of bureaucratic inertia is the rigidification of perceptual assumptions."

40 See D. F. Fleming, in *The Cold War and its Origins, 1917-1960,* 2 vols. (Garden City, N.Y.: Doubleday, 1961), Walter La Febre, in *America, Russia, and the Cold War, 1945-1966* (New York: Wiley, 1968), and Nathan and Oliver, in *United States Foreign Policy,* all of whom stress the importance of initial American images of the Soviet Union in shaping subsequent policy. For an interesting theoretical analysis of this problem, see, Glenn H. Snyder, "'Prisoner's Dillemma' and 'Chicken' Models in International Politics," *International Studies Quarterly* 15 (March 1971): 66-103; Jervis, in *Perception and Misperception in International Politics*, pp. 58-111, also stresses the self-fulfilling nature of foreign policy judgements as to the intentions of other nations.

41 Karl W. Deutsch, *The Nerves of Government* (New York: Free Press, 1963), p. 215.

## Defensive Avoidance and Unconscious Conflict

One further decision-making pathology must be considered. The paralysis or erratic steering that can result when defenses, erected to cope with anxiety, break down.

The human mind is particularly adept at developing defenses against information or impulses that threaten the attainment of important goals or the personality structure itself. Some of the more common defenses include repression, rationalization, denial, displacement, and acting out.[42] These defenses are not always effective. Fresh evidence of an unambiguous and unavoidable kind may break through a person's defenses and confront him with the reality he fears. This can encourage adaptive behavior. But it can also prompt him to adopt even more extreme defense mechanisms to cope with the anxiety this evidence generates. This latter response is likely to the extent that there are important causes of decisional conflict at the unconscious level.[43] Even these defenses may prove transitory and ineffective. As a general rule, the more intense and pro-

longed the defense the greater the probability of breakdown when it finally collapses. In the words of a famous pugilist: "The bigger they are the harder they fall."

Psychiatrists find that there is a very common (but not universal) pattern associated with the breakdown of defense and coping mechanisms:

FEAR
    REPRESSION
    CHRONIC ANXIETY
        DECREASE IN DEFENSE AND
        COPING MECHANISMS
        SYNDROMES OF ANXIETY
        REACTIONS[44]

In this formulation fear is a response to an *external* threat whereas anxiety relates to *internal* conflict. As Ernst Kris notes, external stress is reacted to in proportion to the internal tension or anxiety already existing. When internal tension or anxiety is great fear leads to repression. Repression produces chronic anxiety, all or part of which is usually outside of conscious awareness. In conditions of great psychological stress, defense mechanisms may not be effective in repressing anxiety.[45] An "anxiety reaction" may follow.[46]

---

42 The classic description of defense mechanisms is Anna Freud, *The Ego and the Mechanisms of Defense* 1936; (New York: International Universities Press, 1953).

43 Sigmund Freud distinguished between "preconscious" and "unconscious" emotional impulses. The former refer to motivations that a person is unaware of at the time he acts but is capable of recognizing when given appropriate cues by others. Preconscious impulses are more likely to be counteracted by corrective information than are unconscious ones. The latter derive from fundamental sexual and aggressive drives and are kept from consciousness by repression and other defense mechanisms. Janis and Mann, in *Decision Making*, pp. 95-100, argue that preconscious emotional impulses, triggered by fatigue, alcohol, or crowd excitement, prompt impulsive and irrational choices later regretted by the policy-maker.

44 Sigmund Freud, *The Problem of Anxiety* (New York: Norton, 1936); Norman A. Cameron, "Paranoid Reactions," Harold Lieff, "Anxiety Reactions," John C. Nemiah, "Conversion Reactions," and Louis J. West, "Dissociative Reactions," in Freedman and Kaplan, *Comprehensive Textbook of Psychiatry*, pp. 665-76, 875-85.

45 Gross stress can itself produce an insoluble conflict of vital goals or needs. For some of the literature on this subject, see, Abraham Kardiner and H. Spiegel, *War, Stress, and Neurotic Illness* (New York: Harper & Row, 1941); Robert J. Weiss and Henry E. Payson, "Gross Stress Reaction," and Norman Q. Brill, "Gross Stress Reaction: Traumatic War Neuroses," in Freedman and Kaplan, *Comprehensive Textbook of Psychiatry*, pp. 1027-31, 1031-35; Charles D. Spielberger and Irving G. Sarason, eds., *Stress and Anxiety*, 2 vols. (New York: Wiley, 1975).

46 The American Psychiatric Association's *Diagnostic and Statistical Manual, Mental Disorders* (Washington: American Psychiatric Association, 1952), p. 32, defines anxiety reaction as follows: "In this kind of reaction the anxiety is diffuse and not restricted to definite situations or objects, as in the case of phobic reactions. It is not controlled by any specific psychological defense mechanism as in other psycho-neurotic reactions. This reaction is characterized by anxious expectation and frequently associated with somatic symptomatology. The condition is to be differentiated from normal apprehensiveness or fear."

A person suffering from an anxiety reaction almost always displays apprehension, helplessness, and a pervasive sense of nervous tension. Other clinical manifestations include headaches, indigestion, anorexia, palpitations, genitourinary problems, insomnia, irritability, and inability to concentrate. When confronted with the need to act, such a person is likely to be indecisive. He may cast about frantically seeking the advice of others or may oscillate between opposing courses of action, unable to accept responsibility for a decision. He is also likely to mistrust his own judgment and be easily influenced by the views of others. His ability to perform tasks effectively when they relate to the source of anxiety will be low. Commenting on his experience with anxiety reactions, one psychiatrist observes:

> The smallest obstacle may be insurmountable: the next day is the harbinger of death; the next visitor, the bearer of bad news; the next event, the beginning of catastrophe. Overly concerned with what others think of him the patient is constantly trying to make a favorable impression but is never satisfied with his performance. Uncertain of himself, he may belittle and degrade others in a misguided effort to raise his own self-esteem, all the while castigating himself for his failures. Although the patient with an anxiety reaction may exhibit considerable drive, it usually has a compulsive quality and is accompanied by misgivings regarding his competence to perform the task.[47]

Free-floating anxiety may alternatively be manifested in what Eugen Kahn refers to as a "stun reaction," characterized by withdrawal, passivity, and even psychomotor retardation.[48] The person in question attempts to escape anxiety by refusing to contemplate or confront the problem associated with it. The stun reaction is usually of limited duration and may be preliminary to an anxiety reaction which commences upon emergence from withdrawal.

Free-floating anxiety invariably leads to the adoption of more extreme defense mechanisms to cope with the tension associated with it. Two of the most common mechanisms are projection and marked denial. Both are usually ineffectual and transitory in nature.

In projection the individual attributes his own feelings and impulses to another person because he is unable to accept responsibility for them or tolerate the anxiety they produce. Projection also provides an explanation for failure and protects a person from having to acknowledge a painful and humiliating defeat. Projection invariably contains elements of persecution, jealousy, and sometimes compensatory delusions of grandeur. Frequent resort to projection to preserve an unstable personality structure is a classical manifestation of paranoia.[49]

Marked denial, as the term implies, consists of ignoring a threatening experience or its memory when it can no longer be relegated to the subconscious. Like projection, this defense can only be maintained at considerable cost to a person's ability to act effectively. In its extreme form, marked denial is a manifestation of a "dissociative reaction," a state where a person's thoughts, feelings, or actions are not associated or integrated with important information from his environment

47 Lieff, "Anxiety Reactions," p. 865.

48 Eugen Kahn, "The Stun," *American Journal of Psychiatry* 118 (February 1962): 702-4.

49 Sigmund Freud, "The Neuro-Psychoses of Defense," (1894) and "Further Remarks on the Neuro-Psychoses of Defense," in *The Standard Edition of the Complete Psychological Works of Sigmund Freud* (London: Hogarth, 1962), vol. 3, pp. 43-68, 159-85; Norman A. Cameron, "Paranoid Conditions and Paranoia," in Silvano Arieti and Eugene B. Brody, eds., *American Handbook of Psychiatry: Adult Clinical Psychiatry*, 2d ed. (New York: Basic Books, 1974), pp. 675-93; Daniel S. Jaffe, "The Mechanisms of Projection: Its Dual Role in Object Relations," *International Journal of Psycho-Analysis,* 49 (1968), part 4, pp. 662-77; D. Swanson, P. Bohnert, and J. Smith, *The Paranoid* (Boston: Little, Brown, 1970).

as they normally or logically would be. A disso-ciative reaction in effect consists of a jamming of one's circuits. Clinical symptoms include trance states (characterized by unresponsiveness to the environment, immobility, and apparent absorption with something deep within the self), estrange-ments and paramnesia (detachment and disen-gagement from persons, places, situations, and concepts), fugue (flight, entered into abruptly, often with amnesia and lack of care for one's per-son or surroundings), frenzied behavior (episodes of violent, outlandish, or bizarre behavior) and dissociative delirium (including hallucinations, wild emotional outpourings, and release of pri-mary process material).[50]

A dissociative reaction is an extreme means of defending the ego against material that is too threatening to cope with on a conscious or un-conscious level. It is most often manifested dur-ing periods of extreme stress. According to Louis Jolyon West: "Maturational shortcomings, emotional conflicts, and stressful life situations are thus superimposed upon each other to create a trap or impasse that cannot be resolved by the patient because of the overwhelming anxiety inherent in the available possible solutions."[51] The resolution brought about by a dissociative reaction is crippling but usually produces a ben-eficial change in the psychological economy of the individual.

Defense mechanisms can miscarry by leading to self-damaging behavior. Anxiety reactions, projection, and dissociative reactions hinder the willingness and effectiveness of persons to per-form tasks related to the source of anxiety. These persons become indecisive or paralyzed or, if still capable of action, are likely to respond in ways that bear little relationship to the realities of the situation.

The implications of the preceding discussion for crisis management are obvious. Defense mechanisms are most likely to break down when the policy-maker is inescapably confronted with the reality he has hitherto repressed. Such a situ-ation is most likely to develop during the most acute stage of international crisis when the deci-sion for peace or war hangs in the balance. A breakdown in the policy-maker's defenses at this time may result in erratic behavior or his actual paralysis. Either condition is likely to "freeze" policy and contribute to the outbreak of war to the extent that it leaves the protagonists on a collision course.

---

50  The American Psychiatric Association's *Diagnostic and Statistical Manual, Mental Disorders*, p. 32, defines dissociative reaction as follows: "This reaction represents a type of gross personality distortion, the basis of which is a neurotic disturbance, although the diffuse dissociation seen in some cases may occasionally appear psychotic. The personality disorganization may result in running or 'freezing.' The repressed impulse giving rise to the anxiety may be discharged by, or deflected into, various symptomatic expressions, such as depersonalization, dissociated personality, stupor, fugue, amnesia, dream state, somnambulism, etc."

51  Louis J. West, in Freedman and Kaplan, *Comprehensive Textbook of Psychiatry*, p. 889.

# Part III
## Challenges to the International State System

# Introduction

The international system of states has proved resilient. Disruptions and violent cataclysms have led to the destruction or elimination of some sovereign states, but never of the system itself, and norms of international society have reinforced the survival of the sovereign territorial state. Yet the system of states in the twenty-first century appears to be headed toward a crossroads. On the one hand, new forms of cooperation among states and deepening transnational networks of government officials reinforce the sovereign state's importance in world politics. On the other hand, emerging threats to the security and integrity of states might augur the end of the international system of states as we know it. The future remains uncertain, but transformational change is certainly possible. Part III explores the possibility of such change.

One such possibility is that states will cooperate to uphold the rules of international society by collaborating to deter or punish states that violate the rules. Of particular interest is the use of economic sanctions or military intervention against aggressors or potential aggressors. In chapter 25, Andrew Bennett and Joseph Lepgold discuss this notion of collective security, an idea that has long existed in principle but that rarely, if ever, has been realized in practice. Bennett and Lepgold examine three historical attempts to implement collective security, articulate requirements for successful collective security, and analyze the idea through the lenses of international relations theory, broadly construed.

Collective security might be difficult to enforce without widespread participation in international institutions, but not all international relations thinkers agree that formal institutions or organizations are necessary for global governance in international society—and some are of the reasoned opinion that existing institutions are transforming themselves, or being transformed, in various ways. Rhodes for example argues in chapter 26 that the institutions of international relations are, in a sense, unraveling as a consequence of dramatic changes in technology and human capacity, and that new, "flatter" networks are taking shape—and shaping the international system of tomorrow.

While Rhodes focuses on the power of networked individuals, one form of networking in this world of flux might well provide sovereign states with considerable traction. Anne-Marie Slaughter argues in chapter 27 that transnational networks of government officials and regulators facilitate international cooperation, performing the functions of a global government while preserving the influence and relevance of sovereign states. For Slaughter, the state is not disappearing; rather, it is reconfiguring itself to meet the needs and demands of global society.

Networks of course are not uniformly benign, legitimate, or non-violent. The terror attacks on 11 September 2001 demonstrated that non-state armed groups like al Qaeda pose dangerous threats to even the most powerful sovereign states, and the rise of the Islamic State in

Iraq and Syria suggests that non-state armed groups might seek to upend and replace states in some settings. Chapters 29 and 30 investigate the emerging threats posed by non-state actors to the security of states, and perhaps even to the idea of the sovereign state itself. Those chapters however are preceded by an essay that seeks to disrupt categories of thinking associated with the practice of statecraft and the academic discipline of international relations, both of which historically were dominated by men, and perhaps continue to reify elements of patriarchy. Inspired by feminist approaches to international relations, Rhodes in chapter 28 urges us to reconsider categories and concepts (like the state, security, victory in war, and others) that are socially constructed, and to consider the role of identity (gender identity as well as other forms of identity) as a powerful force in international affairs.

Martha Crenshaw's chapter 29 explains causes of terrorism in the modern state system, including both factors and precipitating events that set the stage for terrorist groups or campaigns. Crenshaw examines the logic of terrorism as a political phenomenon and as an individual choice to give readers a deeper understanding of the asymmetric violence directed at states and their citizens by disaffected elites who operate on the fringes. Crenshaw seeks not to parse the Janus-faced problem of categorizing those who choose to engage in this form of political violence (*viz.*, "one man's terrorist is another man's freedom fighter"), but reading this chapter in the wake of Rhodes's essay, one might be prompted to consider issues connected to the power of socially constructed categories and identities.

Readers might also ask the question: can the traditional nation-state prevail against an enemy that is extraordinarily difficult to attack, defend against, and deter?

Terrorist organizations might not be the only sort of armed group to pose such challenges, both for states and for the way we think about international relations. In chapter 30, political sociologist Diane E. Davis broadens the investigation of non-state armed actors to include warlord-led clans, organized crime rings, private security forces, and civilian militias. States that fail to secure the allegiance and physical safety of citizens might find those citizens turning to these other sources of identity and protection. Non-state armed groups therefore compete with states for people's loyalty, and perhaps herald the loss of states' monopoly over the legitimate use of violence—a theme further plumbed by Amy E. Eckert in chapter 31, where she discusses the return of soldiers for hire in the form of private military companies. The "outsourcing" or privatization of war presents a challenge to our thinking about states, their exclusive claim to the legitimate use of violence, and to tenets and provisions of the just war tradition. Eckert's chapter brings the reader back around to key themes from Parts I and II of the volume, and provides a fine capstone for Part III, with its focus on the tensions inherent in today's international state system.

Part III raises as many questions as it answers about the future of the Westphalian state and the international system of states. From this complex picture one conclusion is clear: the international system of states faces new challenges that threaten its existence, but it also has the potential to adapt and survive these challenges.

# 25: Toward Collective Security?

## Andrew Bennett and Joseph Lepgold

### Three Previous Attempts at Collective Security

The great powers have constructed three versions of collective security mechanisms. Such mechanisms partially centralize security arrangements by vesting enforcement of sanctions against breaches of the peace in an international though not supranational forum.[1] They all reject the unrestrained power balancing through competitive alliances that characterize laissez-faire approaches to security.

The first, longest lasting, and most successful attempt at collective security was the Concert of Europe, which helped prevent great-power war from 1815 to 1854. Although enforcement was decentralized, its members supported Europe's great-power equilibrium, shared a strong distaste for war after the costly Napoleonic Wars, and agreed to consult and take joint action in response to threats to peace. From 1815 through 1822 and to a lesser extent until 1854, they also shared a longer and broader conception of self-interest than is usual in international relations, although the shared stakes did not extend beyond the inner club of great powers.[2] These commitments weakened when the more liberal British and French regimes opposed domestic interventions favored by Austria and Russia.

Like the Concert, the League of Nations assumed great-power cooperation. Its founders drew on numerous experiences in addition to the European Concert, including the Hague Conferences and interallied planning during World War I, but it could not overcome identification with the Versailles Treaty's punitive settlement of the war. It lacked a concert of interests, as Germany, Japan, and Italy opposed the postwar status quo. It even lacked a quorum of great powers, since the Soviets joined only in 1934 and were expelled five years later for attacking Finland, while the United States stayed out from the start. The democracies supported the status quo, but would not take responsibility for enforcing it. Britain and France would not isolate Italy after its invasion of Ethiopia for fear of pushing it toward Germany, and they then failed to resist Germany's aggression against Austria and Czechoslovakia.

In the third attempt, the great-power victors of World War II centralized enforcement of collective security in their own hands on the United Nations Security Council (SC) in the belief that postwar peace required continuation of the wartime concert.[3] But with the former common enemy Germany weak and partitioned, Soviet-American cooperation broke down over conflicting ideologies and security concerns, and

---

1 Kenneth W. Thompson, "Collective Security," *International Encyclopedia of the Social Sciences* (New York: Macmillan, 1968), 565.

2 Robert Jervis, "Security Regimes," *International Organization* 36 (Spring 1982): 362–367; Jervis, "From Balance to Concert: A Study of International Security Cooperation," *World Politics* 38 (October 1985): 78.

3 Robert C. Hilderbrand, *Dumbarton Oaks: The Origins of the United Nations and the Search for Postwar Security* (Chapel Hill: University of North Carolina Press, 1990), 34.

Reprinted by permission from Political Science Quarterly, 108 (Summer 1993): 213–237.

the resultant bipolar bloc system undermined the entire mechanism. Except for the Korean operation, made possible by Moscow's temporary absence from the SC, the cold-war UN could not act against breaches of the peace as set out in its charter. The UN regime thereby lost effectiveness and coherence between the 1940s and the 1980s.[4]

## What does Collective Security Require?

With the end of the cold war, a new debate is emerging over what collective security requires. The requirements depend on how the concept is defined; there are two distinct formulations.[5] In one conception, collective security is a regime designed to sustain a particular status quo. If implemented, this "offer[s] the certainty, backed by legal obligation, that *any* aggressor would be confronted with collective sanctions."[6] It requires a common definition of aggression and willingness to act whenever it occurs. The UN General Assembly stipulated in 1974 that "the first use of armed force by a State in contravention of the Charter shall constitute *prima facie* evidence of an act of aggression" (Resolution 3314, Article 2). However, some UN members insisted at the time that not even this general definition was binding,[7] and it has had little apparent impact on SC behavior. The political utility of trying to freeze the status quo thus seems dubious.

In a second definition, collective security seeks only to ensure that change is peaceful and that force is used only in self-defense. It is not tied tightly to existing political arrangements or any explicit definition of aggression. This view is supported by the evolution of the UN Charter, by its specific provisions, and by its use in the Gulf War. Because the League Covenant was tied to the post-World War I status quo that lacked legitimacy in the eyes of many Germans, UN founders deliberately wrote the charter separate from any potential World War II peace settlements. Article 39, the gateway to enforcement provisions under Chapter VII, mentions threats to the peace and breaches of the peace as well as explicit aggression . . .

Under this interpretation, the charter does not limit SC authority to specific acts of aggression; this permits a requisite SC majority to act whenever it deems this necessary to preserve peace. Conversely, when the SC is divided, it is not handcuffed into any particular response by a written definition of aggression . . .

### Realist Views

To many Realists, self-help seems to preclude collective security or at least to pose stringent conditions. Perhaps the least problematic of these is Inis Claude's criterion that power be diffused among "a number of" major states, since this would be satisfied in any multipolar system. The rationale is that no state should be strong enough to resist collective sanctions.[8] Claude refers to the most ambitious manifestation of collective security, in which sanctions would be applied directly to great powers. But the major powers are unlikely to be coerced on

---

4   See Ernst B. Haas, "Regime Decay: Conflict Management and International Organizations," *International Organization* 37 (Spring 1983).

5   We thank Lawrence Finkelstein for pointing this out to us. See also Finkelstein, "From Collective Security to Collective Defense To ..." in *Implications of German Unification for Future All-European Security* (Proceedings of the Seminar for Senior Academics sponsored by the Paul Loebe Institute, Berlin, 1–7 July 1990), 189–197.

6   Inis Claude, *Power and International Relations* (New York: Random House, 1962), 168, quoted in Kupchan and Kupchan, "Concerts, Collective Security, and the Future of Europe "*International Security* 16 (Summer 1991)." (Emphasis added.)

7   Ahmed M. Rifaat, *International Aggression* (Atlantic Highlands, NJ: Humanities Press, 1979), 278.

8   Inis Claude, *Power and International Relations* (New York: Random House, 1962), 195; and Claude, *Swords Into Plowshares*, 4th ed. (New York: Random House, 1971), 256.

vital interests under a collective security system, a fact embodied in the SC veto. What is essential is thus the power differential between the great-power group and others: the major powers must have the economic and military strength to restore peace whenever it is threatened by any combination of other states.

This requires a concert of interests among great powers. In the three attempts at collective security, concerts formed to defeat aspiring hegemons but dissolved when conflicting goals overrode incentives to protect the new status quo. Normally the major powers compete too much among themselves for order to be anything but an accidental by-product. So under what conditions do the fluid, counterbalancing coalitions of a balance-of-power system, in which it is legitimate to use and threaten force within the group,[9] cease to exist among the major powers?

The literature on cooperation under anarchy is helpful here. In single-play games, cooperation requires that actors prefer mutual cooperation to mutual defection. This is true in the Stag Hunt and Prisoners' Dilemma games. The key difference between the two in a single play is that in the Stag Hunt, it is best to cooperate if you know your fellow player will do so, while in Prisoners' Dilemma, it is best to "rat" on your fellow player whether they inform on you or not. But in concerts, which can be likened to iterated games, the preference for mutual cooperation over mutual defection can override incentives to defect.[10]

In addition, even under the Prisoners' Dilemma conditions characteristic of concerts, mutual cooperation is more likely if it is not only preferred to mutual defection but greatly so, if there are few rewards for exploiting others, and if there are few risks or costs for being exploited.[11] The game may even become a Stag Hunt if mutual cooperation becomes more valuable than exploiting the other. Nothing in Realist thought precludes this, especially if the system becomes multipolar, which decreases fear of exploitation by any one great power,[12] and if cooperation is anchored through reliable institutions. These are likely consequences of successful counterhegemonic wars, and each was evident during the early Concert of Europe period. This unusual cooperation to support the status quo lasted until the payoffs returned to their more usual values.[13] More lasting cooperation may be possible now if, as Lawrence Freedman argues, few national interests are now unique as well as vital . . .[14]

Put differently, the shadow of the future must be long: future interactions must be valued more than current ones. This will be true if interactions among the same states are expected to continue; if stakes are fairly uniform in each round (for example, issues do not vary so much in importance that it is tempting to defect on major ones); and if reliable, prompt information on others' actions is available.[15] The first two can be difficult to achieve in security affairs, where knockout blows are possible and interests are often perceived competitively.

Widespread vulnerability to economic sanctions is also essential according to Realists, since war is a last resort.[16] But Realists also emphasize

---

9   Jervis, "From Balance to Concert," throughout.

10  See Robert Axelrod, *The Evolution of Cooperation* (New York: Basic Books, 1984).

11  Kenneth A. Oye, "Explaining Cooperation Under Anarchy: Hypotheses and Strategies," *World Politics* 38 (October 1985).

12  Jervis, "From Balance to Concert," 69–70.

13  Ibid., 64–79.

14  Lawrence Freedman, "Escalators and Quagmires: Expectations and the Use of Force," *International Affairs* 67 (January 1991): 30.

15  Oye, "Explaining Cooperation Under Anarchy," 16–18; Robert O. Keohane and Robert Axelrod, "Achieving Cooperation Under Anarchy: Strategies and Institutions," *World Politics* 38 (October 1985): 232–234.

16  Claude, *Swords Into Plowshares,* 257; Claude, *Power in International Relations,* 195.

the difficulties in achieving this. Sanctions hurt sanctioners as well as targets. There can be large economic rewards for breaking sanctions. Klaus Knorr thus concluded that "coercively wielding economic power . . . is rarely successful."[17] It is even more difficult if the target is already committed to an objective. A recent study ranked sanctioners' goals from "modest policy change" through "disruption of military adventures" and "other major policy changes." Sanctions failed 70 percent of the time in the three most ambitious categories of goals, and their overall success has declined along with America's weight in the world economy.[18]

Realists may undervalue economic sanctions, however. Even if economic coercion cannot often change a target's behavior, it might help deter future transgressions, impose significant costs on an aggressor, and signal the international community's view that an action is illegitimate. Thus David Baldwin, using the same data as Knorr, concludes that sanctions can usefully serve many purposes.[19] And even if sanctions cannot work alone, they might legitimate further enforcement measures. Moreover, nonphysical sanctions can broaden participation in enforcement; not all states can or need to use force.

Finally, according to Realists, partial disarmament is necessary: few states will forcibly resist aggressors if the costs are too high.[20] Fortunately, arms races can be slowed if offensive and defensive weapons are distinguishable, if defending what one has is easier than attacking others, and if exporters agree that arms transfers are counterproductive.[21] The offense-defense distinction is never clear cut, and many states will arm beyond the requirements of territorial defense for insurance, but technology can make it harder as well as easier to take and hold territory. For arms suppliers, economic incentives create a Prisoners' Dilemma, although cooperation could become more valuable as technologies become more dangerous and widespread.[22]

### Liberal Views

Liberal and other national-level theorists pose two more conditions for collective security. First, ideological, ethnic, and cultural affinities and antagonisms between states cannot preclude cooperation or enforcement between any pair. The United States thus set aside its ties to Britain, France, and Israel in the 1956 Suez crisis and pressured them to halt their invasion of Egypt. Failure to achieve such flexibility weakened collective security in the late 1930s, when Soviet-American ideological differences inhibited cooperation against Hitler and compounded their absence from the League. This same problem, together with great-power rivalry, limited East-West cooperation via the UN after World War II. In contrast, the Concert of Europe worked as long as it did because ideological lines "were not so rigidly drawn as to prevent a high degree of . . . collaboration between the [monarchist] eastern and [liberal] western powers."[23]

Second, states must agree on the relationship between international security and internal governance. They might, for example, share a commitment to a particular kind of regime. Disagreements

17 Klaus Knorr, *The Power of Nations* (New York: Basic Books, 1975), chap. 6.

18 The data are from Kimberly Ann Elliott, "The Role of Economic Sanctions in Collective Security" (Institute for International Economics, 1990, Mimeographed); see also David Fromkin, *The Independence of Nations* (New York: Praeger, 1981), 82–84.

19 David Baldwin, *Economic Statecraft* (Princeton, NJ: Princeton University Press, 1985).

20 Claude, *Swords Into Plowshares,* 259.

21 Jervis, "Cooperation Under the Security Dilemma," 186–210.

22 For example, see "East Bloc's Cold War Arsenals Are Arming Ethnics," *Washington Post,* 8 July 1991.

23 Gordon A. Craig and Alexander L. George, *Force and Statecraft,* 2nd ed. (New York: Oxford University Press, 1990), 34.

on this issue weakened the Concert and the UN. Austria's Metternich and Russia's Alexander I tried to use the Concert to preserve existing governments and to prevent liberal revolts against monarchies. Britain and France objected to this, and Britain consequently stopped attending meetings of the great powers' foreign ministers. Similarly, during the cold war, communist and noncommunist UN members did not agree on legitimate forms of government, much less the role of joint action in fostering particular kinds of regimes.

In particular, Liberals provide four arguments for why peace is best guaranteed among market democracies.[24] First, since voters abhor wars' costs, wars need moral as well as practical legitimacy; this is difficult if the enemy is democratic and thus presumptively legitimate. Second, relatively open political processes in democracies help make motives transparent, easing misunderstandings that can drive the security dilemma.[25] Third, democracy requires compromise at home, and this carries over to foreign policy behavior. Finally, market economies allow mutual gains from trade, making peace more profitable than war.[26]

Some of this reasoning is debatable. Democracies have intervened in other democracies (although usually covertly); they can misunderstand one another through the very openness of their communication[27]; democratic processes can feed expansionism as well as accommodation; and close interdependence can induce conflict when relative as well as absolute gains matter.[28]

Still, the evidence is convincing: while democracies have fought virtually no wars against one another for 200 years, other kinds of regimes have often done so.[29] Since democracies have fought other kinds of regimes, the absence of wars among democracies is especially convincing. Thus, to the extent that collective security is based on a regime of great-power democracies, it may be able to inhibit conflict among its members while sustaining common purposes against nondemocratic aggressors.

### Institutionalist Views

Institutionalists highlight the impact on state behavior of shared definitions of problems, convergent expectations, and organizational constraints and tools. In this view, world politics is institutionalized to the degree that actors' expectations converge, that clear rules follow from this, and that institutions are at least somewhat autonomous and can alter their own rules. Unlike Realists and Liberals, who argue respectively that these factors are epiphenomena of the distribution of power among states or the compatibility of their internal systems, Institutionalists acknowledge the roles of international power and internal politics, but argue that norm-governed behavior can be a key intervening variable. So, unlike Idealists, Institutionalists do not assume that rules alone drive behavior. If states' preference rankings do not allow for gains from cooperation, institutionalization is irrelevant.[30]

---

24  Our definition of liberal market democracies follows that of Michael Doyle, "Liberalism and World Politics," *American Political Science Review* 80 (December 1986): 1164.

25  Ibid., 1160, esp. the quotation from Immanuel Kant.

26  Ibid., 1161. See also Robert Keohane and Joseph Nye, *Power and Interdependence* (Boston: Little, Brown, 1977), chap. 7.

27  Richard Neustadt, *Alliance Politics* (New York: Columbia University Press, 1970).

28  For these and other critiques of the Liberal view, see John Mearsheimer, "Back to the Future: Instability in Europe After the Cold War," *International Security* 15 (Summer 1990).

29  See Melvin Small and J. David Singer, "The War-Proneness of Democratic Regimes 1816–1965," *Jerusalem Journal of International Relations* 1 (1976): 50–69; Doyle, "Liberalism and World Politics," and his "Kant, Liberal Legacies, and Foreign Affairs," parts 1 and 2, *Philosophy and Public Affairs* 12 (Summer and Fall 1983): 205–235, 323–353.

30  See Robert O. Keohane, "Neoliberal Institutionalism: A Perspective on World Politics" in Keohane, *International Institutions and State Power* (Boulder, CO: Westview, 1989).

This raises two crucial questions: Can joint gains be realized from a collective security system? Will states focus on those benefits rather than their relative gains? In general, Realists doubt that international anarchy allows states to focus on absolute gains, since strengthening today's partner could strengthen tomorrow's adversary.[31] But this argument crumbles as the number of great powers increases beyond two. In a bipolar system, Realists rightly argue that relative gains readily transform interactions into Prisoners' Dilemma games, in which the dominant strategy is to defect. In contrast, relative gains have less of this effect in multipolarity, since no pair of the major actors tends to define their competition as zero sum. In multipolarity, if states A and B make an agreement that provides joint gains but B gains relative to A, A still gains relative to others.[32] This applies across international issues, including those involving the instruments of force or threats to use force.

Although the security dilemma and the possibility of a preemptive knockout blow make it difficult for states to focus on joint gains in security affairs, this is not an insuperable obstacle.[33] Realists acknowledge that concerts after counterhegemonic wars temporarily change states' payoffs from Prisoners' Dilemmas to games where cooperation is easier. And if a concert is based on compatible internal systems rather than the short-term attenuation of competition that exhausted victors exhibit after a major war, there is no reason for the expected value from joint gains to diminish over time. Most contemporary arguments for a revamped European security system are based on such a multipolar concert.[34]

Institutionalists would thus maintain that support for collective security can be consistent with egoistic assumptions about states' interests if the value of maintaining a regime outweighs that of defecting in any given case. States that defect undercut their overall reputation for cooperation, weakening not only the regime they violate but others as well.[35] Institutions can also make cooperation dependable by increasing transparency and lowering transactions costs. Strong regimes are difficult to create, so states often perpetuate imperfect ones rather than rebuild them from scratch.[36]

Institutions can thus affect states' willingness to cooperate over the long term, as well as the means they employ, by shaping the way problems are defined. For example, by helping to guarantee that stakes in a dispute remain relatively constant over time, a collective security regime can encourage those satisfied with the status quo to take a long view, even of situations involving their major interests.[37] They will be less likely to preempt under pressure if they believe that waiting for collective measures will not put them in a worse competitive position. To accomplish this, the institution must help prevent sudden escalations and attempts at faits accomplis.

Institutionalists thus potentially qualify Realists' objection that collective enforcement can be

---

31 Joseph M. Grieco, "Anarchy and the Limits of Cooperation: A Realist Critique of the Newest Liberal Institutionalism," *International Organization* 42 (Summer 1988).

32 Duncan Snidal shows this formally in "International Cooperation Among Relative Gains Maximizers," *International Studies Quarterly* 35 (December 1991).

33 Jervis, "Security Regimes,"

34 See Kupchan and Kupchan, "Concerts, Collective Security, and the Future of Europe"; and Richard Ullman, *Securing Europe* (Princeton, NJ: Princeton University Press, 1991).

35 Robert O. Keohane, *After Hegemony: Cooperation and Discord in the World Political Economy* (Princeton, NJ: Princeton University Press, 1984), 105; and this reply to Mearsheimer in *International Security* 15 (Fall 1990): 192–194.

36 Keohane, *After Hegemony*, 100–103

37 See Robert Axelrod, *The Evolution of Cooperation* (New York: Basic Books, 1984), 129–130.

guaranteed only when complete great-power agreement makes a collective mechanism unnecessary. To Realists, collective security demands that the great powers share high enforcement costs even when their interests are marginal and that they refrain from unilateral action even when their vital interests are at stake.[38] In part, such concerns led Winston Churchill to advocate UN mechanisms that would accommodate the great powers' regional interests and their lack of interest in small or distant states. To Institutionalists, if joint gains can be realized by a concert on a global basis, the predictability this generates could well make cooperative behavior more reliable across the board.

International institutions are also valuable if they facilitate collective actions that would otherwise be impossible . . .[39]

## Conclusions and Policy Implications

Realists, Liberals, and Institutionalists lay out demanding conditions for collective security, but taken together these views permit more optimism about its prospects than in 1919, 1945, or even 1815. Realists emphasize that collective security must be based on a great-power concert, that these states must agree what is necessary to preserve peace and order in specific cases, that they must prefer mutual cooperation to mutual defection, and that they repeatedly interact. Liberals highlight the absence of national-level ties strong enough to impede enforcement and the potential among market democracies for a pluralistic security community. Institutionalists emphasize a regime's capability to minimize the costs to states of unrequited cooperation.

---

38 Earl C. Ravenal, "An Autopsy of Collective Security," *Political Science Quarterly* 90 (Winter 1975–1976): 706, 707, 711, 712. See also Claude, *Swords Into Plowshares*, 251, 252.

39 Keohane, "Neoliberal Institutionalism," 5.

# 26: Technology, Knowledge, and the Unraveling of the Institutions of International Relations

*Edward Rhodes*

We are currently witnessing a major transformation of 20th-century institutions. It is not that the sovereign state, transnational business corporations, large bureaucratic international organizations such as the United Nations, or the other major institutions of national and international life are going away. These "modern" institutions are, however, "unraveling." They are coming apart in some very basic ways.

Driving this process are two underlying dynamics: the dramatic expansion of information and communication technology and a pervasive expansion of human capacity caused by wider access to education. The unraveling of institutions which results from these dynamics has three key elements. The first is globalization—a fundamental change in time-distance relationships and in the impact of physical and political boundaries. The second is the increased ability of single individuals or informally organized, non-hierarchic groups to solve complex problems, resulting in a "flattening" of effective organizations. The third transformation is the "unbundling" of services, as the ability of organizations to control information and markets declines. These transformations promise to change the relative competitiveness of various institutions.

## The Underlying Dynamics of Change

### Technological Capacity

There are two underlying dynamics that are driving this institutional transformation—that are leading to the unraveling of the state, the modern corporation, and many of our social institutions. These have been widely described by researchers, perhaps most eloquently by the late James Rosenau in his brilliant 1990 work, *Turbulence in World Politics.*[1]

The first, of course, has been the technological revolution that has transformed and that continues to transform how we deal with information. This is, in fact, two revolutions in one: first, a revolution in our ability to analyze information and, second, a revolution in our ability to communicate information.

Statistical analyses that would have taken thousands of individuals working for months with slide rules, or that would have taken banks of trained technicians running vast, and vastly expensive, mainframe computers for hours, can now be performed nearly instantaneously by a bored first-year student with an inexpensive laptop. This is not simply a change in the scope or speed of activity. It is a profound challenge to the

---

1   James N. Rosenau, *Turbulence in World Politics: A Theory of Change and Continuity* (Princeton, N.J.: Princeton University Press, 1990).

organization of institutions. It is not simply that the slide rule is now a primitive tool, and the 1970s mainframe a dinosaur. It is that the institutions that were designed around these are also primitive or dinosaurs.

We see a similar picture when it comes to information storage and retrieval. The vast physical archives of information that were absolutely essential to the operation of complex organizations, housed expensively and staffed by vast numbers of individuals needed to retrieve the books, reports, analyses, or files, or to find the data in the appendices of the books or buried in the files or reports, are going away. And the institutions that were built around the control of these information archives, or the ability to maintain them, are going away as well.

That the analysis of information was labor- or capital-intensive, and that information was stored in physical, rather than electronic or virtual, form meant three important things. First it meant that specialized institutions, or very large organizations with specialized divisions, were necessary to use or to keep information. By being able to monopolize use and effective ownership of information, these institutions— pre-eminently the state and the large corporation— were able to crush their less-well-adapted rival, "pre-modern" institutions as well as to eliminate smaller competitors unable to generate the economies of scale needed to use and keep information effectively. Second, it also meant that access to and use of information could be readily controlled by hierarchic authorities within these institutions: if analyzing data required a building full of clerks and accountants or vastly expensive hours or even minutes of computing time, then this could be regulated from the top. Similarly, if solving a problem required access to physical repositories of information, this access could be easily denied. Third, the fact that information was stored in physical form meant not only that it could be controlled, but that there were physical limits to how many individuals

could use it at any given time and to that the physical information and the individual using it had to be in the same physical space. Two people—or two offices, or to institutions—could not be reading the same file at the same time, unless additional copies were physically produced.

The revolution in information analysis and information storage radically changes all this. Institutions that had evolved over centuries around the physical realities of information analysis and information storage, and had developed complex and cumbersome bureaucratic procedures over a period of centuries to handle these challenges, were now ill-adapted for the new environment.

And we see a similar change in terms of communication. It is not simply that the mass communication technologies and media of the 20th century—television, radio, newspapers—are quaintly old-fashioned and as irrelevant as a horse-drawn carriage, it is that the institutions— such as the 20th-century state—that were built around their ability to produce and control these media are also increasingly irrelevant. The ability to control the dissemination of ideas yields power. Again, three realities about "modern" (that is, 20th-century) communication media and the institutions designed to control these media are worth emphasizing. First, the geographic constraints of 20th-century communication media dictated that certain types of institutions would be privileged, clearly limited ranges, and were susceptible to blocking or jamming outside their permitted territory; the geographic constraints on printed materials were even more significant. Second, the physical task of maintaining the media and preparing and distributing information over it were complex, requiring coordinated activity of many players, from the reporter or camera operator, to the electrician keeping the broadcast equipment running or mechanic keeping the presses operational, to the newspaper delivery boy or television repairman. Third, these media outlets were not simply complex but vastly expensive to maintain and operate.

The territorial component to 20th-century media and the high organizational and economic barriers to entry of course privileged territorially-based institutions and ones that were able to limit access to particular information markets, either through control of legal restrictions or through the use of violence. "Post-modern," 21st-century communication technology puts those institutions that evolved to take advantage of the peculiarities of 20th-century communication technology at a sudden disadvantage.

### *Human capacity*

If change in information and communication technology is the first principal driver of today's institutional unraveling, the second is certainly change in human capacity. Biologists may argue over whether ongoing evolutionary selection pressures and improvement in diet and health mean human beings today are "smarter" than human beings 50 or 100 years ago. But what is clear is that individuals are now more educated than they were 50 or 100 years ago. Literacy, and perhaps equally importantly, the educational and conceptual framework that permits the questioning of authority is now the norm. It is not necessarily the case that members of the elite are better educated. But a much larger proportion of the world's population now has communication and analytical skills that in the past were the property only of the elite. We may or may not be biologically different than we were 100 or 500 years ago. But socially and culturally we are different.

What this change in human capacity implies is a vastly increased ability of humans to understand their world and to impose meaning on what they experience without the direct mediation, intervention, or interpretation of elites. Hierarchy in social organization and all social institutions is profoundly challenged. Obviously, this does not imply that social and cultural hierarchies will cease to exist—that children will cease to honor their parents, or that individuals will stop seeking advice from their priests, their doctors, their lawyers, and their tax accountants. But there is clearly a leveling.

This is obvious in two ways. Individuals now may be able to think through problems for themselves rather than rely on others—teachers, specialists—to do this for them. They possess not only enhanced analytical skills but enhanced ability to take advantage of the technological changes that make information more readily available—to use the internet, for example, to find out what they need to know, without asking for anyone's help or approval. It is possible now to find answers for ourselves to many of the questions that in the past we would have needed to ask a teacher about, and he or she would have needed to consult a librarian, who would have had to request institutional permission to get the necessary books from a central library, that would have required central government funding to operate and whose existence depended on the whim of elected officials. For better and for worse, it is now possible for individuals to form judgments without the mediating impact of members of the elite or dominant social institutions.

But the revolution in human capacity is not simply that individuals can now find information and answer questions for themselves, or to do so even despite the disapproval of authorities. Perhaps more profoundly, it means that the *basis* on which individuals evaluate information and make decisions is changing. In their efforts to understand the world around them and to explain causes and consequences of actions and events, individuals may rely on various types of knowledge. They may rely on *revealed* knowledge—that is, on knowledge that is founded on claims of divinely revelation. Or they may rely on *wisdom*—that is, on knowledge provided by respected human authorities. Or they may rely on *scientific* knowledge—that is, on knowledge whose validity is ultimately based on the ability of the individual to replicate the analysis or replicate the experiment for himself or herself.[2] Obviously, a revolution in human capacity that increases the ability of individuals perform analyses or (mental or physical) experiments himself or herself poses at least a potential danger to social institutions grounded on revealed authority or wisdom.

## Today's Transformations

The combined, interactive impact of these two changes, in information technology and human capacity, is profound and can be seen in three ways.

### *Globalization*

The first is the most obvious and the most widely discussed. It is the declining importance of location and of physical and human geographic boundaries. The time-space relationship has changed and is changing. The popular term for this is "globalization."

Despite the popularity of the term and the frequency with which it tossed around, globalization is not as simple as we usually make it seem. It is not that *all* distances matter less and that *all* boundaries are less important in *all* aspects of our activities. What makes globalization interesting is that *some* distances and *some* boundaries still matter for *some* purposes, and this has important impact on which institutions are able to continue to function effectively and which are ceasing to be competitive.

The key observation is that for the most part, unless one is worrying about the spoilage of fresh fruit, it is *relative* times and *relative* distances that matter, not *absolute* times and distances. What we are witnessing is extraordinary change in the relative speeds and relative ease with which movement happens.

Two quick examples may provide useful illustration. Even into the first half of the nineteenth century, things, people, and ideas moved at essentially the same speed. It took roughly the same amount of time for my cargo, for me, and for my information to get from, say, London to New York. Now, however, my ideas can make this journey essentially instantaneously, I can make the journey in about six hours, and my cargo, if it is bulky, still may take time measured in weeks. Similarly, international borders pose no obstacle at all to the movement of my ideas from the United States to, say, India; I still need a visa to make the journey; and my cargo still needs extensive permission and is potentially subject to taxation and restriction. Much of what can be said about political borders applies equally well to physical ones: the Himalaya Mountains pose no obstacle to the transmission of ideas via satellite, only modest obstacles to the movement of people via airplanes, but a substantial obstacle to a truckload of coal. Obviously, the relative speed with which things, people, and ideas travel, and the relative permeability of borders to each of these, has changed dramatically—and this has implications for institutions which derive power from their control over things, over people, or over ideas.

A second example: when my grandfather went from America to Europe in 1926, it took him a half an hour to get to the port, a few minutes to board his ocean liner, and a week to get across the ocean. When I go to from America to Europe today, it takes me two hours to get across the metropolitan area to the airport, two hours to get through security and board the airplane, and six hours to get across the ocean. Short, local distances now take relatively longer, and in many cases absolutely longer, than they did in the past. Again, institutions that derived their power from the fact that short distances were quick and easy to travel, and that long distances were relatively slow and hard to travel, find themselves uncompetitive.

---

2   I am indebted to my colleague Roy Licklider for this typology and insight.

## Flattening and networking

Arguably, the second transformation is even more interesting and more profound than globalization. This is the increased ability of individuals, or small, relatively non-hierarchic, informally organized groups of individuals, to solve complex problems.

The flip side of this, of course, is the declining effectiveness, efficiency, and ultimately importance of large, hierarchic, formally organized institutions. It would be rash to make the claim that such institutions—the most important of which are the sovereign state and the business corporation—will be driven to extinction. But it is easily argued that they will change substantially to survive.

Both the state and the business corporation are based on bureaucracy. They are based on hierarchic structuring of control over functionally arranged units and individuals, organized to solve specified tasks. Max Weber saw all this. These organizations are necessary because finding solutions and implementing solutions was beyond the capacity of any single individual, or any small network of individuals bound together by bonds of trust or kinship.

Consider the problem of national security. In the past, if a group wanted the tools of violence that would allow one to protect oneself (or to deter attack or to take what one believed rightly belonged to one), one needed a disciplined regiment of soldiers, or a fleet of battleships, or a squadron of aircraft. Constructing these required a vast organization, to design and build the weapons, train the combatants, and keep the combatants fed and paid. In other words, it required a modern, hierarchic, bureaucratic state.

Weapons of mass destruction—nuclear, biological, or chemical—are not easy to make or use. But they do not require a state. An informal network of individuals can construct and use these. What do sovereign states now see as the principal threat to themselves? Increasingly it is not other sovereign states, or even large transnational corporations with their vast economic power. It is networks of individuals, able to launch terrorist attacks or to hack into vital cyber systems.

Again, at differential rates in different places and in different spheres of activity, we are seeing profound changes in the institutional qualities that are valuable. The postmodern 21st-century state seeks to be nimbler and less hierarchic than the modern 20th-century state was. We see many of the same pressures in corporations. The organizational design of Nike shoes or Google, with regard to the number of employees and management structure, is profoundly different than the organizational design of Ford Motor Company or *The New York Times*. In terms of management architecture and in terms of how much of their production process they seek to keep under direct "corporate" control, competitive institutions of today are very different from competitive institutions of a generation ago. They are 'flattened' organizationally, and they increasingly "outsource." In other words, both corporations and states increasingly reduce the formality of relationships, hierarchy, and size.

## Unbundling

The third change is perhaps the most interesting part of the unraveling of 20th-century institutions. This is the "unbundling" of services. Empowered individuals—empowered by their education and by the information technology at their disposal—are able to make more choices unmediated by large institutions. They are thus better able to "buy" directly from providers and to seek the lowest cost or highest quality for each of the components or particular services they seek, rather than find themselves limited to a monopoly provider of bundles or packages of goods or services.

Again, an example from the travel industry may be illustrative: in the 1960s when Americans traveled on vacation to Europe, they went to a travel agent, who relied on a few major providers to offer up packages of services. Given the information available to ordinary individuals regarding the quality and cost of transportation, hotel, food, and other travel services, the slowness of trans-Atlantic mail service and the prohibitive price of trans-Atlantic telephone calls, and the difficulty of cross-language communication, buying a package from a limited number of package providers or relying on an "expert" who worked with a limited number of preferred vendors were the only realistic options. To get an affordable airfare, they stayed in a hotel they disliked, or had to buy as well a city tour they did not need. Their choice was only between competing bundles of services. Today, when Americans travel to Europe, they skip the "service bundler" and buy air travel from one provider, hotel services from another, ground transportation from a third, meals from a fourth, and so on. Today, travelers pick and choose in a way that was not possible before. And the institutions that had wielded enormous power before—tour providers and travel agents—are either out of business or relegated to working in travel to unusual destinations (where information, communication technology, and language are still barriers) or working with relatively poorly-endowed customers who lack the skills, knowledge, or technological access to work effectively in the post-modern environment.

Obviously this is a trivial example. But it is easy to find more profound ones.

One of the great 'bundling' institutions is one that students are very familiar with: the modern university. The university bundles various courses (some well-taught and useful, some less so), accreditation of knowledge acquired (that is, a recognized degree or certificate), and provision of life-long alumni networks, and perhaps room and board, textbooks (through a campus bookstore), gyms, health services, and counseling services. The university loses money on some of these services, and makes up for the loss on others. It may excel in some of the services it provides, while underperforming and overcharging in others. What we are seeing in America, however, is that this ability to bundle is coming apart quickly. Students now pick and choose: they take courses at multiple institutions, earn "badges" instead of degrees, build a social network online rather than at school, live off-campus (perhaps even in a different city or country), and buy other services on the open market.

This has profound impact on students' relationships—undercutting social hierarchies for example. But it also will put out of business many institutions that can survive only by bundling services.

But the biggest "bundler" of all in today's world is obviously the modern state. The modern state provides a bundle of services—security, education, health, transportation, and so on—and charges a price in terms of taxes, obedience to laws, and mandatory military service. This is the essence of the corporate, bureaucratic, state institution that took the world by storm beginning in the 17th century. But the state's ability to bundle is coming apart.

It is not simply that states are outsourcing services that they used to produce or provide themselves. It is also that (at least in democracies, where individuals have the ability to make such choices) individuals increasingly turn to lower cost providers for particular services, and refuse to pay the higher price the state would charge. Many Americans would rather rely on private security firms than pay the taxes necessary to have sufficient public police protection. Many Americans would rather rely on private schools than pay the taxes sufficient to have adequate quality public schools. New highways are increasingly financed and owned by private corporations rather than by the state. Reform of the retirement system creates increased reliance on the private market. Because individuals prefer the flexibility that this unbundling provides, institutions that rely on selling a bundle of unrelated, or separable, goods find themselves challenged.

## Conclusions and Implications

All this suggests that the institutions shaping the rules and norms of behavior in tomorrow's world will be different from those of yesterday's world. It also suggests, however, three other, final conclusions.

The first is that politicians, professors, opinion leaders, and ordinary people can rail against globalization, flattening-and-networking, and unbundling. And they can fight against them. But they—and we—need to acknowledge the two dynamics that are driving them: information technology and education. In other words, the institutional transformations we are witnessing are being driven by enhancements in knowledge. It is possible to fight against the advancement of knowledge. It is even possible to fight successfully against it. World history has not been a smooth, upward trend-line. But especially in the long run it is hard to fight against the advancement of knowledge, at least without paying a high price.

The second closing observation is that while we have been examining the partial unraveling of 20th century institutions, particularly the state and large corporations, we could equally well describe our topic as the creation of the new 21st-century institutions. We are witnessing a process of creative destruction, not simply destruction. We are not moving into a world without institutions, or possessing only weakened institutions. New institutions, better suited to globalized, flattened, unbundled conditions, are emerging. Looking at the corporations, the organizations, and the governance bodies that are thriving in today's world, we get a clear picture of some of the institution-building going on.

The third, final, perhaps less obvious observation involves one of the unusual institutional "winners" in the postmodern world. One of the key elements in the functioning of an unraveled, globalized, networked, unbundled world is the dramatic strengthening of a very different type of institution: the rule of law. The new 21st-century institutions require enormous levels of trust in order to function. This will require substantial expansion of shared trust in formal legal frameworks. It requires confidence that laws will be made (and not un-made). It requires confidence that judgments on whether laws and agreements have been broken will be made fairly. And it requires confidence that there be reliable enforcement mechanisms.

But note, too, that tomorrow's rule of law will be different from yesterday's. These rule-of-law institutions will not be created and maintained centrally. These new rule-of-law institutions will themselves also be globalized, flattened-and-networked, and unbundled, for precisely the same reasons that states and corporations will be.

This will be a strange new world—but no stranger than those that humanity has constructed in the past.

# 27: Toward Transgovernmental Networks

*Anne-Marie Slaughter*

Terrorists, arms dealers, money launderers, drug dealers, traffickers in women and children, and the modern pirates of intellectual property all operate through global networks.[1] So, increasingly, do governments. Networks of government officials—police investigators, financial regulators, even judges and legislators—increasingly exchange information and coordinate activity to combat global crime and address common problems on a global scale. These government networks are a key feature of world order in the twenty-first century, but they are underappreciated, undersupported, and underused to address the central problems of global governance.

Consider the examples just in the wake of September 11. The Bush administration immediately set about assembling an ad hoc coalition of states to aid in the war on terrorism. Public attention focused on military cooperation, but the networks of financial regulators working to identify and freeze terrorist assets, of law enforcement officials sharing vital information on terrorist suspects, and of intelligence operatives working to preempt the next attack have been equally important. Indeed, the leading expert in the "new security" of borders and container bombs insists that the domestic agencies responsible for customs, food safety, and regulation of all kinds must extend their reach abroad, through reorganization and much closer cooperation with their foreign counterparts.[2] And after the United States concluded that it did not have authority under international law to interdict a shipment of missiles from North Korea to Yemen, it turned to national law enforcement authorities to coordinate the extraterritorial enforcement of their national criminal laws.[3] Networked threats require a networked response.

Turning to the global economy, networks of finance ministers and central bankers have been critical players in responding to national and regional financial crises. The G-8 is as much a network of finance ministers as of heads of state; it is the finance ministers who make key decisions on how to respond to calls for debt relief for the most highly indebted countries. The finance ministers and central bankers hold separate news conferences to announce policy responses to crises such as the East Asian financial crisis in 1997 and the Russian crisis in 1998.[4] The G-20, a network specifically created to help prevent future crises, is led by the Indian finance minister and is composed of the finance ministers of twenty developed and developing countries. More broadly, the International Organization of Securities Commissioners (IOSCO) emerged in 1984. It was followed in the 1990s by the creation of the International Association of Insurance Supervisors and a network of all three of these organizations and other national and

---

1  Naím, "Five Wars of Globalization," 29.
2  Flynn, "America The Vulnerable," 60.
3  Sanger, "The World: When Laws Don't Apply; Cracking Down on the Terror-Arms Trade," *New York Times*, 15 June 2003, Sect. 4, 4.
4  Chote, "A World in the Woods," *Financial Times*, 2 November 1998, 20.

international officials responsible for financial stability around the world called the Financial Stability Forum.[5]

Beyond national security and the global economy, networks of national officials are working to improve environmental policy across borders. Within the North American Free Trade Agreement (NAFTA), U.S., Mexican, and Canadian environmental agencies have created an environmental enforcement network, which has enhanced the effectiveness of environmental regulation in all three states, particularly in Mexico. Globally, the Environmental Protection Agency (EPA) and its Dutch equivalent have founded the International Network for Environmental Compliance and Enforcement (INECE), which offers technical assistance to environmental agencies around the world, holds global conferences at which environmental regulators learn and exchange information, and sponsors a website with training videos and other information.

Nor are regulators the only ones networking. National judges are exchanging decisions with one another through conferences, judicial organizations, and the Internet. Constitutional judges increasingly cite one another's decisions on issues from free speech to privacy rights. Indeed, Justice Anthony Kennedy of the U.S. Supreme Court cited a decision by the European Court of Justice (ECJ) in an important 2003 opinion overturning a Texas antisodomy law. Bankruptcy judges in different countries negotiate mini-treaties to resolve complicated international cases; judges in transnational commercial disputes have begun to see themselves as part of a global judicial system. National judges are also interacting directly with their supranational counterparts on trade and human rights issues.

Finally, even legislators, the most naturally parochial government officials due to their direct ties to territorially rooted constituents, are reaching across borders. International parliamentary organizations have been traditionally well meaning though ineffective, but today national parliamentarians are meeting to adopt and publicize common positions on the death penalty, human rights, and environmental issues. They support one another in legislative initiatives and offer training programs and technical assistance.[6]

Each of these networks has specific aims and activities, depending on its subject area, membership, and history, but taken together, they also perform certain common functions. They expand regulatory reach, allowing national government officials to keep up with corporations, civic organizations, and criminals. They build trust and establish relationships among their participants that then create incentives to establish a good reputation and avoid a bad one. These are the conditions essential for long-term cooperation. They exchange regular information about their own activities and develop databases of best practices,

---

5   The Financial Stability Forum was initiated by the finance ministers and central bank governors of the Group of Seven (G-7) industrial countries in February 1999, following a report on international cooperation and coordination in the area of financial market supervision and surveillance by the president of the Deutsche Bundesbank. In addition to representatives from the Basel Committee, IOSCO, and the International Association of Insurance Supervisors (IAIS), its members include senior representatives from national authorities responsible for financial stability in significant international financial centers; international financial institutions such as the Bank for International Settlements (BIS), the IMF, the Organization of Economic Cooperation and Development (OECD), and the World Bank; and committees of central bank experts. "A Guide to Committees, Groups and Clubs," on on the International Monetary Fund homepage (cited 7 July 2003); available from *http://imf.org/external/np/exr/facts/ groups.htm#FSF.*

6   American readers may be skeptical of these reports due to the widespread and completely false statistic about how few members of Congress have a passport. In fact, 93 percent of all members hold passports and average two trips abroad a year. Indeed, 20 percent claim to speak a foreign language. Eric Schmitt and Elizabeth Becker, "Insular Congress Appears to be Myth," *New York Times*, 4 November 2000, sect. A, 9. What is true is that some members fear that their constituents will identify trips to meet their counterparts abroad with "junkets," but that is a matter of public education.

or, in the judicial case, different approaches to common legal issues. They offer technical assistance and professional socialization to members from less developed nations, whether regulators, judges, or legislators.

In a world of global markets, global travel, and global information networks, of weapons of mass destruction and looming environmental disasters of global magnitude, governments must have global reach. In a world in which their ability to use their hard power is often limited, governments must be able to exploit the uses of soft power: the power of persuasion and information.[7] Similarly, in a world in which a major set of obstacles to effective global regulation is a simple inability on the part of many developing countries to translate paper rules into changes in actual behavior, governments must be able not only to negotiate treaties but also to create the capacity to comply with them.

Understood as a form of global governance, government networks meet these needs. As commercial and civic organizations have already discovered, their networked form is ideal for providing the speed and flexibility necessary to function effectively in an information age. But unlike amorphous "global policy networks" championed by UN Secretary General Kofi Annan, in which it is never clear who is exercising power on behalf of whom, these are networks composed of national government officials, either appointed by elected officials or directly elected themselves. Best of all, they can perform many of the functions of a world government—legislation, administration, and adjudication—without the form . . .

Yet to see these networks as they exist, much less to imagine what they could become, requires a *deeper* conceptual shift. Stop imagining the international system as a system of states—unitary entities like billiard balls or black boxes—subject to rules created by international institutions that

are apart from, "above" these states. Start thinking about a world of governments, with all the different institutions that perform the basic functions of governments—legislation, adjudication, implementation—interacting both with each other domestically and also with their foreign and supranational counterparts. States still exist in this world; indeed, they are crucial actors. But they are "disaggregated." They relate to each other not only through the Foreign Office, but also through regulatory, judicial, and legislative channels . . .

Seeing the world through the lenses of disaggregated rather than unitary states allows leaders, policymakers, analysts, or simply concerned citizens to see features of the global political system that were previously hidden. Government networks suddenly pop up everywhere, from the Financial Action Task Force (FATF), a network of finance ministers and other financial regulators taking charge of pursuing money launderers and financers of terrorism, to the Free Trade Commission, a network of trade ministers charged with interpreting NAFTA, to a network of ministers in charge of border controls working to create a new regime of safe borders in the wake of September 11. At the same time, it is possible to disaggregate international organizations as well, to see "vertical networks" between national regulators and judges and their supranational counterparts. Examples include relations between national European courts and the ECJ or between national U.S., Mexican, and Canadian courts and NAFTA arbitral tribunals.

Equally important, these different lenses make it possible to imagine a genuinely new set of possibilities for a future world order. The building blocks of this order would not be states but parts of states: courts, regulatory agencies, ministries, legislatures. The government officials within these various institutions

---

7   Nye, *Paradox of American Power,* 9.

would participate in many different types of networks, creating links across national borders and between national and supranational institutions. The result could be a world that looks like the globe hoisted by Atlas at Rockefeller Center, crisscrossed by an increasingly dense web of networks.

This world would still include traditional international organizations, such as the United Nations and the World Trade Organization (WTO), although many of these organizations would be likely to become hosts for and sources of government networks. It would still feature states interacting as unitary states on important issues, particularly in security matters. And it would certainly still be a world in which military and economic power mattered; government networks are not likely to substitute for either armies or treasuries.

At the same time, however, a world of government networks would be a more effective and potentially more just world order than either what we have today or a world government in which a set of global institutions perched above nation-states enforced global rules. In a networked world order, primary political authority would remain at the national level except in those cases in which national governments had explicitly delegated their authority to supranational institutions. National government officials would be increasingly enmeshed in networks of personal and institutional relations. They would each be operating both in the domestic and the international arenas, exercising their national authority to implement their transgovernmental and international obligations and representing the interests of their country while working with their foreign and supranational counterparts to disseminate and distill information, cooperate in enforcing national and international laws, harmonizing national laws and regulations, and addressing common problems.

## The Globalization Paradox: Needing More Government and Fearing It

Peoples and their governments around the world need global institutions to solve collective problems that can only be addressed on a global scale. They must be able to make and enforce global rules on a variety of subjects and through a variety of means. Further, it has become commonplace to claim that the international institutions created in the late 1940s, after a very different war and facing a host of different threats from those we face today, are outdated and inadequate to meet contemporary challenges. They must be reformed or even reinvented; new ones must be created.

Yet world government is both infeasible and undesirable. The size and scope of such a government presents an unavoidable and dangerous threat to individual liberty. Further, the diversity of the peoples to be governed makes it almost impossible to conceive of a global demos. No form of democracy within the current global repertoire seems capable of overcoming these obstacles.

This is the globalization paradox. We need more government on a global and a regional scale, but we don't want the centralization of decision-making power and coercive authority so far from the people actually to be governed. It is the paradox identified in the European Union by Renaud Dehousse and by Robert Keohane in his millennial presidential address to the American Political Science Association. The European Union has pioneered "regulation by networks," which Dehousse describes as the response to a basic dilemma in EU governance: "On the one hand, increased uniformity is certainly needed; on the other hand, greater centralization is politically inconceivable, and probably undesirable."[8] The EU alternative is the "transnational option"—the use of an organized network of national officials to ensure "that the actors in

---

8  Dehousse, "Regulation by Networks in the European Community," 259.

charge of the implementation of Community policies behave in a similar manner."[9]

Worldwide, Keohane argues that globalization "creates potential gains from cooperation" if institutions can be created to harness those gains;[10] however, institutions themselves are potentially oppressive.[11] The result is "the Governance Dilemma: although institutions are essential for human life, they are also dangerous."[12] The challenge facing political scientists and policymakers at the dawn of the twenty-first century is discovering how well-structured institutions could enable the world to have "a rebirth of freedom."[13]

Addressing the paradox at the global level is further complicated by the additional concern of accountability. In the 1990s the conventional reaction to the problem of "world government" was instead to champion "global governance," a much looser and less threatening concept of collective organization and regulation without coercion. A major element of global governance, in turn, has been the rise of global policy networks, celebrated for their ability to bring together all public and private actors on issues critical to the global public interest.[14]

Global policy networks, in turn, grow out of various "reinventing government" projects, both academic and practical. These projects focus on the many ways in which private actors now can and do perform government functions, from providing expertise to monitoring compliance with regulations to negotiating the substance of those regulations, both domestically and internationally.

The problem, however, is ensuring that these private actors uphold the public trust.

Conservative critics have been most sensitive to this problem. Assistant Secretary of State John Bolton, while still in the private sector, argued that "it is precisely the detachment from governments that makes international civil society so troubling, at least for democracies." "Indeed," he continues, "the civil society idea actually suggests a 'corporativist' approach to international decision-making that is dramatically troubling for democratic theory because it posits 'interests' (whether NGOs or businesses) as legitimate actors along with popularly elected governments." Corporatism, in turn, at least in Mussolini's view, was the core of fascism. Hence Bolton's bottom line: "Mussolini would smile on the Forum of Civil Society. Americanists do not."[15]

Somewhat more calmly, Martin Shapiro argues that the shift from government to governance marks "a significant erosion of the boundaries separating what lies inside a government and its administration and what lies outside them."[16] The result is to advantage "experts and enthusiasts," the two groups outside government that have the greatest incentive and desire to participate in governance processes;[17] however, "while the ticket to participation in governance is knowledge and/or passion, both knowledge and passion generate perspectives that are not those of the rest of us. Few of us would actually enjoy living in a Frank Lloyd Wright house."[18] The network form, with its loose, informal, and nonhierarchical structure, only exacerbates this problem.

---

9   Ibid., 254.

10  Robert O. Keohane, "Governance in a Partially Globalized World," presidential address, annual meeting of the American Political Science Association, 2000, *American Political Science Review* 95 (March 2001): 1.

11  Ibid., 5.

12  Ibid., 1.

13  Ibid., 12, quoting Abraham Lincoln, "The Gettysburg Address," 19 November 1863.

14  Annan, *We the Peoples*. 70; see also Reinicke and Deng, *Critical Choices* and Reinicke, "The Other World Wide Web."

15  Bolton, "Should We Take Global Governance Seriously?" 206.

16  Shapiro, "Administrative Law Unbounded," 369.

17  Ibid., 376.

18  Ibid., 374.

The governance dilemma thus becomes a tri-lemma: we need global rules without centralized power but with government actors who can be held to account through a variety of political mechanisms. These government actors can and should interact with a wide range of nongovernmental organizations (NGOs), but their role in governance bears distinct and different responsibilities. They must represent all their different constituencies, at least in a democracy; corporate and civic actors may be driven by profits and passions, respectively. "Governance" must not become a cover for the blurring of these lines, even if it is both possible and necessary for these various actors to work together on common problems.

In this context, a world order based on government networks, working alongside and even in place of more traditional international institutions, holds great potential . . . Government networks established for limited purposes such as postal and telecommunications have existed for almost a century.

What is new is the scale, scope, and type of transgovernmental ties. Links between government officials from two, four, or even a dozen countries have become sufficiently dense as to warrant their own organization—witness IOSCO or INECE. Government networks have developed their own identity and autonomy in specific issue areas, such as the G-7 or the G-20. They perform a wider array of functions than in the past, from collecting and distilling information on global or regional best practices to actively offering technical assistance to poorer and less experienced members. And they have spread far beyond regulators to judges and legislators.

More broadly, government networks have become recognized and semiformalized ways of doing business within loose international groupings like the Commonwealth and the Asian-Pacific Economic Cooperation (APEC). At the same time, they have become the signature form of governance for the European Union, which is itself pioneering a new form of regional collective governance that is likely to prove far more relevant to global governance than the experience of traditional federal states. Most important, they are driven by many of the multiple factors that drive the hydra-headed phenomenon of globalization itself, leading to the simple need for national officials of all kinds to communicate and negotiate across borders to do business they could once accomplish solely at home . . .

Government networks can help address the governance tri-lemma, offering a flexible and relatively fast way to conduct the business of global governance, coordinating and even harmonizing national government action while initiating and monitoring different solutions to global problems. Yet they are decentralized and dispersed, incapable of exercising centralized coercive authority. Further, they are government actors. They can interact with a wide range of NGOs, civic and corporate, but their responsibilities and constituencies are far broader. These constituencies should be able to devise ways to hold them accountable, at least to the same extent that they are accountable for their purely domestic activity.

### The Disaggregated State

Participants in the decade-long public and academic discussion of globalization have routinely focused on two major shifts: from national to global and from government to governance. They have paid far less attention to the third shift, from the unitary state to the disaggregated state.

The disaggregated state sounds vaguely Frankenstinian—a shambling, headless bureaucratic monster. In fact, it is nothing so sinister. It is simply the rising need for and capacity of different domestic government institutions to engage in activities beyond their borders, often with their foreign counterparts. It is regulators pursuing the subjects of their regulations across borders; judges negotiating minitreaties with their foreign brethren to resolve complex transnational cases; and legislators consulting on the best ways to frame and pass legislation affecting human rights or the environment.

The significance of the concept of the disaggregated state only becomes fully apparent in contrast to the unitary state, a concept that has long dominated international legal and political analysis. International lawyers and international relations theorists have always known that the entities they describe and analyze as "states" interacting with one another are in fact much more complex entities, but the fiction of a unitary will and capacity for action has worked well enough for purposes of description and prediction of outcomes in the international system . . .

In an international legal system premised on unitary states, the paradigmatic form of international cooperation is the multilateral international convention, negotiated over many years in various international watering holes, signed and ratified with attendant flourish and formality, and given continuing life through the efforts of an international secretariat whose members prod and assist ongoing rounds of negotiation aimed at securing compliance with obligations already undertaken and at expanding the scope and precision of existing rules.[19] The "states" participating in these negotiations are presumed to speak with one voice—a voice represented by either the head of state or the foreign minister. Any differences between the different parts of a particular government are to be worked out domestically; the analytical lens of the unitary state obscures the very existence of these different government institutions.

The result is the willful adoption of analytical blinders, allowing us to see the "international system" only in the terms that we ourselves have imposed. Compare our approach to domestic government: we know it to be an aggregate of different institutions. We call it "the government," but we can simultaneously distinguish the activities of the courts, Congress, regulatory agencies, and the White House itself. We do not choose to screen out everything except what the president does or says, or what Congress does or says, or what the Supreme Court does or says. But effectively, in the international system, we do.

Looking at the international system through the lens of unitary states leads us to focus on traditional international organizations and institutions created by and composed of formal state delegations. Conversely, however, thinking about states the way we think about domestic governments—as aggregations of distinct institutions with separate roles and capacities—provides a lens that allows us to see a new international landscape. Government networks pop up everywhere.

Horizontal government networks—links between counterpart national officials across borders—are easiest to spot. Far less frequent, but potentially very important, are vertical government networks, those between national government officials and their supranational counterparts. The prerequisite for a vertical government network is the relatively rare decision by states to delegate their sovereignty to an institution above them with real power—a court or a regulatory commission . . .

## A New World Order

Appreciating the extent and nature of existing government networks, both horizontal and vertical, makes it possible to envision a genuinely new world order. "World order," for these purposes, describes a system of global governance that institutionalizes cooperation and sufficiently contains conflict such that all nations and their peoples may achieve greater peace and prosperity, improve their stewardship of the earth, and reach minimum standards of human dignity. The concept of a "new world order" has been used and overused to refer to everything from George H. W. Bush's vision of a post–Cold War world to the post-9/11

---

19 See, e.g., the process of international rule-making described in Chayes and Chayes, *The New Sovereignty.*

geopolitical landscape. Nevertheless, I use it to describe a different conceptual framework for the actual infrastructure of world order—an order based on an intricate three-dimensional web of links between disaggregated state institutions . . .

To appreciate the full implications of this vision, consider again our implicit mental maps of "the international system" or even "world order." It's a flat map, pre-Columbian, with states at the level of the land and the international system floating above them somewhere. International organizations also inhabit this floating realm— they are apart from and somehow above the states that are their members. To the extent that they are actually seen as governing the international system or establishing global order, they must constitute an international bureaucracy equivalent in form and function to the multiple domestic bureaucracies of the states "underneath" them.

In a world of government networks, by contrast, the same officials who are judging, regulating, and legislating domestically are also reaching out to their foreign counterparts to help address the governance problems that arise when national actors and issues spill beyond their borders. Global governance, from this perspective, is not a matter of regulating states the way states regulate their citizens, but rather of addressing the issues and resolving the problems that result from citizens going global—from crime to commerce to civic engagement. Even where genuinely supranational officials participate in vertical government networks—meaning judges or regulators who exercise actual sovereign authority delegated to them by a group of states—they must work very closely with their national counterparts and must harness national coercive power to be effective.

Scholars and commentators in different issue areas have begun to identify various pieces of this infrastructure. Financial regulators, for

instance, are becoming accustomed to describing the new international financial architecture as a combination of networks—G-7, G-8, and G-20, the Basel Committee, and IOSCO among them—with traditional international institutions, such as the International Monetary Fund (IMF) and the World Bank. Scholars of the European Union, as noted above, are increasingly familiar with the concept of "regulation by network." Environmental activists would readily recognize some of the institutions associated with the North American Free Trade Agreement (NAFTA) as "environmental enforcement networks" composed of the environmental protection agencies of the United States, Canada, and Mexico.[20] And constitutional law scholars, human rights activists, and transnational litigators would not balk at the idea of transnational judicial networks to describe the various ways in which courts around the world are increasingly interacting with one another.

Further, different regional and political organizations around the world have already consciously adopted this form of organization. Beyond the European Union, both APEC and the Nordic System are essentially "networks of networks," organizations composed of networks of national ministers and parliamentarians. The Commonwealth has also long been structured this way, although its myriad networks of regulators, judges, and legislators have evolved more gradually over time. And the OECD is an international institution that has as its chief function the convening of different networks of national regulators to address common problems and propose model solutions . . .

***Premises*** There can, of course, be no one blue-print for world order. The proposal advanced here is part of an active and ongoing debate. In the spirit of such debate, it is important to

---

20 Fulton and Sperling, "The Network of Environmental Enforcement and Compliance Cooperation in North America and the Western Hemisphere," 111.

acknowledge that the model of world order I put forward rests on a combination of descriptive and predictive empirical claims, which can be summarized in basic terms:

- The state is not the only actor in the international system, but it is still the most important actor.
- The state is not disappearing, but it is disaggregating into its component institutions, which are increasingly interacting principally with their foreign counterparts across borders.
- These institutions still represent distinct national or state interests, even as they also recognize common professional identities and substantive experience as judges, regulators, ministers, and legislators.
- Different states have evolved and will continue to evolve mechanisms for reaggregating the interests of their distinct institutions when necessary. In many circumstances, therefore, states will still interact with one another as unitary actors in more traditional ways.
- Government networks exist alongside and sometimes within more traditional international organizations.

. . . I am not arguing that a new world order of government networks will replace the existing infrastructure of international institutions, but rather complement and strengthen it. States can be disaggregated for many purposes and in many contexts and still be completely unitary actors when necessary, such as in decisions to go to war. And even their component parts still represent national interests in various ways.

### Horizontal Networks

The structural core of a disaggregated world order is a set of horizontal networks among national government officials in their respective issue areas, ranging from central banking through antitrust regulation and environmental protection to law enforcement and human rights protection. These networks operate both between high-level officials directly responsive to the national political process—the ministerial level—as well as between lower level national regulators. They may be surprisingly spontaneous—informal, flexible, and of varying membership—or institutionalized within official international organizations. For instance, national finance ministers meet regularly under the auspices of the G-7 and the G-20, but also as members of the IMF Board of Governors. The extent and the kind of power they may exercise within these two forums differ in significant ways, but the basic structure of governance and the identity of the governors remains the same.

Horizontal information networks, as the name suggests, bring together regulators, judges, or legislators to exchange information and to collect and distill best practices. This information exchange can also take place through technical assistance and training programs provided by one country's officials to another. The direction of such training is not always developed country to developing country, either; it can also be from developed country to developed country, as when U.S. antitrust officials spent six months training their New Zealand counterparts.

Enforcement networks typically spring up due to the inability of government officials in one country to enforce that country's laws, either by means of a regulatory agency or through a court. But enforcement cooperation must also inevitably involve a great deal of information exchange and can also involve assistance programs of various types. Legislators can also collaborate on how to draft complementary legislation so as to avoid enforcement loopholes.

Finally, harmonization networks, which are typically authorized by treaty or executive agreement, bring regulators together to ensure that their rules in a particular substantive area conform to a common regulatory standard.

Judges can also engage in the equivalent activity, but in a much more ad hoc manner. Harmonization is often politically very controversial, with critics charging that the "technical" process of achieving convergence ignores the many winners and losers in domestic publics, most of whom do not have any input into the process.

### Vertical Networks

In a disaggregated world order, horizontal government networks would be more numerous than vertical networks, but vertical networks would have a crucial role to play. Although a core principle of such an order is the importance of keeping global governance functions primarily in the hands of domestic government officials, in some circumstances states do come together the way citizens might and choose to delegate their individual governing authority to a "higher" organization—a "supranational" organization that does exist, at least conceptually, above the state. The officials of these organizations do in fact replicate the governing functions that states exercise regarding their citizens. Thus, for instance, states can truly decide that the only way to reduce tariffs or subsidies is to adopt a body of rules prohibiting them and allow an independent court or tribunal to enforce those rules. Alternatively, states can come together and give an international court the power to try war criminals—the same function that national courts perform—in circumstances in which national courts are unwilling or unable to do so.

These supranational organizations can be far more effective in performing the functions states charge them to perform if they can link up directly with national government institutions. Absent a world government, it is impossible to grant supranational officials genuine coercive power: judges on supranational tribunals cannot call in the global equivalent of federal marshals if their judgments are not obeyed; global regulators cannot impose fines and enforce them through global courts. Their only hope of being able to marshal such authority is to harness the cooperation of their domestic counterparts—to effectively "borrow" the coercive power of domestic government officials to implement supranational rules and decisions. This harnessing has been the secret of the ECJ's success in creating and enforcing a genuine European legal system within the European Union. At the global level, it can make supranational organizations more powerful and effective than many of their creators ever dreamed.

Close ties between supranational officials— judges, regulators, legislators—and their domestic government counterparts are vertical government networks. They depend on the disaggregation of the state no less than do horizontal government networks. Whereas the traditional model of international law and international courts assumed that a tribunal such as the International Court of Justice in the Hague—traditionally known as the World Court—would hand down a judgment applicable to "states," and thus up to "states" to enforce or ignore, the EU legal system devolves primary responsibility for enforcing ECJ judgments not onto EU "member-states," per se, but on to the national judges of those states. Another version of a vertical judicial network, operating on a global scale, is the jurisdictional provisions of the Rome Statute establishing an International Criminal Court (ICC).[21] Under this system, national courts are to exercise primary jurisdiction over cases involving genocide, war crimes, and crimes against humanity, but will be required to cede power to the ICC if they prove unable or unwilling to carry out a particular prosecution. Beyond judges, the European Union is also pioneering a vertical administrative network between the antitrust authority of the

---

21 Rome Statute of the International Criminal Court, UN Doc. A/CONF.183/9, reprinted in *International Legal Materials* 37 (1998): 999. For a detailed discussion of complementarity in and prior to the Rome Statute, see El Zeidy, "The Principle of Complementarity: A New Mechanism to Implement International Criminal Law."

European Commission and national antitrust regulators that will allow the commission to charge national authorities with implementing EU rules in accordance with their particular national traditions.[22]

These vertical networks are enforcement networks. But they can also operate as harmonization networks, in the sense that they will bring national rules and supranational rules closer together. Still other vertical networks are principally information networks. The environmental ministers of NAFTA countries, for instance, benefit by working with the Commission on Environmental Cooperation (CEC), a NAFTA supranational institution charged with gathering information on environmental enforcement policies and compiling a record of complaints of nonenforcement by private actors. This is an attempt to enhance enforcement through the provision of information. Similarly, the European Union is beginning to create Europe-level "information agencies," designed to collect and disseminate information needed by networks of national regulators.[23] Such agencies can also provide benchmarks of progress for their national counterparts against accepted global or regional standards.

### *Disaggregated International Organizations*

Thinking about world order in terms of both horizontal and vertical government networks challenges our current concept of an "international organization." Many international organizations are primarily convening structures for horizontal networks of national officials. Others are genuinely "supranational," in the sense that they constitute an entity distinct from national governments that has a separate identity and loyalty and which exercises some measure of

genuine autonomous power. For example, the Ministerial Conference of the WTO is a gathering of national trade ministers, who can only exercise power by consensus. Dispute-resolution panels of the WTO, by contrast, are composed of three independent experts charged with interpreting and enforcing the rules of the WTO against national governments.

Both of these types of international/supranational organization differ from traditional international organizations—most notably the United Nations itself—that are composed of formal delegations from each of the member states, typically headed by an ambassador serving in the capacity of permanent representative. The Organization of American States (OAS), the Organization of African Unity (OAU), and the Organization for Security and Cooperation in Europe (OSCE) all fit this model. More specialized international organizations, on the other hand, such as the International Postal Union, the World Health Organization (WHO), and the Food and Agriculture Organization, address less overtly "political" subject areas than international and regional security and have long been a forum for meetings of the relevant national ministers. Organizations such as the IMF and the World Bank are hybrid in this regard—national finance ministers and central bankers effectively run them, but they have weighted voting arrangements (like the five permanent members of the United Nations who are able to exercise a veto) that make them far more than convening structures for networks.

In a world of disaggregated states that nevertheless still act as unitary actors under some circumstances, it is important to be able to distinguish between different types of international organizations in terms both of the relevant government officials who represent their

---

22 *"Council Regulation (EC) No 1/2003* of 16 December 2002." See Europa homepage (cited 23 June 2003); available from *http://europa.eu.int/comm/competition/citizen/citizen_antitrust.html#role.*

23 Dehousse, "Regulation by Network."

states within them and the degree and type of autonomous power they can exercise. Where international organizations have become sufficiently specialized to develop the equivalent of an executive, judicial, and even legislative branch, vertical government networks become possible. Where they are specialized in a specific issue area but exercise little or no autonomous power, they can be hosts for horizontal government networks. But when they are regional or global organizations charged with assuring peace and security, or similar very general functions, they represent an older and much more formal model of international cooperation, conducted by diplomats more than domestic government officials . . .

***Global Impact*** A critical piece of the puzzle is still missing. Government networks can provide the structure of a new world order, but how do we know that they actually have, or will have, any impact on addressing the problems that the world needs to solve? How do they, or will they, contribute to increasing peace and prosperity, protecting the planet and the individuals who inhabit it? . . .

Government networks currently contribute to world order: (1) by creating convergence and informed divergence; (2) by improving compliance with international rules; and (3) by increasing the scope, nature, and quality of international cooperation. Kal Raustiala, a young legal scholar and political scientist, has demonstrated ways in which government networks lead to "regulatory export" of rules and practices from one country to another. The result can be sufficient policy convergence to make it possible over the longer term to conclude a more formal international agreement setting forth a common regulatory regime.[24] Soft law codes of conduct issued by transgovernmental regulatory organizations, as

well as the simple dissemination of credible and authoritative information, also promote convergence. Promoting convergence, on the other hand, can also give rise to informed divergence, where a national governmental institution or the government as a whole acknowledges a prevailing standard or trend and deliberately chooses to diverge from it for reasons of national history, culture, or politics.

Government networks also improve compliance with international treaties and customary law. Vertical enforcement networks do this explicitly and directly by providing a supranational court or regulatory authority with a direct link to a national government institution that can exercise actual coercive authority on its behalf. Equally important, however, are the ways in which technical assistance flowing through horizontal networks can build regulatory or judicial capacity in states where there may be a willingness to enforce international legal obligations but the infrastructure is weak.

Finally, government networks enhance existing international cooperation by providing the mechanisms for transferring regulatory approaches that are proving increasingly successful domestically to the international arena. Most important is regulation by information, which allows regulators to move away from traditional command-and-control methods and instead provide individuals and corporations with the information and ideas they need to figure out how to improve their own performance against benchmarked standards. This approach is gaining popularity in the United States, is increasingly prevalent in the European Union, and is being tried at the United Nations. Government networks create regional and even global transmission belts for information that can readily expand to include as many nations as can usefully participate. In addition, government

---

24  See Raustiala, "The Architecture of International Cooperation: Transgovernmental Networks and The Future of International Law," 1.

networks are the ideal mechanism of international cooperation on international problems that have domestic roots, as they directly engage the participation and the credibility of the individuals who must ultimately be responsible for addressing those problems . . .

If government networks exist not only to address specific regulatory, judicial, and legislative problems, but also as self-consciously constituted professional associations of regulators, judges, and legislators, they should be able develop and enforce global standards of honesty, integrity, competence, and independence in performing the various functions that constitute a government.

They could socialize their members in a variety of ways that would create a perceived cost in deviating from these standards. But they could also bolster their members by enhancing the prestige of membership in a particular government network enough to give government officials who want to adhere to high professional standards ammunition against countervailing domestic forces. Just as international organizations from the European Union to the Community of Democracies have done, government networks could condition admission on meeting specified criteria designed to reinforce network norms.[25] A particular advantage of selective strengthening of individual government institutions this way is that it avoids the pernicious problem of labeling an entire state as bad or good, liberal or illiberal, tyrannical or democratic. It focuses instead on performance at a much lower level, recognizing that in any country and in any government different forces will be contending for power and privilege. It is critical to support those who are willing to practice what they preach in both their own laws and their obligations under international law.

At the same time, these networks could be empowered to provide much more technical assistance of the kind needed to build governance capacity in many countries around the world. They could be tasked with everything from developing codes of conduct to tackling specific policy problems. They could be designated interlocutors for the multitudes of nongovernmental actors, who must be engaged in global governance as they are in domestic governance. Vertical government networks could similarly be designed to implement international rules and strengthen domestic institutions in any number of ways. How well will they do? We cannot know until we try . . .

Vertical networks can also strengthen, encourage, backstop, and trigger the better functioning of their counterpart domestic institutions. Consider again the jurisdictional scheme of the ICC. It reflects a conception of a global criminal justice system that functions above all to try to ensure that nations try their own war criminals or perpetrators of genocide or crimes against humanity. The purpose of a supranational global criminal court is to create an entire range of incentives that maximize the likelihood of those domestic trials taking place, from strengthening the hand of domestic groups who would favor such a course to reminding the domestic courts in question that the international community is monitoring their performance. In part, the aim here, as would be true of a wide variety of horizontal government networks, would be to strengthen domestic government officials as a preventive measure to head off a crisis.

Government networks that were consciously constituted as mechanisms of global governance could also acknowledge the power of discussion and argument in helping generate high-quality solutions to complex problems. For certain types of problems, vigorous discussion and debate is likely to produce the most creative and legitimate alternatives. In addition, government networks constituted in this way could harness the

---

25 In Council for a Community of Democracies homepage (cited 7 July 2003): available from *http://www.ccd21.org.*

positive power of conflict as the foundation of lasting political and social relationships. This understanding of conflict is familiar within democratic societies; it is only within the world of diplomacy, where conflict can escalate to fatal dimensions, that conflict per se is a danger, if not an evil. Among disaggregated government institutions, national and supranational, conflict should be resolved, but not necessarily avoided. It is likely to be the long-term engine of trust.

Note that government networks, both as they exist now and as they could exist, exercise different types of power to accomplish results. They have access to traditional "hard," or coercive, power. The central role of national government officials in government networks means that when the participants make a decision that requires implementation, the power to implement already exists at the national level. The power to induce behavior through selective admission requirements is also a form of hard power. At the same time, much of the work of many horizontal government networks depends on "soft" power—the power of information, socialization, persuasion, and discussion. An effective world order needs to harness every kind of power available . . .

## Conclusion: Pushing the Paradigm

The state is not disappearing; it is disaggregating. Its component institutions—regulators, judges, and even legislators—are all reaching out beyond national borders in various ways, finding that their once "domestic" jobs have a growing international dimension. As they venture into foreign territory, they encounter their foreign counterparts—regulators, judges, and legislators—and create horizontal networks, concluding memoranda of understanding to govern their relations, instituting regular meetings, and even creating their own transgovernmental organizations. They are also, although much less frequently, encountering their supranational counterparts, judge to judge, regulator

to regulator, or legislator to legislator, and establishing vertical networks.

The official observers of the international scene—scholars, pundits, policymakers—cannot fully see and appreciate this phenomenon because they are handicapped by the conceptual lenses of the unitary state. Although they are accustomed to thinking of "governments" domestically—as complex conglomerates of different institutions responsible for different governance functions—they think of "states" internationally. These are purportedly unitary actors represented by the head of state and the foreign minister, represented in other countries and international organizations by professional diplomats. These representatives, in turn, purportedly articulate and pursue a single national interest.

The conception of the unitary state is a fiction, but it has been a useful fiction, allowing analysts to reduce the complexities of the international system to a relatively simple map of political, economic, and military powers interacting with one another both directly and through international organizations. But today it is a fiction that is no longer good enough for government work. It still holds for some critical activity such as decisions to go to war, to engage in a new round of trade negotiations, or to establish new international institutions to tackle specific global problems. But it hides as much as it helps.

Abandoning that fiction and making it possible to see and appreciate these networks is particularly important in a world confronting both the globalization paradox—needing more government but fearing it at the global level—and the rising importance of nonstate actors in the corporate, civic, and criminal sectors. Global governance through government networks would mean harnessing national government officials to address international problems. It would be global governance through national governments, except in circumstances in which those governments concluded that a genuine supranational institution was necessary to exercise genuine global authority.

In those circumstances, which would be the exception rather than the rule, the supranational institutions would be more effective than ever before through the operation of vertical government networks.

At the same time, government networks can significantly expand the capacity of national governments to engage the host of nonstate actors who are themselves operating through networks. Networks of specific national government officials—from environmental regulators to constitutional judges—can anchor broader networks of nonstate actors pursuing global agendas of various types while still retaining a distinct governmental character and specific government responsibilities to their constituents. They can expand regulatory reach far beyond the capacity of any one national government. They can bolster and support their members in adhering to norms of good governance at home and abroad by building trust, cohesion, and common purpose among their members. They can enhance compliance with existing international agreements and deepen and broaden cooperation to create new ones.

But this is only the beginning. Push the paradigm a few steps further and imagine the possibilities. A key identifying feature of current government networks is that they are necessarily informal. Their informality flows not only from the fluidity of networks as an organizational structure, but also, and much more importantly, from the conceptual blind spot that this book seeks to repair: separate government institutions have no independent or formally recognized status in international law and politics. They exist only as part of the abstract and unitary state, aggregated together with all their fellow government institutions. Even those networks that have formalized their interactions, in the sense of establishing an organization such as the Basel Committee or the IOSCO,

have no actual formal status in international law. They operate in the political equivalent of the informal economy, alongside formal international institutions . . .

In practical terms, what this informality means is, crucially, that individual government institutions cannot be subjected to specific obligations or duties under international law. Nor can they exercise specific rights. Sovereignty is possessed by the state as a whole, not by its component parts. Yet suppose individual national government institutions could become bearers of the rights and responsibilities of sovereignty in the global arena. Suppose sovereignty itself could be disaggregated, that it attached to specific government institutions such as courts, regulatory agencies, and legislators or legislative committees. But as exercised by these institutions, the core characteristic of sovereignty would shift from autonomy from outside interference to the capacity to participate in transgovernmental networks of all types.[26] This concept of sovereignty as participation, or status, means that disaggregated sovereignty would empower government institutions around the world to engage with each other in networks that would strengthen them and improve their ability to perform their designated government tasks individually and collectively.

In the process, they could help rebuild states ravaged by conflict, weakened by poverty, disease, and privatization, or stalled in a transition from dictatorship to democracy. If transgovernmental organizations of judges, regulators, or legislators had formal status at the level of international law, they could adopt formal membership criteria and standards of conduct that would create many more pressure points for the global community to act upon a wayward state, but also many more incentives and sources of support for national government officials aspiring to be full

---

[26] Chayes and Chayes, *The New Sovereignty*, 107.

members of the global community yet so often lacking capacity or political and material reinforcement in the domestic struggle against corruption or the arbitrary and often concentrated use of power. Aid, pressure, socialization, and education would no longer flow state to state, but would penetrate the state to the level of specific individuals who constitute a government and must make and implement decisions on the ground.

# 28: The Meaning of Xs and Ys: Social Construction, Gender, and Global Security

*Edward Rhodes*

Medical researchers have long observed significant differences, on average, between the lifetime health problems of individuals born in the first six months of the year and of individuals born in the last six months of the year.[1] The precise reason for these differences is not fully understood. The most common guess offered by researchers is that it is a consequence of the different pre-natal environments experienced *in utero*. On average, mothers-to-be come into contact with more viruses, eat different diets (for example, fewer fresh fruits and vegetables), and are exposed to less sunlight during the winter months than during the summer months. There is also evidence that the seasonal pattern of childbirth in wealthier, more educated families is different from that in poorer, less educated families;[2] this, too, might possibly explain or help to explain the difference in lifetime health patterns among children born at various times in the year.

But whatever the cause, the outcomes are well-documented. Regarded as a group, humans born during the first six months of the year are modestly but statistically significantly more likely to develop a variety of psychological, personality, or learning disorders (schizophrenia, manic/depression, autism, narcolepsy, dyslexia, and diagnosed learning disabilities), to experience diminished fertility earlier, and, in later life, to develop degenerative diseases (Alzheimer's syndrome, multiple sclerosis, Lou Gehrig's disease [ALS], and Parkinson's disease). By contrast, as a group those humans born during the last six months of the year are more

---

1 For a summary of findings see, for example, Marc Lallanilla, "Research Links Month of Birth to Disease," ABCNews, February 3, 2005, http://abcnews.go.com/Health/story?id=118260&page=1, downloaded January 5, 2010. For examples of the research on which these conclusions are based see: Christen J. Willer, David A. Dyment, Dessa Sadovnick, Peter M. Rothwell, T. Jock Murray, George C. Ebers, "Timing of Birth and Risk of Multiple Sclerosis: Population Based Study," *BMJ,* 330:120 (2005), http://bmjcom.highwire.org/cgi/content/abstract/330/7483/120, downloaded January 5, 2010; H.R. Anderson, P.A. Bailey, and J.M. Bland, "The Effect of Birth Month on Asthma, Eczema, Hayfever, Respiratory Symptoms, Lung Function, and Hospital Admissions for Asthma," *International Journal of Epidemiology,* 10:1 (1981), http://ije.oxfordjournals.org/cgi/content/abstract/10/1/45, downloaded January 5, 2010; E. Fuller Torry, Judy Miller, Robert Rawling, Robert H. Yolken, "Seasonal Birth Patterns of Neurological Disorders," *Neuro-epidemiology,* 19:4 (2000), http://content.karger.com/ProdukteDB/produkte.asp?Aktion=ShowAbstract&ArtikelNr=26253&Ausgabe=226236&ProduktNr=224263, downloaded January 5, 2010; "Birth Month Can Affect Your Fertility," *Bio-Medicine,* May 13, 2005, http://www.bio-medicine.org/medicine-news/Birth-month-can-affect-your-fertility-0D-0A-3571-1/, downloaded January 5, 2010.

2 See Justin Lahart, "New Light on the Plight of Winter Babies," WSJ.com, September 22, 2009, http://online.wsj.com/article/SB125356566517528879.html?mod=yhoofront, downloaded January 5, 2010. The research on which this is based can be found at: Kasey Buckles and Daniel M. Hungerman, "Season of Birth and Later Outcomes: Old Questions, New Answers," NBER Working Paper 14573, December 2008, http://www.nd.edu/~dhungerm/w14573.pdf, downloaded January 5, 2010. Note that in neither the usual explanation for health outcome differences (that the season of birth is correlated with different likelihood of exposure to viruses, nutrition, or other input *in utero*) or the possibility raised by Buckles's and Hungerman's finding (that season of birth is correlated with the likelihood of being born into families with different resources) does the month of birth actually *cause* the health outcome. Birth month is simply correlated with some causal factor (e.g., viruses, nutrients, sunlight, or parental and household conditions).

likely to suffer from digestive disorders and breathing problems (for example, celiac disease, Crohn's disease, certain types of asthma, and respiratory syncytial virus [RSV]).

Obviously, not everyone born in the first half of the year will experience cognitive or psychological problems, fertility difficulties, or degenerative disease, and not everyone born in the second half of the year will be free from these. Conversely not everyone born in the second half of the year will develop digestive or breathing difficulties, and not everyone born in the first half of the year will be free from them. One can not even say that any particular individual born in the first half of the year is more (or less) likely to experience one of these medical problems than any particular individual born in the second half of the year. Many other things matter, many of them of them a great deal more than the timing of one's birth. All the evidence does suggest is that *as a group* people born in one half of the year or the other are more (or less) likely to develop particular illnesses or disabilities than is the *group* of people born in the other half of the year. And in fact, the greater or lesser risk is modest: one needs to have the medical records of large populations in order to see that these patterns do exist.

But these patterns *do* exist. Taken as a group, people born in the first half of the year are statistically different from—again, taken as a group—people born in the second half of the year. The medical differences between the groups are *physical* realities. They exist whether or not we are aware of them and whether or not we choose to acknowledge them.

Quite probably there are interesting wider physical implications of these medical differences. Given the nature of the medical problems, one would reasonably expect that on average, the group of humans born in the first half of the year is likely to be stronger and more energetic than the group of humans individuals born in the second half (because members of the January-through-June birth group aren't as likely to suffer from the digestive and respiratory problems). While strong and energetic, the January-through-June group is, on average, also more likely to have trouble learning in school, to be mentally unbalanced, and to degenerate after middle age. By contrast, the July-through-December group is, on average, more likely to be physically weaker, but to be more successful as students, to be better able to cope with society and its complexities, to be better able to bear children, and to stay healthy longer into old age.

## The Social Construction of Identity

*Now, the Star-Belly Sneetches*
*Had bellies with stars.*
*The Plain-Belly Sneetches*
*Had none upon thars.*

*Those stars weren't so big. They were really so small*
*You might think such a thing wouldn't matter at all.*
*But, because they had stars, all the Star-Belly Sneetches*
*Would brag, "We're the best kind of Sneetch on the beaches."*

Dr. Seuss
*The Sneetches and Other Stories*[3]

Our society ignores the significance of birth month (as well as of any star-shaped birthmarks on our bellies). Except for the astrologers among us, we do not categorize individuals according to their birth month. Who we are—how we identify ourselves and are identified by others—is not typically defined by our month of birth.

Imagine for a moment, though, a society that took the real, physical differences between the January-through-June and July-through-December

---

3   Dr. Seuss (Theodor Seuss Geisel), *The Sneetches and Other Stories* (New York: Random House, 1961), pp. 3-4. "The Sneetches", from *The Sneetches and Other Stories* by Dr. Seuss, Trademark™ & Copyright © by Dr. Seuss Enterprises, L.P. 1953, 1954, 1961, renewed 1989. Used by permission of Random House Children's Books, a division of Random House, Inc.

groups seriously, divided its people into two categories based on birth month, and tried to make "appropriate" adjustments to take these differences into account. Children born in the first half of the year might be labeled "earlies." Children born in the second half of the year might be known as "lates."

In such a society, so that everyone would know who was who and would treat everyone appropriately, some sort of identifying marks would be used—for example, earlies might have their hair shaved or cut short, while lates would have their hair left long. To make it visually easier for parents and teachers to tell earlies from lates, children would also be clothed differently: earlies would be dressed in one color (say, black or dark blue) and lates in another color (say, white or light red).

In such a society, because it was understood and accepted that earlies would (at least viewed as a group) be stronger and more active, they would typically be given clothes that facilitated physical activity and comfortable shoes for running and jumping and climbing. Bearing in mind that lates, as a group, would be more susceptible to respiratory problems and would need to watch out for colds, they would be given clothes that discouraged activities that would risk exposure to the elements or to germs, and shoes that would keep their feet warm and dry or that were attractively designed for calm, indoor activities.

Given the physical differences between the groups, society would also develop different expectations about behavior. Earlies would be expected to be more active and, bearing this in mind, earlies would be praised and idealized for their strength, vigor, and athletic ability. A "good" early would be defined as one who was strong and active and courageous, excelled at sports, and displayed substantial muscle mass and coordination. Lates, by contrast, would be expected to be more bookish. Lates would be commended for reading and studying. While not expected to be strong, they would be expected to be smart and artistic, to excel at (or at least to

work very hard at) music and painting. And since they would not be running around building up bulky muscles, breaking bones, and getting dirty, they would be expected to be good looking. While homeliness—even ugliness—for an early would not be a significant social disadvantage, any lack of beauty in a late would be a disgrace.

Teachers and parents would have different expectations about social behavior as well. Given their energy, physical vigor, and learning problems, it would be considered perfectly normal for earlies to be unruly, disruptive, and even to have a violent edge. After all, by nature they are strong and a bit unbalanced. As they got older, society would accept that earlies would be likely to be more violent and confrontational, more likely to solve problems by brute force than by discussion or negotiation, more likely to accept risk, and more likely to be authoritative and demanding. Lates, by contrast, would be expected to be gentle and well-behaved, to seek compromise, and to be risk averse. Given these behavioral expectations, society would view it as normal if social interactions between earlies and lates were often characterized by the earlies being aggressive toward the lates—picking on them, exploiting them, perhaps physically abusing them—and by the lates accepting this treatment, trying to appease the earlies through submission, since fighting back would only outrage the earlies.

Because physical strength is important to earlies—and because all of their training and social treatment emphasizes this—and because earlies are also more susceptible to degenerative physical, mental, and psychological diseases, earlies will peak early. They will regard themselves—and society as a whole will regard them—as shooting stars that flash across life's sky in a blaze of brilliance before burning out. An "old" early is a useless thing. Lates, by contrast, will peak late. They will be expected to keep on getting smarter and to live long lives, at least if they pamper their lungs and digestive tracts as society will urge them to do.

Because they peak early, and because they are expected to be "virile" and physical, society expects earlies to be very interested in sex, and to be proud of their sexual conquests. An early who isn't sexually active at an early age doesn't live up to the "early" reputation. Other earlies are likely to regard sexually inactive or sexually modest earlies with pity (or disdain), and lates may wonder what is wrong with them. Society expects earlies to behave in a promiscuous and sexually aggressive fashion. Earlies will be earlies. By contrast, lates see an advantage in waiting. Lates will want to postpone families, to hold off from sex, until they are better established. "Good" lates will be shy and coy—which is a bit of a problem because lates, remember, are the good-looking ones. Lates who have sex, or who admit to being interested in it, are violating society's expectations for them.

Given that society expects them to peak early and to be successful sexual conquerors at an early age, a successful early will also be expected to make money—lots of money—fast. They need to make money while they are strong; they need to make money to give them sexual allure (especially bearing in mind that it is the lates who are regarded as good looking). Knowing this, of course, families and teachers will be likely to point them toward careers that will allow them to make lots of money. Earlies will be encouraged to be derivatives traders, investment bankers, businessmen, trial lawyers, surgeons. For those earlies who do not seem to have a good head for money, as an alternative they may be pointed toward careers which convey a great deal of power and visibility—for example, careers in politics or the military. Either way, where there is danger, risk, and the potential for money, power, or sex, that's where earlies ought, in society's view, to end up.

Lates, by contrast, are always getting abused and pushed around by the earlies, who are stronger and who have always been encouraged to be physical, head-strong, and violent. Knowing that lates are vulnerable to this sort of exploitation, and wanting to protect them as much as possible from the earlies, families and teachers will point lates toward jobs where they can work at home or in settings where the potential for violence is limited, and where the late's brains and caring qualities will be valued. Lates, for example, get trained to be teachers or nurses.

By the time they are mature young adults, the comparison between earlies and lates in this society is quite striking. Earlies are making (or are expected to be trying to make) lots of money and are (or are expected to be trying to be) in the public eye. If successful, they are a huge credit to their families, and can support their aging parents. Lates, on the other hand, tend to stay at home, make less money, bring less prestige to the family, and are a financial drag on the household (for which they are expected to try to compensate by being useful in whatever other way they can).

If there aren't enough resources to go around, as is the case in many societies in many parts of the world, how will families behave? Given the relative value of earlies and lates, it makes sense (and is accepted by society as making sense) for families to give the resources to the earlies. Food, medicine, schooling will go to the earlies first. The lates will get the leftovers, and if there aren't any leftovers they will go without.

Knowing all this, the birth of an early is celebrated. The birth of a late will be regarded as an unfortunate event. Thinking ahead, families may engage in selective birth control or abortions to do their best to ensure that their children are earlies. This, combined with selective access to health care and to nutrition, means that societies will tend to be skewed in numbers toward earlies.

With time—perhaps not even much time—all of these expectations about the behavior of earlies, the behavior of lates, and the sensible way for society to treat individuals depending on whether they have been labeled as an "early" or a "late" come to be ingrained and regarded as normal by everyone. "Everyone," of course, includes the earlies and lates themselves.

What has emerged in this hypothetical society is a *socially constructed reality.* Based on an identifiable physical, "real" difference—the month of birth—society has *constructed* a social reality. Society has constructed two different categories—"early" and "late"—and has assigned different expectations, behaviors, roles, and treatment to individuals based on which of these categories—that is, based on which of these two "boxes"—an individual, through no fault of his or her own, is put in at the time of birth. In shaping behavior, in creating "institutions" (that is, predictable patterns of behavior around which expectations converge), and in generating rules that are regarded as "normal," this social reality is no less "real" and no less consequential than physical reality.

## Sex and Gender

*First of all there is one thing you should know. Am I a boy? Or am I a girl? Well, I'll tell you. I am a _____."*

—Dr. Seuss and Roy McKie
*My Book about Me,* page 1.[4]

Obviously, no society puts individuals in a lifelong "box" at the time of birth based on what month he or she was born in. But nearly all (indeed, arguably all) societies *do* put individuals in a lifelong box at the time of birth based on the individual's sex.

Sex, like month of birth, is a physical fact. It exists whether we pay attention to it or not. Human males have a Y chromosome as well as an X chromosome. Human females have two X chromosomes.[5] This difference exists *prior to* and *independent of* any human awareness of the fact. Similarly, there are physical differences between the two sexes that are typically a consequence of the genetic difference, and these differences exist regardless of human awareness of them. Human males usually develop testes. Human females usually develop ovaries. It is usual for the two sexes to have different hormonal mixes, which affects the development of a wide variety of organs as well as directly affecting behavior. On average, human males taken as a group are larger and stronger than human females,

---

4  Dr. Seuss (Theodor Seuss Geisel) and Roy McKie, *My Book about Me* (New York: Random House, 1969), p. 1. Actually, the *first* thing—even before the first page of the book, on the inside cover and the facing page—is "My name is _____. I don't care if you like my name or not. *That's* my name. It's the only name I've got." But the first *collective* identity in Dr. Seuss's world, and in the world that Dr. Seuss helps children construct for themselves, is gender. This gender identity—am I a boy or a girl?—comes immediately after and is secondary only to *individual* identity, which for a liberal of course must be prior to all else. For Dr. Seuss and the children using his book, gender comes before any *physical* description (size, physical development, appearance) or any political or economic identifier (nation-state; number of beds, pictures, forks, lights, clocks, mirrors, or taps in the house). More important than knowing whether one is big or small, Afghan or Albanian, rich in things or poor in things, is knowing whether one is a boy or a girl. From *My Book About Me* by Dr. Seuss, illustrated by Roy McKie, Trademark™ & Copyright © by Dr. Seuss Enterprises, L. P. 1969, renewed 1997. Used by permission of Random House Children's Books, a division of Random House, Inc.

5  One can of course argue whether there are or are not exactly two sexes and whether the sexes are altogether distinct from each other. Certain relatively unusual genetic occurrences, such as Klinefelter's syndrome and Turner's syndrome, involve chromosomal compositions other than the typical XX and XY – XXY in the case of Klinefelter's syndrome and a single X in the case of Turner's. If "male" is defined as an XY chromosomal makeup and "female" is defined as an XX chromosomal makeup, there are a small but nontrivial number of human beings who are neither male nor female. That is the *number* of sexes is socially constructed: societies may insist there are only two (and choose to lump individuals with chromosomal compositions other than XX or XY either into the "male" sex box or the "female" sex box), or they may conclude there are three (male, female, and "intersex"), or they may conclude there are some number greater than three. Further, even in the case of individuals with "normal" XX or XY chromosomal makeup, atypical development of sexual organs and unusual hormonal balances are not infrequent. The 2009 case of South African runner Caster Semenya is illustrative. Thus to say that sex is a physical reality is *not* to say that it is always obvious what an individual's sex is, or that reasonable people will all agree about the sex of a particular individual, or that sex is necessarily an either (male)/or (female) dichotomy. Further complicating the picture, "sex change" operations to remove organs and to change physical structures and hormonal conditions are possible; if maleness or femaleness is judged by the presence or absence of particular organs, physical structures, or hormones, human sex is not an unalterable physical reality. (For a good discussion of some of these issues, see Anne Fausto-Sterling, *Sexing the Body* (New York: Basic Books, 2000).) None of this, however, impacts the argument that follows.

though this is a statistical difference—some females are larger and stronger than some males. Human females typically live longer than human males, particularly if they do not die during childbirth. Again, this is a statistical difference: some males live longer than some females. On average, human males are more prone to certain psychological and cognitive disorders. Again, this is a statistical difference: some men do not suffer from these disorders and some women do. In sum, males as a collective group are not unlike January-through-June babies as a collective group in our earlier example, and females not unlike the July-through-December group.

Like month of birth, in humans *sex* is a physical reality. It is not a socially constructed one.[6]

But what *is* a social construction is *gender.* Like the categories "early" and "late," the categories "man" (or "boy" or "masculine") and "woman" (or "girl" or "feminine") are ones that societies create. An XY chromosomal endowment—being a male—is a physical reality, but the category "man" exists only because society has created it. Similarly, the category "woman" exists only because society has created it. Our society (indeed every human society that we know of) thinks that sex matters. And it has created two boxes. At the time of our birth, society puts us into one of these two boxes, based on whether we have two X chromosomes or just one (or, more accurately, based on whether we have a penis). In the era before ultrasound and other pre-natal testing, an obstetrician's first pronouncement after delivery was expected to be "it's a boy" or "it's a girl." From that very first introduction—even prior to being given an individual name or even being named by a family name—we are put in a gender box. We are identified by our gender. Each gender box carries with it certain expectations—expectations about how we will behave, how we will treat

others and be treated by them, what we will do with our lives, and how much our lives will be cherished or valued.

Whether a physician, or parents, or society at large pronounces the fact or not, a child is a male or a female. It *becomes* a boy or a girl, a man or a woman, only because it and society identify it as one. (And there may be disagreements: sometimes society identifies an individual as a man, while that individual self-identifies as a woman, or vice-versa. In this case the individual's gender, unlike his or her sex, is problematic.)

As with the "early"/"late" illustration above, the social construction of "man" and "woman" may in some way be based upon physical differences that, on average, exist between the individuals who are put into each of these boxes. But some females are bigger and stronger and exhibit more "male" physique than some males. And some males are smaller and less strong and exhibit more "female" physique than some females. This does not change their gender assignment, the roles and behaviors society assigns to them or expects from them, or the "rights" that society assigns to them in claims on the distribution of power, authority, and social benefits.

As feminist theorists have observed, the "man/woman" distinction that is socially constructed in societies around the world virtually always constructs these categories in ways which suggest that men *ought* to rule over women, and that women *ought* to be ruled over by men. This is the idea of *patriarchy.* Patriarchy implies a construction of manliness in terms of what has been described as "hegemonic masculinity."[7] Hegemonic masculinity suggests that the essence of being a man—that is, of meeting the expectations that are socially created for those that society has put in the category or "box" of man—is dominance over the "other," woman.

---

6  Interestingly, in some animals, sex *is* socially constructed: in some species, an individual will change from male to female—that is, will lose male sex organs and develop female ones—or the reverse depending on the social environment in which that individual finds itself. As biologically fascinating as this is, however, it is not relevant to humans.

7  See, for example, R.W. Connell, *Masculinities,* second edition (Cambridge, UK: Polity, 2005).

This patriarchal construction of identity not only privileges men over women, but privileges gender as an identity: it assumes that gender is a critical way of defining who we are—that gender matters. It assumes, as does Dr. Seuss in *My Book about Me,* that gender is the first, or one of the first, things one must know about someone in order to create social relationships and establish social order. Much as a Marxist construction of social reality suggests that what truly matters, what truly defines our interests and creates the real foundation for ordered (or misordered) human interaction, is economic class not the false consciousness of national identity, a patriarchal construction of social reality concludes that what essentially shapes our interests and our understanding of them is our gender.

## Gender and World Politics

*What are our fathers made of, made of?*
*What are our fathers made of?*
*Pipes and smoke and collars choke;*
*That's what our fathers are made of.*

*What are our mothers made of, made of?*
*What are our mothers made of?*
*Ribbons and laces and sweet pretty faces;*
*That's what our mothers are made of.*
　　　　　　　　—Traditional Nursery Rhyme[8]

Feminist theorists have pointed out the harm done by the gendering of identity and by patriarchal constructions of gender. The harm to women is perhaps most obvious: women are rendered subservient. More perniciously, their social identities are constructed in such a way that women are likely to come to believe that it is right and good to be subservient (or at least for *them* to be subservient—men, of course, would be unmanly if they were subservient). This construction not only denies them authority in the community and authority over their own lives, but denies them the belief—even in their own minds—that they *ought* to have authority in the community or over their own lives.

But feminist theorists astutely note that men, too, are harmed by patriarchy, much as the master as well as the slave is harmed by a master/slave relationship. By defining gender as a central element in individual identity and defining manliness in terms of domination, patriarchy twists and warps men into dominators, leading them to measure their success in achieving their essence in terms of their ability to hold others in subordination. Men are trapped by this construction of reality in a constant struggle to dominate others, and to avoid the loss of "masculinity" associated with failing in this effort.

Feminist theorists note the centrality of gendered identity and pervasiveness of patriarchy throughout social relationships and social institutions, including political ones. As feminist theorists have noted, patriarchy has a critical impact on where societies draw the divide between "public" activities and "private" ones. Because the dominance of men over women is regarded as normal, political institutions set aside a "private" sphere of life, outside the realm of public interference or regulation, in which men are permitted to dominate over women. In activities in this private sphere, men are granted sovereignty—highest authority—over women, as they are over children and others appropriately held in subordination. The public sphere, by contrast, is one in which men struggle for authority and dominance over each other.

What do these insights from feminist theory regarding gender, gendered identity, and patriarchy, suggest about world politics? Recognition of the socially constructed nature of gender and the pervasiveness of patriarchy leads to five important observations. While distinct, these five observations are interlinked in important ways.[9]

---

8　"What Folks Are Made Of," attributed to Robert Southey (1774–1843). First known publication by Burton Stevenson, Copyright © 1820.

9　For an excellent summary of feminist insights into international relations, see Denise M. Horn, "Feminist Approaches to International Relations," in Mary Hawkesworth and Maurice Kogan, eds., *Encyclopedia of Government and Politics,* second edition (London: Routledge, 2003).

(1) The first of these observations is the stunning—and stunningly overlooked—failure of the modern state in the performance of its essential function, that of providing security. Roughly half of the subjects of the world's states are, by virtue of their gender identity, victims or potential victims of a variety of kinds of violence, abuse, or discrimination. They are outside the state's protection, at least to the extent that the violence against them is a "private" matter within the family. They are targets simply because they have been labeled as women. If they were denied the state's protection or were harmed or discriminated because they were of a particular race, ethnicity, language, or religion, what we observe would in all likelihood be condemned by the world community, and international intervention would be a real possibility. But because harm done to women generally occurs within a family setting, it is typically regarded by the state—and by society—as a "private" matter. It is not a public concern. It is invisible.

The magnitude of "private" violence against women is simply astounding. In India, for example, something in the neighborhood of 4% or 5% of females are either aborted as fetuses or are killed in their first six years of life from deliberate infanticide, neglect, or selective denial of resources, simply because they have been categorized as women and not worth keeping alive. In China, the preference for boy children over girl children and the availability of sex-selective abortion has meant that the gender ratio among newborns is now on the order of 118 boys for each 100 girls. Since a normal ratio is about 105 boys for each 100 girls, this suggests that even before birth, approximately 5% of all female fetuses were aborted for no other reason than they would have resulted in girls. In some parts of China, the imbalance may well be twice as great. Estimates are that, globally, there are about 100 million women "missing" today—individuals that, statistically, given the number of men alive today and what we know about natural birth and mortality rates, we would expect to see alive but are not. The missing individuals were aborted for no reason other than the fact that prenatal testing indicated the fetus was female, or fell prey to gender-based infanticide, abuse, or neglect.[10] Their crime? Simply being categorized as women or potential women. To put the 100 million number in perspective, consider that the world's most deadly war, World War II, resulted in "only" 25 million military fatalities and perhaps another 40 or 50 million civilian deaths, including those from starvation and disease. In other words, violence and discrimination against women has had a substantially higher death toll than World War II.

Nor is that the end of it. Women who survive are disproportionately deprived of opportunities to be economically productive.[11] The two ingredients needed to increase the productivity of labor—access to capital and access to education—are routinely denied to individuals simply because they have been labeled "women." Again, were access to capital or to education so routinely denied on the basis of race, ethnicity, language, or religion, it would be regarded by the world political community as a serious matter. The pervasiveness of patriarchy and the public/private divide that places "family" decisions outside of political bounds, however, has permitted the continuation of this sort of structural violence.

---

10  See, for example, Amartya Sen, "More Than 100 Million Women Are Missing," *New York Review of Books,* 37:20 (December 20, 1990), http://www.nybooks.com/articles/3408, downloaded January 5, 2010.

11  The United Nations Development Program has claimed that 70% of the world's poor are women. The empirical basis for this claim is unclear, however, and it probably overstates the reality. See, for example, Alain Mercoux of the UN Food and Agriculture Organization: Mercoux, "The Feminization of Poverty," *SD Dimensions,* June 1997, http://www.fao.org/sd/wpdirect/wpan0015.htm, downloaded January 5, 2010.

While, arguably, progress is being made in reducing gender disparities in education and access to capital, the problem of "missing women" is growing. Observed globally, imbalances in gender ratios continue to increase.

If the modern state system is understood as a set of political institutions designed to control and limit violence, then in a profound sense these data suggest the state system is failing today. It is only the cloak of invisibility thrown over this violence by patriarchy that prevents recognition of this fact.

(2) The second observation is the gendered nature of the state itself. The simplest version of this argument is that the state has typically been the domain of men and a tool of men's domination. The fact that some women have occupied positions of political authority, even as heads of state and heads of government, can not obscure the fact that state institutions of power have typically been dominated by men. "Statesmen"—literally, men governing the state, working the levers of its power, and operating as its agents—have been, and are, typically *men*. And the policies that states have pursued have, in general, passively endorsed or actively supported the preservation of patriarchy in national and international society.

A more complex version of the argument is that the state's very nature is an expression of a patriarchal understanding of political life. The ordering principles of the state are those of hierarchy and domination. The relationship of state to subject, as well as the relationship of individuals within the state, is one of domination and subordination, mirroring the relationship between man and woman. The relationship between states is analogous to that between men: whatever the nominal *de jure* equality of the participants, the relationship is a constant struggle to dominate and to avoid domination. As

some feminist theorists have suggested, just as men fear the loss of manliness that would come from being dominated by another man (and therefore seek to prove their manliness by dominating not only women but other men), states fear the loss of "stateness" that would come if other states could dominate them (and therefore seek to prove their "stateness" by dominating other states as well as their own subjects).[12]

Interestingly, what we witness in today's world is the emergence of a second set of political institutions—organized on different principles, often run by women, and addressing today's security problems using very different strategies. These new political institutions are non-governmental organizations (NGOs). In general these are much less hierarchical in internal organization, rely on networking rather than command, and have *volunteer* members rather than *subjects*. Unlike states, they do not seek to "rule" or to solve problems through the subjugation of others and the imposition of will—in other words, they do not behave in a patriarchal fashion.

(3) The third observation is that it is hard to see any way to solve the central problems of the "new" global security agenda that has emerged with globalization without increasing reliance on this new, second set of political institutions now emerging and without protecting and empowering women. Globalization—the decreasing importance of physical location and of political boundaries, as technology reduces the difficulties of moving things, people, and ideas around the world—is transforming a variety of threats to human security that were formerly typically local or national ones into regional or global ones. Disease, crime, poverty, environmental degradation, urbanization, and migration now are unlikely to be controllable by local or even national authorities. Equally important,

---

12 On the fundamentally androcentric construction of the state and state system, see for example J. Ann Tickner, "Hans Morgenthau's Principles of Political Realism: A Feminist Reformulation," in Rebecca Grant and Kathleen Newlands, eds., *Gender and International Relations* (Bloomington: Indiana University Press, 1991).

they are interlinked problems: it is difficult to imagine satisfactorily addressing any of them without making substantial progress on the others.

Both because of its limited territorial reach and because of its hierarchical, bureaucratic structure, the state is sub-optimally designed to address this global nexus of problems. Indeed, NGOs and other network-based institutional models seem destined to play a critical supporting role, at a minimum, in addressing most of these problems and may well play the leading role in addressing at least some.

It is also very difficult to imagine successfully addressing at least some of these "new" global security problems—for example, poverty—without empowering women. Development economists have long observed the importance of women in solving the problem of economic underdevelopment. Women's labor is underutilized when women are denied equal access to education and capital. More interestingly, development economists have documented that women typically make better, more efficient use of education and capital than do men: expenditures on women's education and provision of capital to women do not merely pay returns equivalent to their provision to men, they pay greater returns. Patriarchal constructions of identity that subordinate women and deny them the ability to compete for resources like education and capital are thus a substantial obstacle to addressing today's new global security issues.

(4) In his adaptation of *Pygmalion,* playwright George Bernard Shaw has his protagonist, Professor Henry Higgins, complain, "Why can't a woman be more like a man?" The fourth observation is that when it comes to addressing the "old" security agenda (that is, the problem of classical interstate war), Shaw and Higgins may have got the problem exactly backward. Given the increasing costliness, destructiveness, and indecisiveness of interstate war, the question we arguably need to be asking is: "Why can't a man be more like a woman?"

If feminist theory's central argument regarding patriarchy is correct, patriarchy constructs men to seek solutions through power and domination. The manly man is a warrior and victor, not a mediator or compromiser. Collective, cooperative solutions are disdained. Real men win. They don't resolve.

But "winning" wars is difficult in today's world. A war between the great powers, if fought to "victory," would be unimaginably destructive. Even were globally catastrophic consequences like nuclear winter avoided, it is easy to imagine the survivors envying the dead. Wars between great powers and smaller powers—for example, the U.S. war in Iraq—appear increasingly unlikely to yield decisive political results. More broadly, one could argue that as the world moves closer toward what political scientists Robert Keohane and Joseph Nye long ago described as "complex interdependence,"[13] the utility of military force, and of threats of military force, in achieving desired political outcomes diminishes.

Increasingly, then, what is needed is an approach and a mindset that focuses not on winning, on victory, on domination, and on the imposition of one's will on the "other," but on compromise, collaboration, and finding solutions to dilemmas of collective action. So long as patriarchy-shaped notions of identity dominate, this is unlikely.

(5) The final observation is that patriarchal institutions not only fail to provide security but contain within themselves the seeds of their own destruction. The devaluation of women results in underproduction of females—that is, given the lower value of women in a patriarchal society,

---

13  Robert Keohane and Joseph Nye, *Power and Interdependence* (Boston: Little, Brown, 1977).

individuals and families will find ways to minimize the number of women produced by their households, resulting in shortages of marriageable women and a "surplus" of men unable to perform the roles dictated for them by patriarchy. As political scientists Valerie Hudson and Andrea den Boer have observed, however, historical evidence suggests that as gender imbalances increase, societal stability decreases and it becomes increasingly difficult for the state to maintain domestic order and for states to eschew war.[14] As men struggle to find ways to perform the roles dictated by patriarchy, the state's ability to dominate and to control and limit violence within patriarchal norms ultimately collapses. Unfettered patriarchy thus threatens to destroy patriarchal institutions.

## Conclusions

*Where have all the young girls gone?*
*Taken husbands every one*
*When will they ever learn?*
*When will they ever learn?. . . .*

*Where have all the young men gone?*
*Gone for soldiers every one*
*When will they ever learn?*
*When will they ever learn?. . . .*
—"Where Have All the Flowers Gone?"
Pete Seeger[15]

We live in a world not simply of physical realities, but of socially constructed ones. Human behavior is shaped not simply by physical realities but by our socially constructed understanding of these realities and by the meanings we read into them. Identity is an obvious example of a socially constructed reality. Our identity matters—it

defines how we think of ourselves in relation to others, what obligations or rights we feel in dealings with others, and what behaviors we conclude are normal, necessary, or appropriate in our interaction with others. But our identity is not a physical reality. Rather, it emerges—that is, it is constructed—through our interaction with others. We learn who we are and what our roles and relationships should and will be like through praxis and communication—that is, through our dealings with each other. The "markers" we use in identifying ourselves and the "other" may well involve physical realities—the month of our birth, the presence or absence of star-shaped birthmarks on our abdomens, our skin color, the length of our hair, the presence or absence of a penis, whether we have had ritual scarring or tattooing performed on our body, our height, whether or not our genitals have been "circumcised." Some of these "markers" may be ones we were born with. Others may be the consequence of things done by us or to us, either with our consent or without it. Some "markers" may not even be physical—they may, for example, involve the language we speak, the religion we observe, the type of breakfast we eat, or the kind of music to which we listen.[16] But in any case, these are simply markers. Whether or not any particular marker or identifier *matters* is a matter of social construction.

Feminist theorists have observed that gendered identity and patriarchal constructions of gender identity have significant implications for political life and for global politics. The violence and structural violence inherent in patriarchy, as well as the patriarchal construction of certain key political institutions such as the state, result in a global political system that fails in the fundamental task of providing human security.

---

14 Valerie Hudson and Andrea den Boer, *Bare Branches* (Cambridge: MIT University Press, 2004).

15 From *Where Have All the Flowers Gone?* by Pete Seeger. Copyright © 1981 by Sanga Music/Figs. D Music. Reprinted by permission.

16 Dr. Seuss, for example, imagines two peoples, Yooks and Zooks, whose only noticeable distinguishing characteristic is whether they eat their bread with the buttered side up or down. The consequences are not as amusing, Seuss argues, as the premises. See Dr. Seuss (Theodor Seuss Geisel and Audrey S. Geisel), *The Butter Battle Book* (New York: Random House, 1984).

Feminist theory thus offers an important perspective on the problem of violence, on the peculiar and flawed nature of the institutions (for example, the modern state) that have been established to deal with violence, and the changes that would be necessary to reduce violence. The implication that flows from this argument is that, ultimately, success in addressing global security issues will require de-gendering identity or, at the very minimum, creating gendered identities that break traditional molds associated with patriarchy.

# 29: The Causes of Terrorism

## Martha Crenshaw

Terrorism occurs both in the context of violent resistance to the state as well as in the service of state interests. If we focus on terrorism directed against governments for purposes of political change, we are considering the premeditated use or threat of symbolic, low-level violence by conspiratorial organizations. Terrorist violence communicates a political message; its ends go beyond damaging an enemy's material resources.[1] The victims or objects of terrorist attack have little intrinsic value to the terrorist group but represent a larger human audience whose reaction the terrorists seek. Violence characterized by spontaneity, mass participation, or a primary intent of physical destruction can therefore be excluded from our investigation.

The study of terrorism can be organized around three questions: why terrorism occurs, how the process of terrorism works, and what its social and political effects are. Here the objective is to outline an approach to the analysis of the causes of terrorism, based on comparison of different cases of terrorism, in order to distinguish a common pattern of causation from the historically unique.

We would not wish to claim that a general explanation of the sources of terrorism is a simple task, but it is possible to make a useful beginning by establishing a theoretical order for different types and levels of causes. We approach terrorism as a form of political behavior resulting from the deliberate choice of a basically rational actor, the terrorist organization. A comprehensive explanation, however, must also take into account the environment in which terrorism occurs and address the question of whether broad political, social, and economic conditions make terrorism more likely in some contexts than in others. What sort of circumstances lead to the formation of a terrorist group? On the other hand, only a few of the people who experience a given situation practice terrorism. Not even all individuals who share the goals of a terrorist organization agree that terrorism is the best means. It is essential to consider the psychological variables that may encourage or inhibit individual participation in terrorist actions . . .

To develop a framework for the analysis of likely settings for terrorism, we must establish conceptual distinctions among different types of factors. First, a significant difference exists between *preconditions,* factors that set the stage for terrorism over the long run, and *precipitants,* specific events that immediately precede the occurrence of terrorism. Second, a further classification divides preconditions into enabling or permissive factors, which provide opportunities for terrorism to happen, and situations that directly inspire and motivate terrorist campaigns. Precipitants are similar to the direct causes of

---

1 For discussions of the meaning of the concept of terrorism, see Thomas P. Thornton, "Terror as a Weapon of Political Agitation," in Harry Eckstein, ed. *Internal War* (New York, 1964), pp. 71–99; Martha Crenshaw Hutchinson, "The Concept of Revolutionary Terrorism," *Revolutionary Terrorism: The FLN in Algeria, 1954–1962* (Stanford: The Hoover Institution Press, 1978) chap. 2; and E. Victor Walter, *Terror and Resistance* (New York, 1969).

From *Journal of Comparative Politics, Volume 13, Issue 4, July 1981* by Martha Crenshaw. Copyright © 1981 by City University of New York. Reprinted by permission.

terrorism.[2] Furthermore, no factor is neatly compartmentalized in a single nation-state; each has a transnational dimension that complicates the analysis.

First, modernization produces an interrelated set of factors that is a significant permissive cause of terrorism, as increased complexity on all levels of society and economy creates opportunities and vulnerabilities. Sophisticated networks of transportation and communication offer mobility and the means of publicity for terrorists. The terrorists of Narodnaya Volya would have been unable to operate without Russia's newly established rail system, and the Popular Front for the Liberaton of Palestine could not indulge in hijacking without the jet aircraft. In Algeria, the FLN only adopted a strategy of urban bombings when they were able to acquire plastic explosives. In 1907, the Combat Organization of the Socialist-Revolutionary party paid 20,000 rubles to an inventor who was working on an aircraft in the futile hope of bombing the Russian imperial palaces from the air.[3] Today we fear that terrorists will exploit the potential of nuclear power, but it was in 1867 that Nobel's invention of dynamite made bombings a convenient terrorist tactic.

Urbanization is part of the modern trend toward aggregation and complexity, which increases the number and accessibility of targets and methods. P.N. Grabosky has recently argued that cities are a significant cause of terrorism in that they provide an opportunity (a multitude of targets, mobility, communications, anonymity, and audiences) and a recruiting ground among the politicized and volatile inhabitants.[4]

Social "facilitation," which Gurr found to be extremely powerful in bringing about civil strife in general, is also an important permissive factor. This concept refers to social habits and historical traditions that sanction the use of violence against the government, making it morally and politically justifiable, and even dictating an appropriate form, such as demonstrations, coups, or terrorism. Social myths, traditions, and habits permit the development of terrorism as an established political custom. An excellent example of such a tradition is the case of Ireland, where the tradition of physical force dates from the eighteenth century, and the legend of Michael Collins in 1919–21 still inspires and partially excuses the much less discriminate and less effective terrorism of the contemporary Provisional IRA in Northern Ireland.

Moreover, broad attitudes and beliefs that condone terrorism are communicated transnationally. Revolutionary ideologies have always crossed borders with ease. In the nineteenth and early twentieth centuries, such ideas were primarily a European preserve, stemming from the French and Bolshevik Revolutions. Since the Second World War, Third World revolutions— China, Cuba. Algeria—and intellectuals such as Frantz Fanon and Carlos Marighela[5] have significantly influenced terrorist movements in the developed West by promoting the development of terrorism as routine behavior.

The most salient political factor in the category of permissive causes is a government's

---

2 A distinction between preconditions and precipitants is found in Eckstein, "On the Etiology of Internal Wars," *History and Theory,* 4 (1965), 133–62. Kenneth Waltz also differentiates between the framework for action as a permissive or underlying cause and special reasons as immediate or efficient causes. In some cases we can say of terrorism, as he says of war, that it occurs because there is nothing to prevent it. See *Man, the State and War* (New York, 1959), p. 232.

3 Boris Savinkov, *Memoirs of a Terrorist,* trans. Joseph Shaplen (New York: A. & C. Boni, 1931), pp. 286–87.

4 Grabosky, "The Urban Context of Political Terrorism," in Michael Stohl, ed., pp. 51–76.

5 See Amy Sands Redlick, "The Transnational Flow of Information as a Cause of Terrorism," in Yonah Alexander, David Carlton, and Wilkinson, eds. *Terrorism: Theory and Practice* (Boulder, 1979), pp. 73–95. See also Manus I. Midlarsky, Martha Crenshaw, and Fumihiko Yoshida, "Why Violence Spreads: The Contagion of International Terrorism," *International Studies Quarterly,* 24 (June 1980), 262–98.

inability or unwillingness to prevent terrorism. The absence of adequate prevention by police and intelligence services permits the spread of conspiracy. However, since terrorist organizatons are small and clandestine, the majority of states can be placed in the permissive category. Inefficiency or leniency can be found in a broad range of all but the most brutally efficient dictatorships, including incompetent authoritarian states such as tsarist Russia on the eve of the emergence of Narodnaya Volya as well as modern liberal democratic states whose desire to protect civil liberties constrains security measures.

Turning now to a consideration of the direct causes of terrorism, we focus on background conditions that positively encourage resistance to the state. These instigating circumstances go beyond merely creating an environment in which terrorism is possible; they provide motivation and direction for the terrorist movement. We are dealing here with reasons rather than opportunities.

The first condition that can be considered a direct cause of terrorism is the existence of concrete grievances among an identifiable subgroup of a larger population, such as an ethnic minority discriminated against by the majority. A social movement develops in order to redress these grievances and to gain either equal rights or a separate state; terrorism is then the resort of an extremist faction of this broader movement. In practice, terrorism has frequently arisen in such situations: in modern states, separatist nationalism among Basques, Bretons, and Québeçois has motivated terrorism. In the colonial era, nationalist movements commonly turned to terrorism.

The second condition that creates motivations for terrorism is the lack of opportunity for political participation. Regimes that deny access to power and persecute dissenters create dissatisfaction. In this case, grievances are primarily political, without social or economic overtones. Discrimination is not directed against any ethnic,

religious, or racial subgroup of the population. The terrorist organization is not necessarily part of a broader social movement; indeed, the population may be largely apathetic. In situations where paths to the legal expression of opposition are blocked, but where the regime's repression is inefficient, revolutionary terrorism is doubly likely, as permissive and direct causes coincide. An example of this situation is tsarist Russia in the 1870s.

Context is especially significant as a direct cause of terrorism when it affects an elite, not the mass population. Terrorism is essentially the result of elite disaffection; it represents the strategy of a minority, who may act on behalf of a wider popular constituency who have not been consulted about, and do not necessarily approve of, the terrorists' aims or methods. There is remarkable relevance in E.J. Hobsbawn's comments on the political conspirators of post-Napoleonic Europe: "All revolutionaries regarded themselves, with some justification, as small elites of the emancipated and progressive operating among, and for the eventual benefit of, a vast and inert mass of the ignorant and misled common people, which would no doubt welcome liberation when it came, but could not be expected to take much part in preparing it."[6] Many terrorists today are young, well-educated, and middle class in background. Such students or young professionals, with prior political experience, are disillusioned with the prospects of changing society and see little chance of access to the system despite their privileged status. Much terrorism has grown out of student unrest; this was the case in nineteenth century Russia as well as post-World War II West Germany, Italy, the United States, Japan, and Uruguay.

The last category of situational factors involves the concept of a precipitating event that immediately precedes outbreaks of terrorism. Although it is generally thought that precipitants

---

6   E.J. Hobsbawm, *Revolutionaries: Contemporary Essays* (New York; 1973), p. 143.

are the most unpredictable of causes, there does seem to be a common pattern of government actions that act as catalysts for terrorism. Government use of unexpected and unusual force in response to protest or reform attempts often compels terrorist retaliation. The development of such an action-reaction syndrome then establishes the structure of the conflict between the regime and its challengers. There are numerous historical examples of a campaign of terrorism precipitated by a government's reliance on excessive force to quell protest or squash dissent. The tsarist regime's severity in dealing with the populist movement was a factor in the development of Narodaya Volya as a terrorist organization in 1879. The French government's persecution of anarchists was a factor in subsequent anarchist terrorism in the 1890s. The British government's execution of the heros of the Easter Rising set the stage for Michael Collins and the IRA. The Protestant violence that met the Catholic civil rights movement in Northern Ireland in 1969 pushed the Provisional IRA to retaliate. In West Germany, the death of Beno Ohnesorg at the hands of the police in a demonstration against the Shah of Iran in 1968 contributed to the emergence of the RAF.

This analysis of the background conditions for terrorism indicates that we must look at the terrorist organization's perception and interpretation of the situation. Terrorists view the context as permissive, making terrorism a viable option. In a material sense, the means are placed at their disposal by the environment. Circumstances also provide the terrorists with compelling reasons for seeking political change. Finally, an event occurs that snaps the terrorists' patience with the regime. Government action is now seen as intolerably unjust, and terrorism becomes not only a possible decision but a morally acceptable one.

The regime has forfeited its status as the standard of legitimacy. For the terrorist, the end may now excuse the means.

## The Reasons for Terrorism

Significant campaigns of terrorism depend on rational political choice. As purposeful activity, terrorism is the result of an organization's decision that it is a politically useful means to oppose a government. The argument that terrorist behavior should be analyzed as "rational" is based on the assumption that terrorist organizations possess internally consistent sets of values, beliefs, and images of the environment. Terrorism is seen collectively as a logical means to advance desired ends. The terrorist organization engages in decision-making calculations that an analyst can approximate. In short, the terrorist group's reasons for resorting to terrorism constitute an important factor in the process of causation.[7]

Terrorism serves a variety of goals, both revolutionary and subrevolutionary. Terrorists may be revolutionaries (such as the Combat Organization of the Socialist-Revolutionary Party in the nineteenth century or the Tupamaros of the twentieth); nationalists fighting against foreign occupiers (the Algerian FLN, the IRA of 1919–21, or the Irgun); minority separatists combatting indigenous regimes (such as the Corsican, Breton, and Basque movements, and the Provisional IRA); reformists (the bombing of nuclear construction sites, for example, is meant to halt nuclear power, not to overthrow governments); anarchists or millenarians (such as the original anarchist movement of the nineteenth century and modern millenarian groups such as the Red Army faction in West Germany, the Italian Red Brigades, and the Japanese Red Army); or reactionaries acting to prevent change

---

7    See Barbara Salert's critique of the rational choice model of revolutionary participation in *Revolutions and Revolutionaries* (New York, 1976). In addition, Abraham Kaplan discusses the distinction between reasons and causes in "The Psychodynamics of Terrorism," *Terrorism—An International Journal,* 1, 3 and 4 (1978), 237–54.

from the top (such as the Secret Army Organization during the Algerian war or the contemporary Ulster Defence Association in Northern Ireland).[8]

However diverse the long-run goals of terrorist groups, there is a common pattern of proximate or short-run objectives of a terrorist strategy. Proximate objectives are defined in terms of the reactions that terrorists want to achieve in their different audiences.[9] The most basic reason for terrorism is to gain recognition or attention— what Thornton called advertisement of the cause. Violence and bloodshed always excite human curiosity, and the theatricality, suspense, and threat of danger inherent in terrorism enhance its attention-getting qualities. In fact, publicity may be the highest goal of some groups. For example, terrorists who are fundamentally protesters might be satisfied with airing their grievances before the world. Today, in an interdependent world, the need for international recognition encourages transnational terrorist activities, with escalation to ever more destructive and spectacular violence. As the audience grows larger, more diverse, and more accustomed to terrorism, terrorists must go to extreme lengths to shock.

Terrorism is also often designed to disrupt and discredit the processes of government, by weakening it administratively and impairing normal operations. Terrorism as a direct attack on the regime aims at the insecurity and demoralization of government officials, independent of any impact on public opinion. An excellent example of this strategy is Michael Collins's campaign against the British intelligence system

in Ireland in 1919-21. This form of terrorism often accompanies rural guerrilla warfare, as the insurgents try to weaken the government's control over its territory.

Terrorism also affects public attitudes in both a positive and a negative sense, aiming at creating either sympathy in a potential constituency or fear and hostility in an audience identified as the "enemy." These two functions are interrelated, since intimidating the "enemy" impresses both sympathizers and the uncommitted. At the same time, terrorism may be used to enforce obedience in an audience from whom the terrorists demand allegiance. The FLN in Algeria, for example, claimed more Algerian than French victims. Fear and respect were not incompatible with solidarity against the French.[10] When terrorism is part of a struggle between incumbents and challengers, polarization of public opinion undermines the government's legitimacy.

Terrorism may also be intended to provoke a counterreaction from the government, to increase publicity for the terrorists' cause and to demonstrate to the people that their charges against the regime are well founded. The terrorists mean to force the state to show its true repressive face, thereby driving the people into the arms of the challengers. For example, Carlos Marighela argued that the way to win popular support was to provoke the regime to measures of greater repression and persecution.[11] Provocative terrorism is designed to bring about revolutionary conditions rather than to exploit them. The FLN against the French, the Palestinians against Israel, and the RAF against the

---

8  For a typology of terrorist organizations, see Wilkinson, *Political Terrorism* (New York, 1975). These classes are not mutually exclusive, and they depend on an outside assessment of goals. For example, the Basque ETA would consider itself revolutionary as well as separatist. The RAF considered itself a classic national liberation movement, and the Provisional IRA insists that it is combatting a foreign oppressor, not an indigenous regime.

9  See Thornton's analysis of proximate goals in "Terror as a Weapon of Political Agitation," in Eckstein, ed. pp. 82–88.

10  Walter's discussion of the concept of "forced choice" explains how direct audiences, from whom the victims are drawn, may accept terrorism as legitimate; see *Terror and Resistance,* pp. 285–89.

11  Carlos Marighela, *For the Liberation of Brazil* (Harmondsworth: Penguin Books, 1971), pp. 94–95. The West German RAF apparently adopted the idea of provocation as part of a general national liberation strategy borrowed from the Third World.

Federal Republic all appear to have used terrorism as provocation.

Terrorism is a logical choice when oppositions have such goals and when the power ratio of government to challenger is high. The observation that terrorism is a weapon of the weak is hackneyed but apt. At least when initially adopted, terrorism is the strategy of a minority that by its own judgment lacks other means. When the group perceives its options as limited, terrorism is attractive because it is a relatively inexpensive and simple alternative, and because its potential reward is high.

Some groups are weak because weakness is imposed on them by the political system they operate in, others because of unpopularity. We are therefore making value judgments about the potential legitimacy of terrorist organizations. In some cases resistance groups are genuinely desperate, in others they have alternatives to violence. Nor do we want to forget that nonviolent resistance has been chosen in other circumstances, for example, by Gandhi and by Martin Luther King. Terrorists may argue that they had no choice, but their perceptions may be flawed.[12]

In addition to weakness, an important rationale in the decision to adopt a strategy of terrorism is impatience. Action becomes imperative. For a variety of reasons, the challenge to the state cannot be left to the future. Given a perception of limited means, the group often sees the choice as between action as survival and inaction as the death of resistance.

## Individual Motivation and Participation

Terrorism is neither an automatic reaction to conditions nor a purely calculated strategy. What psychological factors motivate the terrorist and influence his or her perceptions and interpretations of reality? Terrorists are only a small minority of people with similar personal backgrounds, experiencing the same conditions, who might thus be expected to reach identical conclusions based on logical reasoning about the utility of terrorism as a technique of political influence.

Why individuals engage in political violence is a complicated problem, and the question why they engage in terrorism is still more difficult.[13] As most simply and frequently posed, the question of a psychological explanation of terrorism is whether or not there is a "terrorist personality," similar to the authoritarian personality, whose emotional traits we can specify with some exactitude.[14] An identifiable pattern of attitudes and behavior in the terrorism-prone individual would result from a combination of ego-defensive needs, cognitive processes, and socialization, in interaction with a specific situation. In pursuing this line of inquiry, it is important to avoid stereotyping the terrorist or oversimplifying the sources of terrorist actions. No single motivation or personality can be valid for all circumstances.

The outstanding common characteristic of terrorists is their normality. Terrorism often seems to be the connecting link among widely varying personalities. Psychoanalysis might

---

12  See Michael Walzer's analysis of the morality of terrorism in *Just and Unjust Wars* (New York, 1977), pp. 197–206. See also Bernard Avishai, "In Cold Blood," *The New York Review of Books,* March 8, 1979, pp. 41–44, for a critical appraisal of the failure of recent works on terrorism to discuss moral issues. The question of the availability of alternatives to terrorism is related to the problem of discrimination in the selection of victims. Where victims are clearly responsible for a regime's denial of opportunity, terrorism is more justifiable than where they are not.

13  See Jeffrey Goldstein, *Aggression and Crimes of Violence* (New York, 1975).

14  A study of the West German New Left, for example, concludes that social psychological models of authoritarianism do help explain the dynamics of radicalism and even the transformation from protest to terrorism. See S. Robert Lichter, "A Psychopolitical Study of West German Male Radical Students," *Comparative Politics,* 12 (October 1979), pp. 27–48.

penetrate beneath superficial normality to expose some unifying or pathological trait, but this is scarcely a workable research method, even if the likelihood of the existence of such a characteristic could be demonstrated . . .

An unbiased examination of conscious attitudes might be more revealing than a study of subconscious predispositions or personalities. For example, if terrorists perceive the state as unjust, morally corrupt, and violent, then terrorism may seem legitimate and justified. For example, Blumenthal and her coauthors found that "the stronger the perception of an act as violence, the more violence is thought to be an appropriate response."[15] The evidence also indicates that many terrorists are activists with prior political experience in nonviolent opposition to the state. How do these experiences in participation influence later attitudes? Furthermore, how do terrorists view their victims? Do we find extreme devaluation, depersonalization, or stereotyping? Is there "us versus them" polarization or ethnic or religious prejudice that might sanction or prompt violence toward an out-group? How do terrorists justify and rationalize violence? Is remorse a theme? . . .

An alternative approach to analyzing the psychology of terrorism is to use a deductive method based on what we know about terrorism as an activity, rather than an inductive method yielding general propositions from statements of the particular. What sort of characteristics would make an individual suited for terrorism? What are the role requirements of the terrorist?

Since terrorism involves premeditated, not impulsive, violence, the terrorist's awareness of the risks is maximized. Thus, although terrorists may simply be people who enjoy or disregard risk,[16] It is more likely that they are people who tolerate high risk because of intense commitment to a cause. Their commitment is strong enough to make the risk of personal harm acceptable and perhaps to outweigh the cost of society's rejection, although defiance of the majority may be a reward in itself. In either case, the violent activity is not gratifying per se.

It is perhaps even more significant that terrorism is a group activity, involving intimate relationships among a small number of people. Interactions among members of the group may be more important in determining behavior than the psychological predispositions of individual members. Terrorists live and make decisions under conditions of extreme stress. As a clandestine minority, the members of a terrorist group are isolated from society, even if they live in what Menachem Begin called the "open underground."[17]

Terrorists can confide in and trust only each other. The nature of their commitment cuts them off from society; they inhabit a closed community that is forsaken only at great cost. Isolation and the perception of a hostile environment intensify shared belief and commitment and make faith in the cause imperative. A pattern of mutual reassurance, solidarity, and comradeship develops, in which the members of the group reinforce each other's self-righteousness, image of a hostile world, and sense of mission. Because of the real danger terrorists confront, the strain they live under, and the moral conflicts they undergo, they value solidarity highly.[18] Terrorists are not necessarily people who seek "belonging"

15 Monica D. Blumenthal, et al., *More about Justifying Violence*. Methodological Studies of Attitudes and Behavior (Ann Arbor: Survey Research Center, Institute for Social Research, University of Michigan, 1975), p. 182.

16 Psychiatrist Frederick Hacker, for example, argues that terrorists are by nature indifferent to risk; see *Crusaders, Criminals and Crazies* (New York, 1976), p. 13.

17 Menachem Begin, *The Revolt* (London: W.H. Allen, 1951).

18 J. Glenn Gray, "The Enduring Appeals of Battle," *The Warriors: Reflections on Men in Battle* (New York, 1970), chap. 2, describes similar experiences among soldiers in combat.

or personal integration through ideological commitment, but once embarked on the path of terrorism, they desperately need the group and the cause . . .

If there is a single common emotion that drives the individual to become a terrorist, it is vengeance on behalf of comrades or even the constituency the terrorist aspires to represent. (At the same time, the demand for retribution serves as public justification or excuse.) A regime thus encourages terrorism when it creates martyrs to be avenged. Anger at what is perceived as unjust persecution inspires demands for revenge, and as the regime responds to terrorism with greater force, violence escalates out of control.

There are numerous historical demonstrations of the central role vengeance plays as motivation for terrorism. It is seen as one of the principal causes of anarchist terrorism in France in the 1890s. The infamous Ravachol acted to avenge the "martyrs of Clichy," two possibly innocent anarchists who were beaten by the police and sentenced to prison. Subsequent bombings and assassinations, for instance that of President Carnot, were intended to avenge Ravachol's execution.[19]

The terrorists' willingness to accept high risks may also be related to the belief that one's death will be avenged. The prospect of retribution gives the act of terrorism and the death of the terrorist meaning and continuity, even fame and immortality. Vengeance may be not only a function of anger but of a desire for transcendence.

Shared guilt is surely a strong force in binding members of the terrorist group together. Almost all terrorists seem compelled to justify their behavior and this anxiety cannot be explained solely by reference to their desire to create a public image of virtuous sincerity. Terrorists usually show acute concern for morality, especially for sexual purity, and believe that they act in terms of a higher good. Justifications usually focus on past suffering, on the glorious future to be created, and on the regime's illegitimacy and violence, to which terrorism is the only available response. Shared guilt and anxiety increase the group's interdependence and mutual commitment and may also make followers more dependent on leaders and on the common ideology as sources of moral authority.

Guilt may also lead terrorists to seek punishment and danger rather than avoid it. The motive of self-sacrifice notably influenced many Russian terrorists of the nineteenth century. Kaliayev, for example, felt that only his death could atone for the murder he committed. Even to Camus, the risk of death for the terrorist is a form of personal absolution.[20]

It is clear that once a terrorist group embarks on a strategy of terrorism, whatever its purpose and whatever its successes or failures, psychological factors make it very difficult to halt. Terrorism as a process gathers its own momentum, independent of external events.

## Conclusions

Terrorism per se is not usually a reflection of mass discontent or deep cleavages in society. More often it represents the disaffection of a fragment of the elite, who may take it upon themselves to act on the behalf of a majority unaware of its plight, unwilling to take action to remedy grievances, or unable to express dissent. This discontent, however subjective in origin or minor in scope, is blamed on the government and its supporters. Since the sources of terrorism are manifold, any society or polity that permits opportunities for terrorism is vulnerable.

---

19 Jean Maitron, *Histoire du mouvement anarchiste en France (1880–1914)* (Paris: Societé universitaire d'éditions et de librairie, 1955), pp. 242–43.

20 See "Les meurtriers délicats" in *L'Homme Révolté* (Paris: Gallimard, 1965), pp. 571–79.

Given some source of disaffection—and in the centralized modern state with its faceless bureaucracies, lack of responsiveness to demands is ubiquitous—terrorism is an attractive strategy for small organizations of diverse ideological persuasions who want to attract attention for their cause, provoke the government, intimidate opponents, appeal for sympathy, impress an audience, or promote the adherence of the faithful.

Terrorism is the result of a gradual growth of commitment and opposition, a group development that furthermore depends on government action. The psychological relationships within the terrorist group—the interplay of commitment, risk, solidarity, loyalty, guilt, revenge, and isolation—discourage terrorists from changing the direction they have taken. This may explain why—even if objective circumstances change when, for example, grievances are satisfied, or if the logic of the situation changes when, for example, the terrorists are offered other alternatives for the expression of opposition—terrorism may endure until the terrorist group is physically destroyed.

# 30: Identity, Domestic Security, and the Future of the Nation-State

## Diane E. Davis

In a world of growing security challenges where random and targeted violence generate public anxiety and government concern, non-state armed actors have captured significant scholarly attention, particularly in failed or fragile states where institutions of governance and overall state legitimacy are weakened or under siege . . .[1]

Among non-state armed actors who proliferate in the contemporary period, a large and growing number focus their attention on urban economies[2] and transnational networks of trade and accumulation,[3] with some of them even structured around clandestine networks of remittances,[4] thereby flying under the radar screen (if not catapulting over) the broadly cast domains of governance and sovereignty associated with the nation-state. Likewise, a considerable number of these non-state armed actors use violence to secure markets, networks, and the supply of goods or activities for economic survival, suggesting that their targets are as likely to be other market or supply chain competitors (and sometimes even other actors in civil society, including other non-state armed actors) as the sovereign state itself.[5]

Examples of these non-state armed actors include armed drug lords in urban Brazil and Mexico, international smuggling rings in Central and Southeast Asia, new mafia organizations in Russia, community-based vigilantes in South Africa, Guatemala, and Indonesia, and most striking perhaps, an astounding number of armed private security forces or citizen militias taking on policing functions in politically stable and unstable countries alike, ranging from Mexico to Pakistan to Iraq. All these activities

1   Peter Huber and Cordula Reimann, *Non-State Armed Actors: An Annotated Bibliography* (Geneva: Swiss Piece Center for Peacebuilding, 2006); William Reno, 'The Changing Nature of Warfare and the Absence of State-building in West Africa,' in Diane E. Davis and Anthony W. Pereira (eds), *Irregular Armed Forces and their Role in Politics and State Formation* (Cambridge: Cambridge University Press, 2004), pp. 322-45.

2   Vadim Volkov, *Violent Entrepreneurs: The Use of Force in Making Russian Capitalism* (Ithaca, NY: Cornell University Press, 2002).

3   Peter Lupsha, 'Transnational Crime versus the Nation-State', *Transnational Organized Crime*, Vol. 2, No. 1 (Spring 1996), pp. 21-48; Marcel Fafchamps, 'Networks, Communities and Markets in Sub-Saharan Africa: Implications for Firm Growth and Investment', *Journal of African Economies*, Vol. 10, AERC Supplement 2 (2001), pp. 109-42.

4   Abdou Maliq Simone, 'Pirate Towns: Reworking Social and Symbolic Infrastructures in Johannesburg and Douala', *Urban Studies*, Vol. 43, No. 2 (February 2006), pp. 357-70; S. Maimbo (ed.) 'Remittances and Economic Development in Somalia: An Overview', *Social Development Papers* No. 38 (Washington DC: World Bank, 2006).

5   Enrique Desmond Arias, 'The Dynamics of Criminal Governance: Networks and Social Order in Rio de Janeiro', *Journal of Latin American Studies*, Vol. 38, No. 2 (2006) pp. 1-32; Nat J. Coletta and Michelle L. Cullen. 'The Nexus Between Violent Conflict, Social Capital and Social Cohesion: Case Studies from Cambodia and Rwanda', Social Capital Working Paper No. 23. (Washington DC: World Bank, 2000), p. A1.

rely on armed actors who fuel violence and generate conditions akin to warfare, but without identifying the state or political upheaval as their main objective . . .

Further complicating conventional wisdom on the subject, preliminary evidence suggests that some of the above-mentioned categories of non-state armed actors have been known to act clandestinely *on behalf of* states—or in conjunction with the state's own armed actors, sometimes as formal or informal contract employees—as much as against the regime in power. Examples not only include the government's deployment of paid mercenaries to fill gaps where official military operations have failed, but also the use of citizen militias, privately contracted paramilitaries, neighbourhood 'posses', and other civil society-based associations or independent providers of security to achieve the policing or military aims necessary for establishing the state's hegemony.[6] Perhaps the most complicated of such arrangements is that currently seen in Iraq, where the so-called 'Awakening' militias can be considered both a social movement and an enforcer group working both for citizens and the state, albeit indirectly and with the formal identity as a non-state armed actor.[7]

Lest one think that such instances are epiphenomenal, or tied specifically to the current conflict in Iraq and Afghanistan, evidence suggests that these types of coercive actors, straddling both the state and civil society, are far more common than has been generally recognized in the contemporary literature on non-state actors, let alone in the literature on violence and insecurity. Recent research by Desmond Arias show that armed groups in Brazil interact directly with the state in 'social networks', providing financial or narcotic kick-backs to security forces, who in turn provide armed groups with weaponry and a modicum of unconstrained manoeuvrability in their respective communities;[8] while Ralph Rozema has identified a version of such collaborations in his study of the relations between criminal networks and paramilitaries in Colombia.[9] Historical evidence further shows that the state-sanctioned deployment of citizen militias or privately operated paramilitary forces has been a common response to political instability and/or industrial, agrarian, and communal violence in cases as diverse as 19th-century Greece, 20th-century Mexico and Peru, and contemporary Colombia.[10] The current United States government's reliance on paid mercenaries and other contract employees to achieve its military aims in Iraq and Afghanistan, and the general use of paid mercenaries by militaries around the world, suggests that the practice continues in new forms and should not be relegated to the past.[11]

Finally, the accelerating growth of private security forces on a world-wide scale may be the most important challenge to conventional thinking on non-state armed actors, in theoretical if

---

6 Jane Perlez and Pir Subair Shah, 'As Taliban Overwhelm the Police, Pakistanis Fight Back', *New York Times*, 2 November 2008.

7 Erica Goode, 'Handshake Defuses a Standoff in Baghdad', *New York Times*, 4 September 2008, p. 1.

8 Enrique Desmond Arias, *Drugs and Democracy in Rio de Janeiro: Trafficking, Social Networks, and Public Security* (Durham, NC: University of North Carolina Press, 2006).

9 Ralph Rozema, 'Urban DDR-Processes: Paramilitaries and Criminal Networks in Medellin, Colombia', *Journal of Latin American Studies*, Vol. 40, No. 3 (2008), pp. 423-52.

10 Diane E. Davis and Anthony W. Pereira (eds), *Irregular Armed Forces and their Role in Politics and State Formation* (Cambridge: Cambridge University Press, 2004).

11 Marc von Voencken, 'The Business of War,' *Peace and Conflict Monitor*, 15 December 2003; Report of the United Nations Working Group on the Use of Mercenaries, 24 August 2007; 'Iraqi Premier Says Blackwater Shootings Challenge His Nation's Sovereignty', *New York Times*, 24 September 2007.

not empirical terms, because it signals the widespread transfer of security functions from the state to civil society.[12] The fact that private police are evident in rich and poor countries alike, democratic and otherwise, further suggests that this shift may be as much about contemporary times and reflective of larger patterns of security reorganization seen in the widespread transfer of policing functions from the public to the private sphere, as it is about poverty, state fragility, and democratic institutions and practices (or their lack thereof). To the extent that private police exist alongside public police, rather than in replacement of them, also means that this phenomenon blurs the line between a state and non-state monopoly of the means of violence . . .

Given the complexity of this picture, it may be time to re-think prevailing assumptions about non-state armed actors and consider a new analytical agenda for studying who they are and what their impact is on security and violence in the contemporary era. We must be prepared to question our definition of what, exactly, constitutes a non-state armed actor and whether such actors, despite the nomenclature, might also systematically maintain some clandestine or informal relationship to the state, even in the absence of formal linkages. How hard and fast is the analytical distinction between state and non-state armed actors; and what is the theoretical rationale for preserving it in future scholarship? Why do we distinguish between political versus economic motivations in our categorization of non-state armed actors? Are clans, tribes, warlords, and rebels all that different from mafias, gangs, and drug lords; in what ways and why? Further, we must be prepared to examine and perhaps move beyond conventional understandings of the conditions under which non-state armed actors will emerge, thrive, employ violence, and thus contribute to conditions of insecurity. In

today's world, the functions and territorial reach of nation-states are in flux; progress on democratic transition has itself generated a proliferation of non-state armed state actors; new global economic practices and international networks link non-state actors with varying economic or political agendas to each other in commodity or supply chains that know no territorial bounds; and insecurity abounds, even for the wealthiest, but more tragically so for the poor . . .[13]

## States, Sovereignties, and Non-Armed State Actors: Theoretical and Conceptual Foundations

The basic argument is that in order to defend or establish its sovereignty, a state engages in warfare (usually against other existent or putative states), with inter-state violence fuelling both the fires of warfare and modern state-formation. To the extent that engaging armed actors to fight war requires resources, the state in turn creates new institutions (government bureaucracies), new revenue sources (taxes), and new avenues for securing legitimacy (citizenship rights) that allow it to extract funds and moral support from the citizenry, in the process building stronger state-society connections. These institutions, revenues, and legitimacy claims form the basic building blocks of the modern state, whose capacity to endure and strengthen its sovereignty rests on the capacity of its own coercive forces (military, police, and other state armed actors) to monopolize the means of violence. In short, the struggle to establish state sovereignty rests on armed force, even as the institutional and fiscal capacity to use armed force rests on state power. A closer examination of non-state armed actors suggests that a parallel dynamic may be at play, albeit in non-state domains, where armed

---

12 Simon Chesterman and Chia Lehnardt, *From Mercenaries to Market: The Rise and Regulation of Private Security Companies* (New York: Oxford University Press, 2007).

13 Diane E. Davis, 'Speaking to the Silences: Do We Need a Sociology for the Post-9/11 World?' *International Journal of Politics, Culture, and Society*, Vol. 18, Nos. 3-4 (2005), pp. 293-311.

actors without allegiance to the nation-state are also engaged in struggles over sovereignty and allegiance.

To be more specific: in a globalizing world where neoliberal political and economic policies are ascendant, citizens become less connected to national states as a source of political support or social and economic claim-making,[14] and more tied to alternative 'imagined communities' of loyalties built either on essentialist identities like ethnicity, race or religion or on spatially-circumscribed allegiances and networks of social and economic production and reproduction.[15] These processes are speeded by 'the societal changes associated with the accessibility of information technology that stimulate networked organizational forms', in turn affecting the nature of conflict and crime by empowering 'non-state entities' and altering the global political landscape.[16] To the extent that alternative imagined communities of allegiance and reciprocity provide new forms of welfare, employment, and meaning, they often operate as the functional equivalents of states, thus encouraging new forms of 'non-state sovereignty'[17] that contrast to the imagined national communities that sustained modern nation-state formation and traditional patterns of sovereignty, along the lines articulated by Benedict Anderson.[18] When these new imagined communities exist apart from (if not in opposition

to) traditional nation-states, they often choose (or are forced) to rely on their own armed actors to sustain, nurture, or protect their activities and dominion, especially when they conflict with national state priorities.

This dynamic could readily describe the sets of allegiances, loyalties, and impacts of guerrilla forces and other more conventionally defined non-state armed actors who might conceptualize themselves as an alternative 'imagined community' of rebels fighting against an oppressive nation-state, as seen in Sudan, Somalia, Congo, and other countries caught in the vicious cycle of civil war or politicized armed conflicts.[19] But it is becoming increasingly clear that these same general dynamics are evident in the activities and priorities of those who have not conventionally been studied in the literature on non-state armed actors, including drug smugglers, mafias, youth gangs, and citizen militias in more stable democratic countries who use armed force but also share social loyalties and common economic objectives in ways that sustain alternative reciprocities and solidarity to each other rather than the state.

Granted the concept of imagined communities was developed in order to account for the emergence of a territorially bounded nationalism predominant in the 19th and 20th centuries, built

---

14 Saskia Sassen, *Territory, Authority, Rights: From Medieval to Global Assemblages* (Princeton, NJ: Princeton University Press, 2007); Matthew Sparke, *In the Space of theory: Post-foundational Geographies of the Nation-state* (Minneapolis: University of Minnesota Press, 2005).

15 Margaret Keck and Kathryn Sikkink, *Transnational Issue Networks in International Politics* (Princeton, NJ: Princeton University Press, 1997); Andrew Linklater, *The Transformation of Political Community: Ethical Foundations of the Post-Westphalian Era* (Cambridge: Cambridge University Press, 1993); Matthew Sparke, 'A Neoliberal Nexus: Citizenship, Security and the Future of the Border', *Political Geography*, Vol. 25, No. 2 (2006), pp. 151-80.

16 John P. Sullivan and Robert J. Bunker, 'Drug Cartels, Street Gangs, and Warlords', in Robert J. Bunker (ed.) *Non-State Threats and Future Wars* (New York: Frank Cass, 2003), p. 40.

17 Linklater, *The Transformation of Political Community* (note 15); Richard Devetak and Richard Higgott, 'Justice Unbound? Globalisation, States, and the Transformation of the Social Bond', CSGR Working Paper No. 29/99 (May), University of Warwick; Jane Kelsey, 'Globalisation, Nationalism, Sovereignty, and Citizenship', University of Auckland School of Law, http://www.pcpd.org.nz/sr/pubs.html.

18 Benedict Anderson, *Imagined Communities: Reflections on the Origins and Spread of Nationalism* (London: Verso, 1983).

19 Robert Jackson, *Quasi-States: Sovereignty, International Relations, and the Third World* (Cambridge: Cambridge University Press, 1990); Nat J. Colletta and Michelle L. Cullen, *Violent Conflict and the Transformation of Social Capital: Lessons from Cambodia, Rwanda, Guatemala and Somalia* (Washington, DC: World Bank, 2000).

around a limited and sovereign political community based on 'deep, horizontal comradeship'.[20] That is, this notion was built on an understanding of strong and visceral connections within and between citizens and the state, and thus it is hard to think of drug lords and street gangs fitting neatly into such a conceptual apparatus, not just in terms of their disengagement with formal nationalism but also in terms of strong connections with a wide range of citizens. All too often, in fact, these types of activities alienate neighbours and residents who are caught up in the violence generated by these non-state armed actors. But . . . there are significant elements that suggest the continued relevance of the concept of imagined community, albeit rethought to account for the shifting territorial bases of sovereignty and allegiance that also make more contemporary imagined communities 'new' or different from the past . . .

The territorialities of today suggest that political communities of reciprocity are no longer limited in the same way as before, owing to globalization and transnational flows of peoples and ideas, and to the fact that states are neither uniformly legitimate nor the only authority in an increasingly inter-connected and globalized world. But this does not mean political communities of reciprocity (or imagined communities) have disappeared, only that they are transforming in scale and scope—hence our desire to accommodate an understanding of these changes and recast them in the context of a 'new imagined community' nomenclature . . .

An example of just this type of new imagined community, built on both local and transnationally linked armed actions and loyalties, appeared last spring in the Mexican industrial city of Laredo, in the Northern state of Nuevo Laredo not far from the US-Mexican border. A renowned drug mafia cartel called the *Zetas* hung a banner on a downtown pedestrian bridge calling for 'military recruits and ex-military men . . . seeking a good salary, food, and help for their families' to join them and support their activities. The banner promised no more 'suffering maltreatment or hunger', while a local phone number was posted for contact.[21] The hubris of a drug mafia publicly announcing efforts to recruit new loyalists to a countervailing social and political project defined in direct opposition to a sovereign state and its rule of law, but using the same principles of welfare reciprocity and solidarity, would have been almost unimaginable a decade ago. But in the contemporary era, transnational crime networks are as visible—and almost as legitimate—as national states in many parts of the world, finding loyalty and a sense of community among citizen supporters whose lives become spatially or socially embedded in their powerful criminal orbits.[22] Indeed, after the Laredo announcement citizens in 11 other cities across Mexico responded by hanging public banners asking the country's president to take a 'neutral' stance in the fight against drug-traffickers, so as not to tip the balance towards either the military or the *narcos*, a plea they justified by underscoring the fact that many of Mexico own military personnel were as corrupted and involved in the drug trade as the *Zetas* . . .[23]

What *most* distinguishes the contemporary situation from the pre-modern, however, as well as the immediate past is the fact that these new imagined communities are struggling for 'alternative forms of sovereignty'—power, authority,

---

20  Anderson, *Imagined Communities* (note 18); see also T.J. Clark, 'In a Pomegranate Chandelier', *London Review of Books*, available at http://www.lrb.co.uk/v28/n18/print/clar05_.html.

21  'Incitan a la deserción militar', *El Mañana*, 14 April 2008, p. 1, available at http://www.elmanana.com.mx/notas.asp?id=51677.

22  Enrique Desmond Arias, 'Faith in Our Neighbors: Networks and Social Order in Three Brazilian Favelas', *Latin American Politics and Society*, Vol. 46, No. 1 (2004), pp. 1-38.

23  'Exigen un combate neutral ad narco: colocan mantas en el estados', *El Universal*, 26 October 2008, p. 1, available at http://www.vanguardia.com.mx/diario/noticia/seguridad/nacional/exigen_un_combate_neutral_al_narco;_colocan_mantas_en_7_estados/ 246251

independence, and self-governance on a variety of territorial scales, whether formal or informal—in an environment *where traditional institutions of national sovereignty and the power of the nation-state still exist and must be reckoned with.*[24] Stated simply, the new imagined communities of the contemporary world do not exist in an historical vacuum. They co-exist and overlap with the modern state, and by so doing have a feedback effect on 'old' imagined communities (e.g. the national state) and their relationship to society, by virtue of their capacity to de-legitimize, weaken, or challenge political allegiance to the nation-state. The challenge for contemporary security studies scholarship is to examine both overlapping and competing states, sovereignties, and non-state armed actors, and to examine their impact on violence and insecurity both with respect to nation-states and society as a whole . . .

### New Territorial Dynamics of Non-State Armed Action: The Urban Frontlines of Conflict

In prior epochs of more conventional war-making, when state armed actors monopolized the means of violence, sovereignty used to be about asserting and legitimizing political power over a fixed territorial domain that established the same national boundaries of allegiance for citizens and state alike. Capital, whether globally or locally extracted, served as a source of funds for arming state actors who engaged in war to protect national boundaries and the citizens within them. States frequently made alliances with local capitalists to supplant the

state's territorial sovereignty and war-making aims; in return they protected markets, so that flows of resources could be guaranteed for state activities, war-related or not. All this constituted what Charles Tilly so aptly identified as a protection racket.[25] In today's world, many non-state armed actors also rely on sources of global and local capital, and by so doing they diminish both the legitimacy and resource-extraction capacities of national states, even as they relocate the territorial domain and reach of protection rackets to other scales, both sub-national and international. This has brought new networks of individuals and economic activities connected in and across transnational or sub-national territories, in which armed actors acting on behalf of these new networks—or protection rackets—sometimes wield as much coercive power than do their 'host' nation-states, at least in particular locations and territories.

Such trends are evident by focusing on the main purveyors of violence in the contemporary era, and by highlighting their territorial location. Two or more decades ago, the military, paramilitary, and police tended to monopolize the means of violence, using repressive actions against rebellious citizens identified with warlike terminology as 'enemies of the state'. Much of this conflict centred in rural areas or in regions excluded from the urban-based or elite-dominated developmental gains that accompanied late development. Today, although civil wars, agrarian or rural-based rebel movements still persist in a select subset of countries around the world, violence and 'warfare' are more likely to unfold in cities, especially capital cities.[26] They also are just as likely to be associated with the activities

---

24 Brennan Kraxberger, 'Strangers, Indigenes, and Settlers: Contested Geographies of Citizenship in Nigeria', *Space and Polity*, Vol. 9, No. 1 (April 2005), pp. 9-27; Ralph A. Litzinger, 'Contested Sovereignties and the Critical Ecosystem Partnership Fund', *PoLAR: Political and Legal Anthropology Review*, Vol. 29, No. 1 (2006), pp. 66-87.

25 Charles Tilly, 'Warmaking and Statemaking as Organized Crime', in Dietrich Rueschemeyer, Peter Evans, and Theda Skocpol (eds), *Bringing the State Back In* (Cambridge: Cambridge University Press, 1985), pp. 169-91.

26 Marika Landau-Wells. 'Capital Cities in Civil Wars: The Locational Dimensions of Sovereign Authority', Occasional Paper 6, Crisis States Research Center, London School of Economics, April 2008.

of drug cartels, mafias, non-state militias, citizens acting as vigilantes, and private police (providing protection for both individuals and firms) as with political insurgency. Moreover, whereas in the past much of the armed violence was associated with roaming rebel or guerrilla opposition, in today's world non-state armed actors locate their command and control functions in fixed settings, in neighbourhoods and communities strategically located in large cities and/or in strategic border or exchange areas, many of which sustain their transnational reach.

Several of these dynamics are embodied in the activities and identities of the Mara Salvatrucha, known widely as 'los Maras', a gang whose social and economic activities link a network of Spanish-speaking youth from their origins in Los Angeles through Mexico down into the major cities of Guatemala and El Salvador in a self-identified community of loyalties, whose strength has only accelerated in the wake of state efforts to incarcerate urban gang members (where they only strengthen their networks, plan new operations, and become more strategic opponents to the state). But what is most significant about the Maras is not so much their self-identified gang status but their origins as a group of city-based youth who turned to criminal activity because of the lack of employment alternatives in the large metropolitan areas of California, Mexico, and Central America. Both the urban and employment aspects of their formation as a transnational 'alternative imagined community' speak loudly to the prevalence of city-based, non-state armed actors all over the burgeoning metropolises of the global south, even as they

underscore the temporality of this phenomenon.[27] Indeed the rapid growth of cities in the developing world has become one of the major social, economic, and demographic challenges of the contemporary era. We are entering an age where almost half the world is urban and where the majority of population growth will be concentrated in large cities in formerly poor countries of the world, most predominantly in East Asia, South Asia, Latin America, and the Middle East. Rapid urbanization has brought with it a huge set of problems, primarily employment and housing scarcities, which if not resolved will destroy old bonds of community and solidarity among citizens, and which also fuel insecurity and the resort to armed force.[28]

In the rapidly transforming urban environments of the global south, residents find few job opportunities in the industrial sector, a situation which forces larger numbers of residents into informal employment (in commerce and trade primarily) or other means of securing their livelihood.[29] In Mexico City, for example, official estimates identify close to 70 per cent of the urban labour force as employed in the informal sector, and within this category, petty commerce and street vending often predominate. Such employment, which barely meets subsistence needs for many stuck within it, has become ever more 'illicit' as protectionist barriers drop and fewer domestic goods for re-sale are produced, and as the globalization of trade in contraband and illegal goods picks up the slack. As a result, much informal employment is physically and socially situated within an illicit world of violence and impunity, not just because of the sheer illegality of many of the goods traded, but

27 Dennis Rodgers, 'Slum Wars of the 21st Century: The New Geography of Conflict in Central America', Working Paper No. 10, Crisis States Research Centre, London School of Economics, 2007.

28 Diane E. Davis, 'Insecure and Secure Cities: Towards a Reclassification of World Cities in a Global Era', *Sociologia Urbana e Rurale*, Vol. 29, No. 82, (2007), pp. 67-82. (Reprinted in *MITIR: The MIT International Review*, Spring 2008, available at http://web.mit.edu/mitir/2008/spring/insecure.html).

29 Manuel Castells and Alejandro Portes, 'World Underneath: The Origins, Dynamics, and Effects of the Informal Economy', in Manuel Castells, Alejandro Portes and Lauren A. Benton (eds), *The Informal Economy: Studies in Advanced and Less Developed Countries* (Baltimore, MD: Johns Hopkins University Press, 1989).

also because to be involved in guns, drugs, and other contraband products (pirated CDs, knock-off designer goods, valuable gems in the case of natural resource-rich African cities) frequently necessitates the deployment of one's own 'armed forces' for protection against the long arm of the state, whether the police or customs inspectors.[30] These forces also fight amongst themselves for control of illicit supply chains, further creating an environment of violence.

Well-organized cadres involved in these illicit activities often take on the functionally equivalent role of mini-states by monopolizing the means of violence and providing protection in exchange for loyalty and territorial dominion.[31] But as mini-states they also participate in their own form of 'foreign policy', that is negotiating, baiting, or cooperating with the sovereign states in whose territory they operate. The result is often the development of clandestine connections between local police, mafias, and the informal sector, as well as the isolation of certain territorial areas as locations for these activities.[32]

The physical concentration of dangerous illegal activities in territorial locations that function as 'no man's lands' outside state control further drives the problems of impunity, insecurity, and violence on the part of non-state armed actors. Historically, border areas between nation-states have played this role, with constantly shifting populations preventing networks of reciprocity and social control to strengthen sufficiently to insure that violence and danger would still flourish, despite the efforts of authorities to control movement in and out of border areas. But as urbanization changes cities into dense conglomerations of peoples and activities, and as illicit trade becomes a principal source of livelihood, we see the same patterns in cities. Certain areas begin to serve the refuge for illegal activities and shifting flows of people and goods. In many cities of the global south, these dangerous areas sit nestled against old central business districts (CBD), where local chambers of commerce face a declining manufacturing base and are especially desperate to attract high-end corporate investors and financial services. Some of this owes to the importance of maintaining a physical proximity to large markets of consumers who will buy informal or illegal goods. But whatever the origin, these spacial dynamics further drive the conflict as the upper and lower ends of the commercial spectrum compete to control the same space. When the successful introduction of urban mega-projects or other downtown development schemes physically displaces those who earn their living in informal sector, their sources of economic livelihood are disrupted, driving more and more to illegal activities and the use of violence to maintain their supply chains. Yet the presence of so much informality and violence in centrally located areas of large cities is often what motivates high-end developers to push for urban renewal and other major renovations of central business districts in the first place.[33]

Globalization has added even more urgency to these contradictory processes as real estate development and the physical creation of upscale 'global cities' has emerged as a key source of grease for the wheels of capital accumulation in

---

30 Kees Koonings and Dirk Kruijt (eds), *Fractured Cities: Social Exclusion, Urban Violence, and Contested Spaces in Latin America* (London: Zed Books, 2007).

31 Elizabeth Leeds, 'Parallel Politics in the Brazilian Urban Periphery: Constraints on Local-Level Democracy', *Latin American Research Review*, Vol. 31, No. 3 (2006), pp. 41-83; Teresa Caldeira, *City of Walls: Crime, Segregation and Citizenship in São Paulo* (Berkeley: University of California Press, 2001).

32 Mingardi Guaracy, 'O trabalho da inteligencia no controle do crime organizado', *Estudos Avancados*, Vol. 21, No. 61 (2007), pp. 51-69.

33 Dennis Rodgers, 'Disembedding the City: Crime, Insecurity, and Spatial Organisation in Managua, Nicaragua', *Environment and Urbanization*, Vol. 16, No. 2 (2004), pp. 113-24.

the global economy.[34] The upshot is a clash of forces, if not development models, between competing sets of actors both seeking to maintain their dominion in strategically located urban spaces, with non-state armed actors involved in protecting illegal and informal activities a key set of actors embroiled in this larger conflict.[35]

These struggles parallel yet depart from the traditional forms of political struggle waged by non-state armed actors against states discussed in much of the conventional literature. On one hand, the state is involved in this conflict by virtue of its deployment of urban planners and police to displace the local populations who fight to maintain their locations and activities downtown. But the non-state armed actors who are involved in protecting their turf and physical territory, and who assert their political and economic power through illicit rather than licit networks of trade and distribution, are not struggling for political dominion, control of the state, or a reversal in patterns of political exclusion. Rather, they seek economic dominion, and their desire is to not to politically control national territory (as states do), so much as to control key local nodes and transnational networks that make their economic activities possible.[36] Accordingly, they are as likely to use armed force in a defensive way, that is, to keep the state out of their affairs, rather than to insert themselves in the state's affairs.

To be sure, not all informal sector workers in cities of the global south should be classified as non-state armed actors involved in illegal or illicit activities. Nor do they all operate in a transnational orbit of illegality that drives them to use armed force to protect themselves and their means of livelihood from state intervention. But what many of these poor urban residents do hold in common in the contemporary era is a network of obligations and reciprocities in a given spatial context that is not necessarily coincident with the nation-state.[37] The more transnational the supply chain of goods in which these citizens are involved, the more likely that money and/or commodity exchange fuels the connections; while the larger the sums of money are involved, the more likely will these networks of reciprocity will fuel an environment illegality and thus violence. And to the extent that these communities of non-state armed actors involved in transnational networks of violence have the capacity to challenge the national-state's control of the means of coercion, the state and its hold on sovereignty and security is under direct challenge.

In these and other regards, the problems produced by many of these 'non-conventional' non-state armed actors may be as debilitating and threatening to the institutional capacities and democratic character of the state as were the more 'conventional' non-state armed actors (guerrillas, rebels, etc.) that dominated the literature in prior decades. This has been clearly shown in Mexico, in the actions of drug mafias and other armed actors, who have waged war against local police and military in an ongoing battle that has pushed the state to introduce authoritarian measures and legislation that limit general civil liberties and concentrate power in a small circle of high-level officials.[38] Such patterns are also clear in other countries or regions of the world, with Brazil, Argentina, Russia, and

---

34 Diane E. Davis, 'Conflict, Cooperation, and Convergence: Globalization and the Politics of Downtown Development in Mexico City', *Research in Political Sociology*, Vol. 15 (2006), pp. 143-78.

35 Arif Hasan, 'The Changing Nature of the Informal Sector in Karachi as a Result of Global Restructuring and Liberalization', *Environment & Urbanization*, Vol. 14, No. 1 (2002), pp. 69-78.

36 Elizabeth H. Campbell, 'Economic Globalization from Below: Transnational Refugee Trade Networks in Nairobi', in Martin Murray and Garth Myers (eds), *Cities in Contemporary Africa* (Basingstoke: Palgrave Macmillan, 2006), pp. 125-47.

37 Cathy McIlwaine and Caroline Moser, 'Violence and Social Capital in Urban Poor Communities', *Journal of International Development*, Vol. 13, No. 7 (2001), pp. 965-84.

South Africa only a few of the many nations where smuggling rings that rely on armed protection have come into violent conflict with the state or citizens.[39] Additionally, in some of these settings the power and influence of mafias has at times been so great, owing to the huge sums of money involved, that mafia elements directly infiltrate those state's agencies charged with coercion.[40] Infiltration or rampant rent-seeking further limits the state's capacity to reduce overall violence and insecurity. With inside knowledge of the state's strategies and intelligence gathering breached, the state cannot function as an all-powerful sovereign entity, nor is it capable of upholding a rule of law, despite its democratic status and electorally legitimate hold on power.

Such conditions not only undermine the state's effective sovereignty; they also require new political or legislative strategies for dealing with these highly elusive yet economically consequential non-state armed actors, ranging from restructuring or eliminating entire state agencies to instituting new legal measures or constitutional changes for defining criminality and empowering the courts, police, and military to fight against non-state armed actors without violating the established norms of governance. These requisites have a direct feedback effect on the nature of the state and its institutional structures, the most visible of which are reflected in efforts to centralize power and authority in new coercive apparatuses capable of controlling or eliminating non-state armed actors. Yet these reforms hold the capacity to undermine the state's

democratic underpinnings by promoting the unfettered use of state violence to stem a losing battle against corruption, mafias, and drug trade.

## Urban Nation, State Formation, and the Peculiarities of Late Development

The proliferation of non-state armed actors rooted in cities throughout the global south, but who operate transnationally and thus escape effective regulation, is not merely a problem for individual cities or states and their capacities to govern and/or monopolize the means of coercion. The presence of so many armed actors involved in illegal and illicit supply chains has dramatically transformed the quality of life more generally, with the declining security situation generating citizen unhappiness with the state and, at times, even with democratic institutions. Not that long ago optimism reigned in many developing countries about benefits to be gained by the democratic transition; but dreams of progress have steadily dimmed as problems of violence, crime, and insecurity have proliferated with a vengeance, especially in cities.[41]

Citizens are frustrated with the state, mainly because little headway has been made in eliminating urban crime and violence. This is a result not just of the infiltration of criminal elements into the governing state apparatus, as noted earlier, but also because those charged with keeping order and guaranteeing the rule of law on behalf of the state, that is the police and/or the military, are themselves frequently implicated in abusive

---

38 Diane E. Davis, 'Undermining the Rule of Law: Democratization and the Dark Side of Police Reform in Mexico', *Latin American Politics and Society*, Vol. 48, No. 1 (Spring 2006), pp. 55-86.; John Bailey and Roy Godson (eds), *Organized Crime and Democratic Governability: Mexico and the US-Mexican Borderlands* (Pittsburg, PA: University of Pittsburgh Press, 2000).

39 Graham Denyer Willis, 'Deadly Symbiosis? The PCC, the State and Institutionalized Violence in Sao Paulo', in Gareth A. Jones and Dennis Rodgers (eds), *Youth Violence in Latin America* (New York: Palgrave Macmillan, forthcoming).

40 Marc Lacy, 'Officials Say Drug Cartels Infiltrated Mexican Law Unit', *New York Times*, 26 October 2008, p. A9; see also Bailey and Godson, *Organized Crime* (note 38).

41 Susana Rotker, Katherine Goldman, and Jorge Balan (eds), *Citizens of Fear: Urban Violence in Latin America* (Camden, NJ: Rutgers University Press, 2003); Bailey and Godson, *Organized Crime* (note 38); Caldeira, *City of Walls* (note 31).

practices or criminality.[42] And although patterns of urban violence are linked to illicit activities undertaken by mafias and criminal gangs who run the supply and distribution of contraband, these activities persist with the tacit support of the police and even the military, whose priorities are often protection of their own institutional sovereignty and/or involvement in these black market activities rather than protection of citizens who suffer in the precarious urban environment where informality flourishes and the rule of law remains elusive.

The result is growing cynicism and a renewed sense of hopelessness about both the future and the potential of a democratic political system to deal with extra-legal violence and impunity. State legitimacy is on the decline; instead of letting elected officials and their regulatory agents fight the problems of crime, growing numbers of citizens reject formal political channels and look for their own answers to the problems of insecurity in everyday life. The upside of this trend may be that citizens mobilize among themselves or become directly involved in civil society efforts to monitor crime and reduce insecurity.[43] But there also is a downside. Anxiety about the urban security situation and the state's inability to guarantee order has become so extreme in certain contexts that citizens turn to violence themselves—whether in the form of vigilantism, seen as a last-gasp measure for achieving some sense of citizen justice, whether by self-arming or other forms of protection, or whether through the embrace of a life of crime, so as to be on the giving rather than the receiving end of a growing environment of insecurity—in order to establish some control over their daily existence.[44] In this

way, violence originally generated by non-state armed actors involved in illegal, illicit activities lays the contours for a declining urban security situation, which in turn widens the circle of armed action by pushing urban citizens into the world of violence as well, sometimes even motivating them to deploy violence against others out of sheer frustration with the state's incapacity to deliver security . . .

### From the State to Civil Society? Shifting Domains of Armed Force and the Decline of State Sovereignty

. . . When citizens bypass state channels and turn to non-state actors like private police for protection, the state itself loses a key function and some of its legitimacy, even if the logic seems quite appropriate. To some extent, this is a vicious cycle: if citizens do not struggle for government accountability and transparency in rooting out corruption and cleaning up the police, the state will not go the extra mile in attacking the police, since this is a costly and uphill battle. Yet in the absence of concrete gains in rooting out police corruption, citizens become further alienated from the government, driving them to alternative imagined communities of reciprocity to solve the insecurity problem. This new imagined community might be one of outraged citizens mobilizing against the state for greater security, as seen recently in Mexico City in the mass mobilizations of hundreds of thousands. It might be seen in the form of creating new business-citizen partnerships around security provision, a model used in Johannesburg in the form of a Business Improvement District (BID). Yet it might also be seen in

42 Caroline Moser, 'Urban Violence and Insecurity: An Introductory Roadmap', *Environment & Urbanization*, Vol. 16, No. 2 (2004), pp. 3-16; Mercedes S. Hinton and Tim Newburn (eds) *Policing Developing Democracies* (New York: Routledge, 2009).
43 Philip Oxhorn and Graciela Ducatenzeiler, *What Kind of Democracy? What Kind of Market? Latin America in the Age of Neoliberalism* (University Park, PA: Penn State Press, 1998).
44 David Pratten and Atryee Sen, *Global Vigilantes* (New York: Columbia University Press, 2003); Daniel Goldstein, *The Spectacular City: Violence and Performance and in Urban Bolivia* (Durham, NC: Duke University Press, 2003).

the form of local citizens taking on policing activities themselves, whether in the form of lynching or vigilantism.

But such anarchic citizen responses have a direct impact on the state and its legitimate sovereignty, even as they raise troubling questions about democracy and the rule of law more generally. When ever more individuals start bearing arms as a condition of their employment in private security services, and citizens themselves start to carry guns for self-protection from criminals and police alike, violent 'resolutions' to questions of public insecurity become the norm, thereby fuelling the vicious circle of violence and insecurity. The overall security situation can deteriorate further when 'private' police compete with 'public' police for a monopoly over the means of violence and the legitimacy to use force. In both Mexico City and Johannesburg, two highly violent cities, there have been instances of 'public' and 'private' police forces, not to mention communities themselves, engaging in conflict over who has the right to protect and arrest citizens. Such tensions between different 'imagined communities' of reciprocity bring a collision of loyalties and allegiances, with private police serving and protecting their clients and public police acting on behalf of a sovereign state and its rule of law. The upshot is an environment of fear and insecurity where competing or overlapping imagined communities struggle to hold dominion. Such a situation is well seen in the *favelas* of Rio de Janeiro and Sao Paolo, where citizens are as likely to support local drug lords because they guarantee protection and 'local sovereignty' better than do police or the state.[45]

Complicating matters, as private police grow in numbers and citizens rely on them for protection, there is less discussion about the larger social contract in which security is to be guaranteed as well as increasing ambiguity about the conditions under which private police can take on public police functions, or vice-versa. In the most democratic nations, where there is strong and relatively widespread commitment to a shared social and political contract between ruler and ruled, as in South Africa, citizens are trying to monitor the situation so as to limit private police powers. Citizens and politicians have worked to impose legislative controls on private police, and they have deliberated over how to insure that public police still protect citizens, in ways that reinforce the state's role as guarantor of the constitution and rule of law. But in those nations where democracy is less well entrenched, where the state remains weak, or where the citizenry is divided about how much trust it will put in the police or the state, very little headway has been made in limiting the power of private police vis-á-vis public police.

In Mexico, for example, where democratic transition has exacerbated vicious conflict between political parties and interest groups so as to make police reform almost impossible, corruption remains rampant and people turn to private police for security. As a result, it is hard to find public support to limit private police actions, and they have become almost as unaccountable as public police. This fact is evidenced by rising complaints about human-rights abuses lodged against private police by citizens, a state of affairs echoed in Brazil as well, where some citizens claim that off-duty cops who take on the role of private police are responsible for more extrajudicial killings than the public police. In an environment where there is insufficient state or citizen capacity to limit private security forces, we also see private police withholding evidence from public police in order to protect their own 'monopolization' of the means of coercion, meaning prior legal procedures and democratic

---

45 Elizabeth Leeds, 'Rio de Janeiro', pp. 23-35 in Koonings, and Kruijt, *Fractured Cities* (note 30), Arias, 'The Dynamics of Criminal Governance' (note 5).

fundamentals associated with a single rule of law start to break down. This only encourages the fragmentation of the citizenry into distinct imagined communities, if you will—further legitimizing the proliferation of more non-state armed actors, each protecting their sub-national or transnational network of clients, imagined communities, and alternative sovereignties.

The problem is not just competition between state and non-state armed actors, however. In some countries the problem is the overlap, or a blurring of lines, between armed forces working in and outside the state. This is not only clear in those countries like Mexico, where poorly paid public police frequently moonlight as private police at night; it also occurs in situations when those who are expelled from public police service for corruption (as in Mexico) or after regime change (as in South Africa after apartheid) become private police. Whatever the source, when the same individuals or networks of armed professionals move back and forth between the state and civil society, sharing knowledge and personal relations, it is harder for citizens to leverage institutional accountability, and abuse of coercive power is more likely to continue.

The *de facto* blurring of lines between public and private police, much like the overlaps between civilian and state-based armed actors evidenced by the clandestine reciprocities between criminals and police, poses several challenges to conventional research on state and non-state armed actors. First, both examples support our originating concerns about the ambiguities in definition, even as they raise questions about which category of armed state actors would be most likely to undermine (or uphold) a stable and sovereign state and its rule of law. Increasingly, it is hard for citizens to know whether public police, private police, the military, local vigilante groups, or even criminal mafias will be most likely to protect them from harm, or to know whether any or all of these armed actors will use violence against them. In the absence of any certainty about which armed actors or state/non-state institutions are most likely to guarantee protection and security, citizens turn to their own informal institutions and mechanisms for protection. By and large, these informal practices bypass the nation-state, further undermining its legitimate sovereignty.

More important perhaps, the conceptual blurring of lines between different types of armed actors poses new security concerns that have implications for both theory and practical action. One of the most troubling is evident in yet a third form of categorical 'boundary crossing', one that has become increasingly common in the contemporary era as new armed state action continues to grow in importance and visibility: the growing interconnections between conventionally defined armed actors politically focused on battles for state power, and 'alternative' non-state armed actors focused on securing or strengthening economic dominion. With global smuggling on the rise in a world of ever more fluid national boundaries, and with the imagined community of the nation-state decreasing in relation to alternative local and transnational networks of allegiance, there are increasing opportunities for old-style political insurgents with nationalist political projects to take advantage of the power and activities of non-state armed actors.[46] This is evidenced by the fact that rebels, terrorists and guerrillas—or those more conventionally defined as non-state armed actors concerned with political regime change—increasingly fuel their political activities through connections with 'newer' forms of non-state armed actors who seek economic advantage, that is, those involved in contraband and illicit trade activities, and vice-versa. Some examples include Hezbollah's reliance on Colombia drug traffickers

---

46  Christine Jojarth, *Crime, War, and Global Trafficking: Designing International Coordination* (New York: Cambridge University Press 2009).

for funds, the Taliban's use of the opium trade for financial resources, and Somali rebels' engagement with pirates and other criminal groups who control trade running through waters off the African coast . . .

These examples suggest that one key challenge of the contemporary epoch is to come to terms with the fact that we are living in a 'coercive transition'. That is, we seem to be exiting a Westphalian world where most coercive force has been monopolized in the hands of nation-states, and entering a new epoch where local and transnational non-state actors take on those roles, either because the nation-state is weak or non-state actors are overly strong, or because the strength of the latter fuels the weakness of the former, and vice-versa.[47] This pattern, which dominated in the pre-modern era before the rise of nation-states, used to be confined primarily to the poor and non-democratic countries and regions of the world that never fully consolidated state power. But now it is expanding in geographic scope, and appears in middle-income countries of the global south. To the extent that the wealthier and more democratic nations of the world, whether England or the United States, are being pulled into this global orbit through transnational activities that cross developmental boundaries, then we really must see this as a global and temporal transition that affects us all. In the face of these changes, new questions arise. How will security be guaranteed on a local, national, or global scale if these scales are connected not only through transnational networks but also through fused imagined communities that reject standard allegiances to a single nation-state? And what will this mean for the future for democracy, security, and the global order?

---

47 Kees Koonings and Dirk Krujit, *Armed Actors: Organized Violence and State Failure in Latin America* (London: Zed Books, 2005).

# 31: Private Military Companies, the State, and Just War

*Amy E. Eckert*

While the rise of the state did lead to the consolidation of authority within states as territorial entities,[1] the state system did not immediately drive out nonstate actors engaged in the use of force. This reality is belied by contemporary understandings of the state that rely heavily on Max Weber's (1964) definition of the state as the entity with a monopoly over the legitimate use of force.

The state did not eliminate nonstate actors such as mercenaries for some time after the Peace of Westphalia. On the contrary, like their counterparts in the Middle Ages, early Westphalian sovereigns continued to rely extensively on the provision of force by nonstate actors. Prior to the French Revolution, the use of mercenaries was the rule rather than the exception (Avant 2000). Only with the success of revolutionary France's army did national forces begin to replace the multinational forces composed largely of mercenaries that states had relied on up until that point. The military successes enjoyed by France after the revolution inspired other states to imitate the French model of a citizen army and eschew the hired soldiers that had previously formed the core of their militaries. Likewise, the Enlightenment ideals of nationalism made fighting out of patriotism more noble than fighting for profit.

Rousseau's discussion of mercenaries in *The Social Contract* captures this shift. Rousseau (1997, 28) associates mercenaries with tyrannical oppression and citizen armies with the more noble cause of defense of the homeland. Rousseau's treatment of mercenarism implies that the cause of self-defense will draw patriotic citizen soldiers to serve in the military out of a sense of nationalism. In contrast to the nobility of these citizen armies who were motivated by their dedication to the common cause, Rousseau wrote, the worth of mercenaries "could be judged by the price at which they sold themselves" and they would rather be "henchmen of Caesar than defenders of Rome" (29).

The emergence of national armies, which coincided with limits on mercenarism, reflected a real and significant shift in the relationship between a state and its citizens (Bukovansky 1999). The principles of the American Neutrality Act of 1794, which limited the right of US citizens to participate in foreign militaries, suggested how this relationship was changing. Led by the efforts of the United States in the early 1800s, the state now "claimed a monopoly on the authority to organize violence within its borders, even if it were organized for deployment beyond those borders" (Thomson 1994, 86). This new attitude toward the relationship

---

1   Even this consolidation was not instantaneous. Some aspects of the Westphalian state system emerged prior to the Peace of Westphalia and others would not be consolidated until much later.

between state and citizen, and in particular the state's assertion of control over its citizens' military service, meant that individuals were no longer free to sell their force on the open market. Private actors engaged in the use of force became delegitimized. . . . mercenaries who continued to operate were generally lone individuals who would hire themselves out in an underground market (Singer 2003, 37). The rise of the national army had relegated them to the margins of the international system.

Although the state did not immediately displace these other private actors after the Peace of Westphalia had been signed, the emergence of the state did transform the political landscape in a manner that had some significant implications for just war tradition. On one hand, unlike the decentralized feudal system, the state concentrated authority over its territory within a single central authority. On the other hand, in contrast to a more hierarchical form of political organization like the Church or an empire, the society of sovereign states consisted of political entities that were juridically equal to one another. The emergence of the sovereign state precluded the possibility that a higher authority could authoritatively assess the justice of any particular war (Miller 1964, 255). This meant that each state had the ability to assess both its own right to wage war and the claims made by other states with respect to justice and war. The new society of states now lacked any other actor with the authority to determine whether states' claims of just cause or just conduct were legitimate. Instead, each state was in the position of asserting and assessing claims based on the standards developed within the society of states. Vattel's (1916) discussion of just war standards . . . suggested that states actually owed each other an explanation of their decision to wage war in terms of the principles of just war tradition.[2]

The question of right authority, which had bedeviled the just war theorists of the Middle Ages, became resolved in favor of the state. By the seventeenth century, Hugo Grotius (2004) granted the sovereign states a privileged position with respect to rights. This privilege is especially pronounced with respect to the right to use force. While he did not rule out war by nonstate actors in extraordinary circumstances, Grotius "does give an especially prominent place to states as opposed to individual persons and nonstate entities" (Bull 1992, 84) . . .

Secularization and the shifting of nonstate actors to the margins of the legitimate use of force reflects the rising position of the state and the diminishing significance of nonstate actors that previously exercised considerably more authority and influence within the system.

## The State System and the Transformation of the Just War Tradition

The emergence of the state and the international system also transformed jus ad bellum norms. Related to the emergence of the state system and the decline of more centralized forms of authority, the substance of jus ad bellum became less important relative to the process of deliberation about whether the principles were satisfied. This was in part because the function of sovereign equality within the international system precluded a "final" decision on whether or not a claim was substantively just. With the decline of substantive considerations, the procedural aspects of jus ad bellum came to the forefront. Determining whether one state had been injured by another, or whether waging war to avenge it was proportional, was complex. In the absence of an authoritative decision maker, each state could potentially reach a different conclusion.

---

2   This is similar to the function of what John Rawls (1999a) would later call "public reason," a set of principles that citizens use to justify their positions to one another. Rawls argues that states should operate in the same way by using the principles to which they share a common commitment to explain their actions to one another. In his account of international justice, the principles of the Law of People fulfill this function.

Michael Walzer's (2000) treatment of the state system exemplifies the significance of the state for the just war tradition at this stage of its development. Walzer likens the political independence and territory of the state to the freedom and life of the individual. Like an assault on the individual, "Every violation of the territorial integrity or political sovereignty is called aggression" (52). The preservation of states, and the political communities that they contained, constitutes the archetypical example of just cause for Walzer and for the contemporary just war tradition. In his domestic analogy, aggression at the level of international society is the equivalent of robbery or murder in domestic society. International society lacks the centralization of domestic society, meaning that enforcement of the prohibition on aggression falls to the citizens of international society, the states. This law enforcement function is a key component of the justification for wars of self-defense. But this conception of international society as populated exclusively by states leaves little room for nonstate actors.

This exclusion of nonstate actors belies their growing significance and the ways in which their activities can skew the application of ethical principles even to states within the international system.

### Internationalism and Just War Principles

The lack of a central authority to enforce common standards does not mean that states did not seek to agree about restricting the use of force. The state era, and the twentieth century in particular, is distinguished by a number of collective efforts to place limitations on states' right to wage war. The League of Nations, formed in the aftermath of World War I, was an early effort to restrict the use of force by its members, though its restrictions were more procedural than substantive, requiring states to exhaust certain remedies before initiating war (O'Driscoll 2009, 27). Specifically, the League

Covenant institutionalized something like the "last resort" criterion by mandating that member states attempt to resolve disputes peacefully before using force and by providing an institutional mechanism to support those dispute resolution efforts. The League of Nations enjoyed some modest successes in resolving some international disputes, but its highly visible failures to prevent or punish aggression in places like Manchuria or Czechoslovakia ultimately led to the organization's demise.

The UN Charter contained more restrictive provisions on the use of force in addition to collective security provisions that the League of Nations had lacked (O'Driscoll 2009, 28). Bellamy observes that the UN Charter provisions on war "tightened the principle that sovereigns had an obligation to justify themselves to their peers whenever they decided to use force" (2006, 107). The Charter contains the principles, accepted by the UN member states, from which states can draw to justify their use of force. The key Charter restriction on the use of force, Article 2(4), mandates that

> all Members shall refrain in their international relations from the threat or use of force against the territorial integrity or political independence of any state, or in any other manner inconsistent with the Purposes of the United Nations.

This broadly worded prohibition forbids nearly all use of force. The Charter carves out an exception for emergency self-defense measures in Article 51 and, in Chapter VII of the Charter, for the authorization of force by the UN Security Council in response to an act of aggression or a breach of or threat to peace and security. . . .

The UN system reflects the statist norms of the international system in both its principles and its institutional structure, leaving no real space for nonstate actors.

States have also struggled to incorporate nonstate actors into jus in bello principles, in part because the first serious efforts to develop these norms occurred within the context of the state system. These jus in bello principles were translated into the legal system in the form of conventions on the law of armed conflict. The first comprehensive efforts were the Hague Conventions of 1899 and 1907, which were precursors to the contemporary Geneva Conventions that were adopted after World War II. Another international organization, the International Committee of the Red Cross (ICRC) facilitated the negotiation of the Geneva Conventions and subsequent documents that codified the law of armed conflict (Bellamy 2006,108–9) . . . and extended many principles from the growing body of jus in bello thought. However, these principles reflect a particular definition of combatants based on statist assumptions. In particular, the Geneva Conventions assume a sharp divide between soldiers and civilians. The former category includes those who are part of a hierarchical military system set apart from the peaceful realm of civilian life.

## Postinternationalism?

This state-centric formulation of jus in bello norms has come under stress from other sources, including the rise of civil war and irregular warfare.

The shift away from violence between states to violence within states has chipped away at core assumptions of the just war tradition as presently formulated, particularly with respect to the principle of legitimate authority . . . While policymakers were relatively quick to recognize this shift, the just war tradition lagged behind, maintaining its focus on international war and avoiding the issues posed by internal strife (Johnson 1999, 12). The just war tradition has struggled to incorporate these belligerent movements, and international law has done only marginally better with the adoption of Protocol II to the Geneva Conventions in 1977. Protocol II

provides for the recognition of belligerencies, which extends to belligerent movements some rights and responsibilities under the law of armed conflict.

Belligerent movements are in some respects the tip of the iceberg with respect to the decentralization of force. The weakening of the state, at least in relative terms, has created openings for other actors to begin performing many of the functions that were once the exclusive domain of states. The process of globalization has brought to the state system changes so sweeping that some now refer to the system as postinternational (Ferguson and Mansbach 2004; Rosenau 2003). In this global order, war itself is becoming transformed into what Mary Kaldor calls "new wars," which

> involve a blurring of the distinctions between war (usually defined as violence between states or organized political groups for political motives), organized crime (violence undertaken by privately organized groups for private purposes, usually financial gain) and large-scale violations of human rights (violence undertaken by states or politically organized groups against individuals). (2007, 2)

Christopher Kinsey (2006) draws a connection between these new wars and Private Military Companies (PMCs). These new wars, he argues, contribute to the commercialization of politics (123). This commercialization, which blurs distinctions between the conduct of states and nonstate actors, is a key component of the context within which PMCs now operate. Kaldor locates the emergence of new wars within the context of the eroding of the state's monopoly on force and the rise, at least in relative terms, of nonstate actors.

Just as the rise of the state altered the political culture of the international system, so the growing role of private actors will also change the political culture of the international system. Nevertheless, the present political culture of the international system is statist. As such, states continue to enjoy a special position in international ethical reasoning, as they do in contemporary formulations of the just war tradition. But the changes that prompt some to characterize this order as postinternational do fundamentally alter the context within which states operate, giving rise to a more active and significant private sphere at the international level.

The challenge posed by PMCs differs from that of belligerent movements. First, belligerent actors resemble states in important ways. Cecile Fabre (2008, 968) suggests that in the modern era, wars are fought in defense of "state interests" like territory or political authority. Lawful belligerents, she argues, defend the same interests. While rebel movements are not states, they aspire to control of the state. If successful, national liberation movements or rebel movements assume control of the state apparatus and become the legitimate authority of the state over which they seek control. Second, PMCs enjoy a degree of legitimacy that is conferred on them by the state itself. Unlike belligerent movements and other nonstate actors, PMCs operate with a degree of legitimacy that other actors do not possess. The state, which has come to be defined as the entity enjoying a monopoly over the legitimate use of force, has delegated a degree of its legitimacy to other actors.

## *The Reversal of the State Monopoly on Force*

The reprivatization of force has been driven by a number of dynamics with the evolving international system. The first of these is the dynamic of supply and demand that drives any free market. Several developments within the international political system created a supply of individuals ready, willing, and able to provide their services on the private market. These political developments included the end of the Cold War and the subsequent dissolution of the Soviet Union, which prompted both the United States and the newly independent former Soviet republics to reduce the size of their militaries. The end of the apartheid government in South Africa prompted a similar downsizing. The end of the Cold War or of white minority rule in South Africa did not mean an end to the need for military intervention across the entire international system, however. The end of the Cold War in particular had a destabilizing effect within some states. A number of civil conflicts that had been suppressed during the Cold War soon boiled over. While the international community was initially happy to intervene through the UN or regional organizations, they soon developed a fatigue that rendered them unwilling to intervene in situations where they would previously have taken action. This unmet need created a demand for the services that the now-unemployed military personnel were prepared to provide.

The second factor behind the rise of the PMC industry is globalization and, perhaps more importantly, the ideology that underlies it. A number of conservative governments in the 1980s and 1990s pursued a path of privatization because of their ideological preference for the free market (Spearin 2004, 41). In the US case, the belief that relying on private forces yields more "bang for the buck" has created a preference for reliance on PMCs (Spearin 2003, 29). US political culture has long favored a small government and a robust civil society. Globalization has diffused these particular values across the global political institutions. Since then, these ideological preferences have been institutionalized at the international level in the form of the free trade regime. The neoliberal ideological underpinnings of globalization push the resolution of this particular supply and demand problem toward a particular outcome, which is the reprivatization of force (Singer 2005, 120). This has had the effect of promoting privatization both globally and within states. One hallmark of the globalization regime has been the "outsourcing" of manufacturing or services from areas perceived as less efficient to those seen as more efficient. The privatization of war fighting is both the apparent logical extension of this proprivatization ideology and the potential transformation of the state system, as the state outsources its core functions to private actors.

The performance of these core sovereign functions by private actors has some potentially serious implications for the state system. While PMCs are waging war and performing other security functions much like states have done, they are also ultimately corporate actors. This means that their loyalties are starkly different from those of national militaries. National militaries are part of the state apparatus. PMCs have no accountability or loyalty to the states that hire them beyond their contractual obligations. David Simons stated aptly that the loyalties of PMCs "shift with each contract" (2004, 68). Even these obligations are secondary to the PMCs' ultimate responsibility to their shareholders.

As with any corporation, a PMC is accountable to its shareholders, meaning that it is obliged to maximize profits for those investors. A PMC has no inherent interest in the state system or in the survival of any particular state. Its interests lie in pursuing which ever course is more profitable.

The reprivatization of force is occurring in an era in which the state is the dominant actor in the international system and is closely associated with a monopoly on the legitimate use of force. As nonstate actors engaging in the use of force, PMCs are now operating in an international system that has no theoretical space for them. Principles of international ethics are ill-equipped to deal with the realities of nonstate actors performing the functions previously carried out exclusively by states. The preoccupation with the state has created a division between the public political sphere and the private sphere on the international level. This divide relegates certain actors—states—to the "public" political sphere and leaves the remaining actors—even those that now perform state functions—in the hidden "private" sphere. Though largely unseen, the behavior of nonstate actors forms part of the political terrain. The activities of private actors can create hidden distortions in this terrain that frustrate a meaningful application of ethical principles that were formulated for public actors.

Despite the growing PMC involvement in armed conflict, states still make jus ad bellum assessments when they decide to wage war. Likewise, the state makes the decision to outsource that war, whether that decision is one of choice (in the case of highly capable states) or necessity (in the case of weak or failing states). Because these are choices that lie within the scope of the state's agency, it is appropriate to hold the state accountable for these choices and the consequences of them. This is not to suggest that the availability of PMCs to participate in the conflict does not influence the decisions about going to war that jus ad bellum standards regulate. The ability to effectively purchase additional capabilities might make an otherwise impossible war possible or an unpopular war feasible or improve a state's possibility of attaining the (presumably) just cause for which it fights. Despite this influence, the decision to wage war is a political decision that is ultimately made by the state. As such, the actions of PMCs that bear on jus ad bellum standards can and should be attributable to the state that contracted with them to wage the war.

Jus in bello standards, by contrast, apply to those who actually wage the war. While the state decides to wage the war, and to some extent determines how that war will be waged, those who actually do the fighting also bear responsibility for complying with the rules that apply to that fighting. Whether these are state or private actors, these fighters bear responsibility for any violations of jus in bello rules that they commit. Who bears responsibility for a particular violation is, of course, a question of fact that can only be determined by examining the circumstances of that violation. But, to the extent that the individuals affiliated with PMCs and even the PMCs themselves can possess moral agency, both can and should be held responsible—along with the state actors, where applicable—for the jus in bello violations that occur during wartime.

While the context within which states operate has changed in a real and significant way, the just war tradition can still apply in this new, more privatized international system, albeit with some key adjustments. Like other theoretical traditions, the just war tradition is less a set of specific rules than a collection of principles that evolves over time.

Just as the centralization of authority and force under the authority of the state altered the trajectory of the just war tradition, the reprivatization of force through the rise of the PMC industry will have similarly important effects on the future of the just war tradition. The reemergence of private actors in warfare erodes the privilege that state actors enjoy with respect to the use of force and, by extension, within the just war tradition. Even where PMCs act on behalf of state interests, they chip away at the state's monopoly on the use of force because the state is pursuing its interests through private actors engaged in the use of force. States of all degrees of capability—in addition to nonstate actors like international organizations or corporations—can and do contract for the force that they need. Some states lack the capability to use force on their own, and they privatize out of necessity. Other states believe in the market as a more efficient solution and they privatize out of choice. In either case, the legitimate use of force by nonstate actors has changed the face of war.

## References

Avant, Deborah. 2000. "From Mercenary to Citizen Armies: Explaining Change in the Practice of War." *International Organization* no. 54(1): 41–72.

Bellamy, Alex J. 2006. *Just Wars: From Cicero to Iraq.* Cambridge: Polity Press.

Bukovansky, Mlada. 1999. "The Altered State and the State of Nature: The French Revolution and International Politics." *Review of International Studies* no. 25(2): 197–216.

Bull, Hedley. 1992. "The Importance of Grotius in the Study of International Relations." In *Hugo Grotius and International Relations,* edited by Hedley Bull, Benedict Kingsbury, and Adam Roberts, 65–94. Oxford: Clarendon Press.

Fabre, Cecile. 2008. "Cosmopolitanism, Just War Theory and Legitimate Authority." *International Affairs* no. 84(5): 963–76.

Ferguson, Yale H., and Richard W. Mansbach. 2004. *Remapping Global Politics: History's Revenge and Future Shock, Cambridge Studies in International Relations.* Cambridge: Cambridge University Press.

Grotius, Hugo. 2004. *On the Law of War and Peace.* Whitefish, MT: Kessinger Publishing.

Johnson, James Turner. 1999. *Morality and Contemporary Warfare.* New Haven, CT: Yale University Press.

Kaldor, Mary. 2007. *New and Old Wars: Organized Violence in a Global Era.* 2nd ed. Stanford, CA: Stanford University Press.

Kinsey, Christopher. 2006. *Corporate Soldiers and International Security: The Rise of Private Military Companies.* New York: Routledge.

Miller, Lynn H. 1964. "The Contemporary Significance of the Doctrine of Just War." *World Politics* no. 16(2): 254–86.

O'Driscoll, Cian. 2009. "From Versailles to 9/11: Non-State Actors and Just War in the Twentieth Century." In *Ethics, Authority, and War: Non-State Actors and the Just War Tradition,* edited by Eric A. Heinze and Brent J. Steele, 21–46. New York: Palgrave Macmillan.

Rawls, John. 1999a. *The Law of Peoples; with "The Idea of Public Reason Revisited."* Cambridge, MA: Harvard University Press.

Rosenau, James N. 2003. *Distant Proximities: Dynamics beyond Globalization.* Princeton, NJ: Princeton University Press.

Rousseau, Jean-Jacques. 1997. *The Social Contract and Other Later Political Writings.* Edited by Victor Gourevitch. Cambridge: Cambridge University Press.

Simons, David. 2004. "Occupation for Hire: Private Military Companies and Their Role in Iraq." *RUSI Journal* no. 149(3): 68–71.

Singer, P.W. 2003. *Corporate Warriors: The Rise of the Privatized Military Industry.* Ithaca, NY: Cornell University Press.

Singer, P.W. 2005. "Outsourcing War." *Foreign Affairs* no. 84(2): 119–32.

Spearin, Christopher. 2003. "American Hegemony Incorporated: The Importance and Implications of Military Contractors in Iraq." *Contemporary Security Policy* no. 24(3): 26–47.

Spearin, Christopher. 2004. "The Emperor's Leased Clothes: Military Contractors and Their Implications in Combating International Terrorism." *International Politics* no. 41: 243–64.

Thomson, Janice E. 1994. *Mercenaries, Pirates, and Sovereigns: State-Building and Extraterritorial Violence in Early Modern Europe.* Princeton, NJ: Princeton University Press.

Vattel, E. de. 1916. *The Law of Nations or the Principles of Natural Law Applied to the Conduct and the Affairs of Nations and of Sovereigns.* Washington, DC: Carnegie Institution.

Walzer, Michael. 2000. *Just and Unjust Wars: A Moral Argument with Historical Illustrations.* 3rd ed. New York: Basic Books.

Weber, Max. 1964. *The Theory of Social and Economic Organization.* Translated by Alexander Morell Henderson and Talcott Parsons. New York: Free Press.

Part IV
The Problem of Explanation

# Introduction

Our examination of international relations and of the phenomenon of war has suggested a variety of different understandings and explanations. How are we to choose among them? How do we decide what answers to our questions about how world politics works, what happened in the past, and what is likely to happen in the future are "better" and what answers are "worse"? On what basis do political scientists and historians claim to "know," and how can we formulate conclusions that are convincing to us and to others? This is the problem of epistemology.

Ultimately, any understanding or explanation relies on simplification. Like a map, it is a reduction of a complex reality into a more manageable form, leaving out an overwhelming wealth of knowledge and detail. It is, in short, a generalization or abstraction. As we draw our simplified map of how international politics operates, determining what facts are important and what weight to give them becomes a critical issue. Self-conscious awareness of the difficulties and challenges we face is valuable, lest we overestimate the sureness of our conclusions or prefer a dubious explanation to a more probable one.

In chapter 34, James Rosenau and Mary Durfee discuss the importance of thinking theoretically—that is, of searching for patterns and constructing general explanations of the phenomena about which we are interested. In constructing our explanations, though, we need to recognize that while facts are critically important, these facts do not speak for themselves. As J. David Singer points out in chapter 35, our understanding of history may be enhanced by applying the structure and rigor of social science to our analyses of the past—thus putting singular events in broader perspective, and improving the quality of the historical lessons we draw. Finally, in chapter 36, Roy Licklider contrasts two methods for building understanding: what he terms the "wisdom" approach and the scientific one.

# 32: Thinking Theoretically

*James N. Rosenau and Mary Durfee*

It is sheer craziness to dare to understand world affairs. There are so many collective actors— states, international organizations, transnational associations, social movements, and subnational groups—and billions of individuals, each with different histories, capabilities, and goals, interacting to create historical patterns that are at all times susceptible to change. Put more simply, world affairs are pervaded with endless details— far more than one can hope to comprehend in their entirety.

And if these myriad details seem overwhelming during relatively stable periods, they seem that much more confounding at those times when dynamism and change become predominant. Such is the case as the twentieth century draws to a close. In all parts of the world, long-established traditions, institutions, and relationships are undergoing profound and bewildering transformations. Indeed, the pace of change has been so rapid, with the collapse of the Soviet Union following so soon after the end of the Cold War—to mention only the most dramatic of the changes that have cascaded across the global landscape—that it becomes reasonable to assert that change is the only constant in world affairs.

And we dare to think we can make sense of this complex, swift-moving world, with its welter of details, intricate relationships, mushrooming conflicts, and moments of cooperation! How nervy! How utterly absurd! What sheer craziness!

But the alternatives to seeking comprehension are too noxious to contemplate, ranging as they do from resorting to simplistic and ideological interpretations to being propelled by forces we can neither discern nor influence. So dare we must! However far-fetched and arrogant it may seem, we have no choice as concerned persons but to seek to fathom the meaning and implications of the events and stunning changes that bombard us from every corner of the world.

Happily, there are at least two handy mechanisms available for easing the task. One involves a sense of humility. If we can remain in awe of the complexities and changes at work in the world, ever ready to concede confusion and always reminding ourselves that our conclusions must perforce be tentative, then it should be possible to avoid excessive simplicity and intellectual paralysis. Second, and much more important, we can self-consciously rely on the core practices of theory to assist us in bringing a measure of order out of the seeming chaos that confronts us. For it is through theorizing that we can hope to tease meaningful patterns out of the endless details and inordinate complexities that sustain world politics.

## Moving up the Ladder of Abstraction

Being self-consciously theoretical is not nearly as difficult as it may seem at first glance. For inevitably we engage in a form of theorizing whenever we observe world affairs. It is impossible to perceive and describe all that has occurred (or is occurring), and there is just too much detail to depict every aspect of any situation, much less numerous overlapping situations. Put more forcefully, asking a student of world affairs to account for all the dimensions of an event is like asking geographers to draw a life-sized map of the world. Clearly, such a map could not be drawn (where would they store it?); thus, one is compelled to make choices among all the possible details that could be described, to select some as important and dismiss others as trivial for the purposes at hand (much as geographers might select mountains and rivers as salient and treat hills and streams as irrelevant). And it is at the very point when one starts selecting the relevant details that one begins to theorize. For we do not make the selections at random, for no reason, capriciously. Rather, crude and imprecise as they may be, our observations derive from some notion of what is significant and what is not—distinctions that amount to a form of theory, a sorting mechanism that enables us to move on to the next observation.

To acknowledge that the selection process always accompanies effort to develop understanding is not, however, to insure a self-consciousness about theory. It is all too tempting to lapse into thinking that the aspects of a situation selected form an objective reality that any observer would perceive. From the perspective of our unrecognized theories, everything can seem so self-evident that we may be inclined to equate our understanding of events with the "truth" about them, a practice that can lead to all kinds of problems once we try to share our understandings with others.

To avoid or overcome these difficulties, and thereby heighten our theoretical sensitivities, it is useful to conceive of raw observations—the endless details noted above—as located at the lowest rung on a huge ladder of abstraction. One then ascends the ladder each time one clusters details at a given level into a more encompassing pattern. The broader the generalizations one makes, of course, the higher one goes on the ladder, stopping the ascent at that rung where one is satisfied that the kind of understanding one seeks has been achieved. In a like manner, one descends the ladder when one perceives that more detail is needed to clarify the understanding developed at higher rungs.

The notion of understanding arrayed at different levels of abstraction promotes theoretical self-consciousness because it constantly reminds us that we are inescapably involved in a process of selecting some details as important and dismissing others as trivial. Aware that, perforce, we must teeter precariously on a rung of delicately balanced interpretations whenever we move beyond raw facts, we are continuously impelled to treat any observation we make as partly a product of our premises about the way things work in world politics.

Another way of developing a keen sensitivity to the imperatives of theorizing is to evolve a habit of always asking about any phenomenon we observe, "Of what is this an instance?" Though brief, the question is powerful because it forces us to move up the ladder of abstraction in order to identify a more encompassing class of phenomena of which the observed event is an instance. Suppose, for example, one is investigating the Soviet Union and observes that in 1991 it underwent a coup d'ètat that failed, and further suppose that one then asks of what is this failure an instance. Immediately one comes upon a number of possible answers at different rungs on the ladder. At the next highest rung the coup attempt may loom as a botched power grab by a small clique of politicians frustrated by their progressive loss of influence. At a higher rung it can be seen as an instance of factional and ideological tension among an elite accustomed to unquestioned leadership. At a still higher rung it might be interpreted as an instance of the kind of political tensions that follow when an economy enters a period of steep decline. Near the top rung the failed coup can readily be viewed as an instance of profound change in a long-stagnant society. At the very top it might be seen as the final stage in a long process of systemic collapse.

In the sense that they are broadly explanatory, each of these interpretations is profoundly theoretical. None of them is more correct than any other—since they offer explanations at different levels of aggregation—but all of them select certain aspects of the failed coup as relevant and impute meaning to them. And, in so doing, they nicely demonstrate how the of-what-is-this-an-instance question impels us to use theory as a means of enlarging our understanding. More than that, the several interpretations of the coup highlight the satisfactions inherent in the theoretical enterprise. For there is little to get excited about at the lowest rungs on the ladder of abstraction. To be sure, the raw facts and historical details are important—one could hardly theorize without them—but it is only as one moves up the ladder that the interesting questions begin to arise and allow one's mind to come alive, to probe and ponder, to delve and discard, to roam and revise. Taken by itself, the failed coup in August 1991 was no more than nine men imprisoning a president and issuing orders; but as an instance of more encompassing processes, it was one of the most dynamic moments of recent history.

## The Refinements of Theory

It follows that at least crude forms of theorizing are at work whenever we undertake observation. The facts of history or current events do not speak to us. They do not cry out for attention and impose themselves upon us. Rather, it is we who make the facts speak, accord them salience, give them meaning, and in so doing endlessly engage in the theoretical enterprise. Since this is the case irrespective of whether we are aware of ourselves as theoreticians, it is obviously preferable to move consciously up and down the ladder of abstraction. Indeed, since theorizing is the surest and most expeditious route to understanding, there is much to be said for making a habit out of the of-what-is-this-an-instance question, of training oneself to ask it constantly in order to insure that one proceeds explicitly from observation to inference to explanation. By being habitual about the question, that is, one assures always seeing larger meanings even as one focuses on particular events. And by being explicit, one can identify

where one may have erred if it turns out that an interpretation proves unwarranted in the light of subsequent developments.

Explicitness, in other words, is a crucial refinement of the theoretical enterprise. It is what allows us to test and revise our theories. By being explicit we can not only check our reasoning against further observations but also submit our theories to the scrutiny of those who doubt the soundness of our theorizing. In this way knowledge cumulates and both specific events and broad trends come into focus and pave the way for ever more enriched understanding. Thus is a task that may seem like sheer craziness transformed by the theorist into a challenging and rewarding endeavor.

There are, of course, many other rules and procedures that underlie the theoretical enterprise. Theory is not a means of giving vent to one's intuitions, of randomly asserting whatever pops to mind as a response to the of-what-is-this-an-instance question. A hunch or impression may serve as an initial stimulus to theory building, but no observation acquires a theoretical context until such time as it is integrated into a coherent and more encompassing framework and then subjected to the rigors of systematic analysis. Like any other intellectual enterprise, in other words, theorizing is founded on rules—in this case, rules for transforming raw observations into refined hypotheses and meaningful understandings. In themselves, the rules are neutral; they allow for weak theory as well as powerful theory, for narrow theory that explains a limited set of observations as well as broad theory that purports to account for a wide array of phenomena. Whatever the strength and scope of any theory, however, it is unlikely to advance understanding if it strays far from the core rules that underlie the enterprise.

## Toward the Higher Rungs

[T]he higher one moves up the ladder of abstraction, the less one worries about anomalous situations and the more one focuses on patterns that reflect central tendencies. At the top of the ladder sit comprehensive perspectives that organize our overall understanding of cause and effect. We all have such theories, even if we are not consciously aware of them. Pluralists, for example, understand social life to be moved by a variety of groups with differing agendas that may nevertheless intersect. Any such broad perspective is consistent with several more specific theories; pluralism implies interest-group liberalism or "world society" approaches. Even though such theories require somewhat different testable hypotheses, they are fundamentally related in that they share basic axioms about social and political life.

Consequently, as one approaches the rungs at the top of the ladder, one's theories subsume diverse details and become all-encompassing, ranging across the full gamut of human affairs. At the highest rung, a theory may also be called a paradigm or a model, terms that refer to an integrated set of propositions that account for any development within the purview of the theory. Virtually by definition, therefore, paradigmatic formulations rest on simple propositions that subsume many diverse forms of activity and thus cannot be readily overturned or embarrassed by exceptions to the central tendencies they depict. Put differently, paradigms tend to be closed systems of thought that cannot be broken by the recitation of specific examples that run counter to their premises. A thoroughgoing paradigm closes off the anomalies by resort to deeper explanations that bring the exceptions within the scope of its central tendencies. Marxists, for example, were long able to preserve their paradigm by treating any challenge to their theoretical perspective as conditioned by class consciousness and thus as explicable within the context of their core premises. It follows that the only way one can break free of an entrapping paradigm is by rejecting its core premises and framing new ones that account in a different way for both the central tendencies and the anomalies. Once one develops a new formulation out of the new premises, of course, one acquires a new paradigm that, in turn, is both all-encompassing and all-entrapping.

In short, we inevitably bring to world politics a broad paradigmatic perspective that enables us to infuse meaning into the latest development. And inescapably, too, we are bound to feel quarrelsome with respect to those who rely on different paradigms to explain the same events.

Notwithstanding the combative impulses induced by paradigmatic commitments and the occasional moments of insecurity over being entrapped in a conceptual jail of one's own making, the higher rungs of the ladder serve the valuable purpose of infusing coherence into all that we observe in global politics. The paradigm of our choice may be excessively simple and it may be closed to all challenges, but it does guide us through the complexities of an ever more interdependent world. Our perch high on the ladder of abstraction enables us to identify key questions and develop a perspective on how to answer them. Without a self-conscious paradigmatic commitment, one is destined for endless confusion, for seeing everything as relevant and thus being unable to tease meaning out of the welter of events, situations, trends, and circumstances that make up international affairs at any and every moment in time. Without a readiness to rely on the interlocking premises of a particular paradigm, our efforts at understanding would be, at best, transitory, and at worst they would be arbitrary, filled with gaping holes and glaring contradictions.

# 33: Learning from History as Social Scientists

*J. David Singer*

With the advent of nuclear weapons and ballistic missile delivery systems in the years following World War II, some social scientists in the West began to consider seriously whether they might now have a more useful role to play. It was appreciated that war over the past few centuries had been increasingly destructive, but now we were confronted with the possibility of devastation so massive and so swift as to make even the havoc of the two world wars modest by comparison. Could social scientists shed much light on the conditions and events that might make nuclear war more—or less—likely, and more to the point, could their research make a difference?

By the mid-1950s, we began to see a modest coming together of those who hoped to respond to this unprecedented challenge. They came not only from history and political science but from psychology, sociology, economics, and anthropology as well, and 1957 saw the establishment—at the University of Michigan—of both the *Journal of Conflict Resolution* and the Center for Research on Conflict Resolution. While some of these scholars turned to the results of laboratory and field research, a fair number of us looked to history as a source of lessons that might shed some light on the strategies of conflict management and war avoidance.

Those of us who chose to look to international history for the relevant lessons were not especially blessed with a solid set of scholarly precedents that might serve as a point of departure. To be sure, people such as Buckle (1885),

Condorcet, and Bagehot had pondered the possibility of bringing scientific method and history together, and more recently we could turn to the pioneering efforts of Bloch (1899), Richardson (1939), and Wright (1942), but there certainly was no sustained body of work, nor even a shared norm that history—political, diplomatic, or military—might be treated in the scientific style. To the contrary, the dominant tradition was that of "ransacking history" in pursuit of those particular cases that might illuminate a problem, or worse yet, support a given contention. Despite the above pioneers, most political scientists continued on the one hand to cite Santayana (to the effect that those who fail to learn the lessons of history are doomed to repeat it) while at the same time acting as if history were merely "one damned thing after another."

Be that as it may, a good many of us have decided that history *is* the most promising source of such knowledge as may help understand, and avoid, the processes that culminate in war. . . .

Other strategies come to mind, but my intention here is to concentrate on the prospects—and pitfalls—of learning from history.

Choosing history as our potential source of knowledge concerning the dynamics of war and peace is more than merely turning to History. Without that discipline and its gifted practitioners, the social scientist could hardly begin to ply her or his trade; historians have done, and continue to do, an impressive job in sorting out the empirical facts, evaluating assertions, and tracking down the elusive, the ambiguous, and the disputed. They also offer up a rich, and often dizzying, variety of interpretations, all of which are essential grist for the social science mill. But, with only a few bold exceptions, they shy away from any explicit search for generalizations, preferring rather to give us a rich, textured, subtle, and thorough analysis of a given episode, era, or locale.

To begin, the relevant geographical-temporal domain must be specified, and second, *all* relevant cases from that domain must be examined. Third, the cases or situations must be compared with one another in a rigorous fashion, and in terms of characteristics that are both precisely defined and clearly germane to the case at hand. To illustrate, when the American foreign secretary Dean Rusk asserted that the "lessons of Munich" were applicable to the Indochina confrontation in 1967, journalists, members of Congress, and citizens should have posed the following questions: "Along which dimensions were these two cases similar? How similar? Along which dimensions were they different? How different? How many cases of this type do we find since, let us say, the Congress of Vienna? In which cases were which policies pursued? Which cases turned out which way? In sum, Mr. Secretary, please tell us about Fashoda, Agadir, Constantinople, and Sarajevo, as well as about the one case that you happen to like!" Rusk was, of course, neither the first nor the last of those diplomats who frequently "fell into a habit which can be neither cured nor pardoned: making history into the proof of their theories" (Acton 1909). . . .

As already suggested, we cannot expect to learn much from history if we merely use the past as a grab bag from which we select the cases that support our views of the moment, while putting back into the bag those cases that contradict these prejudices. Only a well-defined total population of cases, or a carefully and explicitly drawn sample of that population, can serve as a legitimate basis for generalization; a biased or distorted population or sample of cases will inevitably give us distorted results.

But that is not the only requirement for discovering the lessons of history. A second requirement is that each of the phenomena about which we seek to generalize must be converted into very clear verbal forms (that is, a variable) and thence into unamibiguous quantitative forms that can serve as an indicator of the variable. This is achieved by "operationalizing" the variable, on the basis of one or the other processes of quantification (Singer 1982). The most obvious type of quantification is that of *measurement*: height in centimeters, temperature in degrees, earthquake severity in the logarithmic Richter scale units, velocity in kilometers per hour; many physical phenomena are operationally quantified by measuring them against a scientifically accepted scale. Less obvious, but equally familiar, is quantification by *enumeration*: the percentage of women in a parliamentary body, the number of bottles in a case of wine, the fraction of the work force that is unemployed, the number of tanks in an armored division; many physical and social phenomena are operationally quantified by enumeration, or counting.

However, accurate counting requires unambiguous classification, and that is easier when it comes to women, bottles, workers, or tanks than when it comes to less easily defined phenomena like crises, manic-depressives, small businesses, political radicals, great musicians, effective teachers, or economic depressions. The criteria for inclusion and exclusion of our cases in or out of these categories are often not sufficiently clear and operational, and even if they are, there may well be some disagreement over the classification criteria or "coding rules." Thus, when it comes to events or conditions that are not ordinarily treated as quantifiable—such as national security or military preparedness—we need first to articulate our coding rules.

If most of the specialists in a given area of competence agree on these coding rules and how to apply them, so much the better. That seldom happens at the beginning, and it often takes years or decades before they come to general agreement on how to identify a genius, a delinquent, and a typhoon, or how to measure the hardness of a steel alloy, the viscosity of a liquid, the permeability of a membrane, the severity of a war, the culpability of a criminal's accomplice, and the duration of a business cycle. Eventually, however, certain conventions emerge, and general agreement is reached on the procedures for inclusion-exclusion and measurement, permitting us to produce scientifically useful sets of data. Hence, in the field of international politics today, we find a rather clear consensus on how to identify sovereign states, major powers, militarized disputes, civil wars, and international wars, and on how to measure national capabilities, diplomatic importance, and the severity and magnitude of a war. (Small and Singer 1982; Gochman and Maoz 1984; and Singer and Diehl 1991.) . . .

There is, finally, a third major requirement to be satisfied if we are to learn from history. We must not only operationalize our concepts and examine all of the relevant cases; we must also statistically analyze the resulting sets of data in such a fashion that our expectations or preferences do not predetermine the results of the investigation. Our analysis must not be allowed to "load the dice" in favor of, or against, a given theoretical position, and we must look not only at those patterns that point in the hypothesized direction, but also at those that point in other directions as well. In the same vein, our statistics must tell us how probable it is that the observed patterns could have occurred by chance alone, so as to distinguish between historical accident and randomness on the one hand and robust empirical findings on the other.

Having considered both the relevance of international history, and some of the criteria to be kept in mind if we hope to draw accurate generalizations from the historical record, let me now put some of these principles to work. There would seem to be two major uses that can be made of observed regularities in the relevant past. One is essentially scholarly, driven primarily by the hope of adding to our knowledge via the testing of hypotheses or the construction of a theory or both. In that application, we ask whether a given pattern is repeated over and over, how frequently it occurs, and whether it rises or falls over time or whether it is cyclical. Further, we ask the extent to which certain variables rise and fall together, whether that relationship holds only in some regions or some decades or is more general in time and space. Of course, with Bernard de Voto (1952), we recognize that "history abhors determinism," but unlike him, recognize that it can indeed "tolerate chance." The occasional naive critic to the contrary, then, we rarely expect, and even more rarely find, that the same relationship between or among variables will obtain in every case or every spatial-temporal context. As noted earlier, we generate data in an operational way to ascertain what happens when, where, and under what conditions, and we analyze those data statistically to measure the regularity of a given pattern and its likelihood of having occurred by chance alone.

Shifting from theory to practice (and in this case the expression is used literally), a second use is to build our policies on a more solid foundation than provided by those cases that were most recent, most dramatic, most successful, most disastrous, or most easily remembered. Rather, the hope is to examine *all* relevant cases.

The idea here is to generate what might be called a "contingent forecast," by which we mean that the historical evidence permits us to say that "if we do this, under these circumstances, the most likely result is such and such." That is, by examining all the cases since perhaps the Congress of Vienna or World War I involving disputes between, let us say, two major powers of approximately equal strength, the record can show which moves and countermoves culminated in which types of outcome with given frequencies. To be sure, there is no certainty in such a forecast, given the tentative and incomplete nature of our knowledge base, the possibility of faulty classification (assigning the case at hand to an inappropriate class of cases), and, of course, the fact that the international system—like all social and biological systems—is a developing one in which the relationships between variables do not remain constant over time.

Worth noting here is the intimate connection between the theoretical and the practical; as the cliché has it, "there is nothing as practical as a good theory." Whereas a fair amount of competent scientific research can indeed generate the findings on which to base an impressive array of contingent forecasts, these remain in the realm of correlational knowledge—useful as far as they go. But if the right kinds of research are combined with creative speculation in a recurrent and iterative fashion, we might come up with a reasonably coherent theory for the explanation of different (and as yet unknown) types of international war. . . .

People in the policy community often assert that "history teaches us" some lesson or other, when history may indeed *not* teach us that, or might even—if studied systematically—teach us quite the opposite. Quite clearly, when such general assumptions are widely shared, it is essential that they be well grounded in the historical facts; otherwise, the likelihood of disaster becomes all too high. . . . Work that is to be relevant to the issues of war, peace, and international security needs to be numerate as well as literate, and when it is both it can provide the sort of knowledge that may well guide the nations away from policies that range from costly to catastrophic, and toward those that increase the likelihood of making the global village safe for human habitation and conducive to human survival.

## References

Acton, Baron, J. E. 1909. *The History of Freedom and Other Essays.* London: Macmillan and Co.

Bloch, J. de. 1899. *The Future of War.* New York: Doubleday and McClure.

Buckle, H. T. 1885. *History of Civilization in England.* London: Longmans, Green.

de Voto, B. 1952. *The Course of Empire.* Boston: Houghton Mifflin.

Gochman, C., and Z. Maoz. 1984. "Militarized Interstate Disputes, 1816–1976." *Journal of Conflict Resolution* 28: 585–615.

Richardson, L. F. 1939. "Generalized Foreign Politics." *British Journal of Psychology* (June): 1–89.

Singer, J. D. 1982. "Variables, Indicators, and Data: The Measurement Problem in Macro-Political Research." *Social Science History* 6(2): 181–217.

Singer, J. D., and P. Diehl. 1991. *Measuring the Correlates of War.* Ann Arbor: University of Michigan Press.

Small, M., and J. D. Singer. 1982. *Resort to Arms.* Beverly Hills, CA: Sage.

Wright, Q. 1942. *Study of War.* Chicago: University of Chicago Press.

# 34: How Do We Know What We Know?[1]

*Roy Licklider*

How do we know and learn about international relations? This question in turn is a part of the larger issue of *epistemology*: How do we know about reality in general?

What kind of questions do we want to answer? Sometimes we want to know why specific things happen. Why does Lebanon seem to be in a constant state of civil war, while Switzerland has had no major civil strife for several hundred years? Will China continue to be a repressive society, or is it likely to change in the future? Sometimes we want the answer to specific *policy* questions. What should the U.S. government do in response to a terrorist attack? Should the United Nations get involved in Southern Africa? Should the U.S. give aid to the Kurdish rebels in Iraq or to the Bosnian government? Sometimes we are interested in broader, more general questions. Why is there war? Why are some countries rich and others poor? Why do some political groups resort to terrorism and others use nonviolence? These questions are very different, but our responses have similarities.

We can start by breaking down any such question into *empirical* issues (those relating to facts) and *normative* issues (those relating to values). If someone sets off a bomb in South Africa, *empirical* questions will include (1) who did it, (2) what did he or she intend to achieve, and (3) what will happen as a result. We may have some difficulty in answering these questions, but they are all questions of *fact,* of what

has or what will actually occur. In principle, if we knew everything about what has and will happen, we could agree on the answers to these questions; greater *knowledge* will allow us to resolve these issues. *Normative* questions would be (1) whether or not the person should have set off the bomb, (2) who is morally responsible for the destruction, and (3) how other groups, including the United States government, should respond to the event. Note that these questions cannot be settled simply by more knowledge; their answers depend on the *values* held by people.

This distinction is sometimes hard to make. One of the *empirical* questions in the previous example is what values did the bomber have, which seems to contradict the idea that *normative* questions center around values. The difference is that what values a person actually *had* at a particular time is a fact; what values the person *should* have had is a normative issue. Similarly, facts may be essential to allow us to reach normative conclusions. The number of people killed and their degree of responsibility for South African government policy (empirical questions) may be important to allow individuals to decide how they will respond to the attack; if the bomb was in a police station, for example, some people would feel differently than if it were in a department store. However, in this case the facts themselves do not determine your response; instead it is the values that you attach to the facts, whether

---

1   The general approach of this paper draws heavily on the ideas of James Rosenau, especially the first edition of his *The Dramas of Politics* (Boston: Little, Brown & Company, 1972), and J. David Singer, in particular from his "The Behavioral Science Approach to International Relations: Payoffs and Prospects" in James N. Rosenau (ed.), *International Relations and Foreign Policy,* Revised Edition (New York: The Free Press, 1969), pp. 65–69.

or not you regard attacks on police as more "just" than attacks on civilians (remembering that different people will have different concepts of justice).

The study of normative or value questions is extremely important. . . . However, we will focus here on two particular ways to answer *empirical* questions, which we can loosely call the science and the wisdom methods. These methods are different ways to create agreement on empirical questions, even among people whose values fundamentally differ. Each is useful, and each has its own limitations, as we shall see. However, neither is much help in resolving normative issues. For example, either or both may be helpful in determining whether human rights violations *will be* more or less likely if the U.S. intervenes in Bosnia, but neither can tell whether the U.S. *should* go do so rather than accept the status quo. . . .

## The Epistemological Problem

Why is it necessary to worry about how we answer empirical questions? Surely we can just learn all the facts and answer the questions. In fact, however, we cannot learn all the facts for at least two reasons. We perceive reality through our five senses: sight, sound, smell, touch, and taste. However, we know two things about this process.

(1) Our senses can be fooled rather easily. We rely heavily on sight, for example, but it is notoriously fallible. One example is "moving pictures," which don't move at all; instead, the projector flashes a series of still pictures so quickly that we "see" motion. Similarly, a television picture is a series of dots on a screen, fairly close together; we "see" a whole picture rather than the separate dots.

If you look down a set of railroad tracks, you will "see" that they come closer together in the distance, even though you "know" that they remain the same distance apart. The earth looks flat to us, even though we are told that it is round

or pear-shaped. Visible light is only a small section of the electromagnetic spectrum; what would the world look like if we could "see" radio or infrared waves instead?

It is not hard to find similar examples of problems with our other senses. Most animals have keener senses of hearing and smell than ours. In a game called "telephone," one child whispers a complex message to another, who in turn whispers it to a third; the fun of the game is that, by the time the message gets back to the first child, it is quite different. When we have a cold, our sense of taste practically disappears. We know that some people can distinguish more complex tastes and smells than others; indeed some make a living as professional tasters of coffee or wine. But where does that leave the rest of us, who don't have these "advanced" senses, which in turn aren't as good as those of animals or machines? *We cannot depend on our senses to tell us what reality is, but we have no other choice.*

(2) However, fallible senses are not our only problem. If we define "facts" as *things perceived by our senses,* our brains are so limited that we cannot retain all the facts which our senses produce. When you have read an assignment, you will not be able to recite the whole thing word for word, and no one expects you to do so. Instead you must *select* the most "important" facts, and different people will select different facts as most important (which can be a problem when you and your teacher disagree, for instance). Teachers who have spent eighty minutes in front of a class cannot describe each student in detail, much less what each student did during each minute; they too will selectively perceive reality. We think of our mind as preserving pictures of reality; actually, it keeps only a small set of selected impressions of reality, rather like a map, and different maps will highlight different aspects of the same reality. Our perceptions are thus inevitably a distortion of reality. One easy way to see this is to talk to family members or old friends about something that happened many years ago. Almost always they either don't

remember it at all or remember it quite differently than you do; this exercise gives one new insight into the problems of being a historian.

Thus, we work under two major handicaps when we attempt to perceive external reality: *we rely on our senses*, which are fallible, and *we must select only a few of the impressions which our senses gather*. We can call this situation the epistemological problem. The implication is clear: *we cannot know external reality with great confidence*. As we shall see, this puts us under an enormous handicap in international relations (not to mention most other areas of our lives).

One other problem should be noted: particularly in international relations, our knowledge is usually *indirect*, since we almost never observe the important facts ourselves. I have taught college classes about the Vietnam War for almost thirty years, but since I never went there myself, I have no *direct* way of confirming that the war existed. Supposedly, there is a group of people who believe that the earth is flat and that things like space shots are elaborate fakes by the government; we may think this is unlikely, but we cannot disprove it from our own direct knowledge.

Typically we depend on other people, often people whom we do not know, to tell us "what is happening." These people suffer from the same handicaps of limited senses and the necessity to select facts that we do; in addition we have no way of knowing how their personal or institutional biases affect the facts they select. We have to evaluate their assertions and decide for ourselves what to believe. In order to be intelligent *consumers* of knowledge produced by others, we have to know the strengths and weaknesses of different ways of grappling with the epistemological problem.

## Consequences of the Epistemological Problem

Let us focus on the second part of the epistemological problem, our inability to perceive "all the facts." How do we select what we will retain?

We have ideas about reality within our brains which we call *concepts*. These concepts are important because they tell us what "facts" to look for and which ones to ignore. If you see a person running down the street waving a gun and yelling, your reaction may depend on whether or not you "see" that person as a policeman or not. This in turn will depend on your definition of the concept "policeman"; perhaps you expect a particular kind of uniform, for example. If your definition of policeman does not include hair color, you may ignore this "fact" in trying to classify the individual. Definitions of concepts can change; fifty years ago, racial and sexual identity were important parts of most Americans' definition of the concept "policeman" (only white males were expected to be policemen), while today they are probably not. It is the "concept" which tells you which "facts" are "relevant" and which are not, which facts you must notice and which you can ignore, and the concept is just an idea in your head.

Concepts dominate our perception of reality so much that we often "see" things that are not there. In amusement parks, floors can be on an angle, but if furniture is fastened so that it looks straight up and down, most people will "see" the floor as level because their concept of a room (flat floors, right angles between floors, walls, and ceilings, etc.) makes them alter the "facts" their eyes perceive, at least until they try to walk on the floors. Similarly, we can give people words with several incorrect letters; they will often "not see" the errors because they have a concept of what words should be which makes them "select" those perceptions which confirm the concept and ignore those which do not. (This is why it is hard to proofread a paper just after you have written it. You know what it "should" be, and as a result you "see" that it actually is like that, even when it isn't. The solution is to have someone else read it or to wait a day or two until you have forgotten precisely what you were trying to say.) The implications of these problems are clear: we may well simply not "see" important facts which contradict our preconceptions; we see what we expect to see.

The epistemological problem has at least two different sorts of implications.

(1) It makes it very difficult for us to be confident that our *own* perceptions of reality are correct. We know that we do not have "all the facts," and we have no guarantee that we have the ones we need or that our "facts" are correct. We therefore cannot tell with confidence what *objective* reality is. However, most of us usually ignore this problem and are content to *assume* that our limited, personal, *subjective* view of reality is "the truth" or objective reality.

(2) A more serious problem is *persuading other people to accept our view of reality*. This is essential since almost any interesting social activity requires that a large number of people cooperate. If we want to change the future in some way, we will have to get lots of people to work with us. One of the best ways to do this is get others to share a single view of reality; then, if we can agree on goals and the consequences of particular actions, we will presumably cooperate voluntarily. To put it differently, we want to replace our own individual, *subjective* view of reality with an *intersubjective consensus,* a subjective view of reality that is *shared* with others. Given the epistemological problem, this is the best we can hope for.

However, the epistemological problem makes it very difficult to persuade others to abandon their view of reality and accept ours. Such disagreements are common in international affairs. In many cases there is real disagreement about what happened in a particular situation. There are, for example, debates over the extent to which Japan adopted a pro-Arab foreign policy after the Arab oil embargo of 1973–1974, whether the Soviet Union was responsible for the assassination attempt on the Pope several

years ago, and whether the violent acts of the Irish Republican Army are supported by most Catholics in Northern Ireland. All of these are differences about *facts.*

We thus can sympathize with historians who find it difficult to resolve debates about what happened in the past. However, political scientists are usually more concerned with the *future,* and that is even more difficult, since we have *no direct knowledge* about the future. To borrow an analogy, we are trying to navigate the river of time while going down it facing backwards.[2] We cannot predict the future if it has no connection with the past, since our senses give us information only about the past. However, previous failed predictions suggest that this connection is at best very difficult to find and at worst practically non-existent. Of course, the fact that we disagree about the past itself doesn't help.

For example, we are often concerned with the *consequences* of acts. If the United States significantly reduces military spending, will it be more or less likely to become involved in war in the future? If Serbia is victorious in Yugoslavia, will it then move against other states like Macedonia or be content with its victory? Would an independent Palestinian state make war between Arabs and Israelis more or less likely? If Argentina gets some help in paying off its foreign debt, will world financial collapse be more or less likely? If the U.S. withholds investments from Russia, will Russia abandon or intensify its move toward a free market economy?

Note that these questions are all empirical, since they concern what *will happen* under certain situations, not what we think *ought to happen.* Unlike the first set of questions, however, they focus on what will happen in the *future,* not what has already happened. We therefore must first know not only on what has happened in the past but also how this will relate

---

2  Eugene J. Meehan, *Social Inquiry: Needs, Possibilities, Limits* (Chatham, NJ: Chatham House Publishers, 1994), pp. 11-12. This book is recommended for anyone interested in a more sophisticated treatment of some of these issues.

to future events. It is very difficult to persuade other people to agree on the answers to these questions. We will shortly look at two methods for doing so, called "wisdom" and "science."

We must remember that being able to answer these *empirical* questions will not by itself allow us to agree on what *policy* should be followed. For example, someone might support strict economic sanctions against Haiti, believing they will coerce the current government to allow democracy to be established there. Thus, persuading her that sanctions will make it more difficult for poor Haitians to get food would not, by itself, get her to oppose sanctions; she would have to decide what she values the most, making democracy more likely or making hunger less likely. Typically, policy questions involve this mixture of normative and empirical questions, and it is important to remember that we are here focusing only on questions of fact. On the other hand, if we can get agreement on empirical questions, we will at least understand that we are debating values when our policies differ.

## Alternative Responses to the Epistemological Problem[3]

How then can we respond to this problem? Since we cannot know "all the facts" (since our senses can be fooled and since our brains will in any case ignore most of what we learn), how can we *select* facts so as to get other people to agree on our answers to empirical questions, even if some of those people have fundamentally different values? Alternatively, when someone tries to persuade us that her view is correct, how should we evaluate her ideas? This is the central issue of this paper. We can distinguish at least two different approaches

which are popular today in the United States; we will also note some others in passing.

## The Wisdom Method

The wisdom method involves gaining *intensive knowledge* of a *limited area;* this involves *specialization*. The classic example of this technique is the area specialist, who has often spent many years intensively studying a particular geographic area. In most political science departments you can find, among others, specialists on the U.S., Latin America, the Middle East, China, Japan, Western Europe, and Russia.

In the wisdom method you learn so much about your subject that you *become part of it*. Wisdom specialists select the "relevant" facts by a kind of educated intuition, by putting themselves in the place of the people they are studying. This ability to assume the identity of your subjects requires *intensive study* and *experience*. Thus specialists on Japan will typically have spent many years studying the language and culture of Japan. They will usually have lived in Japan itself for some time. They will have learned, not simply the politics of Japan, but its culture, religion, geography, history, myths, humor, even its climate.

I once attended a conference in the United States on the subject of French politics. The people attending were mostly Americans who had studied France intensively. Although they were Americans, they looked and behaved like Frenchmen. There were exuberant greetings, heated arguments, and people wearing berets. The speeches were usually in English, but the jokes were always in French. These people had studied France so long that they had become like Frenchmen; this similarity enabled them to make

---

3  Many of the ideas in this section, including the distinction between science and wisdom, are taken from Charles McClelland, "International Relations: Wisdom or Science?" in James N. Rosenau (ed.), *International Relations and Foreign Policy*, Revised Edition (New York: The Free Press, 1969), pp. 3-5.

judgments about how people in France would behave under certain circumstances.

It is not necessary to specialize in a geographic area to use the wisdom method. Anyone who studies a limited area in great depth in order to develop an educated intuition about how the subject will behave uses the same approach. But it has been widespread in international relations because of the necessity to deal with countries with widely different cultures and languages; indeed it is probably fair to call it the *traditional* or *classical* way to gain knowledge about international affairs. In fact, most of what we know about international relations has come from the wisdom method. And at its best it is remarkably good, predicting the behavior of people from foreign cultures with uncanny insight, noting qualities which make each country different from others, and interpreting "strange acts" to foreigners who need to understand.

Nonetheless, there are fundamental problems with the approach.

(1) Their specialization means that wisdom researchers are *reluctant to make generalizations,* to talk about things or countries they do not know intimately. Since any one person can only know a few things intensively, it is necessary to bring *groups of specialists* together to analyze problems which cut across national boundaries, and by definition most international problems do just that. Such groups of specialists often disagree among themselves, and as we shall see below, it is very difficult to resolve such disagreements among wisdom specialists.

(2) There are over 160 separate countries in the world; it is very *difficult to train and maintain separate specialists in all of them.* This is a problem for universities, which often have "gaps" in their faculty; certain areas simply don't get covered. It is a more serious problem for corporations and governments, many of whom cannot afford such "gaps"; India is not less important to the United States just because we have few specialists who can interpret it for us. Before World War II, the U.S. could run a

reasonable foreign policy just knowing about the major European powers; most of the Third World was not politically independent, and non-European powers such as Japan were less important. This is not true today, where many of our most perplexing problems occur in Third World countries such as Lebanon, Peru, North Korea, and Somalia.

(3) Wisdom specialists can sometimes be *caught off guard by major changes* in their countries. Most Western scholars were surprised by the 1979 Iranian revolution, both that a revolution had occurred at all, and that the final result was a religious government rather than a military one. Similarly the Russian and Chinese revolutions, because they changed the countries and peoples involved so much, made it difficult for outsiders to "keep up" with the changing moods of both the peoples and their governments. When confronted with such radical changes, it is sometimes more useful to look at examples of major change in other countries rather than at the prerevolutionary history of the country in turmoil, but this runs contrary to the wisdom method.

(4) Most importantly, *there is no way to check up* on a wisdom method analyst to see how well the research is being done. For example, a wisdom specialist might well tell an American president that the revolutionary groups in Peru will succeed because the government has too little popular support. If the President asks why the analyst thinks this is true, she might cite a number of "facts": land is distributed very inequitably in Peru, the high population growth rate has increased urban poverty, the government troops have often killed civilians needlessly, etc.

However, this may not end the argument. It is hard to argue that such facts are not *true,* but people can reasonably dispute what they *mean*; facts never "speak for themselves." Thus a President might ask why the wisdom specialist omitted *other facts* which might suggest that the government can in fact defeat the revolution with American help, such as the reduction in death squad activity, the high levels of voting in national elections, the ability of American assistance to curb the excesses of the armed forces, and the bizarre nature of some of the revolutionary leaders.

The wisdom specialist will reply that she doesn't think those facts are as important. However, she made that judgment on the basis of her experience, because of her ability to *empathize* with the people of Peru. As a result, she really has no way of persuasively explaining to anyone who has not shared her own experiences why one set of facts is more "relevant" than another. It is this personal knowledge (or "wisdom") which is the end result of the wisdom method, and ultimately an outsider must either accept it or reject it depending on his analysis of the *quality of the wisdom researcher,* whether or not she seems to know what she is talking about.

The problem is even more complex because specialists often do not agree among themselves. Thus, to continue with our Peruvian example, it is quite possible that different wisdom specialists with intense personal knowledge of the country will disagree, that some will predict the current government will survive while others will expect it to fall. This complicates the problem of the outsider who usually doesn't know much about the country but has to pick one set of specialists over another. The selection is very difficult because the specialists themselves will not be able to agree on an explanation of why they differ so widely, even though they "know" the same "facts." The ultimate product of the wisdom method is the *good judgment of individuals*, and we have no "objective" ways to determine who has the best judgment.

### The Science Method

If the wisdom method involves intensive study of a limited area, the method we will call "science" is the search for *patterns*. The first goal of the science analyst is to establish *generalizations,* statements of patterns of behavior which apply to *many examples*. When confronted with a single

event, say the revolution in Peru, the wisdom specialist examines its background in depth. The science analyst, on the other hand, asks "Of what general pattern is this an example?" and "What does this tell us about other events in other places?" Thus the science analyst might say it is an example of revolution and try to see how it was similar to or different from revolutions in other countries and other times. Note that both types of analysts necessarily perceive reality selectively; the important point is that they use different criteria to select "relevant" facts.

The underlying idea in the science method is to *test general statements against reality* to see if they are true in such a way that the results can be accepted as true by many different people, even those who do not share the same values. This is very difficult, as noted earlier, because of the epistemological problem. The science analyst's "solution" to the problem has two parts.

(1) Her research design must allow her own guesses to be proven wrong by reality. Thus science analysis is phrased in terms of testing ideas against reality, not defending a position like a lawyer; we call such testing against reality *falsifiability,* because it allows the analyst to be proven wrong.

(2) The analyst must explain the process by which she tests her idea against reality so clearly that the reader believes that he would be able to repeat the analyst's work and reach the same conclusions. This ability to *repeat the work of the analyst* in order to check up on her is called *replication,* and it is a central part of the science method. After all, if you would have reached the same conclusion yourself, then it doesn't matter who actually did the work. You may respect that person or not, but in science you should be concerned with *what she did*, not *who she is*. Thus the results of science analysis are *independent of the researcher*, while in wisdom the quality of the researcher is critical. Good science can be done by fools or (more likely) by people who do not share your values; the idea of science is that, if the *process* is followed, you will accept the results as

valid. Because of the epistemological problem, we will never know objective reality, but replication is the mechanism by which science is supposed to establish *intersubjective consensus* about reality.

But what *is* the process of science analysis?

(1) The first step is to *state the pattern or relationship you wish to test*. This statement is called a *hypothesis*. The hypothesis is crucial to science research because it determines what you are testing. A hypothesis is a *general, empirical, comparative, testable statement*. Let us examine some of these terms more closely.

A *general* statement refers to a *group of events* (or *cases* as we often call them), not to a single event. A general statement has no proper nouns. "Harriet and Bill did poorly on the exam" is a specific statement; "the students did quite well" is a general statement. As noted earlier, *empirical* means relating to facts rather than to values, "is" instead of "ought." "She is not driving very fast" is an empirical statement; "she should not be driving so fast" is a normative statement.

A *comparative* statement focuses on the similarities and differences between *at least two groups* (remember that we are dealing with general statements, so it will be groups rather than single events). Many everyday statements are comparative, but the comparison is often not explicit. Indeed, both of our previous examples imply comparison: the students "doing well" are doing better than something or someone, and "driving fast" means fast in comparison to something. Obviously it makes a difference whether we are comparing the students to their peers or to Nobel prize winners and whether we are comparing the driver to others on the New Jersey Turnpike or to a jet airplane. In a hypothesis the comparison must be *explicit*. Last, the hypothesis must be *testable*, able to be tested by comparing it to reality. For example, the statement "war will be less likely when people no longer have to fear death by illness or old age than it is today" cannot be tested against reality because we do not know what the future will be (note that it is general, empirical and comparative but not a hypothesis.).

(2) The second stage of the science method is to compare the hypothesis to a portion of reality

in a way that can be *replicated* by others if necessary. Replication has two aspects.

(a) We have already noted that *concepts* are ideas which allow us to select "relevant" facts from the many which are available to us. We call such "relevant" facts, selected by applying concepts to a segment of reality, *data*. The *definitions of concepts* are crucial to replication; the science analyst must define her concepts so clearly that *any reader, using the analyst's definitions and looking at the same piece of reality, would select the same set of facts as data*. We call such clear definitions *operational*. Without operational definitions, science research is not replicable and therefore loses much of its power to persuade other people.

It is often very difficult to make definitions operational, particularly in social science where concepts are rather vague. For example, what is a war? One definition might be a conflict between the armed forces of two or more countries. This would include World Wars I and II, but what about civil wars, where one side is a state and the other is not? Does a war have to be declared to be a real war? Was it war when the Israeli army and the Palestinian Liberation Organization fought? When one country's armed forces killed civilians of another country (as when the U.S. bombed German and Japanese cities in World War II)? When revolutionary groups killed civilians (a process we sometimes call terrorism)? When the Black Liberation Army killed policemen in the U.S.? When countries were in conflict over many issues and issued military threats without actually killing anyone? When a member of the Soviet army shot an American military officer in East Germany? When the U.S. launched a commando attack on Iran to try to rescue hostages?

There is no "right" definition of a term; words mean what people want them to mean. Clearly, different people mean different things by the word "war." However, any *single* piece of science analysis must have *operational* definitions of all important terms. For example, J. David Singer and Melvin Small define a war *for their research* as a conflict which involves the armed forces of at least one side with at least 1000 battle deaths between 1815 and 1945.[4] They then list each conflict which they call a war and explain why. The idea is to persuade the reader that, if she applied their definition to the same historical time period, she would choose as data the same set of "wars" that they did.

Of course, this kind of explicit statement of your meaning allows the reader to decide that your definitions are inappropriate or that you have omitted some important evidence. The hazard of the science method is that you deliberately open yourself to criticism from your readers. Thus, if someone thinks that Singer and Small's definition of war is silly, that, for example, only declared wars are really wars, she can quite reasonably dismiss their thirty years of work as futile and pointless. On the other hand, if the reader accepts the definitions, she may well find the selected "facts" persuasive because of the belief that, if she had done the research, she would have selected the same ones as data.

(b) However, operational definitions are not enough. Once you have made data from facts, you then have to *use* the data to see if the hypothesis is correct or not. Sometimes that is a fairly routine activity. . . . At other times, it can involve complex decisions about how the data will be applied, how great differences must be to be considered significant, and so on. Regardless, the rule is the same: the analyst must be so clear about what she has done with the data that the reader could redo the work himself and reach the same conclusion. Only then should the results be persuasive, according to the science method.

(3) The third step of the science method is to *summarize the results of your analysis and draw conclusions.* If the hypothesis has been shown to be incorrect, this often involves creating a new hypothesis, starting the cycle all over again. Again, the basis for drawing the conclusions must be explicitly stated so that the reader understands how they were reached. It is often useful to summarize a good deal of information by a simple statistic such as a percentage.

Note that the application of the science method in international relations has major problems.

(1) At a high level of generality, there are serious questions about whether in fact humans behave in patterned, predictable fashion at all. At one level this argument is frivolous; we all stake our lives on the predicted, patterned behavior of unknown people every day, whether at traffic lights or in receiving the food, clothing, and shelter which most of us cannot produce by ourselves. However, the problem is particularly acute in international affairs where unusual individuals like Hitler, Gandhi, Churchill, Castro, or Khoumeni can alter events directly and where social and technological change occur so fast that it's hard to know what events are really "comparative."

(2) Another problem is science's focus on general statements. Because science looks for patterns of behavior to establish general statements, it uses the concept of probability. Indeed, it is often argued that probability cannot apply to a single case; it implies a *group of cases or events.* Perhaps the easiest way to show this is to look at weather forecasts, which are sometimes phrased as "a 30% chance of rain tomorrow." This statement is nonsense. It will either rain tomorrow in one place or it will not; 30% doesn't mean anything. In fact, what this statement means is that, if there were a million days with conditions just like those which are predicted for tomorrow, it would rain on 30% of them. The analyst has taken a single case in which he is interested (tomorrow) and has transformed it into a *group of cases.* He can make science statements about the group. Note, however, that he cannot tell whether it will rain tomorrow or not; he can only say it is more or less likely to rain tomorrow than on some other day (a comparative statement). Even if science

---

4  This is the basic definition of war used in the Correlates of War project. A useful summary of the data-making phases of the project is J. David Singer and Melvin Small, "National Alliance Commitments and War Involvement, 1818–1945," reprinted in James N. Rosenau (ed.), *International Relations and Foreign Policy,* Revised Edition (New York: The Free Press, 1969), pp. 513–542.

can establish the truth or validity of general statements, foreign policy is usually concerned with a particular case or problem, and there is no scientific way to move from the general statement to the particular case with confidence. Science is a little like a tote sheet for betting on a horse race; it tries to give you the odds, but it can't tell you whether the animal will win on any given day, which is often just what you want to know.

(3) There are major problems in applying the model of science research to international affairs. The idea of replicable research is attractive, but in fact analyses are often so complex that replication seldom occurs, and readers wind up taking the results on faith as if the author were a wisdom specialist. Science focuses on what cases have in common, since it looks for patterns; it therefore has trouble dealing with the unusual or unprecedented events which seem so common in international relations. Last, because science needs many cases, it tends to divert its analysts into areas where data can be created (such as United Nations voting), regardless of whether or not this behavior is really significant;

it thus produces a great deal of trivial and useless research. Because science requires many cases, its analysts have to spend little time on each, ignoring the qualities which make it distinctive.

## Comparing Wisdom and Science

Science and wisdom are *different* methods of learning about the world. Their goals are similar, to establish *intersubjective consensus* on what the world is like within the limitations on human knowledge posed by the epistemological problem. However, their approaches are fundamentally different. The same *person* can use both methods but *not at the same time*. Each has its own strengths and weaknesses, each is better suited for answering some kinds of questions than others, and anyone interested in international affairs should be familiar with both approaches.

If we imagined all relevant knowledge in international affairs as being a chart with countries in columns and different areas of knowledge in rows, the top left-hand corner might look something like this:

U.S. Russia China Chad Tibet Chile. . . .

Wars
G.N.P.
Literature
Language
Religion
Ethnic divisions
Armed forces quality
Technological level
National morale
History
Traditional rivalries
National unity
.
.
.
.

(The dots at the bottom and on the right hand side indicate that the chart would go on further, listing more topics and more countries.)

Ideally we would learn everything on this chart. However, we can't do this. Our senses can't perceive accurately, and our brains can't hold anywhere near the required amounts of information. We must *perceive selectively,* and the wisdom and science methods do so differently. The wisdom method involves selecting a country or other particular specialty area and learning everything about it, a *vertical column* on this chart. The science method involves looking for patterns among a number of different countries on only a few qualities or variables, a *horizontal bar* on this graph.

The wisdom method stresses what is *unique* about a particular country or problem; science looks for what it has *in common with* other cases. Wisdom depends on the *quality of the individual researcher;* the goal of science is to be *independent of the quality of the researcher.* Wisdom requires intensive study over a long period of time; science requires familiarity with a method rather than a substantive area.

### Other Methods of Learning about Reality

People learn about the external world in ways other than through their senses. One way is by personal revelation from divinity. A close friend once told me that, when he was broke, God told him to go to a particular bank and ask for a loan. He got the loan, his business prospered, and the last time I saw him my friend was driving a Mercedes. My aunt used astrology to guide her decisions buying and selling stocks; she seemed to do pretty well. Historically this way of knowing things was not uncommon, and there are important modern political figures such as the Ayatollah Khoumeni who seem to use it; indeed revelation from divinity probably still persuades more people in the world than science. However, in our society today this kind of knowledge is not often persuasive to others.

Reference to some kind of belief system or ideology is another method. One advantage of Marxism-Leninism as practiced in the Soviet Union was that it gave its adherents *certain knowledge* of how things will work out in the real world. Any person who believes this is very difficult to reason with; by definition anyone who argues with her doesn't understand reality and can be ignored. When events do not conform to expectations, that means that she has somehow misunderstood the ideology. Changing such an ideology is very difficult indeed. Such ideologies were not unique to the former Soviet bloc; some of the ideas of liberal democracy (democratic governments are better than non-democratic governments; democratic governments are peaceful; therefore if democratic states are involved in war, they must have been attacked) look remarkably like ideologies, but there seems to be too little agreement in the U.S. today to call it an ideological country. At any rate, for most people in the U.S. today, the approaches of wisdom and science remain the most useful means by which to overcome the epistemological problem and learn enough about international affairs so as to be able to act effectively or to judge the actions of others.

Another possible alternative is suggested by the ideas of *post-modernism,* which argues that science is an inadequate response to the epistemological problem: the heart of science is testing theory against reality, but since we cannot perceive reality directly, this can't be done; therefore the findings of science are no more persuasive than those of any other method. Indeed, the whole idea that some things are caused by others cannot really be proven either. This is a powerful *argument,* pointing up the fact that acceptance of science results requires a *common faith* that this method is the best available. However, this approach has not yet developed an *alternative* way to create intersubjective agreement among people which will help us act together. Such an alternative may in fact appear and be more persuasive than the science method (also known as positivism). However, at this time in this society, many people find the idea of testing theories against reality in a way that can be replicated more persuasive than any other. Therefore, even if you do not believe it yourself, you need to be able to understand and use the method in order to participate in the scholarly and public debates of our time.